IN GOD'S IMAGE

In God's Image

How Western Civilization Was Shaped
by a Revolutionary Idea

Tomer Persico

Translated from Hebrew by Eylon Levy

NEW YORK UNIVERSITY PRESS

New York

NEW YORK UNIVERSITY PRESS
New York
www.nyupress.org

Please contact the Library of Congress for Cataloging-in-Publication data.

ISBN: 9781479835713 (hardback)
ISBN: 9781479835744 (library ebook)
ISBN: 9781479835720 (consumer ebook)

This book is printed on acid-free paper, and its binding materials are chosen for strength
and durability. We strive to use environmentally responsible suppliers and materials to the
greatest extent possible in publishing our books.

The manufacturer's authorized representative in the EU for product safety is Mare
Nostrum Group B.V., Mauritskade 21D, 1091 GC Amsterdam, The Netherlands.
Email: gpsr@mare-nostrum.co.uk.

Manufactured in the United States of America

Also available as an ebook

Dedicated to my father, Michael Persico,
so much of whom exists in me.

CONTENTS

Introduction

The Big Question

Has anything truly significant happened over the past few centuries? Are the Enlightenment, the scientific revolution, secularism, humanism, feminism, and liberal democracy major and unprecedented developments in human history, or are these no more than ordinary events cast over the course of humankind's arduous journey on earth; normal developments, interesting in themselves but unexceptional in any important sense, on the long and grueling path that began with Homo Sapiens' emergence from the earth's genetic jungle some one hundred millennia ago?

This question is important. Arguably, it is more foundational and fundamental than other "big questions," such as the existence of God or the meaning of life. That is because our answer to it will determine how we approach these other questions and how we judge their relevance to our lives. Answering this big question might also help us to understand the answers that we have tried to offer to other queries, such as the existence of free will or the truth of any particular account of divine revelation. In other words, the answer to this question—this is the argument I am making—is a paradigmatic verdict on our life. It implies an ethical evaluation of our current state: an assessment of the nature of the present, prior to the facts and framing them.

Let's fine-tune this inquiry. Nobody can ignore the momentous upheavals that have rocked the world over the past few centuries. Humanity has undeniably experienced some pivotal changes, if only in the fields of medicine and technology. When we speak of "significant" changes, however, we mean changes that go beyond those ushered in by accumulative developments, namely improvements in our material lives. Even religious fundamentalists will (usually) admit that modern medicine, unlike its antecedents, is able to immunize our children against polio or successfully treat lung infections. We all are also aware that electricity, which could not be harnessed barely a century ago, has made our lives immeasurably easier.

These are all facts, which are all—with the exception of regrettable cases of voluntary ignorance—indisputable. But significant changes are not those that have changed the world, but those that changed our basic conceptions of the world. Thus, for example, the scientific revolution is not just about the invention of new technologies, but about a new method for, and conception of, discovering and accumulating knowledge. Secularism does not simply entail the dwindling power of organized religion, but new perceptions of liberty and ethics. Democracy is not only a more or less efficient system of governance, but an expression of a new understanding about the value and significance of human life and about the source of legitimate authority.

Our question, therefore, is not whether our world is different from the world that existed a few hundred years ago, but *whether our understanding of the world, including our conception of humanity, has fundamentally changed in an unprecedented manner.* An affirmative answer to this question will compel us, quite inescapably, to grapple with earlier generations' conception of humanity, which gave rise to manifold frameworks of political life, tradition, and religion. Once we understand that we do not think of ourselves and of each other like our ancestors thought of themselves, we have not only the legitimacy but the moral obligation to explore how our traditions and ethical frameworks should respond to these changes. We shall have to reattune and rebalance our own lives, knowing that we think of them and of the world completely differently from the way people did in previous millennia.

The Modern Self Has a History

I maintain that something did happen over the past few centuries, and that it was indeed significant. This book sets out to explain the dramatic transformation that compelled this development. It does so by exploring the intellectual history of the modern era. We shall demonstrate that Western individuals' fundamental beliefs about themselves, about sources of authority, about moral principles, and about matters of identity have undergone a major metamorphosis in recent centuries.

Nowadays we all grasp the world completely differently from how our ancestors did 1,000 years ago, and even just 300 years ago. We not only have more access to information; this information is based on different premises. We not only know more about the world; we also hold as valid different sources of knowledge. Put simply, we believe that what is true about our lives, about our reality, and about good and bad can be understood not through divinely mandated traditions, but from within ourselves, through individual reason and the human conscience.

We also conceive of ourselves differently. It is typically understood nowadays that we are all autonomous subjects; that our connections with our surroundings, with our families, with our communities, and with the culture into which we were born are all accidental; that we have no obligation to adhere to them, and that we are free to disassociate ourselves from them as we wish. Whereas in the pre-modern past people saw themselves as organic and integral parts of a given social and cultural fabric, as extended limbs of their own families, clans, tribes, ritual traditions, and so forth, at present Western people conceive of themselves as individuals: as essentially unencumbered by their surroundings, free to get up, leave, and change their lifestyles, families, homes, professions, and even sex and gender—all as a matter of personal preference and free choice. This way of thinking would have been inconceivable mere centuries ago.

One of the most widespread illusions is that, unlike nations, countries, and religions—ideas have no history. While we may blithely dismiss the naïve notion that the Swedish nation, for example, has always existed in its current form, we rarely hesitate before accepting the no less naïve notion that ideas such as liberty, faith, or God have remained constant for hundreds if not thousands of years. Many of us assume, for example, that what the ancient Israelites referred to as their exodus from "from slavery to liberty," and what we presently understand as "slavery" and "liberty," are the same. But this is a precarious illusion and it blinds us in several important regards.

First, it bars us from understanding our present reality. It is a mistake to think that our worldview, our conception of ourselves and of each other, is a fixed, undifferentiated constant, which requires no reflection. We are of course capable of distinguishing between different shades of our own understanding of reality (left-wing vs. right-wing politics, faith vs. atheism, high culture vs. low culture), but we fail to grasp that this understanding in its totality, the entire framework by which we conceive of ourselves and the society in which we live, merits investigation and analysis.

Second, the illusion that our conception of the world transcends history and evolution blinds us to the realization that our way of life is not the only possible form, that there are alternatives, that other people once thought differently. Once again, it bears stressing: they thought differently not just because they had religious faith and we do not, or because they were ethnocentric and we are not—but because their fundamental conception of the world was different. They never even considered, for example, that it was rationally or morally possible not to believe in God. They did not ask, for example, to coalesce into nation-states, because the maximum scope of loyalty that they could imagine was the specific clan or tribe to which they belonged.

Abandoning this illusion does not mean simply learning that ideas do indeed have their own histories. It means explicitly and specifically studying certain ideas, exploring their histories, and investigating how people understood them differently in the past. Such an inquiry will enable us to understand our world and ourselves, and also to imagine our world and ourselves in a different manner. It will not only broaden our horizons but is the gateway to personal and social creativity and genuine change.

This book seeks to foster such an inquiry.

The Image of God as the Ancient Herald of Modernity

Exploring the evolution of modernity or of the modern world would be a monumental and immensely complicated undertaking, far beyond my capabilities. I make no pretense of doing so, but only of offering a few directions in which we may examine the intellectual development of several of the foundational principles that produced the modern world. We shall do so from the specific angle of the principle of the image of God.

This book sets out to demonstrate that the idea that all humans bear the image of God—an ancient idea that was familiar in various guises to the peoples of the ancient Near East, and which received its most prominent and dramatic expression in the book of Genesis—exercised a profound and decisive influence on the history of the West.

In doing so, I shall propose an answer to another of the big questions that attracts much interest nowadays: Why the West? Why, of all places, did Europe and then North America leap forward and become hegemonic world powers, economically, scientifically, and culturally, beginning in the seventeenth century? This question, which has alternatively been phrased as "why Christianity?"[1] "why Europe?"[2] or "why Anglo-American culture?"[3] has in the past been given theological and metaphysical, ethnocentric and nationalist, racialist and racist answers, and more recently economic, geographic, and technological answers. The sheer multiplicity of such answers illustrates not only the tremendous interest in this question but also the difficulty, both intellectual and moral, of proposing a simple formula to answer it.

This book seeks to answer this question from an angle that has received insufficient attention: the perspective of ideas, both theological and ideological. At its core is the proposition that the idea that all human beings were created in God's image was seminal to the creation of the modern West. In other words, the fact that the West, or the Christian tradition in its Protestant articulation, grew out of ideas rooted deeply in this notion, played a critical role in their development and in the position they have claimed for themselves in the modern age. The absence of a similar idea in other cultures explains, at least partially, their alternative conceptions of humanity and their different vectors of development.

The analysis of the West in this book will take place from a largely Anglocentric perspective. While I do not of course deny or ignore the influence of other cultures and communities, I maintain that it is in England that a certain kind of emphasis on the autonomy of the individual developed, a "possessive individualism," as the famous articulation of C. B. Macpherson puts it.[4] This accentuated to a measure nowhere else realized certain trajectories drawn from the development of the idea that humans were created in the image of God. England became the first Protestant nation, was the first to dispose of its king in a revolution, and it is in England, arguably, that for the first time a concept of selfhood was articulated that was characterized by an interiority that manifested a unique, expressive individual identity—a modern notion of identity.[5] As an island, England could let its Protestantism and parliamentarism gestate to their most radical and elaborate expressions—a gestation that was continued, mostly unperturbed, by the same radical groups in the New World. Understanding liberty as personal autonomy, the English were more willing to question traditional and political authority, accept change, and tolerate dissent, and they spread these attitudes, along with their understanding of selfhood, throughout the British empire, which at its peak covered over a quarter of the earth. Then they saw them yet amplified in one specific former colony and future empire, the United States of America.

These developments came, of course, long after the idea of humanity's likeness to the divine first gained adherence and centuries after it was adopted by the Catholic Church. Indeed, the fact that it was primarily (though not solely) one direction of Protestantism—Anglo-Saxon, and especially English Calvinist Puritan—that shaped how that ancient idea formed and informed the modern West suggests that the process that will be elaborated here is by no means deterministic. There is no justification in thinking that planting the idea of the image of God at a certain point in a certain culture will produce the Western liberal order 3000 years later. It can just as well produce the Vatican or the Russian Empire or Jewish Ultra-Orthodoxy. An astonishing set of conditions must coalesce and integrate for it to come to fruition, of which that idea is but one. It is by no means a sufficient condition. Though perhaps it is a necessary one.

Furthermore, as we shall see, the evolution of Western culture—individualistic, liberal, and secular—out of the idea that all humans were created in God's image came not without a price. Western individuals—us—live in a world in which the conception of liberty as individual autonomy eclipses all other conceptions of liberty, much as conceptions of romantic love or the nation-state conceal from view other conceptions of love or community. The Western conception of progress, in other words, stops us from seeing aspects of our lives in which we have not made "progress" but have rather become poorer. The major changes unleashed by the past few centuries have not all been positive.

That is not to say that we do not enjoy the Western world, and specifically the liberal order that allows for maximal personal autonomy, protections for human rights, freedom of religion, and unprecedented material abundance. We do, and rightly so. It is an incredible achievement. What is nevertheless pertinent is to understand what constitutes this world, what has allowed for these gains and accounts for our blind spots. We must understand the conditions that made its development possible. This book seeks to explore one of the most important of those conditions: the notion that all humans bear a resemblance, or an essence, that they share with their Creator.

The Structure of This Book

In God's Image begins by exploring the role of the notion of the divine image in the ancient Near East. In contrast to Mesopotamian cultures, which applied this idea to royalty alone, ancient Hebrew civilization insisted on its universal application, championing an essential equality common to all persons.

The uniqueness of this approach is explored through a comparison of ancient legal codes—specifically Assyrian and Babylonian law, to biblical law—focusing on different conceptualizations of the sanctity of human life and the application of law in cases involving sexual offenses and issues of life and death. By examining these laws, we grapple with what it meant in antiquity *not* to be an individual but rather an appendage of a patriarch or a paterfamilias, exploring an existence that we would regard as foreign (and frightening). We then explore the deepest roots of individualism and **selfhood** though the evolution of conceptions of human beings as distinct legal subjects.

Chapter 1 ends with a comparison and analysis of biblical and modern laws concerning rape. Biblical law does not consider rape itself a crime or a sin, but rather focuses on the offense against the man to whom the woman was considered to belong: either her father or her husband. Illicit sex was that which transgressed social structures and harmed men. In contrast, modern law treats consent, or the lack thereof, as the key feature distinguishing licit from illicit sex. The latter is that which harms a subject by transgressing her or his will. Through this example, we witness the completion of the process of internalization and subjectification: women were elevated to the status of legal subjects, and individual will or autonomy became the fulcrum of selfhood.

Proceeding to the Christian era, chapter 2 analyzes the Pauline emphasis on the faith and inner metamorphosis of the subject as the foundation of Christianity's internalization of the image of God. We find that here lie the roots of the abstract individual: of personhood unencumbered by ethnicity, class, race, or gender. *Freedom* received a new, personal, perspective, and we see how the adoption of the notion of the value of human life and of human equality in the Christian world resulted in the Christian critique of Roman slavery, leading to the decline of intra-European slavery by the ninth century.

Entering the Middle Ages, we examine the roots of the discourse on human rights as concepts of natural law, human reason, and free will merged, resulting in a new understanding of the image of God. The individual came to be recognized as having dimensions of agency and subjective depth—"rights"—worthy of universal recognition and protection. In the sixteenth century, these developments would influence the first encounters between European colonists and the indigenous cultures of the Americas; in the eighteenth century, they would become the core of the United States Declaration of Independence.

Examining the struggle for freedom of conscience, chapter 3 begins with the Protestant Reformation, in which the role of the *conscience*, also rooted in the idea of the image of God, gained increasing importance. Martin Luther himself places conscience at the center of his refusal to recant his criticism of the Church. The English Civil War and the Glorious Revolution were profoundly influenced by public discourse about freedom of conscience, and we trace the ideas and struggles of the English Puritans, both in Britain and upon their arrival in North America. Exploring figures such as Roger Williams and John Locke, we explore the first tracts that demand that all human beings, of all religious persuasions, be granted religious freedom and even equal civil rights. Beyond freedom of conscience, this is already the beginning of the separation of church and state and the formation of the modern world as we know it.

Taking the "Jewish Question" as a universal question, a prototype for Western societies' adjustment to the rights of minorities and *equality* for all, chapter 4 explores the democratization of the West. The European naturalization of the Jews, Christianity's significant other, created a new, modern, Jewish identity: Judaism as a religion. Jews had traditionally understood themselves as an ethnic minority with their own distinct mode of worship, but with the acquisition of civil rights in modern states, Jews were essentially demanded to renounce their ethnic ties, to cease identifying as a distinct nation or ethnic group, and to reinvent their tradition as a personal faith. Using Judaism's entrance into modernity as a test case, we follow Locke, Schleiermacher, Mendelssohn, Kant, and Napoleon to witness the internalization of Judaism, like the concept of the image of God, as a matter of individual concern.

Finally, we look at the way the idea of the image of God played a crucial role in the emergence of secularism. The rise of modern atheism drew heavily on the struggle for freedom of conscience and personal autonomy. Following thinkers such as Descartes, Tindal, Baron d'Holbach, and Camus, chapter 5 examines how the notion of God (and divine authority in general) shifted from being a precondition for morality, to just another source of morality, and then to a threat to the very possibility of moral conduct. During the Age of Enlightenment, religion and ethics were transformed and gained new *meaning*. By the nineteenth century, the concept of human dignity was no longer embedded in the image of God but instead negated it in the name of a secular conception of humanity.

We thus explore atheism as an ethos and analyze secularization not as a process caused by the scientific revolution or driven by technological progress, but as a moral imperative. Religion was rejected in the name of personal autonomy and a wish to become fully human. The value of the human subject, created through the idea of the image of God, came to demand the repudiation of divine authority—of any and every God. Coming full circle, we conclude by examining religion and secularism in the modern era, understanding the contemporary world as having been built through embracing, and then renouncing, the idea that all humans were created in God's image.

The Foundations of the Modern Mind

The discussion in the forthcoming pages will take us from the ancient Near East, through medieval Christian Europe, and into the evolution of Western civilization in the modern age. We live in a world in which social upheavals have become commonplace, and economic and political struggles are seen as clashes between rival worldviews. This book disputes the extent to which these contemporary battles are truly polarized. The different parties share the same overall intellectual framework, a system of thought rooted in the conception of humans as autonomous individuals. In fact, their disagreements usually pertain only to the degree of autonomy—whether great or absolute—that individuals should properly exercise in different walks of life (religion, economics, politics, sex, gender, etc.).

Fundamentalist religious traditions are of course the exception, disputing the importance (or indeed the reality) of individual autonomy and therefore also the protections that should be afforded to individuals to exercise it. Adherents of such belief systems would answer "no" to the question with which this book began—whether anything truly significant has happened over the past few centuries. For them, history is but a record of the suffering and upheavals between creation and redemption; the mighty shifts that humanity underwent with the dawn of the modern era are merely additional hurdles that the Lord of History has thrown in the way of true believers, who must grit their teeth and plow ahead without accepting change.

The contrary view—that something momentous has indeed happened in the modern era—entails far-reaching conclusions: modernity ushered in a new and different world, in a fundamental and principled sense, from what existed before. These transformations have not only reshaped our lives, practically speaking, but also require us to look at the world differently, ethically speaking, since these changes bore tremendous moral and religious significance.

This book understands the image of God as a principle interwoven into the great symphony of Western history. Studying this principle and its evolution will elucidate the foundations of the modern mind; familiarity with them will allow us to gain a deeper and truer understanding of the condition of our society and of the individual in the present day.

1

Selfhood

The Relationship between People and Law

Historians of the modern era like to speak of the "emergence of the modern subject," as if the subject emerged and the world changed accordingly. But rarely do they explain who exactly the modern subject is and how he or she differs from their premodern predecessor. In what sense, besides a set of beliefs about the universe and the ability to drive a car, are modern people any different from their ancient ancestors? Of course, one can say that modern individuals perceive the world differently, yet this begs the question: how differently? In what ways do we perceive things differently from our forebears? True, we have different opinions about knowledge, authority, and love; whole books have been written about each of these themes. But what do all the shifts in our attitudes toward a whole range of ideas and core tenets have in common?

The emergence of the modern subject was inextricably linked to the rise of the individual. We are all individuals, as we are often told, and perhaps it is difficult for us nowadays to understand what it means *not* to be individuals. Looking at traditional societies, it is noticeable at a first glance that their members do not conceive of themselves as atomized entities but rather as segments in a continuum of generations, enmeshed in a web of familial and communal commitments. Even nowadays, members of traditional societies usually live near their parents (if not physically under the same roof), engage in occupations that are often connected to their family's profession (or at least serve its general well-being), and get married with limited autonomy over their choice of partner (the match depending on their family's decisions, traditional norms, and other considerations over which they have no say). This is not an individualistic existence. It is a life experienced less as an individual and more as a link in an undivided mesh.

In order to explore the growth of the modern subject, of the individual, we must dive into an array of questions about how humans conceive of themselves, their societies, and the world. Needless to say, these factors all shape people and thus whole societies in turn. In this chapter, we shall address two essential dimensions of the transformation from antiquity to modernity. The first pertains to how the law treats people, or how people conceive of themselves legally. The second concerns how people conceive of themselves psychologically, and what boundaries they may or may not draw between their subjective experiences and the world. The first aspect, how the law treats people, will reveal the difference between the laws of the Hebrews and the rest of the ancient Near East: a difference linked to the fact that Hebrew law was based on the ancient premise of humanity's creation in the image of God.

The relationship between people and the law tells us a great deal about relations between people and others around them. Law is a social institution that regulates relationships between individuals and society. It gives basic expression to all forms of human social interactions, and like language and ritual, law is a fundamental basis without which no community can exist. Laws are formulated by communities and shape them in turn; they are constituted by people, and they constitute them. Whereas in the past, the law was seen as rooted in divine authority, in modern times the law has lost its metaphysical anchor and we conceive of it as built on collective human will or on a social contract.

It would be stating the obvious to note that laws create communities, because they define the contours of what is allowed and forbidden, and thus subordinate individuals to a uniform normative order. To reject the validity of the law is tantamount to placing oneself outside a certain group. But beyond this, the law plays an integral part in societies' founding myths, in the metanarrative that tells the story of a particular society to its members. When the law was seen as divinely ordained, the divine obviously played a significant role in a people's cultural narrative. For a society that has a relationship with a particular god, for example, this deity is connected to the society through a metanarrative that places its members not only normatively but also metaphysically inside a world of meaning. They know who they are based on their relationship with their god.

If nowadays the law is understood as an expression of the will of the people or of fixed principles defining individual rights, these entities—

the general will, human rights, etc.—are obviously part of the stories we tell ourselves about the world. The idea of the social contract and the discourse of rights position communities within a narrative that frames certain axioms in a broader story about the birth of human society or these specific communities. Citizens of modern states base their identities, among other things, on their membership in national communities. In any case, the law is an organ in a narrative body, a framework that encompasses a society and explains to those bound by it who they are and what rules they must obey.

In his essay *Nomos and Narrative*, Robert Cover explains it thus:

> The rules and principles of justice, the formal institutions of the law, and the conventions of a social order are . . . but a small part of the normative universe that ought to claim our attention. No set of legal institutions or prescriptions exists apart from the narratives that locate it and give it meaning. For every constitution there is an epic, for each decalogue a scripture. Once understood in the context of the narratives that give it meaning, law becomes not merely a system of rules to be observed, but a world in which we live.[1]

In other words, law is a pragmatic expression of the binding narrative of any given society. It is derived from that narrative, and its existence sustains that narrative. By obeying the law, people validate their narrative and recognize it as carrying binding significance for their community (when observant Jews obey the *mitzvot*, for example, they validate the myth of the Giving of the Law at Mount Sinai). In this sense, the law tells a story and carries narrative meaning. Of course, the law also represents *values* and carries *normative* meaning.

As Cover teaches us, the relationship between the law and the meaning from which it is derived, and which it entails in turn, is not unequivocal. Meaning is much more fluid than law and is permanently open to changes and interpretations. Jewish tradition, for example, is built not only out of new interpretations of old laws but also out of new interpretations of the narratives explaining them: Shabbat is evolving into a social issue, *shemitah* (the practice of letting fields lie fallow every seven years) into an ecological statement, and the Temple Mount in Jerusalem into a national symbol.

The law not only emerges in parallel with and within a certain narrative, as we have seen; it also constitutes and sustains that narrative in turn. Nomos and narrative, law and story, are constantly amplifying and reinforcing each other. We may therefore learn not only about law from narrative, but also about narrative from law. Let us try to do so with respect to laws from antiquity, in order to understand from within these laws how their legislators understood themselves. In other words, we shall seek to understand, from their laws, how they conceived of their fellow human beings, and we shall do so by examining the legal status of the individual, which will serve us as a framework through which we may view their narrative and conceptions of humanity.

What Do Ancient Laws Tell Us about Humans?

What you are about to read is unpleasant. Ancient laws were based on a totally different conception of selfhood, a conception that makes us uncomfortable. Consider a brief series of laws from the Code of Hammurabi, the eighteenth-century BCE king of Babylonia:

> If a man strike a free-born woman so that she lose her unborn child, he
> shall pay ten shekels for her loss.
> If the woman die, his daughter shall be put to death.
> If a woman of the free class lose her child by a blow, he shall pay five
> shekels in money.
> If this woman die, he shall pay half a mina.
> If he strike the maid-servant of a man, and she lose her child, he shall
> pay two shekels in money.
> If this maid-servant die, he shall pay one-third of a mina.[2]

Did people actually behave this way? They probably behaved much worse. It's important to note that much of ancient Mesopotamian society, including the ancient Israelites, lived according to local customs and tribal codes, practiced in actual quarrels and feuds, and at better times according to common law dealt in courts. They usually did not adhere to formal codices such as this, or lists of laws in the Bible. Indeed, we might consider the Code of Hammurabi, and also the ancient Hebrew laws to be discussed later, as paradigmatic frameworks containing the highest moral ideals of these cultures (or their elites), which might have been only rarely applied in daily life—certainly the farther you lived from the seat of the king.[3] Of course, as ideals they carry much importance, and indeed, as we shall see, gradually had a growing and lasting influence on the entire populace. They set commendable values and frames of reference for the society, which shaped it ethically and socially.

What moral ideals did the above clauses instill in Babylonian society? They discuss men who beat pregnant women. From a first glance, we can see that the women fall into three classes: "free-born" women, women "of the free class," and maid-servants. Indeed, we know that in this period in ancient Babylonia, society was divided into three main hierarchical classes: property-owning freemen, the free poor, and slaves. Nevertheless, as these clauses hint, women did not belong straightforwardly to any of these classes, but rather belonged to the *men* who belonged to these classes. A "free-born woman" was the daughter of a property-owning freeman; a "woman of the free class" was the daughter of a free but poor man; and a maid-servant was of course the slave of a freeman (a property-owner being a freeman who owned at least one female slave). Notice that the Code of Hammurabi is silent about women who do not belong to any man. Such women, at the time, simply did not exist. Until the modern age, women were never deemed to exist in their own right. They were not individuals but rather always attached to a man of some sort, defined through the relationships to which they were inseparably tied.

The Babylonian punishment for beating a pregnant woman was based on class: according to the law, the harshest penalty was reserved for the killing of the daughter of a property-owning freeman; the lightest penalty, for killing a maid-servant. But the nature of the punishment is interesting in its own right. The killer of a free-born woman was punished with the execution of his own daughter. Here we must ask: why was the penalty for killing the daughter of a property-owning freeman the execution of the killer's daughter? Why not execute the killer himself, since he was the one who committed the crime? We shall get to the answer soon, but first let us consider another ancient law, this time from the legal code of the Middle Assyrian Empire (most likely from the fifteenth century BCE):

[If a man] takes a virgin from the house of her father, does not return (her) to him; and if she had not been [previously] deflowered and had not been handed over [for marriage], nor held as a claim on the house of her father, any man who whether within a city or outside, whether at night or on a highway or at an eating house, or at a city festival forcibly seizes the virgin and violates her, the father of the virgin takes the wife of the seducer of the virgin and gives her to be ravished. To her husband he does not return her; he takes her away. The father of the ravished girl gives her as a possession to the seducer. If the man [i.e., the seducer] has no wife, then three times the purchase price of the virgin the seducer must give to her father. The seducer who marries her cannot spurn her. If the father does not wish to receive three times the price of the girl, he may give his daughter to any whom he pleases.[4]

This case is about rape. Specifically, the rape of a young woman, or virgin, living in her father's house. From the text, we know that she is a virgin because no man has asked her father for her hand or claims to have slept with her, since she "had not been handed over, nor held as a claim on the house of her father." If this girl is raped by a man, this man's own wife is taken away from him, raped, and is reduced to being the slave of the father of the girl who was raped. The girl who was raped can be given by her father to the rapist to marry, a consequence of the difficulties in marrying off a woman who is not a virgin and the raped girl's need for a man to support her (as we have said, a woman cannot remain alone). If the rapist does not have a wife, he must pay the raped girl's father three times her "price," meaning her price as a bride: the sum that any man who wanted her hand in marriage would otherwise have paid her father.

As with the Code of Hammurabi, here too it is clear that a woman was absolutely the property of another man: her father if she is still unmarried, and her husband when she was married. Even when a raped woman's fate was discussed—should she be given in marriage to her rapist or not?—nobody asked her opinion. The only person who would decide whether she would marry her rapist was her father: "If *the father* does not wish to receive three times the price of the girl, *he* may give his daughter to any whom *he* pleases." Moreover, as in the Code of Hammurabi's discussion of femicide, the criminal himself goes unpunished.

If a man kills a pregnant woman, his *daughter* is executed, and if a man rapes a virgin, it is his *wife* who is given to the raped girl's father to be raped.

We find these laws nauseating, and it is important to notice our reaction. Something inside us is outraged by these clauses, and we are filled with rage, if not also sorrow, at the thought that human societies once behaved or thought this way. There is nothing surprising about our shock. We react this way because our conception of justice is totally different from the one embodied in these ancient laws. The laws that *we* would legislate, and do legislate, are very different. This is not by chance, but because the narrative surrounding our laws is different. We think completely differently about humanity, about criminal responsibility, and of course about the legal and social position of women. Precisely for this reason, it is important to try to understand the overarching story that made possible the legislation of such laws.

In the Framework of the Law

Here is a proposal: let's assume that the inhabitants of ancient Babylonia and Assyria were no more stupid or wicked than we are. Instead of letting them off the hook as "primitive savages" unworthy of discussion, let's try to understand the internal logic structuring their laws. They too aspired to justice and the good, despite obviously defining justice and the good differently. And so the question is how, for these ancient Babylonians and Assyrians, were these laws expressions of justice? Based on what conception or overarching story did they conclude that such a society was a good or moral one? What normative logic guided them?

The logic, it appears, is thus: women were not legal subjects in their own right. A woman belonged to a specific man, and if he was free, then *he* was a legal subject. She was part of him, an extension of his body. Anything done to a woman, therefore, was not done to *her*, per se, but to the man to whom she belonged: the man whose property she was. The rape of a virgin was an injury to her father. The killing of a "free-born" woman was an injury to the man responsible for her, exactly as if someone were to break his hand or gouge out one of his eyes. In line with this logic, the culprits were also not separate individuals but legal subjects comprising their bodies and everything else they owned. They were men who controlled and were consequently responsible for their families and property. In both cases, therefore, the culprits were punished by injury not to their physical bodies but to their legal and social bodies, to their property or to their women (and at the time, there was little difference between the two). An eye for an eye.

Men who harmed women were punished, therefore, even though to us it looks like they evaded punishment. According to our moral and legal logic, it was their daughters or wives who were punished. This is because as modern people, we take for granted the basic premise that *all* human beings, including women, are autonomous legal subjects. First of all, therefore, this entails that women are not "owned" by anyone else, and a crime against a woman is a crime against *her*, and her alone. Second, it means that murderers and rapists must be personally punished. And third, individuals unconnected to the crimes perpetrated by others must not be punished, even if they are relatives of the perpetrators.

For us, these assumptions seem straightforward and axiomatic. But the peoples of the ancient Near East thought otherwise. They did not conceive of all humans as autonomous legal subjects, or as autonomous subjects at all: slaves, women, and children were certainly not such subjects. They remained subject to the custodianship of the men who owned them; they were therefore not only under the jurisdiction of men but also under their legal responsibility and accountability.

Note that this was not simply male chauvinism, but a patriarchal social structure, in the full sense of the term: a way of thinking in which the man of the house was the absolute ruler and owner. This much is clear from other ancient laws, such as a Babylonian law about the professional negligence of builders:

> If a builder build a house for someone, and does not construct it properly, and the house which he built fall in and kill its owner, then that builder shall be put to death. If it kill the son of the owner the son of that builder shall be put to death. If it kill a slave of the owner, then he shall pay slave for slave to the owner of the house. If it ruin goods, he shall make compensation for all that has been ruined.[5]

If a builder negligently causes the death of the owner of the house that he is building, he is executed. But if he causes the death of the owner's son, his own son is executed. If a slave is killed, he replaces the slave with one of his own. And if he causes physical damage, he must provide suitable compensation.

In sum, the driving logic of these laws seems to be constituted by two basic principles. First, *the principle of proportionality*. Any misfortune inflicted on a legal subject must be inflicted exactly in kind on the legal subject responsible for it. Second, the patriarch is *the only legal subject* and the owner of his family and property, and is therefore responsible for everything in his household and for the actions of every member of his household. The combination of these two principles elucidates the simplicity of this law: if a patriarch causes the death of another patriarch, according to the principle of proportionality, he is executed. If he causes the death of the *son* of a patriarch, proportionality dictates that his *son* be executed. The same goes for his slaves and goods: an eye for an eye, a tooth for a tooth, a slave for a slave, a son for a son. These are all under the patriarch's protection and responsibility, just like his daughters in the earlier laws we discussed. In a social framework in which the patriarch is the only legal subject, proportionality requires the punishment of the individual in the corresponding relationship to the offending patriarch as the object of his offence: a patriarch for a patriarch, a son for a son, a daughter for a daughter.

This is not about the intentional oppression of women, therefore (although they were obviously discriminated against, held an inferior rank to men, and would never become legal subjects, a transformation possible only for young males who became grown men), but a different conception of legal personality. Only the paterfamilias was a full legal subject. Everyone else fell under his control, responsibility, and legal jurisdiction.[6]

In various civilizations, including ancient Rome, fathers were allowed to kill their children or simply abandon them. "Ancient Law," writes Henry Maine in his classic study on the subject, "knows next to nothing of Individuals. It is concerned not with Individuals, but with Families, not with single human beings, but groups."[7] In many respects, ancient Hebrew communities were no different in their conception of personhood from neighboring Near Eastern peoples; they certainly shared their patriarchal structure of family and society. But on a few theological points, the ancient Hebrews departed sharply from the norms of the world around them. These unique theological principles were part of a broader narrative that in turn shaped the Hebrews' laws. This narrative, and these legal differences, would have a defining impact on the development of Western culture.

The Principle of the Image of God

The mythological war between the Greek city-states and Troy was also a war between the gods. Various deities had different loyalties to armies on earth, or perhaps more accurately: competing preferences for which warring side should triumph over the other. Thus, for example, Poseidon, Hera, and Athena assisted the invading Greeks, while Apollo, Aphrodite, and Artemis helped the Trojans.

In Book XXI of the *Iliad*, the conflict on earth escalates to the heavens and a fight erupts within the pantheon. The deities curse and reproach each other, and amid all the shouting Apollo turns to Poseidon and questions the wisdom of the war: "Sound of mind you could not call me if I strove with you for the sake of mortals, poor things that they are. Ephemeral as the flamelike budding leaves, men flourish on the ripe wheat of the grain-land, then in spiritless age they waste and die."[8]

What is the point of a battle between the gods, asks Apollo, if it is waged only for the sake of the fate of mere mortals? After all, humans are like leaves: one day they blossom; the next, they wilt. Why should any sane god fight their battles for them? The sentiment expressed here is understandable, and it was eminently clear to every Greek in the ancient world. The gods cared only for themselves.

Readers familiar with the Hebrew Bible, however, might recall another dialogue, between God and man, in which the comparison between human life and plant life is utilized to prove the importance of the former:

> Then the LORD said: "You cared about the plant, which you did not work for and which you did not grow, which appeared overnight and perished overnight. And should not I care about Nineveh, that great city, in which there are more than a hundred and twenty thousand persons who do not yet know their right hand from their left, and many beasts as well!"*

---

* Jonah 4:10–11. Quotes from the Hebrew Bible here and hereafter will be translated according to the Jewish Publication Society version, 1985 edition.

God addresses the prophet Jonah and rebukes him for insufficiently valuing the lives of the inhabitants of the great city of Nineveh. Jonah refuses to fulfill his prophetic calling to warn the Ninevites about God's ire and make them repent, although he eventually acquiesces and thus saves their lives. God draws a distinction between the lives of the Ninevites (who have no relationship with the Jews) and the plant that sprouts overnight and wilts overnight. God orders the prophet to have no less care for human beings than he himself does—that is to say, to care for them greatly.

The God of the Bible creates humankind as the crowning glory of Creation. He would never say, as Zeus does, that "nothing is more wretched than a man, of all things that breathe and move upon the earth."[9] On the contrary: humans are God's most exceptional creation, more worthy and superior. Unlike the Greek deities, the biblical God sees value in humanity and in human life. Humans are not simply created last as a grand finale, but are created in the image and likeness of God.

There can be no overstating the revolutionary importance of the principle that human beings share God's image. As we shall see throughout this book, this principle and its implications in the fields of religion and society have had a critical influence on the Western world. Below we shall examine how the human subject evolved in accordance with translations of the principle of the image of God into ancient Hebrew law, and how the idea that all were created in the divine image engendered a presumption of inherent equality between all people, and of the unique and special existence of each individual. Before moving on to these discussions, however, we must clarify exactly what the term "image of God" means.

Image and Idol

In the Jewish tradition, the word "image" (*tzelem* in Hebrew) has negative connotations because of the Hebrew Bible's strict prohibition on the worship of images. An image was an idol, a statue of a deity used for ritual purposes. In the Midrashic story (the Midrash is a collection of sacred texts that interpret and elaborate on the Bible) about the young Abraham's war against idolatry in Ur, the great city of the Chaldees, we read that Abraham's father, Terach, was an "image-worshiper."[10] The Bible condemns image-worship and tells us of God's instruction to the Israelites to destroy the images of the other nations dwelling in their midst:

> You must destroy all the sites at which the nations you are to dispossess worshiped their gods, whether on lofty mountains and on hills or under any luxuriant tree. Tear down their altars, smash their pillars, put their sacred posts to the fire, and cut down the images of their gods, obliterating their name from that site. (Deuteronomy 12:2–3)[11]

The images were sculptures of foreign deities, which the Israelites were commanded to shun, out of exclusive loyalty to their own God. Image-worship was idolatry and paganism. The Mishnah (the first book of rabbinical law, from the end of the second century CE) describes with horror the placing of an "image in the Sanctuary," referring to the installation of the statue of a foreign god in the Israelites' Holy of Holies. Why, then, would humans be said to exist "in God's image"?

The principle of the image of God makes its first appearance in Genesis 1, at the moment of God's creation of humankind:

> And God said, "Let us make man in our image, after our likeness. They shall rule the fish of the sea, the birds of the sky, the cattle, the whole earth, and all the creeping things that creep on earth." And God created man in His image, in the image of God He created him; male and female He created them. (Genesis 1:26–27)

In the whole of the Hebrew Bible, the principle of the image of God is mentioned only twice more. Genesis 5:1 states that:

> This is the record of Adam's line.—When God created man, He made him in the likeness of God.

The word "image" is not mentioned, but the meaning is the same.[12] And Genesis 9:6 stipulates a law inferred from humanity's creation in the image of God:

> Whoever sheds the blood of man, by man shall his blood be shed; for in His image did God make man.

The combination of the principle of the image of God with law is obviously significant. The conception of the human person as God's image is a central thread in the narrative encompassing and engendering this law. Note the primacy of human beings that results: humans are the only ones of God's creations who bear his image. Humans are created in the image of God as the pinnacle of God's creative oeuvre. They also receive a special role in the process of Creation, therefore, as elucidated in Genesis 1:

> God blessed them and God said to them, "Be fertile and increase, fill the earth and master it; and rule the fish of the sea, the birds of the sky, and all the living things that creep on earth."

Humans are made supreme over the earth and all other lifeforms. Men and women, one could say, are God's representatives on earth. Note that the image of God here is also associated with ownership and control, and we shall see that these principles will prove critical in the evolution of the discourse of human rights.

What Is the Image of God?

The image of God is his likeness. But what exactly does this mean? We are used to understanding the expression "image of God" as referring to human wisdom or free will, to some divine soul or consciousness. These interpretations of this expression emerged in the first century CE in the Hellenistic world (such as in the works of Philo of Alexandria), migrated from there to Christian theology, and started making their way into Judaism only in the tenth century, before being emphatically embraced by Maimonides in the twelfth century. But this was not how the authors of the Hebrew Bible and the ancient Sages of the Talmud understood the term. As we just saw, an image of a god was its idol. For the sages, the image of God was God's physical likeness.

How could this be? Does God have a body? Does he assume corporeal form? In the tenth century CE, Greek philosophy began to penetrate Jewish thought, along with the dualistic conception of humans as composed of two elements: body and soul. In this conception, the soul is the most defining element or even the core of one's existence. The body came to be viewed as secondary, if not entirely negative,

whereas the soul, and especially the intellect, became the most important and positive dimension of human existence. Accordingly, if people
were recast as essentially spiritual beings, then *a fortiori*, so was God.
Furthermore, while humans have bodies that drag them "down," to
the material world, God must be entirely spiritual and transcendent.
In this conception, which sees the soul as spiritual and the body as
earthly, it would certainly be illogical to attach a body to God. This
entailed a need to somehow negate the personified and anthropomor-
phized descriptions of God that appear throughout the Hebrew Bible,
and philosophers and rabbis devoted serious efforts to doing so. The
best known of these figures, who had a critical influence in this regard, was Maimonides, who invested great effort in his *Guide for the
Perplexed* to find allegorical interpretations for descriptions of God in
the Hebrew Bible.

But for the authors of the Hebrew Bible, and indeed for the ancient
Israelites, it was obvious that God had a body. The evidence is manifold and unequivocal.[13] As late-stage heirs of this tradition, monotheists
in the modern world have learned to interpret every mention of God's
body as a metaphor, but without preconceptions that make us dismiss
the literal meaning of the Hebrew Bible, we would have no reason not to
understand the biblical God as corporeal. There is not a single verse in
the whole Hebrew Bible that denies God's corporeality, nor that he has a
shape that can be grasped, and there are many verses that refer to God's
organs or events in which humans plainly saw him.

As early as the creation of humans in God's image, we are told that
God creates them "in our image, after our likeness," and the tautology
serves to clarify and emphasize: for anyone who has not understood
exactly what an image is, it means his *likeness*—the likeness of God. The
Hebrew Bible repeatedly uses these, "image" (*tzelem*) and "likeness"
(*demut*), to refer to concrete, physical forms. And why impute them to
God if not to use them in the same sense? "Let us make man in our
image, after our likeness" is not, therefore, a metaphor but the literal
creation of man and woman in God's likeness.

It is also clear, therefore, that for the Jewish Sages of the Second Temple era and early first millennium, the "image of God" referred to God's
physical form. The Sages' understanding of God's image is the subject
of an illuminating analysis by Yair Lorberbaum, in which he clearly

shows that for the Sages, humans were created in God's likeness in the most literal sense possible.[14] Lorberbaum produces ample evidence, citing various Midrashic stories that refer to God's body, analyzing this theme through Jewish law about the four methods of capital punishment (which are careful not to cause any physical mutilation) and laws of procreation.

Here is one example: Midrash Genesis Rabbah tells us that "when the Holy One, blessed be He, created Adam, the ministering angels mistook him [for a divine being] and wished to exclaim 'Holy!' before him."[15] Seeing the magnificence of God's creation, the first man, the ministering angels mistake him for God and nearly exalt him in the same terms as God. The reason for this error is, of course, the striking resemblance between man and his creator.

Here is another example: the Talmud elaborates on why *Halakha*—sacred Jewish law—forbids the practice of leaving a human body, after an execution, hanging, and mandates its immediate burial:

> Rabbi Meir says: The Sages told a parable: To what is this matter comparable? It is comparable to two brothers who were twins and lived in the same city. One was appointed king, while the other went out to engage in banditry. The king commanded that his brother be punished, and they hanged his twin brother for his crimes. Anyone who saw the bandit hanging would say: The king was hanged. The king, therefore, commanded that his brother be taken down, and they took the bandit down.[16]

In this analogy, hanging a person is like hanging a bandit who is the brother of a king. Since they look so similar, anyone who sees the bandit at the gallows might think that the king has been hanged, and therefore his body must be taken down immediately. Similarly, it is forbidden by Jewish law to leave any human body hanging, because this would be disrespectful to the King of Kings himself, namely God, given their physical resemblance.

From these two examples, it is clear that from the Sages' perspective, humans' resemblance to God is not a matter of spirit, intellect, or conscience, but of physicality. The "image of God" is therefore none other than God's physical likeness. God gave humans his likeness when he created them in his image.

God's Image as His Presence

The biblical image of God was, therefore, God's form. But these forms should not be understood as representations (that is, symbolic signposts) of God, neither in the case of idols nor, in the Hebrew tradition, in the case of humans. God's image does not *symbolize* him but rather presents him, or *expresses his presence*. Contrary to common wisdom, images in polytheistic religions are not symbolic representations of deities but expressions or manifestations of them. The image of a particular god is not a sign pointing up at him, but a means of making him present down here on earth. An image creates a locus of divine presence. One could even say that an image, in a sublimated and muted sense, is the deity itself.[17]

In contrast, the semiotic conception of an image as distinct from the god whose image it bears was born out of Greek polytheism and adopted by Christianity, thanks to which it is familiar to all of us in the modern world.[18] In ancient Greece, sacred statues of the gods were images sanctified by those gods, and the physical resemblance between statues and gods was supremely important, but statues did not constitute their presence. In the ancient Near East, however, as in Hinduism and other polytheistic religions, images served to summon and invoke divinity, empowering the divine presence wherever they stood.

We can therefore now understand anew the biblical prohibition on making idols and molten gods. If in the biblical era the prevailing theological understanding was that that God had a form, then clearly the prohibition "You shall not make for yourself a sculptured image or any likeness" (Exodus 20:3) was not a statement that God had no form that could possibly be sculpted, but rather a prohibition on sculpting the form that he explicitly had. The reason that it is forbidden to sculpt God's form has to do with the notion of the creation in God's image: humanity's resemblance to God is no coincidence, and it cannot be expressed solely as some aesthetic attribute. Rather, there is tremendous significance in man and woman's existence as the image of God: humans were created in God's image, meaning that they themselves are the image instantiating God's presence. Midrash Deuteronomy Rabbah quotes the third-century rabbi Joshua Ben Levi as saying that wherever a person goes, angels walk before him and announce his imminent arrival. "And what do they say? Make room for the icon of the Holy One, Blessed be He!" An icon (*eikon* in Greek) is of course an idol: an image.

Humans were not made as a copy of the image of God, nor do they partake of the image in some way. The human person *is* the image of God. Indeed, while we commonly say that "man was created in the image of God," a more correct articulation would be that each person was created *as* the image of God.[19]

Now we can understand the radical depth of the Jewish monotheistic revolution: just as an image in a temple instantiates the particular god that it manifests, so too do human beings, in the ancient Hebrew understanding, instantiate the one true God, the Creator of the Universe. The Israelites prohibited idols and molten gods because the most fundamental premise of their tradition was that *humans* were the image of God. Humans give expression to God's presence on earth. It is therefore quite unnecessary and indeed forbidden to create images of God, because these are poor substitutes, if not outright forgeries, of the true image of God: people. In idol-worship, the glorification and cult of images replaces the glorification of humanity and, through it, the glorification of God. Jews must therefore reject idol-worship and embrace human-worship as a means to the worship of God. It is in this context that we must also understand the ethics of the prophets, as indeed of Jesus, who insisted on the primacy of moral obligations over ritual ones: respecting humans is no less important than respecting religious rituals. In fact, anyone who does not honor other humans is turning their back on God and will enjoy no reward from performing cultic sacrifices or obeying ritual law.

The analogy that the ancient Israelite faith drew between the images of deities, made of stone or wood, and the image of God, namely man and woman, is emphasized in a Midrash brought to us about Hillel the Elder, one of the most prominent of the ancient Sages:

Hillel the Elder . . . at the time that he was departing from his students, would walk with them. They said to him, "Rabbi, where are you walking to?" He said to them, "To fulfill a commandment!" They said to him, "And what commandment is this?" He said to them, "To bathe in the bathhouse." They said to him: "But is this really a commandment?" He said to them: "Yes. Just like regarding the icons of kings, that are set up in the theaters and the circuses, the one who is appointed over them bathes them and scrubs them, and they give him sustenance, and furthermore, he attains status with the leaders of the kingdom; I, who was created in the [Divine] Image and Form, as it is written, 'For in the Image of G-d He made Man (Genesis 9:6)', even more so!"[20]

Hillel the Elder draws an equivalence between cleaning "icons"— specifically referring to images of kings, in both temples and public spaces—and the human body. As Lorberbaum explains, in the first century CE, during Hillel's lifetime, statues of the Roman emperor were typically placed in public places, including in population centers around the Land of Israel. According to the Midrash, just as the servant responsible for polishing and buffing the statues of emperors is rewarded every year and rises in rank (because serving the statue, or the presence of the emperor, makes him increasingly important), so too, and all the more so, are people rewarded and exalted when they serve their own bodies, for their bodies are the image of God: the presence of the one true God.

We can hear people today referring to their body as "a temple." Hillel would agree. It is a religious commandment, Hillel argues, to wash one's own body (giving us further proof that the human form, and not some internal spiritual element, was then considered the image of God). The human body is to God what the statue of the emperor is to the emperor: a manifestation of the exalted one and an expression of his presence. It is therefore religiously significant to honor it. Humans, all humans, bear the likeness of the King and wear His crown.[21]

Substantive Equality

Genesis 5:1 emphasizes the universality of the principle of the image of God: the Torah is "the record of Adam's line" (not "the record of Israel's line," for example), because all humans were created in God's image. This likeness of God, imprinted in humans, distinguishes and empowers them—and it does so for all of them equally. There is a fundamental basic equality shared by all of humanity.

The idea of fundamental and inherent human equality was not common in the ancient world. In many cultures, genealogical myths about the dawn of humanity distinguished between groups of humans created in fundamentally different ways. In *The Republic,* Plato invokes a myth (which he concedes is false but useful as popular propaganda) that describes how

> God included gold in the mixture when he was forming those of you who have what it takes to be rulers (which is why the rulers have the greatest privileges), silver when he was forming the auxiliaries, and iron and copper when he was forming the farmers and other workers.[22]

Humans are created by God, according to this myth, as fundamentally different from each other—from different materials, with different worth. Some of them, those who contain gold, are born to rule; others, made with silver, will be functionaries; and those rich in iron and copper are born for hard labor. Aristotle, likewise, is very straightforward in stating that some people, "from the hour of their birth . . . are marked out for subjection, others for rule."[23]

The Rigveda, the most ancient and arguably most revered text in the Hindu Vedic tradition, also invokes a myth describing the creation of humans not as equals but as substantively different from each other:

> A Thousand heads hath Purusha, a thousand eyes, a thousand feet. On every side pervading earth he fills a space ten fingers wide. This Purusha is all that yet hath been and all that is to be; The Lord of immortality which waxes greater still by food. . . . When Gods prepared the sacrifice with Purusha as their offering, its oil was spring, the holy gift was autumn; summer was the wood. . . .
>
> From that great general sacrifice the dripping fat was gathered up. He formed the creatures of the air, and animals both wild and tame. . . .
>
> When they divided Purusha how many portions did they make? What do they call his mouth, his arms? What do they call his thighs and feet? The Brahman was his mouth, of both his arms was the Rajanya made. His thighs became the Vaisya, from his feet the Sudra was produced.[24]

This myth describes the primeval reality that preceded Creation. All that existed then was Purusha, which contained within it the whole of existence. The gods, who somehow managed to exist both as part of Purusha and outside it, sacrificed it. The seasons provided the raw material for this ritual, but when they dissected this enormous body, out sprouted a whole array of things. Humans were also created at this point, but not all of them in the same way. "The Brahman was his mouth, of both his arms was the Rajanya made. His thighs became the Vaisya, from his feet the Sudra was produced"—the priestly caste was created from Purusha's mouth, warriors and leaders from its arms, merchants from its thighs, and the lowest form of menial workers from its feet.

This is of course the most basic division of the Indian caste system (although the correct Sanskrit term is in fact *varna*, meaning "class," "type," or "color"), which establishes four separate classes distinguished by their value and roles. In this narrative, human beings were not initially created equal, but as substantively different from each other. These essential differences determine the direction of their lives, their destiny, and their fate. Hindu law would be created in accordance with this narrative: the caste system would be created out of thousands of clauses of discriminatory and exclusionary laws.

The creation of man and woman in the image of God establishes a different human order. All humans are created equal, as expressions of the divine image. We need only look at the words of the U.S. Declaration of Independence—"We hold these truths to be self-evident, that all men are created equal"—to understand how far-reaching the consequences of this basic principle would be for the evolution of Western society.[25]

When Not All Humans Were Created Equal

This is not the only difference, however, between the ancient Hebrew myth of Creation and other creation myths. Attitudes toward the basic concept of the image of God also developed differently between the ancient Hebrew civilization and equivalent ideas in the ancient Near East, as the Hebrew tradition was not alone in casting human beings in the image of God (or rather, of the gods, in the case of other cultures).

We have already noted that in the most basic respect, an image is an idol of a deity. The idea of images, like idolatry in general, was widespread in the ancient world, and they were indeed connected: the image in an ancient temple was a deity, and the creation of an object in the image of the god was the conventional way to establish a relationship with this deity and to establish its presence on earth. The creation of images was how people empowered objects that would manifest the presence of their deities.[26] Similarly, God's creation of a living being in his own image was a way to form a relationship with these creations and to empower them.

Unlike in the Hebrew Bible, however, in other ancient myths not all humans were created in God's image—only a precious few were. Thus, for example, in the ancient Mesopotamian myth of the *Epic of Gilgamesh*, from the late third millennium BCE, the city elders of Uruk beg the god of the heavens, the king of the gods, Anu, to create a double for their king, Gilgamesh, because in his boredom he is harassing them. Anu obliges and addresses the goddess Aruru, who according to Mesopotamian mythology had created Gilgamesh first (and according to a certain myth, also the rest of humanity, although not in her image):

> "Thou, Aruru, didst create [Gilgamesh];
> Create now his double [*zikru*];
> His stormy heart let him match.
> Let them contend, that Uruk may have peace!"
> When Aruru heard this,
> A double [*zikru*] of Anu she conceived within her.
> Aruru washed her hands,
> Pinched off clay and cast it on the steppe.
> [On the steppe] she created valiant Enkidu,
> offspring of . . . essence of Ninurta.[27]

The word *zikru* here can be translated here as "idea," "double," or "image," similar to the biblical verse that posits humans as not only God's "image" but also his "likeness." The meaning is in any case clear: Anu asks Aruru to create a replica, as it were, of Gilgamesh, in order to create an equal to "his stormy heart." Aruru creates Enkidu, but as a double, or in the image, of the god Anu. In any case, this creation is lent distinction and power by virtue of its creation in the image of a god: Enkidu is stronger than ordinary humans and matters more, because he was created in the image of the deity Anu. Enkidu is not just another creation, but one that bears the image of a much greater entity.

In the Babylonian myth of *Enūma Eliš* (believed to be from the late second millennium BCE), we also encounter creation in the image of a god. The beginning of the myth describes the first gods, who are created in the innards of the freshwater god Apsu and the sea god Tiamat. Among the new gods are Anshar, the horizon, whose son is Anu, the god of the heavens. The myth recounts that "Anu begot in his image [*tamšīlu*] Nudimmud."[28] Nudimmud is one of the names of Ea, the god of wisdom and magic, who also replaces Apsu as the god of freshwater.[29] This act of creation (or birth) in the image of the gods not only allows for continuity but empowers the next generation.

The difference between these Mesopotamian myths and Genesis is clear: in the former, specific characters are created or born in the image of a god—heroes or deities. In contrast, the Hebrew Bible tells us that *all of humanity* was created in the image of God. This is a critical difference. When a single individual, like Enkidu, is considered special because he was created in God's image, we have a neat myth. That person's life has exceptional meaning and his story attains iconic status. Tales are told about him, festivals celebrated in his honor.

But if all of humanity is special in the same way, then history itself is a myth that we are all writing together. Everyone's life carries exceptional meaning. The whole of humanity—including all human lives, struggles, challenges, and achievements—become meaningful, as does the life of every single individual. Everyone matters. Humanity celebrates its own existence. If the image of God distinguishes and empowers all its bearers, then unlike the Babylonian myths that empowered gods and heroes, the Hebrew Bible empowered each and every member of humankind.[30]

Here is another example: in the ancient Near East, the king was typically described as the image of God. In a letter from the eighth century BCE addressed to king of Assyria, the writer exalts and praises him as follows: "The father of the king my lord was the image of Bel, and the king my lord is likewise in the image of Bel."[31] In other words, the men of the Assyrian royal family are said to bear the image of the god Bel. In an even earlier period, the sixteenth century BCE in Egypt, the pharaoh is described as "the image of [the god] Ra" and the "image of [the god] Atum." Elsewhere, the god Amun-Re tells Pharaoh Amenophis, who reigned in the fifteenth to fourteenth century BCE: "You are my beloved son, who came forth from my members, my image, whom I have put on earth. I have given to you to rule the earth in peace."[32]

These examples tell us exactly what it means for a specific being to carry the image of God: to be special, powerful, and in control. Once again, in complete contrast to the first chapter of Genesis, the image of God in these examples is reserved exclusively to the king. Only the king was created in the image of God; none of his subjects were. They were therefore inferior, and their lives mattered less than the king's. This, of course, is why the king rules them and they are subordinate to him. The contrary view, that all humans were created in God's image, also bears political significance. It nullifies the assumed legitimacy for rule based on the extraordinary status of the one created in god's image. Indeed it is directly connected to the rise of democracy in the West: if everyone was created in the image of God, then everyone deserves a share of power.

Each Person as a Unique Image

But the notion of the image of God is even more intricate. All statues of an emperor look the same, but people all look different. Unlike idols of deities, which are sculpted to match a specific iconography and must adhere strictly to a list of exact characteristics (with a single inaccuracy ritualistically voiding the image), no two individuals are identical. On the contrary, although all human beings share important traits in common, outwardly they all look different. In Sanhedrin 4:5, the Mishnah explains:

> Therefore, Adam was created alone, to teach that anyone who destroys one soul, the verse ascribes him blame as if he destroyed an entire world. And conversely, anyone who sustains one soul, the verse ascribes him credit as if he sustained an entire world. . . .
>
> And this serves to tell of the greatness of the Holy One, Blessed be He, as when a person stamps several coins with one seal, they are all similar to each other. But the supreme King of kings, the Holy One, Blessed be He, stamped all people with the seal of Adam the first man, and not one of them is similar to another. Therefore, each and every person is obligated to say: The world was created for me.

The Mishnah elucidates two points. First of all, the first man, Adam, was created alone in order to teach that individual humans are entire worlds unto themselves. Just as the first human was the crowning glory of Creation, a unique entity in the world, so too is every individual considered an exceptional, inimitable pinnacle of existence—an entire world. Second, we are told that every person is unique: not only was every human being created in God's image, but like God, humans are one-of-a-kind.

When a person (a king) mints coins in his own image, the coins all come out the same, bearing the same image. But when the King of Kings created human beings, none of them came out looking the same. Each person, therefore, exists in their own right as a world unto themselves. Hence the dictum that whoever takes a single life, it is as if he has destroyed a whole world, and whoever saves a single life, it is as if he has saved a whole world.[33] What we have, therefore, is the idea that in a fundamental sense, not only are all humans equal, but each and every person possess a *unique, singular value*. Every person bears the image of God and manifests its form in a distinct, irreplaceable manner.

"There was something quite innovative and distinctive in the Sages' thought, in emphasizing the differences between people and exalting the value of each and every individual as a unique model of humanity," writes the scholar of Jewish thought Alexander Altmann.[34] The notion of each individual's uniqueness was indeed extremely innovative and audacious, especially in the context of ancient civilizations' collectivist conceptions of the family and community. And whereas the Sages' counterparts at this time—the Gnostics, the authors of the *Corpus Hermeticum*, and the Hellenistic philosophers—understood the body as distinct from the soul and mortals as defective, fallen creatures far removed from the perfection of the realm of ideals or the "world of souls," the Sages discerned a divine presence in humanity and deemed every human a special, unique instantiation of this presence. This was revolutionary.

The notion of man and woman as the image of God serves to counterbalance the conception of humanity as God's submissive servants. Empowered as a bearer of divine presence, humans can, for example, stand before God and argue with him about principles of justice and morality, like Abraham in the story of Sodom ("Shall not the Judge of all the earth deal justly?" in Genesis 18:25) and Moses on many occasions ("When one man sins, will You be wrathful with the whole community?" in Numbers 16:22; see also Exodus 32:11–13 and 32:32, and Numbers 14:13–19). One is not merely God's obedient creation but a thinking, innovating, assertive being. Bearing God's presence, humans are both creations and creators.

This principle would prove tremendously important for the whole of Western civilization. It would become the font of individualism and human rights discourse and it would shape the evolution of the human subject from antiquity to the present. As we shall see, the notion of the image of God would enter the Christian tradition and plant a seed there that would grow over the course of centuries into an expansive tree. But before we address this, let us return to ancient Hebrew law and the ways in which it expressed the principle of the image of God, in the context of our study of the laws of the ancient Near East and the narratives that nourished them and were nourished by them in turn.

"A Person Shall Be Put to Death Only for His Own Crime"

Besides the idea of the law as the direct will of God and the notion of God as the supreme legal subject, ancient Hebrew law was also distinguished by its principle of the image of God. The conception of humans as God's image rendered them, as we have seen, God's representatives and markers of his presence. Humans are God's ambassadors on earth, and all individuals bring to bear a distinct quality of the divine presence. Every person is a world unto themselves.

Since law is a practical expression of the narrative sustaining a particular society, biblical law understandably expresses the principle of the image of God. Thus, for example, we read that whoever kills another person must also be killed ("He who fatally strikes a man shall be put to death," Exodus 22:12). According to biblical law, anyone who deliberately takes another life, as attested by two witnesses, must be put to death. This might not be particularly surprising, but note that in some ancient legal codes, it was acceptable to give compensation for the life of the murder victim. Assyria, for example, had a law permitting the brother of a murder victim to kill the murderer or alternatively to exchange his life for a share of the killer's inheritance.[35] This made pragmatic sense because ancient communities always needed working hands, and the execution of an adult would have kneecapped the work force. Sometimes a murderer could offer somebody else in his stead (usually a relative or a slave). But no such possibilities exist in biblical law, because human life has no substitute. The Hebrew Bible does not allow for somebody else to be executed in the murderer's place, nor can a death sentence be converted for money:

> You may not accept a ransom for the life of a murderer who is guilty of a capital crime; he must be put to death. (Numbers 35:31)[36]

Moreover, not only is human life sacred, but individual human lives are also sacred, because each individual is a unique image of God, a world unto himself or herself. Therefore, the Torah states that "parents shall not be put to death for children, nor children be put to death for parents: a person shall be put to death only for his own crime" (Deuteronomy 24:15). The Bible scholar Moshe Greenberg emphasizes that the statement that "a person shall be put to death only for his own crime" stands in complete contrast to all other ancient Near Eastern legal codes.[37] As we have seen, in Babylonia and Assyria it was taken for granted that proportional punishment meant killing (or raping) a person who stood in the same relationship to the patriarch to whom they were subordinate as the person who was killed (or raped) by the criminal patriarch. The situation here is completely different, and it is different because the basic assumptions underpinning the law are different. The story that the ancient Hebrews told themselves about humans, about their status and worth, was different.

The principle of the image of God thereby received expression. Since, in the Hebrew Bible, humankind's possession of the image of God makes each and every individual exceptionally important, no one may be substituted for another and executed in somebody else's stead. The image of God means not only that humans and God share a fundamental resemblance, but also that every person is unique and irreplaceable. On the one hand, all humans are equal in virtue of their resemblance to God; on the other, every individual is special in virtue of the uniqueness of this same resemblance to God. The Hebrew Bible therefore states: "Whoever sheds the blood of man, by man shall *his* blood be shed; for in His image did God make man" (Genesis 9:6—emphasis mine). Murderers shall be put to death—but *they* are the ones who shall be put to death, and they may not be substituted, for anyone else or for money. Why? Because God created each person in his image. It is the image of God that makes every human a singular, supremely important individual. Conversely, therefore, whereas theft was punishable by death in the laws of Babylonia and Assyria, the Hebrew Bible mandates compensation alone. Human life is too important and precious to be lost on account of property crimes.

This principle was not accepted immediately or straightforwardly. The prevailing view among the Hebrews in the ancient world was the same as in other Near Eastern nations, and it took time for these verses to become axiomatic. Consider this example: in the book of Joshua, we read the story of Achan, who sins by taking plunder from the battle of Jericho (Joshua 7). God tells Joshua that Israel's defeat against the city of Ai was a result of Achan's sins, and Joshua sentences Achan to death. But not only he is executed: so are his sons and daughters and his ox, his donkey, his flock, his tent, "and all his belongings." Achan is the patriarch, the head of his household, and therefore everyone and everything related to him are his, exactly like his arms and legs. He is the only legal subject, and his selfhood includes all of his property. Achan's family are also his possessions, and therefore they too must be punished:

> And Joshua said, "What calamity you have brought upon us! The LORD will bring calamity upon you this day." And all Israel pelted him with stones. They put them to the fire and stoned them. (Joshua 7:25)

The Bible scholar James Kugel notes the peculiar phrasing in this verse, using "they" and "he" interchangeably to refer to those being stoned: they pelted *him* with stones, put *them* to the fire, and stoned *them*. "It is as if the narrator assumes that Achan's offspring and possessions are an extension of his own person," writes Kugel, "as if they are not individuals in our sense, but expressions of a single collective experience."[38] It would seem that in this period, the Hebrews had not yet internalized, or perhaps had not even developed yet, the principle of the image of God and its derivative implications.

In contrast, the prophet Ezekiel showed that he understood those implications when he wrote:

> What do you mean by quoting this proverb upon the soil of Israel, "Parents eat sour grapes and their children's teeth are blunted"? As I live—

declares the Lord GOD—this proverb shall no longer be current among you in Israel. Consider, all lives are Mine; the life of the parent and the life of the child are both Mine. The person who sins, only he shall die. (Ezekiel 18:2–4)

"Parents eat sour grapes and their children's teeth are blunted"? Ezekiel, who prophesied in the sixth century BCE, takes care to emphasize that things should not be this way, because as God says, "all lives are mine." All humans belong to God, and they are all equal before him. Nobody belongs to anybody else, not even a son to his father, and therefore nobody can replace anyone else in receiving their rightful punishment. "The person who sins, only he shall die," states Ezekiel, and later in the chapter he repeats this case:

The person who sins, he alone shall die. A child shall not share the burden of a parent's guilt, nor shall a parent share the burden of a child's guilt; the righteousness of the righteous shall be accounted to him alone, and the wickedness of the wicked shall be accounted to him alone. (Ezekiel 18:20)

Ezekiel's repeated emphasis of this principle suggests that some people had not yet grasped this point and still believed in the concept of "ancestral sin."[39] It would take time before nobody else would be punished for the sins of another person, but this time would come. The principle, in any case, is clear: all human beings are unique and irreplaceable. We are all complete legal subjects and must therefore be punished personally for our sins. In time, this principle would engender the understanding that individuals are exclusively responsible for their own deeds, and from it the notion that autonomy is a necessary condition for self-worth and self-determination would develop. Subsequently the idea of the image of God would be secularized and transformed into the concept of dignity—secularizing the Western world with it.

Our Self-Conception: The Boundary between Inside and Out

In the previous section, we examined the importance of law as an expression of an entire social narrative. We saw that the laws of the ancient Near East did not treat people as individuals but as elements of social structures headed by patriarchs. We also noted that Hebrew law contained the first seeds of the recognition of, and even respect for, the life of the human individual. We elaborated, therefore, on the social dimensions of human life in antiquity, which found expression in the laws and theological principles underpinning them.

Let us now proceed to examine another aspect of human life, one that characterizes human psychology. Understanding it will allow us to explore another major difference between humans in the past and in modern times. This will give us a better understanding of what is it like *not* to be an individual, how the modern subject emerged and how it is connected to the principle of the image of God. This matter appears simple: one's conception of oneself and the boundary between oneself and the world.

It bears saying a few preliminary words about our sense of selfhood. In short: it is not fixed. There is no simple conception of selfhood common to all humanity, everywhere and at every time. We conceive of ourselves, that is, of our lives as self-conscious entities, in manifold ways. At the most basic level, we see variations between different people's sense of self, or between the same person's sense of self at different times, as when we examine their conscious state under the influence of intoxicating or hallucinogenic substances or during spiritual or mystical experiences. To use an extreme example, one who feels "at one with the world" and another who honestly reports having "lost his sense of self" experience themselves completely differently from the rest of us. The former, we may say, experiences himself as a totality, as the whole of existence; the latter, as an absence or emptiness. Without delving into the nature of these experiences now (and it does not matter whether they are ontologically valid—this is about how people experience *themselves*), these examples attest to the potential malleability of the human sense of self.

It is clear to the scientific world nowadays that there is no "center" or "core" in the brain that contains our sense of self. There is no "command and control center" that receives our sensory data and returns instructions to our limbs. The mind, as we now understand it, is not a linear system operating from a single point but a decentralized network operating in parallel and complementary manners. Out of these operations, the mind creates a certain model of selfhood: a sense of self that distinguishes between "me" and "not me."[40] This boundary, between the self and the not-self, and the classification of thoughts, memories, and feelings as belonging or not belonging to oneself, are the axes along which the sense of self varies between different people, and of course between different societies and historical periods. Indeed, my argument here, following philosophers such as Charles Taylor and scholars such as James Kugel, is that the contours of the self have changed over the past 2,000 years.[41]

Interestingly, the human self, which was much less consolidated in the ancient past, used to experience wishes, feelings, and desires not as internal but as externally sourced. Down the ages, our sense of self gradually became closed and came to be positioned, or so it seemed, in a subjective and private "internal" sphere. That was when the self appropriated for itself those elements that would previously have been considered foreign or external.

In the West, this process attained unique dimensions. Modern Westerners have a different conception of the self from others around the world, and indeed from others in the past. Specifically, most of us feel ourselves to be autonomous individuals, independent of and not necessarily connected to our surroundings, and we do so in a fairly extreme manner without historical precedent. As the American social psychologist Walter Anderson writes:

> Most people in the past were probably not individual selves in the modern Western sense, and people in some parts of the world probably are not now. That is, they do not experience themselves as clearly bounded, but rather as seamlessly embedded in their tribes and their ecosystems; they do not think of themselves as unique, but rather as more or less identical to others of their kind; and they do not think of themselves as neatly integrated, but rather as invaded by strange spirits and forces that may pull them in many different directions.[42]

Anderson presents a clear dichotomy. In practice, as we shall see, there exists a continuum along which the boundary between the self and the not-self, and the potential for certain mental features to be experienced as part of the self or as foreign, vary in their frequency and intensity. The distinction between Western and non-Western is not as sharp as it is often taken to be. But the key point is that our conception of the self as modern Westerners (a conception that is extreme in its closure to its surroundings and affirmation of individual autonomy), is only one of many possibilities.[43] As Clifford Geertz writes in a celebrated article,

> The Western conception of the person as a bounded, unique, more or less integrated motivational and cognitive universe; a dynamic center of awareness, emotion, judgment, and action organized into a distinctive whole . . . is, however incorrigible it may seem to us, a rather peculiar idea within the context of the world's cultures.[44]

We shall see that this conception emerged from within Christendom, especially in the English-speaking world, and draws fundamentally on the principle of the image of God. In the ancient Near East, including in the Hebrew kingdoms, selfhood was connected to the body, and the body, as we have seen, was connected to the family, specifically the paterfamilias, and beyond all this, to dynastic ancestors and to one's broader tribe. In fact, according to Ayelet Hoffmann Libson, who has studied the development of the subjective self in the writings of the Jewish Sages, only between the second and fourth centuries CE did a new sensitivity develop toward an internal sense of self, attaching unprecedented importance to the world of feeling and consciousness.[45] The Hebrew Bible and the earlier Tannaitic Midrashim placed no such emphasis on the internal world. The rise of Christianity played a critical role in this regard, but for this revolution, it drew on ancient Jewish ideas.

Fear of God and God-Given Courage

If the conception of the self "as a bounded, unique, more or less integrated motivational and cognitive universe; a dynamic center of awareness, emotion, judgment, and action," as Geertz puts it, is primarily a modern Western story, then we must understand what other forms of the self looked like. For this purpose, we shall explore ancient sources attesting to a conception of selfhood in which there was no clear boundary between the self and what lay beyond it, and we shall examine how this boundary gradually came into focus. In other words, we shall seek to uncover the process whereby we evolved from having a weak and fluid sense of self to consolidating a sense of self that was closed and personal. In order to do so and to check how a different conception of selfhood found expression in antiquity, we begin with an ideal, or a value, that played a central role in ancient cultures: heroism.

Heroism was one of the most important values in the ancient world. Fighting on the battlefield, assuming personal risks, displaying bravery, achieving victory over one's enemies, acquiring glory, and making a name for oneself—all these stand at the core of many of the mythological texts that have survived and been handed down to us. From Babylon to Greece, heroes were those who exhibited great courage and were glorified almost exclusively for this trait. In contrast to the ideal presented by the Sages and adopted by the early Christian world, these daring warriors' heroism was expressed neither in their self-restraint nor in their ability to conquer their desires, but in their willingness to risk their lives and chop off their enemies' limbs. Had these heroes not exhibited courage on the battlefield and brought back their enemies' scalps (or worse), they would probably not have been considered heroic at all.

But when we look more closely at how acts of heroism are depicted in these myths, or more precisely, how heroism itself is described, we notice that the ancients did not conceive of courage in the same way as we do. In fact, although nowadays we can easily identify with ideals such as battlefield bravery, we cannot identify with how people grasped them in the distant past.

Thus, for example, in the Mesopotamian *Epic of Gilgamesh*, which we touched on earlier in addressing the conception of the image of God in the ancient Near East, Gilgamesh together with his good friend Enkidu plot to kill the monster Huwawa. But when he stands before Huwawa, after a grueling journey, he is overcome with fear. The myth tells us how events unfolded:

> By all this hubbub Gilgamesh disturbed Huwawa in his den,
> (Huwawa) let loose his terrifying radiance against him.
> Gilgamesh . . . was held as if in deep sleep,
> [Enkidu] was in a stupor.[46]

Gilgamesh awakens Huwawa from its slumber, and the monster immediately unleashes its "terrifying radiance" against him and instills him with cowardice. Gilgamesh is "held as if in deep sleep," the ancient myth tells us, and our hero requires words of encouragement from Enkidu, which wake him up and envelop him (as we read in the next lines), "like a wooden garment." Notice that fear enters Gilgamesh from the outside, and so does courage. The fear is the "terrifying radiance" emitted by the monster in front of him;[47] courage is the armor that protects him against this radiance—armor built of the words of encouragement of Enkidu (who as we recall, is not a mere mortal but the handiwork of the goddess of creation Aruru, created in the image of the god Anu). It is important to note: Gilgamesh does not muster courage as an internal mental resource; his heroism is entirely imported from the outside.

In the *Iliad*, the Greek epic ascribed to Homer, we see a similar pattern. The *Iliad* was probably completed around 750 BCE but was based on much more ancient material. It tells the story of the mythological Battle of Troy, waged between the armies of Agamemnon and Paris, Prince of Troy, after the latter kidnaps Helen, the beautiful wife of King Menelaus of Sparta. It contains many tales of battlefield heroism, which understandably form a central theme of the myth, but here too, heroism often enters the hero from the outside-in.

Thus, for example, the kidnapped Queen Helen's husband Menelaus is the subject of a whole paean in the *Iliad* exalting his heroism. The Spartan king approaches the walls of Troy in order to rescue the body of Patroclus, one of the fallen heroes of the forces besieging Troy. Before this act of heroism, the goddess Athena imbues him with strength and courage:

> At this the grey-eyed goddess [Athena] secretly
> took pleasure, that of all the gods he chose
> to make his prayer to her. Power in his shoulders
> she instilled, and gristle in his knees,
> and in his heart the boldness of a shad-fly,
> fiercely brushed away but mad to bite,
> as human blood is ambrosial drink to him.
> So furious daring swelled in Menelaus's
> dark chest-cave, and he regained his place
> above Patroclus, levelling his spear.[48]

The "furious daring" that Athena instills in Menelaus, along with the strength given to his shoulders and knees, allows him to run beneath the walls of Troy and defend Patroclus's honor. He thus becomes a hero. In the *Iliad*, we encounter many more cases in which the courage required of a hero to perform his act of heroism is given to him, and practically instilled into him, by the gods.[49] This phenomenon, at least for those worthy, is quite common and routine.

It would be a mistake to dismiss these stories as flowery descriptions or metaphors. Ancient Mesopotamian civilizations, much like the ancient Greeks, lived in a world in which the gods existed as a simple and obvious part of reality. Although later generations of Greeks could treat the gods as metaphors or personified forces, during Homer's time and beforehand, the pantheon on Mount Olympus was thought to exist as a straightforward reality. Moreover, for these ancients, the gods not only existed and not only influenced world events, but they also influenced people's feelings and decisions. It was the gods who suffused warriors with courage, stoking their confidence to run into battle.

Note that Menelaus does not develop this courage *as a result* of some positive influence by the goddess. Athena does not offer him encouragement and thus inspire his courage. She does not appear by his side, place a hand on his shoulder, whisper in his ear, "You're the greatest!" and thus cultivate his self-confidence. Such an interpretation would involve the projection of a modern, complete, autonomous self onto a past in which this was not the accepted conception. As we shall see imminently, for our ancestors, the self was not a holistic entity *onto which* external forces exercised an influence. The self was a battlefield, a completely open space *within which* different forces, including gods, operated. Athena does not therefore need to play on Menelaus's mind and manipulate him with flattery or words of encouragement. She simply places courage in Menelaus's chest, and he becomes courageous.

By the same token, prayer is not simply a means of asking the gods to intervene on the battlefield or shape the course of events to the advantage of the person offering the prayer. Prayer is a means of asking the gods to give one courage. "Fill his heart with courage!" Achilles prays to Zeus before his friend Patroclus sets out for battle, the battle in which he is killed. The gods are not only responsible for the course of the warfare but also for the emotional dispositions of the warriors.

This was true not only of Mesopotamia and ancient Greece, but also of Israel. When Saul goes to war against Nahash the Ammonite, it is God who imbues him with might. As the narrative goes, Nahash besieges the town of Jabesh-Gilead, on the eastern bank of the Jordan River. The men of Jabesh-Gilead ask Nahash to spare their lives and offer to become his slaves in exchange. Nahash agrees, but he has a condition for the covenant of their servitude, he insists that "everyone's right eye be gouged out."

> The elders of Jabesh said to him, "Give us seven days' respite, so that we may send messengers throughout the territory of Israel; if no one comes to our aid, we will surrender to you."
>
> When the messengers came to Gibeah of Saul and gave this report in the hearing of the people, all the people broke into weeping. Saul was just coming from the field driving the cattle; and Saul asked, "Why are the people crying?" And they told him about the situation of the men of Jabesh.
>
> When he heard these things, *the spirit of God gripped Saul* and his anger blazed up. He took a yoke of oxen and cut them into pieces, which he sent by messengers throughout the territory of Israel, with the warning, "Thus shall be done to the cattle of anyone who does not follow Saul and Samuel into battle!" Terror from the LORD fell upon the people, and they came out as one man. (I Samuel 11:1–7, emphasis mine)

Nahash's condition for a covenant of servitude was gouging out each man's right eye.[50] The people of Jabesh-Gilead appeal to his mercy and ask for one week to think about his offer, and Nahash, ever the gentleman, obliges. The men use this time to call for help. They send messengers to their compatriots on the western bank of the Jordan, but everyone who hears their story bursts into tears. Who could possibly stand up to Nahash the Ammonite? Saul, who by now has been secretly anointed king by Samuel, is the only one who is filled with rage and a willingness to confront the Ammonites. This is not a fluke, nor is it because of his record of exceptional bravery. The Hebrew Bible tells us that the "spirit of God" grips Saul when he hears this news. It is God who instills him with his fighting spirit, and Saul's actions, inspired by God, put the fear of God in the rest of the people. Only then do they form a united front for war—"Terror from the LORD fell upon the people, and they came out as one man"—and grant Saul his first victory as king.

It seems therefore that heroism, one of the core ideals of antiquity, was understood completely differently from its modern sense. For us, heroism is not the sort of thing that can be instilled in us by an external agent, whether that outside force be a Greek goddess or the God of Israel. Courage for us is not an essence or a substance but a character trait and a mode of behavior. In order to be courageous, it is not enough to appeal to some higher power and ask it to make us courageous. We associate courage with an inner ability to consciously confront danger and with a determination to fight basic instincts such as the urge for flight, the concern for survival, and fear of death. Courageous individuals are those who can balance these against other values or goods (glory, honor, homeland, fellow citizens, our loved ones). For us, the performance of courageous acts involves a difficult and painful mental process of perseverance and determination. In doing so, one can certainly pray to a higher power, but courage is not a gift from God, and it is certainly not a foreign element thrust into one's chest. On the contrary, if a soldier returning from the battlefield were to describe an act of wartime heroism as the consequence of some divine activity inside him, rather than of an autonomous, internal decision, we would not consider his deed courageous. We might view it as religiously significant, or we might consider it a case of self-deception or delusion, but in any case, we would not value it as an act of heroism.

When courage is something that cannot enter one from the outside, it is one's own responsibility. It is not a gift from the gods but the result of personal effort or some inherent quality. When an army hero receives a citation for outstanding service and humbly whispers, "I was only doing my duty," we know that they acted above and beyond the call of duty by placing themselves in personal danger in order to save others. They displayed heroism on the battlefield. If they were to say that they had been gripped by the spirit of God, which propelled them to place explosives next to an enemy bunker, and that other soldiers froze because they were not gripped by the abovementioned spirit, the hero would probably still be awarded his citation—but we would probably feel a bit awkward about it.

Depression Is the Malevolent Spirit of God

Besides the case of his victory over Nahash, King Saul had a long and complicated relationship with various manifestations of the "spirit of

God." It begins in I Samuel 10, where Saul is sent by Samuel to "prophesy": to suffuse himself with the spirit of God by joining forces with a band of prophets using musical instruments to summon the spirit of God to visit them. When the spirit of God falls upon him, he becomes "another man," meaning that he undergoes some inner transformation. This spirit of God is benevolent, therefore, and empowers Saul, and immediately in chapter 11 we understand that it is essential in preventing Saul from breaking into tears like the rest of his countrymen and becoming sufficiently courageous to rally others to war.

But the spirit of God is not always kind to Saul. After several incidents in which he violates God's word, the spirit of God that grips him changes. This happens immediately after Samuel anoints David as king instead of Saul:

> Samuel took the horn of oil and anointed him [David] in the presence of his brothers; and the spirit of the LORD gripped David from that day on. Samuel then set out for Ramah. Now the spirit of the LORD had departed from Saul, and an evil spirit from the LORD began to terrify him. (I Samuel 16:13–14)

The good spirit of God grips David and departs from Saul, who from that day on is haunted by a bad spirit of God.[51] This is his famous case of depression, which Saul will suffer from for the rest of his life. Saul becomes an angry, jealous, and miserable man, susceptible to paroxysms of fury. His courtiers notice this shift immediately and suggest a possible source of relief:

> Saul's courtiers said to him, "An evil spirit of God is terrifying you. Let our lord give the order [and] the courtiers in attendance on you will look for someone who is skilled at playing the lyre; whenever the evil spirit of God comes over you, he will play it and you will feel better." (I Samuel 16:15–16)

It is obvious to Saul's courtiers that his gloomy mood is the result of an "evil spirit of God"—what else could induce depression?—and they propose to find him a lyre player, whose music will improve his mental state (here too, as in chapter 10 of I Samuel, the spirit of God can be invoked through music). This lyre player, of course, is none other than David. And indeed, Saul's courtiers' advice proves to be successful:

> Whenever the [evil] spirit of God came upon Saul, David would take the lyre and play it; Saul would find relief and feel better, and the evil spirit would leave him. (I Samuel 16:23)

The music quite plainly causes the malevolent spirit of God to depart from Saul, whose mood accordingly improves.

Like the *Iliad*, these verses from the book of Samuel were probably written in the sixth century BCE, and like the *Iliad*, here too the material is based on stories that unfolded much earlier (Samuel and Saul, if they were historical figures, lived in the eleventh century BCE).[52] What all these narratives and also the much more ancient *Epic of Gilgamesh* have in common is their conception of humans as perpetually susceptible to external forces. This is not merely in the simple sense of vulnerability to natural disasters or the caprices of the gods. Not only are people's bodies at the mercy of the outside world; so is their self. For the people who wrote these stories, the human mind was a field on which external forces operated. People's mental and psychological lives were not really "theirs," certainly not in the sense that we would understand nowadays. They conceived of the human mentality as open, with outside forces able to freely enter and exit. Gods and monsters could imbue people with fear, courage, joy, or sorrow. The sound of music could allow the good spirit of God to grip one and the evil spirit to leave.

Divine Inspiration

The distinction between the "objective" and "subjective" dimensions is one of the most obvious and fundamental binary divisions in our lives, and it points to how we understand our own minds as private and closed. The mind is something completely different from the outside world, separate and even detachable from it. It is private and belongs to each individual alone. We imagine ourselves to be complete, autonomous entities possessing private mental lives that unfold in our consciousness and belong to us alone.

In ancient times, and in fact to some extent until the dawn of the modern era, the boundaries between inside and outside were exceptionally flimsy. Distinctions were drawn, of course, between the "heart" or the "soul" on the one hand and the visible world of objects, but these were not considered two substantively different and irreconcilable domains but rather two poles of a single reality. The conception that was widely taken for granted was of a single gradated continuum from the heart and all the way up to some higher plane, from one's personal mental domain as far as the horizon. Moreover, the soul was not seen as a single whole but as a composite. Various forces operated inside it, not all of them belonging to the same central entity. Memories, feelings, and desires emerged, disappeared, and intermingled. In the context of such a conception of a totally open and decentralized consciousness, the gods could introduce courage, fear, or depression into people's souls.

In fact, sometimes there was no choice but for the gods to intervene, because the simple understanding was that such transcendent things could not possibly emerge from within ourselves independently. Who are *we*, after all? Therefore both the *Odyssey* and the *Iliad* begin, as customary in the ancient world, with an appeal to the divine muses to give the poet the ability to compose his epic: "Sing, O Muse . . ." Without divine inspiration, there could be no writing. The author of Psalm 51 also asks, "O LORD, open my lips, and let my mouth declare Your praise," for how else could one praise the Lord without the Lord helping out by placing words in one's mouth? These appeals must be understood not as empty blandishments, but as genuine requests for the dubbing powers of heavenly forces. As the Classicist Bruno Snell writes in connection to the *Odyssey* and the *Iliad*:

> Homer, however, could not do without the deity. . . . Homer's man does not yet regard himself as the source of his own decisions. . . . Homer lacks a knowledge of the spontaneity of the human mind; he does not realize that decisions of the will, or any impulses or emotions, have their origin in man himself.[53]

Snell might be exaggerating slightly, because the dichotomy between these possibilities is not entirely clear-cut. It also appears more apt to say that, far from failing to understand something, Homer (like the psalmist), simply had a different conception of the self. Similarly, we are not exactly failing to understand how Homer conceived the world, as much as we simply experience the world differently. But one thing is clear: for our ancestors, external intervention was often required for the self to be able to act—or more precisely, for the self to be operated like a puppet-master operates a marionette.

The Porous Self

This will be evident if we examine the *Testaments of the Twelve Patriarchs*.[54] This apocryphal, extra-canonical text from the first century, if not somewhat earlier, presents the supposed last wills and testaments of the Children of Israel: the sons of the Patriarch Jacob with his two wives and two concubines. One by one, Jacob's sons impart their wisdom and dying wishes. This composition was written, of course, not by Reuben, Gad, Levi, and their brothers, but by an author who lived in a much later period and wished to place his own thinking in their mouths, using their names and authority to lend his words added veracity.

The *Testaments of the Twelve Patriarchs* did not enter the canon, but it teaches us a great deal about people's thinking at the time of its writing. The scroll contains many interesting gems, but we shall focus on its author's proposed explanation for sin. Right at the beginning, in Reuben's last will and testament, the author explains that human beings are fated to sin because evil spirits lurk inside them. Inside the human body,

> are mingled the spirits of error. First, the spirit of fornication is seated in the nature and in the senses; the second, the spirit of insatiableness, in the belly; the third, the spirit of fighting, in the liver and gall. The fourth is the spirit of obsequiousness and chicanery, that through officious attention one may be fair in seeming. The fifth is the spirit of pride, that one may be boastful and arrogant. The sixth is the spirit of lying, in perdition and jealousy to practise deceits, and concealments from kindred and friends. The seventh is the spirit of injustice, with which are thefts and acts of rapacity, that a man may fulfill the desire of his heart; for injustice worketh together with the other spirits by the taking of gifts. And with all these the spirit of sleep is joined which is (that) of error and fantasy. And so perisheth every young man, darkening his mind

from the truth, and not understanding the law of God, nor obeying the admonitions of his fathers as befell me also in my youth.[55]

As we can see from the text, sexual urges, hunger, fighting, obsequiousness, pride, mendacity, injustice, and sleep are but different spirits, "mingling" in the body, and it is these spirits that cause one to sin. The person is not hungry or proud; they simply have spirits inside them that *make them* feel hunger or pride. The intermixture between what we perceive as character traits and purely physical matters is not accidental, but rather points to the author's conception of the human subject: as modern individuals, we draw a distinction between pride, for example, which is a character trait of certain people and indeed fundamental to their selfhood (although in most cases, we think that this trait can be disposed of by means of internal change, be it psychological or spiritual), and hunger or sleep, which are unrelated to the self, but which strike us "from the outside." But for the author of the *Testaments of the Twelve Patriarchs*, pride is external to the self, exactly like hunger.

The modern self is internal, spiritual, and bounded. The self as described in the *Testaments of the Twelve Patriarchs* is spread all throughout the body, as physical as it is spiritual, and open to all directions. The selfhood of the author of this text includes the body, and it is not an internal and autonomous locus of desire or liberty. Human selfhood, in this conception, is decentralized, unbounded, and entirely open to the intrusion of alien forces. These forces change the self from the "inside" and impose wickedness or obsequiousness on it, just as they subject it to hunger or tiredness.

The Canadian philosopher Charles Taylor calls this the "porous self": a conception of selfhood in which the boundaries of the self are open and porous.[56] The porous self was typical of the premodern world, and it situated people in a completely different existential experience from what we, as modern individuals, know. Possessing a porous self, premodern individuals were permanently exposed to a range of forces that might not only influence them from the outside but also penetrate them and cause them to act in certain ways. Gods, demons, angels, and dead souls—the universe was full of entities, some good and some bad, capable of entering us and changing us from within. When, in the *Testaments of the Twelve Patriarchs*, Simeon elaborates on why he sought to kill his brother Joseph (in the famous narrative that we all know as the story of Joseph and his brothers), he explains that "I set my mind against him to destroy him, because the prince of deceit sent forth the spirit of jealousy and blinded my mind, so that I regarded him not as a brother."[57] Simeon set his mind against Joseph (or literally in the original Hebrew, his "heart hardened") because something got inside him: the "spirit of jealousy," sent forth by the "prince of deceit." In such a world, people were at the mercy of alien forces, which forced evil onto them and made them behave accordingly. But this did not absolve them of blame in the eyes of their contemporaries, just as the good spirits that propelled them to acts of heroism did not diminish their heroism, nor deprive them of their rightful glory.

Since people did not possess an internal, autonomous, and cohesive world separate from the "objective" world around them, there was no way for them to conceive of a "subjective" domain as clearly belonging to them—as something private, intimate, and "theirs." Accordingly, there was no way for them to ascribe authenticity or legitimacy to actions originating only in such a subjective realm. One's selfhood, personality, and persona were much more explicitly associated with one's body. A person *was* his body (and everything his body contained and did), and not, as we conceive of it nowadays, an amorphous personality located somewhere *in* the body, be it the heart or the brain or the soul.

This has significant ramifications. Since a person was a body, familial relations were much more important and were in fact considered an integral part of one's personhood. This corresponds to their diminished individuality, of course. One's deeds were also much more important: people were judged much more by their behavior than by their thoughts (note the importance attached in ancient faiths, like Judaism and the religion of ancient Rome, to bodily rituals and commandments). In light of all this, it is also clear why the "image of God" was understood as being something much more corporeal than spiritual.

Note that this was not a matter of faith or a theory about the world, but a basic conceptualization of life and an existential experience. This was how people lived. And this lived experience was quite frightening. In this reality, people were perpetually at the mercy of much greater and more powerful forces. Not only their bodies, but also their psyches, feelings, and even loftiest traits (such as courage and creativity) were a playing field for foreign entities.

People were not independent, not only because they depended on others, but, on a much more profound level, because others were interfering with their very selves. In this reality, individuals had no choice but to constantly seek protection and support from the forces they considered good: saints, angels, and of course—God. As Taylor suggests, it is practically impossible for the porous self to contemplate atheism, but not for lack of knowledge about the world, nor even because the existence of gods and demons is an obvious matter of consensus. Denying the existence of God is near impossible because one experiences the world—and more importantly, oneself—as a battlefield over which one has hardly any control. One is completely dependent on a benevolent god to give one strength, health, life, and protection against the evil forces that are constantly trying to steal all these away. A person cannot do so alone, and cannot imagine ever being able to. One's only recourse is simply to surrender to this higher, protective power.[58]

What Is Melancholy?

If, thousands of years ago, people experienced their selfhood as a battlefield open to external forces, disease was presumably also considered the result of external intervention. Indeed, we know that the word "influenza" comes from the Latin *influentia*, meaning "influence." It is of course the influence of the stars that makes us sick. How else might one explain cold-like symptoms if not through celestial imposition?

What about other illnesses, physical and mental? We have already seen that the ancient texts depicting the gods as directly intervening in the human consciousness, with stories about divine entities filling people's chests with courage, were written before 1000 BCE at the latest. The closer we get to the present, the more we witness forces shaping one's mood gradually ceasing to be seen as external, and becoming internalized. For the Judaism of the Sages, external demonic forces had evolved into an inner *yetzer hara*, or evil impulse, which was no longer situated outside but rather became part of every person's inner being.[59] This *yetzer hara* fights to control people's decisions (or capacity for reason) from inside them.

Socrates, who features in Plato's writings some 400 years after Homer, also tends to consult the *daimonion* that speaks to him from inside him. Socrates's *daimonion* is not an external deity but an inner voice, albeit one that is distinct from the rational part of the self.[60] This voice, which we would now call a "conscience" (we shall address the rise of the conscience as a source of authority later on), is for Socrates an alien, non-human entity. On the other hand, this entity is internal, and Socrates can choose not to listen to it. In this regard, Socrates presents a different conception of selfhood from that of Homeric heroism.

In this reality, people still possessed porous selves, and their mood was still susceptible to direct manipulation, but entities such as gods or demons were no longer routinely intervening in people's psyches, and on the rare occasions when they did so, it was considered worthy of especial praise (as in the case of visitations or visions of angels) or condemnation (as with possession, dybbuks, and similar phenomena). In time, our psychological lives became entirely internalized. The classicist E. R. Dodds famously concluded that, in the first centuries CE, a dividing line emerged between the body and the soul, which was clearly related to the emerging dividing line between the self and the world.[61] In the modern world, this dividing line is already considered obvious.

In order to briefly illustrate the evolution of this process, let us examine the depression that afflicted King Saul. We have seen that it was the result of an "evil spirit of God" terrifying him. Notice that the evil spirit does not *cause* depression: it does not settle in Saul's soul and foster sadness. Such an anachronistic interpretation would confuse the premodern conception of the human subject (as possessing a decentralized, porous self) with the complete modern self ("Saul's soul" as a bounded, clearly circumscribed entity). For the authors of the Hebrew Bible, the evil spirit *is* depression. Depression enters Saul from the outside, and makes him depressed. Similarly, the music of the lyre does not make Saul happy; it takes the evil spirit out of him. It literally lifts his spirits.

The situation changed gradually with the development of humorism, the medical lore of the ancient West, formulated by Hippocrates, the "father of Western medicine," in the fifth-century BCE in Greece. This medical conception is based on the supposed existence of four "humors" (materials of different colors and characteristics) in the human body, which must be balanced in order to ensure good physical and mental health (which are correlated in this system). The rise of humoral medicine led to an internalization: depression was gradually transformed from being an intrusive evil spirit in the body into an excess of "black bile"—that is, an overabundance of a chemical that already existed in the body. Depression, here, was in the most literal sense, the black liquid that constitutes one of the four humors in the body (together with blood, yellow bile, and phlegm).[62] An excess of black bile is depression. As Hippocrates wrote, around the turn of the fourth century BCE: "If a fright or despondency lasts for a long time, it is a melancholic affection."[63]

Depression, sadness itself, a bad mood, comes from black bile, a black liquid in the body. Hippocrates uses the Greek *melas kholé*, which we know as melancholy. *Melas kholé* literally translates as "black bile," and black bile is the source of "fright or despondency." The affliction, then, that in the second millennium BCE was caused by the "terrifying radiance" of a monster or the "evil spirit" of God became, in the mid-first millennium BCE, a black substance in the human body.

It bears emphasizing: black bile does not *cause* depression; it *is* the substance that is the quality of depression. When it exists in excess, *there is depression in the body.* "The emotional life is porous here again; it doesn't simply exist in an inner, mental space,"[64] a space that can supposedly be influenced or not. Our mental lives exist inside our bodies, and our bodies are composed of humors. The result of an excess of black bile is depression, just as the result of an excess of yellow bile is a nasty temper, and of an excess of phlegm is apathy (hence the adjective "phlegmatic").

The change relative to earlier eras was that black bile was not a foreign divinity that caused people to act in certain ways by infiltrating them from the outside, but a chemical that already suffused the body. The boundaries around the body were already much more rigid, and outside forces could no longer enter as easily. On the other hand, people still did not conceive of themselves as autonomous, bounded entities located inside their bodies and influenced by different chemicals, but as decentralized systems of substances and activities. An individual's selfhood *was* this system. The self was not yet a kind of centralized, internal command center but a collection of forces (goodwill, the "evil impulse," wisdom, desire) and substances. Depression was an excess of black bile in the body, and if this black bile returned to its desired proportions and proper balance with the other humors, the result would be health, happiness, and kindness.

This way of thinking is completely different from how we, as modern individuals, experience our own lives. We experience the self as a substantive locus, a center of consciousness and agency located "inside" our bodies. This locus of selfhood supervises and commands our bodies and exists in an interactive relationship of negotiation with the outside world. The outside world, in turn, is distant and different from us. Taylor calls this the "buffered self." A clear buffer exists between inside and outside. The distinction between the internal "subjective" self and the external "objective" world is one of the most natural and obvious parts of how we view the world. In contrast, at a time when *melancholia* was both a chemical and a feeling, clearly such a distinction between the objective and the subjective did not exist.

In the modern world, if we feel despondent, we can point to a physical or psychological cause (such as hormones or PTSD, respectively). The self, bounded and internal, is susceptible to a range of factors but it can also shield itself against them. Although they can influence how we feel, there are no foreign elements that can intervene in our essence. Depression is not a part of us, but something that happens *to* us. The subjective and objective realms are quite distinct.

This understanding places us in a completely different situation. It allows us to treat depression with a certain detachment, which facilitates equanimity. We have control over the situation, because the situation is not us. There is no "depression liquid" that is part of who we are, and there are certainly no foreign forces, whether demons or divine spirits, entering us and changing us from within. We are autonomous and free of external influence upon our selfhood.

This development in our self-awareness is transformative. As Taylor writes,

> winning through to a self-defining identity was accompanied by a sense of exhilaration and power, that the subject need no longer define his perfection or vice, his equilibrium or disharmony, in relation to an external order. With the forging of this modern subjectivity there comes a new notion of freedom.[65]

This new notion of freedom—freedom as autonomy—is seminal to our journey into modernity. It spells empowered individualism, liberalism, and indeed secularism.

Depression at the Dawn of Modernity

The transition toward the modern conception of the self was of course gradual and protracted, but by the eighteenth century, we can already clearly discern the modern individual. In this section, we shall explore its growth by examining how depression was understood in this period. As an illustration, we shall consider a text that offers a clear social and historical representation of the modern era: the *Encyclopédie* by Denis Diderot (1713–1784). The *Encyclopédie*, the first volume of which was published in France in 1751, was one of the most famous attempts to organize humanity's knowledge. It was a quintessential representation of the spirit of the Enlightenment, and it enjoyed dizzying commercial success at the time of its publication. It heralded for its readers a new age of humanism, of the aggregation and study of knowledge that for the first time was considered *human*: of the sort discovered and verified by people, rather than received through divine revelation. Humanity was now assembling in one place the sum of the knowledge that it required, knowledge that it had discovered and could validate. For eighteenth-century Europeans, this was nothing short of a declaration of independence.

In Volume X of the *Encyclopédie*, published in 1765, Diderot offers a definition of melancholy. For Diderot, melancholy is a mental and physical problem caused by "grief, pains of the spirit, passions, as well as all the love and sexual appetites that go unsatisfied."[66] Depression, therefore, is caused by a range of psychological issues. Diderot mocks those who ascribe it to demonic possession: such a diagnosis, he claims, is like a *deus ex machina*, the sudden appearance of a god in a story or play to easily resolve an otherwise problematic plot point.

Diderot also acknowledges that for "the majority of modern people," the existence of "black bile" is "ridiculous and imaginary," although he himself does not dismiss this possibility out of hand. In any case, according to Diderot, the cure for melancholy lies not in balancing the humors but, besides abstinence from smoked and salted meat and from certain liquors, in emotional therapy: therapists must obtain the trust of those suffering from melancholy and lead them, through cooperation with their fantasies rather than resistance to them, to understand that their melancholic beliefs are mere illusions.

In the modern world, therefore, melancholy becomes an *emotional problem* at the level of the individual. It is caused by a range of factors, but the cure lies in therapeutic dialogue with the melancholiac, leading them to understand and recognize that their beliefs are untrue. Diderot thinks that music might help—not by banishing an evil spirit inside the melancholiac, but by distracting them. Nor is there a need to manipulate an internal system of liquids. Melancholy is treated by directly addressing the individual or *subject*: not the forces inside them, which somehow constitute him or her. We meet an autonomous, self-responsible agent that is supposed to undergo a therapeutic process releasing them from depression, which is not a liquid but a mood. The modern individual is here.

The Buffered Self and Secularization

We are modern individuals, but the conception of the porous self, despite being alien to us, is still within reach. People can still believe that they have been possessed by spirits speaking through them, or that the stars affect their mood. In the contemporary world, such thinking is much rarer than it used to be, and it requires a certain effort to maintain. It will never be as obvious and natural to us as it was to our ancestors, but it is certainly conceivable. The important thing is that we do not live *perpetually* and *restrictively* within such thinking. If we wish, we can always retreat into our isolated, subjective, and autonomous selves, separated from the outside world by a very clear buffer.

The erection of a buffer between our inner psyches and the outside world, the creation of a subjective world juxtaposed against the objective world, was the first and necessary step on the road not only to the modern world, but also to secular society. We have seen that from the perspective of the porous self, it is almost impossible not to believe in God (or in many gods). In antiquity, God was the father of all spirits and the king of all forces. He was the only power that could promise to protect mankind, and in theory, that also could keep this promise. The field of forces to which ancient humans were susceptible was not only external; it also existed inside them. Their open-ended selfhood was at the perpetual mercy of outside elements. Nature, stars, demons, wicked deities—all these not only existed as obvious and "natural" parts of the world, but also threatened people's souls in the most profound sense. The spirits of the heavens threatened not only to harass us, but also to infiltrate and seize control of us. Ghosts, the moon, the demon in the big tree trunk at the top of the hill—our selfhood was exposed and accessible to all these forces. In this mentality, one had no choice but to trust the forces of good—or a single, great, benevolent force—for protection. There was nothing inside us that could have withstood these scary external forces, and we had no way to seal ourselves against their influence. We had no choice but to place our trust in God.

The modern subject is characterized by a "buffered" selfhood, and with the rise of the buffered self also came secularism.[67] Only after the emergence of a border between inside and outside, one that protected against external forces, could humans let go of divine protection. Even more importantly: only after the construction of an independent internal world could people search for internal sources of authority and meaning. Only then could human initiative be seen as a positive value, and could humanism coalesce as a fully-fledged ideology. Only then could personal autonomy not only be seen as a possibility but also considered an ideal, which, if unfulfilled, leaves our lives somehow lacking. We shall address all of this later on. Before that, let us return to the beginning of our discussion and connect the dots between the porous psychology of premodern humans and the laws of the ancient Near East. Returning to biblical law, we shall see how the absence of an internal autonomous space shaped understandings of a crime that is related to matters of will and psychology no less than questions of society and community. The crime of rape.

Rape in the Hebrew Bible

Our day and age is characterized by acute sensitivity to sexual crimes. The #MeToo movement brought to widespread attention all sorts of sexual offenses that women experience as a matter of routine. Naturally, this movement emerged once the intellectual climate was ready and receptive to it: it is based on moral principles that we understand and are anxious to defend. These principles—bodily autonomy, the importance of choice and consent, the existence of diverse, deep, and significant emotions—took shape as a result of a process of development over many generations.

At the beginning of this chapter, we discussed a law from the Middle Assyrian Empire concerning rape. We shall now study the laws about rape in the Hebrew Bible and compare them to equivalent laws that modern Jewish legislators have articulated, those of the State of Israel. In this great shift, women went from being considered part of the men to whom they belonged (more or less literally) to being independent subjects, and along the way, also to possessing an internal, subjective, and autonomous personal space, which has correspondingly received social recognition in law. Through the law, we shall understand the various narratives that we tell ourselves, narratives that give rise to law, and that the law in turn sustains.

In the Hebrew Bible, laws concerning rape can be found only in Deuteronomy, which was most probably composed in the seventh century BCE. The laws read as follows:

> If a man is found lying with another man's wife, both of them—the man and the woman with whom he lay—shall die. Thus you will sweep away evil from Israel.
>
> In the case of a virgin who is engaged to a man—if a man comes upon her in town and lies with her, you shall take the two of them out to the gate of that town and stone them to death: the girl because she did not cry for help in the town, and the man because he violated another man's wife. Thus you will sweep away evil from your midst.
>
> But if the man comes upon the engaged girl in the open country, and the man lies with her by force, only the man who lay with her shall die, but you shall do nothing to the girl. The girl did not incur the death penalty, for this case is like that of a man attacking another and murdering him. He came upon her in the open; though the engaged girl cried for help, there was no one to save her.
>
> If a man comes upon a virgin who is not engaged and he seizes her and lies with her, and they are discovered, the man who lay with her shall pay the girl's father fifty [coins of] silver, and she shall be his wife.

Because he has violated her, he can never have the right to divorce her. (Deuteronomy 22:22–29)

At a first glance, it is easy to see that the Hebrew Bible does not use the word "rape." This series of laws discusses forbidden sexual relations, and more specifically, forbidden sexual acts between a man and a woman. The key distinction separating the cases in these four laws concerns the woman's status relative to other men: is she married, engaged, or unmarried (a virgin) living in her father's home. Within this internal distinction, there are differences between sexual relations with an engaged woman in a city compared to the same acts in the open. Let us now examine the different cases in turn.

The first verse is supposedly about adultery. If a man sleeps with a married woman, both are sentenced to death. The Hebrew Bible does not tell us whether there was mutual consent, or whether this was rape. There can also be no atonement for the two engaged in the act, for they have wronged not only the woman's husband, but also God.[68] The woman's wishes are not a relevant factor in the law about adultery (Was she raped? Did she initiate the sexual act? Perhaps she wants to divorce her husband and marry her new lover?), and the wording of this law hints at what lies ahead.

The next laws are about a virgin who is engaged to a man and is raped by another man. If this act takes place in a city, both the woman and the man are put to death. Why? The woman should have cried for help, and it is improbable that people would not have heard her and intervened to save her. Her failure to cry for help brings shame on her fiancé. Both parties are punished, therefore, as in the case of adultery. In the case of rape that takes place in the open, a woman cannot be blamed for not crying for help, because nobody would have heard her anyway. The Hebrew Bible analogizes this crime to murder ("this case is like that of a man attacking another and murdering him") in order to explain that the woman had no real choice. Just as people are murdered against their will, women can also be subjected to sex against their will (there is apparently a need to give the subjects of this law a basic explanation of the concept of rape, because it is not obvious). And indeed, in the case of sexual acts in the open, a woman is not punished, and only the rapist is put to death.

Even though in both cases concerning an engaged woman, the sexual relations are clearly coercive ("the man . . . violated[69] another man's wife," "the man lies with her by force"), notice that the penalty is imposed not because of the rape itself, but because of the injustice caused to the woman's fiancé. If a woman does not cry for help in a city, she wrongs her fiancé, and if a man has sexual relations with her, he is punished because he "violated [not any woman but] another man's wife," that is, because he too wronged the woman's fiancé. This much is quite clear from the following law, concerning a woman who is not engaged.

When we reach the discussion of the rape of a virgin living in her father's home, the situation is different. Here, the punishment is not death, and the rapist must even marry his victim. Why is the death penalty forgone? Because there is no case of adultery here: there is no grave injustice against another man or against God. In other words, there is no crime or sin against a *legal subject*. The girl's father is however wronged: she has lost her virginity, making it difficult to marry her off. Perhaps there has also been an affront to the father's honor. The fifty pieces of silver that the rapist gives the girl's father are most likely the bride-price for her virginity—*mohar* in Hebrew, the traditional payment that a groom makes for the virginity that he receives (or buys)[70]—or perhaps compensation for the damage that he has caused the father. In addition, the rapist must marry his victim, and he is not permitted to divorce her. This solves the problem of how the girl may be married off (the payment that the rapist must make might also serve to deter men wishing to force women into marriage by raping them). Notice that according to the text of the law, there is no need to ask a rape victim whether she consents to marry the man who raped her. Just as her will does not matter during the rape itself, it carries no importance afterwards, either. Nor is there any treatment of the harm, pain, or grief inflicted on her. She is not an individual; she is not a subject.

Rape in the Modern Age

The situation in the modern world is completely different. In the modern Israeli penal code, there is great importance attached to a woman's consent. In fact, the whole definition of rape is built around it:

If a person had intercourse with a woman

(1) without her freely given consent;
(2) with the woman's consent, which was obtained by deceit in respect of the identity of the person or the nature of the act;
(3) when the woman is a minor below age 14, even with her consent;
(4) by exploiting the woman's state of unconsciousness or other condition that prevents her from giving her free consent;
(5) by exploiting the fact that she is mentally ill or deficient, if—because of her illness or mental deficiency—her consent to intercourse did not constitute free consent,

then he committed rape and is liable to sixteen years imprisonment.[71]

The first clause in the law concerns a woman's consent. The absence of a woman's free consent makes the difference between legitimate sexual relations and rape. The following clauses concern cases in which a woman's free consent is limited for various reasons: deceit by the man, or her age, unconsciousness, or some deficiency on her part. Notice that the woman is the person against whom the rapist commits his crime. She is the only person discussed here, and her relationship status—whether she is single or married—is not a relevant criterion at all. Simply put, the woman has become a legal subject.

A simple comparison between these laws, ancient and modern, reveals that although in both cases a crime is committed using a woman's body, in biblical law the crime is perpetrated *against the man* who has the woman under his patronage, whereas in the law of the modern State of Israel, the crime is *against the woman's will*, that is, against her freedom of choice, against her right to bodily autonomy—against her existence as an autonomous person.

The crime of rape is in any case judged in relation to the controlling element. Over time, however, women's bodies have gone from being subject to the control of men to being subject to the control of their own will. Another difference is that, whereas in the Hebrew Bible this crime possessed an objective and absolute nature, considering that the law was God-given, in modern Israel, the same crime is measured by subjective means. Whether a crime was committed depends only on a woman's consent. Adultery is not a crime according the laws of modern democratic states, because both parties engaged in the sexual liaison consent to it.[72]

There has evidently been a genuine revolution in our understanding of forbidden sexual relations. In fact, there have been two revolutions. First, women have become legal subjects in their own right; crimes against their bodies are crimes *against them*, because their bodies belong to them. Second, it is people's consent or volition (and not their social or familial status) that is the critical factor in adjudicating sexual crimes against them. Even when the law states that sexual relations with a person who has been deceived, is underage, is mentally deficient, or has been drugged constitute rape, it does so not because God or society are intolerant of such acts (considering them an "abomination") but because these people are considered incapable of giving genuine consent. Of course, a certain society or divinity may well abhor sexual relations with people who have been deceived or drugged. However, the law does not proscribe such relations because they violate a social norm, but rather because people who have been deceived or drugged simply cannot, in our view, freely and cogently consent to sexual relations.

In fact, when it comes to sex, there are very few cases in which the deciding factor is not a legal subject's consent, but rather prevailing social norms. Incest is of course one example, and polygamy is another, although much less so (polygamous relations are allowed; they simply cannot be officially recognized). Homosexual relations, which were still illegal until a few decades ago because they were socially disapproved of, are now considered by most Westerners as entirely legitimate—as long as both parties consent, of course. The source of authority determining sexual normativity for most of modern Western society has undergone *privatization*, and then *internalization*. First, divinity was abolished as a source of authority, and society itself assumed the role of supreme legislator (on the authority of the "will of the people" or the "social contract"); second, social norms also became irrelevant, with the validity of the law basing itself on an entirely private and subjective domain, the domain of *will*—an internal individual matter. This revolution unfolded along several social and ideational vectors, therefore, including humanism, secularism, feminism, and the internalization of the self. These are all pillars of the narrative that determine the law in the modern world, the narrative that the law in turn sustains.

Life as a Link in a Chain

Let us combine these insights. Premodern individuals possessed, as we have seen, a porous self. Their selfhood was a decentralized repository of qualities and forces, completely exposed, at the mercy of various external forces. At the same time, they conceived of their selfhood as a link in a much longer chain, connected both back in time and in every spatial direction to other links in the same chain. Fathers were named after their sons, sons were named after their fathers, and women were considered men's property. Individuals were seen as extended limbs of their families, limbs whose importance was measured in relation to their proximity to the head—the patriarch, the father of the house.

This way of life was obvious to everyone. When two people met in the street, they did not see each other as individuals, but as particular parts of an extended whole. They valued and related to each other as links in different chains, as limbs of much greater organisms. Quarrels drew in entire families (or clans), and so did marriages. Laws and customs applied to families (or ethnic communities), not to individuals. The primary social distinction in antiquity was not between the public and private spheres, but between the public and the familial.[73] Religion was also a familial, clan-based, tribal, and ethnic matter.[74]

The absence of any conception of a clear buffer around the self gives rise to a form of life fused with one's natural and social environs. Individuals with porous selves are rooted firmly in their surroundings and communities as their organic offshoots. They are integral parts of their world, deeply interwoven into their collective and originating within it.

In his book *The Worldview of Medieval People*, the historian Aron Gurevich explains that these collectives

> were not transient assortments of individuals, but tangible and concrete groups. Thus were classified groups that people during this period imagined as inseparable: married couples, parents with children, relatives, families with their servants, friends, leaders with their soldiers, companions on a journey or a voyage, or in brief—social collectives. These collectives were commonly united around their most senior member: a king, a father, a captain of a ship, and so forth. . . . Thinking about the whole was dominant relative to thinking about individual constituent parts.[75]

Couples, families, and even communities were considered single organisms. When the prophet Jonah, whom we met earlier being reprimanded by God for caring more for a plant than for humans, goes and prophesies to the residents of the great city of Nineveh that "forty days more, and Nineveh shall be overthrown!" (Jonah 3:4), and the people decide to repent, they all fast and wear sackcloth—even the animals: "They shall be covered with sackcloth—man and beast—and shall cry mightily to God" (Jonah 3:8). The whole collective is at fault, and the whole collective repents, down to each individual and every living thing.

Premodern people conceived of the whole as dominant over its component parts. In other words, the whole was considered *prior* to individuals, both chronologically and ontologically. It predates them, and it is *more real* than them. Long before we are individuals, we are limbs in a single body. From here, we deduce the ideals that individuals must realize: "Neither originality nor difference compared to other people, but on the contrary, maximum active integration into a social group, a corporation, a God-given order, the *ordo*—this is the true virtue required of the individual."[76]

Besides certain unique individuals (usually demigods or individuals chosen by God), people were required to integrate, not to stand out; to conform, not to be original. A good life was considered a life of cooperation and obedience, a life of walking the straight and narrow and helping the collective. The authority of the past, tradition, and scripture was considered indisputable, and independent opinions challenging it were considered scandalous.

How did the transition to the world in which we live today unfold? How did Western individuals move from profoundly collectivist ideals to the complete opposite, coming to see themselves as unique individuals, who exist prior to the societies around them, from which they may disengage at will? How did we come to cultivate such ideals as originality and creativity, and to consider the new supreme over the old? How did virtues such as autonomy and negative liberty (the freedom to do as one wishes, without interference) develop? And what role does the principle of the image of God still play?

We shall seek to understand these complicated developments in the next chapters, beginning by exploring how conceptions of liberty changed with the rise of Christianity and Saint Paul's theological revolution. We continue with the transformations that the principle of the image of God underwent, and we shall examine how these shaped the legal status of the individual in Europe and the changes experienced by one of the social institutions that most profoundly challenged the status of individuals and the value of human life: slavery. Finally, we shall explore the critical role that the idea of the image of God played in the emergence of human rights discourse, from the twelfth century and onwards.

2

Freedom

The Ancient Conception of Liberty

People nowadays want to be original, but in the past they did not. In the modern world, people commonly aspire to self-fulfillment, a goal that would have never crossed our ancestors' minds. Modern individuals want to live unique lives and to express themselves through creativity, but Socrates, the Prophet Isaiah, or Thomas Aquinas were not interested in expressive creativity or originality. They cared for none of these ideals, because these are all utterly modern and would have sounded strange and alien until just a few centuries ago. Nevertheless, there is one modern ideal that was ubiquitous thousands of years ago: liberty. Both the ancient Greeks and the Hebrews glorified liberty, as did a host of other ancient civilizations. What they meant by this term, however, was quite different from what we understand it to mean nowadays.

In brief: in antiquity, liberty was primarily understood as political liberty. Individuals were free when they belonged to communities that charted their own course and autonomously determined their own laws. The political liberty of a citizen in ancient Greece was expressed in his participation in the public assemblies of the *polis*, and in Rome, having a share of power was considered a basic condition of liberty: "In aristocracies," wrote Cicero, "the masses can have hardly any share in liberty, since they are deprived of any participation in discussion and decision-making."[1] Writing in the first century about the history of the founding of Rome, Titus Livius (Livy) has Gaius Canuleius, Tribune of the plebs, insist that the commoners have a share in power, because "the mark of true liberty [is that] they are allowed to take their turn, both in obeying the annually elected magistrates and in exercising magisterial power."[2] Anyone who did not have access to political power was unfree. "Liberty has no home in any state except a democracy," Cicero added,[3] expressing the classical conception that liberty cannot exist when the laws imposed on people are not the product of their collective judgement.

The same was true for ancient Judaism. For individuals in the rabbinical Jewish tradition, liberty was the ability to participate in deliberations in the *beit midrash*, where they would interpret the Torah and render halakhic rulings. The Mishnah invokes the passage in Exodus 32:16 that states that "the tablets [of the Ten Commandments] were the work of God, and the writing was the writing of God, graven upon the tablets," and instructs: "Read not *haruth* ['graven'] but *heruth* ['freedom']. For there is no free man but one that occupies himself with the study of the Torah" (Ethics of the Fathers 6:2). Freedom means learning, and legislating, the Torah. Passover, the Jewish festival of liberty, also celebrates collective and political liberty. When the Israelites "departed from bondage to liberty," they emerged from subordination to a foreign ruler and into a state of political autonomy, in the context of which they forged a covenant with God and accepted his laws. Liberty for the People of Israel meant collective liberty. Individual Jews had no freedom to violate the tenets of their broader collective (e.g., desecrating the Sabbath).

The law was therefore the basic framework within which liberty or slavery could exist. Laws imposed on communities from above were a threat to their liberty, turning members of those communities into slaves. States of lawlessness and complete personal autonomy, where everyone does as they please, were also viewed negatively, as expressions not of liberty but of licentiousness and anarchy. The existence of law acceptable to the community was the most basic condition for liberty, and when individuals took part in making that law, they fully realized their status as free human beings. By delivering speeches, engaging in debates, casting votes, or adjudicating cases, citizens were able to give expression to their liberty. There was no liberty outside the framework of the polity, and excluding the context of spiritual sects, any notion of individual or universal liberty was simply meaningless. On the contrary, one's liberty, insofar as this could be spoken of, was always derivative of one's particular social standing, status, and privilege.

The prominent liberal thinker Benjamin Constant (1767–1830), indeed one of the first to proudly call himself "liberal," sought to explain the difference between ancient and modern conceptions of liberty in order to elucidate the importance of individual liberties. According to Constant,

> The aim of the ancients was the sharing of social power among the citizens of the same fatherland: this is what they called liberty. The aim of the moderns is the enjoyment of security in private pleasures; and they call liberty the guarantees accorded by institutions to these pleasures.[4]

The differences between these conceptions of liberty should not surprise us. As we have seen, until the modern era, individuals were rooted firmly in their social contexts and were defined, in a significant but not absolute sense, by their familial and communal ties. A person's conception of their own liberty was derivative from their conception of themselves as part of a greater whole. Their liberty was the liberty of their community, and just as there could be no such thing as a private life, there could be no such thing as private liberty.[5] On the other hand, general liberty *was* individual liberty, so much so that even the redemption of the collective was the redemption of the individual.

From Collective to Individual Redemption

After the destruction of the kingdoms of Israel and Judah, redemption in ancient Jewish tradition came to mean self-rule in the Land of Israel. When the prophets spoke about salvation at the end of days, they were referring to the restoration of the united kingdom of Israel and Judah under a king from the House of David (see Isaiah 11, Hosea 2, Amos 9). Consequently, the Talmud and the Midrash present the position that "the only difference between this world and the days of the Messiah is with regard to servitude to foreign kingdoms alone" (Berakhot 34b, Sanhedrin 92a). In other words, the messianic age would herald liberation from foreign domination.

During the Great Revolt, shortly before the destruction of Jerusalem and the Second Temple in 70 CE, coins were minted in the city bearing the date "Year 2 to the Liberty of Zion." On some coins, "liberty" was replaced with "redemption." Political liberty *was* redemption. Maimonides begins his discussion of redemption in the end of days with the statement that "the King Messiah will arise and re-establish the monarchy of David as it was in former times" (Mishneh Torah, Kings and Wars 11:1). The Jewish People's final redemption, like their first redemption, from Egypt, would be their deliverance to liberty, in the sense of casting off the yoke of foreign rule and regaining their political independence. This was the meaning of true freedom in the minds of the ancients.

The rise of Christianity heralded the privatization of redemption, together with its universalization. In this new view, the life, death, and resurrection of Jesus Christ gave all humanity the possibility of personal redemption from original sin. We are denied redemption not by laws imposed on us by foreign powers, but by our inner essence, which imposes its own dark laws on each and every one of us. The notion that individuals must achieve personal liberation from inner enslavement was found around the last centuries BCE among certain philosophical schools and minor sects in the Mediterranean Basin. The Epicureans, Neoplatonists, Cynics, Skeptics, Stoics, and various Gnostic groups believed that individuals must free themselves from a range of forms of enslavement. Christianity, in its infancy, absorbed certain aspects of these philosophies. Redemption and liberty became private matters. This was a radical change.

In the New Testament (John 8:31–36), we find clear evidence of this transformation, of the transition from collective, political liberty toward personal liberty—and of resistance to this view:

> Then Jesus said to those Jews who believed Him, "If you abide in My word, you are My disciples indeed. And you shall know the truth, and the truth shall make you free." They answered Him, "We are Abraham's descendants, and have never been in bondage to anyone. How can You say, 'You will be made free'?" Jesus answered them, "Most assuredly, I say to you, whoever commits sin is a slave of sin. And a slave does not abide in the house forever, but a son abides forever. Therefore if the Son makes you free, you shall be free indeed."[6]

Jesus explains to his Jewish followers that if they follow his teachings, they will know the truth, and the truth will set them free. The Jews are puzzled by his remarks, because they have never been slaves, so how can they achieve liberty? Most traditional Christian commentators point out the blindness of the Jews, who after all commemorate their slavery in Egypt every year at Passover, and they attribute Jesus's interlocutors' answer to their arrogance. It is also possible, however, that they simply mean that since God delivered them from slavery to liberty, they are *already* free. They themselves were never enslaved. What liberty, therefore, are they supposed to acquire?

Notice that for them, liberty is a political matter: they are descendants of Abraham, who have already been delivered from slavery to liberty, and therefore Jesus's promises to set them free are meaningless. But Jesus disagrees. He explains that they are slaves to sin: personally enslaved to their own sins, and perhaps even to their own general desire to sin. This enslavement is internal; it is personal, not political. And "a slave does not abide in the house forever": unlike family members, Jesus explains, slaves do not fully belong in a household. They dwell in it, but they cannot enjoy it, nor can they enjoy the intimacy of a family. Only the son is an integral part of the household, and only he—the son, Jesus—can make them "free indeed," children of the father of the house: God himself, of course. Liberty is transformed here into an individual matter, a question of standing personally before God and achieving liberation from sin.

A Radical Jew

This new theology was given its most explicit formulation by Saul of Tarsus: Paul, the "Apostle to the Gentiles." Paul made an immense and critical contribution to shaping the basic intellectual and moral contours of the Christian tradition and indeed the whole Western world. By moving the locus of religious life from the collective community to the individual soul, Paul proposed a new and original understanding of such theological principles as redemption and liberty. This internalization of religious life, turning individuals and their inner lives into the focal point of religious drama, was one of the most momentous revolutions in the history of monotheism and indeed of the Western world.

Paul was born a Jew and lived as a Jew, and even after he became Jesus's emissary to the Gentiles and constructed a brilliant and elaborate theological framework for the purpose of this mission, he believed that he was advancing Judaism to its rightful position. In effect,

Paul was a "radical Jew," as Daniel Boyarin calls him: a Jewish thinker who delved into the roots of his culture and faith and leveled an intellectual and social critique against them from within those roots.[7] Paul arrived in Jerusalem and studied Torah there. In several places in the scriptures he identified as a Pharisaic Jew, a zealous follower of the law.[8] Yet as a child of Tarsus (on the northern Mediterranean coast, in modern-day Turkey) and as a citizen of the Roman Empire, he straddled the border between the Jewish cultural-religious ethnos and the Hellenistic world. Out of this hybrid existence, he set about to fix what he saw as serious problems in the covenant between God and Israel. He grappled with his tradition as an educated, observant Jew who had nevertheless discovered something new. He reinterpreted this tradition by synthesizing Jewish conceptions of the world with Hellenistic conceptions of personhood, insisting that his discovery held the key to a better, more authentic relationship with God—and the path to liberty.

Paul dove into the depths of his Judaism, and when he resurfaced, he radically transformed Judaism's conception of a person's relationship with God. He replaced the Jewish concept of the "covenant," whereby a collective committed to a heteronomous framework of political, moral, social, and ritual laws and commandments, with a new covenant: a personal, not collective, one. In the Pauline covenant, individuals would undergo an inner, subjective transformation or metamorphosis, one that would form the basis for their new relationship with God. It was this inner metamorphosis that would connect individual Christians to Christ and thereby redeem them.

It is worth dwelling on Paul's new theology, because it is important to grasp the tremendous shift that he engineered in conceptions of redemption in order to understand the ultimate emergence of the individual. Private redemption became the *source of religious meaning* for individuals, and to a certain extent, which would become more significant later, also the *source of religious authority*. The focal point of religious drama migrated inward, into the individual soul.

Paul's writings addressed a range of social and ethical issues, but their starting point was the internal, spiritual experience and transformation of the individual.[9] The experience of conversion, of a change of heart—as Paul experienced with his revelation on his way to persecuting Jewish Christians in Damascus[10]—launched Paul's Christian journey and remained a core tenet of his religious worldview. The word *metamorphosis* appears twice in Paul's letters: in his Epistle to the Romans (12:2) and his Second Epistle to the Corinthians (3:18). It signifies the spiritual shift (the "renewing of your mind," as Paul writes in his Epistle to the Romans*) that Christians experience when they enter into a new and improved relationship with God. Paul laid the foundations for this redemptive faith—faith in the crucifixion and resurrection of Jesus Christ, the supposed key to redemption from original sin—in the process of inner transformation.[11] As he wrote in his Epistle to the Galatians, his mission was to spread Jesus's gospel "until Christ is formed in you" (Galatians 4:19). Redemption is no longer political dominion but an inner transformation.

And this transformation would be total. According to Paul, whoever Christ is formed *in* would henceforth live *in* Christ. The phrase "in Christ" (*en Christo*) appears dozens of times in Paul's epistles. It refers to the experience of an elevated existence, one understood as life after death: as a state of redemption.[12] For Paul, the experience of living "in Christ" provided the overall context for his life in the period after his Damascene conversion. This was how he lived, and this, he promised, was how anyone who committed his life to Christ would live. "In Christ" one could be cleansed of sin; no longer defiled, one could become free.[13] This was in fact the only real way of becoming free.

Paul concluded that the inner transformation that he had personally experienced, this profound and personal metamorphosis, was open and accessible to everyone else, Jew and non-Jew alike. He invited Jesus's first disciples to live "in Christ" with him and achieve liberation and redemption from sin together. Paul's personal spiritual experience became a model for the whole of humanity and for every individual. Every man and woman could emerge from personal servitude to personal liberty exactly as he had done. Traveling around the Mediterranean Basin, Paul would preach this good news, attract many followers to his cause—and dramatically transform how so many understood liberty and redemption.

---

* Quotes from the New Testament here and hereafter will be translated according to the New King James Version.

Jewish vs. Hellenistic Conceptions of the Mind-Body Relationship

Life "in Christ" was, for Paul, redemption. The internal metamorphosis that he called for therefore heralded a cultural metamorphosis of the notion of salvation, which he privatized and internalized. Redemption was transformed from a communal or national objective into something personally attainable.

How could this possibility have crossed Paul's mind? No spiritual experience, however exciting and enrapturing, could ever by itself have convinced one, for example, that the soul was the focus of religious life. Jewish Sages in the Second Temple era presumably also had spiritual experiences, but none thought that any particular experience was sufficient reason to revise his religious beliefs and reorient his relationship with God to an internal sphere, at the cost of its external dimension. There was nothing stopping those who had religious experiences from rejecting them as meaningless, as mishaps or illusions, or even as pernicious temptations by the *yetzer hara* or Satan. In order to ascribe a positive meaning to their internal experiences, they would have needed an *interpretative context* nourished by certain beliefs about the world.

The following anecdote should illuminate this issue. It comes from the British playwright Tom Stoppard in his play *Jumpers*. Stoppard tells a story about the brilliant philosopher Ludwig Wittgenstein, who once asked a friend: "Tell me, why do people always say that it was *natural* for men to assume that the sun went round the earth rather than that the earth was rotating?" His friend replied that this was fairly obvious: "Well, obviously, because it just looks as if the sun is going round the earth." To which Wittgenstein replied: "Well, what would it have looked like if it had looked as if the earth was rotating?"[14]

This brief exchange elucidates a simple point: appearances, even of something as simple as the sun's movement across the sky, are important but still open to interpretation, and interpretations are determined by our views of the world. Worldviews that place humans center stage encourage them to interpret the sight of the sun's changing location in the sky as if the *sun* were revolving around *them*. Egocentrism leads to geocentrism. If humans were predisposed to think of themselves as marginal creatures or inclined to interpret reality in a non-self-centered manner, they would perhaps have assumed that the Earth revolved around the sun. Our worldviews shape the interpretations that we attach to data, and it was a particular worldview that allowed Paul to interpret his experience in such an original manner, and from there to embark on a new religious journey.

To understand the religious revolution that Paul spearheaded, we must therefore understand the prior assumptions that made it possible. The key lies in the influence of Hellenistic civilization. As a Greek-speaking Jew, Paul was exposed to Hellenistic influence, and the prioritization of the spiritual dimension over the physical therefore came quite naturally to him. This was one of the most fundamental differences between Hebrew and Hellenistic cultures at the time. Unlike the Jewish Sages, who saw the body as the core of human experience (and as the image of God itself, no less), Hellenistic philosophers regarded the psyche, if not the soul, as the defining element of human life.

Indeed, the Jerusalem Talmud describes a human being as a body that is animated by the spirit of God: "The white is from the male, from him are brain, bones, and sinews. The red is from the female, from her are skin, flesh, and blood. But breath, life force, and soul are from the Holy One, may He be praised; all three are partners in him."[15] Plato, in contrast, opines that "what makes each of us to be what he is, is nothing else than the soul, while the body is a semblance which attends on each of us."[16]

The tensions between these two positions are palpable. The Talmud treats humans as metaphysical combinations of three elements: a mother, a father, and God. It is God who breathes a life force into the body, but this soul is not the person themself. If that were the case, the Sages would not have used phrases such as "breathed out his soul" or "returned his soul to the creator" (who exactly is exhaling or returning this soul, if not the body, which is the person?). Nor would they have composed the morning blessings that thank God for creating the soul, which "You guard while it is within me, You take from me and restore within me."[17] (What is meant by "me"? The body, of course.) Nor would the Sages have believed in the resurrection of the dead, for what is the point of resurrecting a dead body if a person is their soul, which is already enjoying the beatific vision in heaven? For the Sages, a person was their body, and the soul gave them life. Plato represented the contrary view: a person was his soul, and the body gave him death. In other words, the body trapped the soul in an inferior earthly structure that dragged it down, before finally—what a relief!—dying. In death, the transient body releases the eternal soul to never-ending life.

Daniel Boyarin succinctly encapsulates these differences:

> Rabbinic Judaism invested significance in the body which in the other formations was invested in the soul. That is, for rabbinic Jews, the human being was defined as a body—animated, to be sure, by a soul—while for Hellenistic Jews (such as Philo) and (at least many Greek-speaking) Christians (such as Paul), the essence of a human being is a soul housed in a body. For most of the Greco-Roman world an ontological dualism became as natural a way of thinking as the conscious and unconscious is for us, but the proto-rabbinite Jews of Palestine seem to have strongly resisted such dualist notions.[18]

Conceptions of Humans and Laws

The Sages of the Mishnah and the Talmud developed Halakha, the corpus of Jewish law, based on their conception of the human person. For them, a person was not a spiritual entity that existed inside a body, which it controlled and subordinated to its will. For the Sages, a person was a single body-soul unit that operated in synchrony vis-à-vis the world. They certainly knew that we possess an "inner" world of thoughts and intentions, but they did not imagine a clear buffer separating this domain from the outside world. This does not only mean that for the Sages, the self was "porous," as we called it earlier. Clearly from their perspective, the inside and outside world existed along a continuum that was more or less unbroken, existing in a constant state of reciprocal influence. But the same was true of the Hellenists and the Christians. What distinguished the Sages even more was that, at the "internal" end of this continuum, they did not imagine some entity that was fundamentally different from the "outside" world, a "spiritual" entity that might be considered a truer instantiation of selfhood than the body.

For the Sages of the Talmud, there did not exist any such "spiritual" entity. Since they understood the human body to be the image of God, the Sages could in no way have regarded it as secondary to the soul.

Conversely, for Hellenistic Jews, the person was a spiritual entity and the body was subsidiary. Philo, the Jewish philosopher who lived in first-century Alexandria, was the quintessential Hellenistic Jew. He interpreted Jewish tradition in line with Hellenistic teachings and understood the notion of the image of God in the same way. For Philo, the image of God could not be the body:

> Let no one think that he is able to judge of this likeness from the characters of the body: for neither is God a being with the form of a man, nor is the human body like the form of God; but the resemblance is spoken with reference to the most important part of the soul, namely the mind.[19]

In his commentary on the first chapter of Genesis, Philo explained that the image of God was not a person's form, but his mind. As a Hellenistic Jew, he could not accept the premise that God had a physical form, much less a body, and that man and woman were created in its likeness.

Since, for the Sages, the body was the most significant focal point of religion, intentions usually bore little halakhic weight. Jews are not required to perform the commandments with intention in order to have fulfilled them.[20] What matters is their actions, which are presumed to be in accordance with their will. As Ishay Rosen-Zvi demonstrates, even when the Sages of the Mishnah discussed intentions as a halakhic criterion, they were merely "internal" continuations of "external" acts. "In the Mishnah," Rosen-Zvi argues, "'thought,' 'intention,' and 'will' are not independent psychic phenomena, but mental gestures which precede or accompany external actions":[21]

> While a mental world does indeed appear in the Mishnah, it is markedly different from the Hellenistic one. There is no "inner person," a soul or logos that stands in contrast to "external" parts of "me" such as my body or my appetites, as in Plato or Paul. . . . The Mishnaic truth cannot be found by looking inwards—as in Augustine—and there is no hidden "inner truth," known only to "me," of the type which created the modern radical dichotomy between inside and out.[22]

For the Sages, one's internal world was simply a continuation of the outside world: an extension of one's body and actions, constituting an expression of God's image. This contrasts with the supreme importance attached to the interior sphere in Hellenistic culture: the psyche, or the soul in later conceptions (Stoic, Gnostic, Christian, Neoplatonic, etc.), is a person's essence; what happens *to* it and *in* it matters more than anything else.

Paul Looks Inside

Let us return to Paul. In the Sages' conception of humanity, exhilarating internal experiences, or "spiritual experiences," were easily dismissible as unimportant, because experiences in general were considered religiously insignificant. Such experiences were not the sorts of things that could induce "changes of heart," the kind that exposed individuals to previously unknown truths. The Torah was the sole source of truth, and one's "internal" life was but an extension of the external image of God, bound in a covenant with God himself. This covenant with God was sustained through observance of his Torah. The only things that carried religious significance were people's actions, or avoidance of certain actions, in accordance with their faithfulness to this covenant, namely the Torah. The body was the center of existence; the soul revolved around it.

In contrast, the Hellenistic view, which distinguished between matter and spirit while giving primacy to the spirit, allowed Paul to interpret his religious experience, on the spiritual plane, as bearing the full force of truth and far-reaching significance. Paul was not a thorough Hellenist like Philo, and he attached importance to the body, but he also attached sufficient importance to his spiritual transformation in order not to dismiss it as an aberration, a problem, or a dangerous temptation by evil forces. On the contrary, Paul chose to lend it supreme authority and to derive from it a new religious paradigm.

For Paul, the soul was the center of existence, around which the body revolved. In accordance with this Hellenistic cultural habitus, Paul was convinced, as a result of his experience, that one was defined more by one's internal world than by one's ethnic group, loyalty to an external system of laws, or belonging to any collective covenant. What mattered most was not an external web of social significance, but rather the experiences of the human soul. This paradigm had momentous implications, and it would resonate throughout the history of the West, as we shall see. It is already clear, however, that it was Paul's openness to this paradigm that turned his unsettling experience into a genuine change of heart. It was this openness that rendered his experience of revelation, entering into a life "in Christ," more than an illusion or a confusion, but rather a genuinely new basis for theological understanding and faith. It was this that transformed Saul of Tarsus into Paul the Apostle.[23]

Out of this paradigm, Paul attributed religious significance and even religious authority to one's inner life, and he anchored his theological conclusions on the spiritual changes that he had personally experienced. Among these conclusions was his criticism of the nature of the rabbinical Jewish connection with God. Having come to believe that the most important locus of religious life was internal, he understandably concluded that anything external was of secondary importance. It was from this position that Paul could claim that the *mitzvot*, the ritual commandments of Jewish law, were null and void:

> But now we have been delivered from the law, having died to what we were held by, so that we should serve in the newness of the Spirit and not in the oldness of the letter. (Romans 7:6)

> That the righteous requirement of the law might be fulfilled in us who do not walk according to the flesh but according to the Spirit. For those who live according to the flesh set their minds on the things of the flesh, but those who live according to the Spirit, the things of the Spirit. For to be carnally minded is death, but to be spiritually minded is life and peace. (Romans 8:4–6)

According to Paul, Christians operated according to the "newness of the Spirit." The transformative experience that he had personally experienced, the rebirth that brought him to dwell "in Christ" and led him to faith, was precisely such a spiritual renewal. Christians would therefore renounce the "oldness of the letter," thoughts of the flesh, and "practice," which for Paul represented tradition and the law, and of course the yoke of the ritual commandments. The focal point of worship migrated from the outside inward, from the physiological to the psychological, or, as Paul would have put it, from the flesh to the spirit.

It is important to note that this shift diminished, in an instant, the importance of the Jewish ethnic community. The Jewish ethnos saw itself as special, both because of its loyalty to the covenant with God and its collective obedience to divine law, and because of its genealogical descent from the Patriarchs—from Abraham, Isaac, and Jacob—who were, in their eyes, the first people to forge a unique covenant with God. Paul maintained that the law was unimportant, if not downright harmful. Unlike faith, "practice" was a "stumbling stone," and the pursuit of righteousness through obedience to the law was futile.[24] The importance of the (fleshly) dynasty that began with Abraham, continued with the sons of Jacob and the twelve tribes, and led all the way to the Jews of the first century CE around him, suddenly paled into insignificance.[25]

The Individual as the Basic Religious Unit

This emphasis on individuals' inner lives, including their feelings, experiences, and beliefs, laid the foundations for a view of the individual's spiritual life as a general, and not only religious, source of meaning and authority. But such a shift would happen over the 1,500 years following Paul's lifetime. In Paul's day, what mattered was the theological shift from the collective to the individual. At a time when the validity of people's actions was determined by their social belonging, by social institutions, by their ethnicity, religion, class, or sex, Paul transformed the question of one's standing before the law, before God, into a personal and internal matter. By extracting people's relationships with God from the familial and communal context given to them by Judaism and anchoring them in the internal life of the individual, Paul not only did away with the family and society as necessary components of the individual's relationship with God, but also transformed the individual into the only vital element in this relationship (albeit as part of a community of believers). This made possible both the privatization and the universalization of religion.[26]

Whereas previously the basic units of religious tradition were the extended family, the tribe, and one's limited geographic area, this role was now given to private individuals. Whereas previously redemption and liberty were to be realized in the context of a polity, a collective, they were now to be achieved at an individual level. Individuals, with inner lives, for the first time became subjects of immense importance. Moses asked God, "Let me behold Your Presence!" (Exodus 33:18), or in other words: show me yourself. Augustine, however, already had a different request: "I beseech you, my God, show me myself."[27] The Church Father was asking God not to reveal himself (God) but himself (Augustine), so that he could know himself. Augustine did not believe that God was unimportant. On the contrary, anyone who reads his *Confessions*, one of the most beautiful and moving religious texts ever composed, can see that proximity to God was supremely important to him. But Augustine believed that the path to God passed through introspection, through internal inquiry. One could only reach heaven through the heart, and without an intimate familiarity with oneself, there could be no true relationship with God. This paradigm was a direct consequence of Paul's theological revolution, and it was built on the basis of Hellenistic civilization.

This paradigm would have implications for every dimension of society. Whereas in the ancient world, the family was the most basic building block of both religion and society, once the individual entered a personal association with God, the family also began to lose its force as a single unit under the control of a patriarch. Every individual became a subject, personally answerable to God, with private duties and obligations toward God and toward others. "The great achievement of the ethical religions," wrote Max Weber, "was to shatter the fetters of the sib [family]. These religions established the superior community of faith and a common ethical way of life in opposition to the community of blood, even to a large extent in opposition to the family."[28]

Christianity subverted the tribal ties of the Jews, and by the same token also the family ties of its own believers. For the first time, a disparity emerged between one's social-familial status and position and one's standing before God. Religious life, in other words, became independent of familial and societal life—and also of political life.[29]

Changing Conceptions of Adultery

Let us consider an example that corresponds with our earlier discussion about laws governing sex and rape. With the rise of Christianity, Jewish Christians' understanding of the laws concerning adultery evolved.

In the Torah, as we have seen, the punishment for adultery is death. In contrast to the Torah's severe view of adultery—"Thou shalt not commit adultery" is one of the Ten Commandments, alongside "Thou shalt not murder" and "Thou shalt not steal"—the Jewish Sages sought to moderate the punishment for adultery and instituted a rule whereby an adulterous woman would be "forbidden to her husband and to her lover." In other words, she would have to divorce her husband and would be forbidden from later marrying the man with whom she had committed adultery. Notice, however, that adultery is a situation in which a man has intercourse with another man's wife, which is considered a sin against the married man. He is wronged by both his unfaithful wife and by her lover. In contrast, a married man who lies with an unmarried woman has *not* committed adultery, according to the bible and the halakhic conception. In principle, a man may take several wives, and sexual intercourse is one way of performing *kiddushin*—the binding act of marriage in Jewish law.

In Paul's new theological framework, in contrast, both men and women were required to be faithful to their spouses. This was a novelty. Paul declared, "Let the husband render to his wife the affection due her, and likewise also the wife to her husband. The wife does not have authority over her own body, but the husband does. And likewise the husband does not have authority over his own body, but the wife does" (1 Corinthians 7:3–4). There is full symmetry between the parties in this arrangement. The Church Fathers, building on Paul's teachings, elucidated this point: "Betrayal of this fidelity [in a couple] is called adultery, when . . . sexual intercourse takes place with another man or woman contrary to the marriage-pact."[30] Thus, whereas in Halakha, a man is not covenantally bound to a single woman, and before the proclamation of the edict known as the Cherem d'Rabbeinu Gershom around 1000 CE, polygamy was permitted for Jews, it was the Church that converted the family from being a single unit subordinate to a patriarch into subsidiary units, each directly subordinate to God and thus each with independent legal standing.

In the ancient Roman world, adultery was also considered a sin that only women could commit, and the idea that a man must also remain faithful began to develop only in the first centuries of the Common Era. The symmetry between the partners in Paul's thinking must be seen as a product of his new conception of humanity. *Men and women were considered private legal subjects* in their relations with God, and following that, also in their relations with other people. When it came to a commitment to sexual exclusivity, both sides were equal—and the conception of adultery changed accordingly.[31]

Alain Badiou on the Pauline Revolution

The revolution in the status of women was connected to the revolution in the status of man. More specifically, it was connected to the fact that for Paul, and later the Church, people became first and foremost individuals, as opposed to extensions of some greater whole. In his book on Paul, the modern French thinker Alain Badiou elaborates on the great idea at the core of Paul's theology.[32]

According to Badiou, Paul originated the notion of the individual universal subject, of the person as above all a single person, of the human being as an entity unchained by any particular ties or associations, unbound by sex or tribe. Man or woman, in this sense, a consciousness unbound by body, law, or history, exists as an eternal subject, a witness to the (divine) truth revealed within them. In Badiou's analysis, Paul understood truth as a personal and subjective principle, conditioned on and constituted by an individual's pronouncements about it. It was Paul who attested that Jesus Christ had revealed himself to him, and this revelation changed the course of his life. According to Paul, truth depends neither on law, as for the Jews, nor reason, as for the Greeks. It requires neither the authority of rabbinical-Pharisaic interpretations of law, nor the authority of the philosophers' reason or logic. Paul's truth shone from within. It was constituted by an event, a revelation, and was therefore acosmic and anomian. It resided outside social hierarchies and was therefore also asocial. In fact, fidelity to such truth means turning one's back on society and law.

It is commitment to this form of truth that constitutes the individual. Badiou points to Paul's internalization of divinity, in stark contrast to its ethnic and communal context in Judaism. God becomes present in individuals' lives through the transformative experience of being born "into Christ." This was in contrast with Halakha, which pushed God further away and retained God as a transcendental being. This shift, empowering human beings as individuals and individuals as human beings, therefore also empowered humans as divine, or at least as bearing the divine within them. This modifies the divine presence, which had previously existed in each person as the image of God. After Paul, God's presence was expressed within one *as an individual in their own right*, not as a member of a covenantal community. This was God's new covenant with humankind.

Badiou highlights the way Paul instigated a total revolution in the conception of the person. He placed at the center of his new doctrine the universal individual: the individual capable of transcending local ties, social status, ethnic belongings, and even sex and gender, and becoming universal "man," bound in a relationship with a universal God. In a seminal essay, Marcel Mauss describes this as a transition away from a conception of personhood as *persona*, as persons embedded in a context, to personhood as *personality*, as persons existing in their own right.[33] Paul spearheaded this transition as a departure from the prevailing conventions of the culture into which he was born—Second Temple Judaism—which believed, with variations, in the existence of fundamental differences between Jews and Gentiles, and men and women, concerning their relationships with God.

Neither Jew Nor Greek

Importantly, the distinction that the ancient Israelites drew between themselves and other nations was not essentialist. They did not believe that they possessed superior souls, that they alone were capable of prophecy, or that their lineage, which they traced to Abraham, endowed them with unique hereditary virtues. Such ideas would only emerge in the tenth century CE onward, with Rabbi Judah Halevi and his *Book of the Kuzari*, and in kabbalistic literature, which adopted the Hellenistic paradigm of the soul as constitutive of personhood.

In the minds of the Jews of the first centuries of the Common Era, the difference between them and non-Jews came down to their special relationship with the one true God, the creator of the universe—a relationship that other nations lacked. God had chosen them, loved them, and brought them into a unique covenant with him. They were his hand-picked stewards, and they were obligated by his special laws, a fact that gave them an exclusive status and role in the whole of creation.

Moreover, Paul's universalist aspirations drew not only on Hellenistic universalism, but also on universalist trends present in Judaism itself, beginning with the Hebrew Bible.[34] We have already seen that universal fraternity is rooted deeply in the Genesis myth about humanity's descent from a single set of parents.[35] Nor was Paul's hope for all nations to enter into a better, closer relationship with the one true God alien to ancient Hebrew tradition, from God's promises to Abraham in Genesis and all the way to the prophetic visions. But Paul advanced his strand of universalism not by placing all the world's nations next to the nation of Israel, but by dismantling all nations, including Israel, by transforming communities into sets of individuals, and by turning the covenant with God into a personal, not collective, matter.

Accordingly, Paul's radical new conceptions of redemption and liberty shook Judaism to its core. No longer did the one true God have a unique and collective relationship with the Jews as a nation, but with each and every person. No longer did redemption involve national freedom and prosperity, but personal, private liberation. Paul proposed a *new covenant*, a covenant forged between each individual and God. He hoped for every human being to undergo the same spiritual metamorphosis that he had experienced, thus forging a personal redemptive relationship with God. This metamorphosis, as we have seen, was an internal, psychological matter, and therefore greatly diminished the importance of the body. Moreover, this also rendered a person's social status and sex far less important.

Since Paul believed that individual redemption must come through spiritual transformation, and since he saw no essential difference between people's souls (as a first-century Jew he saw no essential difference between human beings), the division of humanity into nations, classes, and genders became increasingly insignificant. Paul could therefore declare, in one of the most famous and dramatic pronouncements in his epistles:

> For you are all sons of God through faith in Christ Jesus. For as many of you as were baptized into Christ have put on Christ. There is neither Jew nor Greek, there is neither slave nor free, there is neither male nor female; for you are all one in Christ Jesus. And if you are Christ's, then you are Abraham's seed, and heirs according to the promise. (Galatians 3:26–29)

This is quite a pronouncement for the first century. There was no difference between Jews and Greeks, slaves and freemen—even men and women. These categories were rendered trivial the moment Jesus appeared with his gospel, a message of personal, spiritual redemption. All those who experienced this redemption—the "baptism into Christ" or "clothing in Christ" about which Paul wrote—would be transformed into "Abraham's seed, and heirs according to the promise," or in other words: into the true Israel, *Verus Israel*, the Israel of the spirit, not the flesh. The contours of the Jewish ethnos became irrelevant. This covenant was universal, one that appealed to every human *qua* human.

Conversion into Judaism involved, for the rabbis, study, circumcision, and ritual immersion: "Once he has immersed and emerged," the Talmud teaches, "he is like a born Jew in every sense."[36] But for Paul, "conversion," or admission into the covenantal community, was predicated on faith, the "circumcision of the heart,"[37] and the immersion (or baptism) of the spirit:

> For by one Spirit we were all baptized into one body—whether Jews or Greeks, whether slaves or free—and have all been made to drink into one Spirit. (1 Corinthians 12:13)

With baptism in the spirit, one becomes initiated without distinction as to ethnicity, class, or sex, into redemption in Christ. One becomes a fully-fledged member of Israel, but "Israel" now means the whole of humanity, because the ethnic circle of the Children of Israel bound by God's covenant has been broken and unfurled to include all Children of Adam. No longer is the covenant between God and a specific, special people. Every individual becomes an independent subject, entering into a private covenant with God. All humans are rendered equal through their faith in Christ and internal metamorphosis, and all humans may be baptized "into one body": the universal spiritual corpus.

In later days, Paul's words would prove tremendously significant. Liberalism would base itself precisely on this axiom, that we are all fundamentally the same and equal, and that "external" differences, such as ethnicity, gender, or social status, are ultimately insignificant. When the Declaration of the Rights of Man and the Citizen was proclaimed during the French Revolution (on August 26, 1789), its first paragraph stated:

"Men are born and remain free and equal in rights. Social distinctions may be based only on considerations of the common good"—in other words, not on considerations of an individual's religion or sex or nationality. Such social distinctions are transient, non-essential, and in any case exist only to satisfy particular needs. The only true foundational element is the abstract individual.

The Image of God, Reinterpreted

At the entrance of the University of California, Berkeley, between the campus and the street, stands a lone preacher nearly every day, with combed hair and simple attire. Clutching a megaphone at the gate, he urges repentance. Since he knows what the students crossing his path care about, he makes sure to stress that the redemption will not arrive as a result of their academic achievements, government policies, socialist or Marxist reforms, or the accumulation of wealth. Just a few days before the campus was closed because of the COVID-19 pandemic, I heard him denouncing identity politics. "People talk about identity politics," he hollered, "but when Jesus died on the cross, he didn't die for his skin color. He died for your soul, which has no color but is fallen."

Paul would have approved this message. He elevated the spirit above the flesh, the internal over the external. He was therefore able to downplay ethnicity, class, and sex. For him, psychological changes were more important than physical distinctions, and in these, we are all equal. The soul has no color. It was only natural, therefore, that Paul proposed a new interpretation of the notion of the image of God. For him, God's image was not his physical body, but his spirit. He articulated this explicitly in his Epistle to the Colossians:

> Do not lie to one another, since you have put off the old man with his deeds, and have put on the new man who is renewed in knowledge according to the image of Him who created him, where there is neither Greek nor Jew, circumcised nor uncircumcised, barbarian, Scythian, slave nor free, but Christ is all and in all. (Colossians 3:9–11)

Paul preached that the individual must "put on" Christ, becoming a "new man" and thus experiencing a form of psychological renewal ("renewed in knowledge"). Only thus could they truly become the image of God. Humans were all created in God's image, according to Paul, but in his earthly, physical, and therefore inferior image. Only now, by entering a new covenant with God, could humanity be endowed with God's loftier, spiritual image. This transformation would also render the body into something spiritual:

> "The first man Adam became a living being." The last Adam became a life-giving spirit. . . . And just as we have borne the image of the earthly man, so shall we bear the image of the heavenly Man. (1 Corinthians 15:45–49)

Paul entrusts Jesus with rescuing the image of God, delivering humanity from exile to redemption, from bondage to liberty. For what is redemption if not the completion of Creation itself? Redemption is thus the creation of man and woman in God's image, an objective that has thus far not been fulfilled on account of humanity's sins and an inordinate focus on physical deeds, instead of internal metamorphosis.[38] According to Paul, humans would be endowed anew with the image of God in virtue of Christ, who died and was resurrected. Only after Christ's resurrection, he believed, was it truly possible to achieve this goal and reach the pinnacle of human life:

> Now the Lord is the Spirit; and where the Spirit of the Lord is, there is liberty. But we all, with unveiled face, beholding as in a mirror the glory of the Lord, are being transformed into the same image from glory to glory, just as by the Spirit of the Lord. (2 Corinthians 3:17–18)

Christ is "the Spirit," and when we see him "as in a mirror," i.e., through a process of psychological transformation, we become "the same image," the image of Christ, who is himself the complete image of God. Only then may we transcend from "glory to glory" and realize the complete image of God in ourselves, in the spirit of Christ. "And where the Spirit of the Lord is, there is liberty." Here the process is complete: liberty no longer means participation in independent polity and comes to mean internal, spiritual change. "For you, brethren, have been called to liberty!" cries Paul (Galatians 5:13).

The textual record of early Christian baptism rituals mention this reacquisition of the image of God. There developed an understanding that the first image was corrupted when the first man ate the forbidden fruit of the Tree of Knowledge and that his last image would be given to him by his rebirth in Christ: by an internal metamorphosis and participation in a community of faith. In Paul's writings, this was the image that would make all of humanity—men and women, freemen and slaves, Jews and Gentiles—united in the spiritual body of Christ. This new, internal image would also renew human unity: if the corrupted image of the first man scattered people into distinct groups, the new image would reestablish the primordial unity of humankind.[39]

"The linking of contemplation and the perfecting of the image of God" made the above passage from 2 Corinthians "one of the most important in the history of Christian mysticism," writes Bernard McGinn,[40] as it legitimized a life devoted to contemplation in pursuit of inner transformation and the recovery of the original and perfect image of God. Thus we have a line of Christian mystics yearning to achieve what Paul had: liberty and redemption through restoration of the divine image. Hence Origen (c. 185–c. 253) can write, "Let us always, therefore, contemplate that Image of God so that we can be transformed to his likeness,"[41] and with Augustinian spirituality as well, "the essential task [was] the restoration of the image of God."[42]

To sum up, beginning in the first century CE a new conception of the image of God emerged and was adopted. By injecting Pauline theology into Hellenistic philosophy (of the sort that we have already seen in such thinkers as Philo), the image of God was internalized and Christianized.[43] The Church Fathers, chiefly Augustine, for whom Paul's proposed internalization of God's image was obvious, added to it a new interpretation of biblical mythology and explained that the image of God was corrupted by original sin. The advent of Jesus Christ, who was "the image of the invisible God, the firstborn over all creation" (Colossians 1:15), heralded the possibility of rehabilitating humanity's fallen image. And with this rehabilitation came liberty. Individual liberty.

An Elective and Private Religion

With liberty comes responsibility. Individuals are delivered into liberty, and they are also personally judged for their sins. Christianity, as said, empowers an individual's status as a legal subject. As we have seen, in the ancient Near East, the whole family was a single legal unit, and the sole legal subject—the only one with agency and responsibility, who could be held accountable, who could be rewarded or punished—was the patriarch. Ancient Jewish tradition gave individuals, by virtue of the principle of the image of God, a unique status. This was still, of course, a fiercely patriarchal society, but unprecedented importance was attached to individuals as individuals. They could not be executed for others' crimes, and their lives could not be exchanged for money.

For Paul, individuals acquired an even more important status, because they possessed the responsibility and agency entailed by the potential for personal transformation and personal redemption. Individuals were responsible for their own fate, that is, for their own redemption, which they would achieve neither as members of a nation nor by virtue of ancestral merit, but only by themselves. No longer would their relationship with God be sustained indirectly or by invoking the memory of distant ancestors (a form of nepotism with God's willing consent). From now on, they would have to undergo a metamorphosis, an internal change, and to have faith. They would have to do so by themselves, as individuals. Nobody else could do this on their behalf or in their stead.

It was hugely important that Christianity was a *new* religion. This fact meant that its proposed relationship with God was not only personal but also disconnected from traditional social structures. Here was another reason for the transformation of the individual, detached from his or her family, into a religious subject. In the first century CE, nobody was born a Christian. Christians were not delivered into a tradition, but *chose* it. They did not receive it from their parents, but rather discovered it by themselves. Religion was a private, elective matter. Moreover, for individuals, for the first time there emerged space between their personal identity as recipients of divine law and their social roles. No matter whether they were descended from priests, from common Jews, or from a Samaritan or Roman family, the exact same path to God was open to all. No matter whether they were fathers or sons, wives or daughters, God was accessible to them to the same extent and by the same means.[44]

It bears emphasizing: in the pre-modern world, an individual's religious life and relationship with God was not a hobby, a profession, or a field of social activity. It was the essence of one's life, in the most fundamental sense. People defined themselves in accordance with their relationship with God, and this was the most foundational and meaningful relationship in their lives. With the advent of Christianity, it was precisely here that they became individuals, religious subjects wishing to establish this relationship with God on a personal basis. They were severed from their familial, communal, and ethnic attachments. The liberty that Paul promised was therefore also the relative liberty, still small but set to grow, of the individual from the social networks around him.

The Roots of the Separation of Church and State, and Freedom of Conscience

The transformation of individuals into religious subjects transformed religious communities into voluntary associations. As we have said, the first Christians adopted their religion as adults; they were not born into it. They did not sustain a tradition but invented one. The Church became an assemblage of individuals, and membership was conditional on an individual's consent.[45] For the early Christians, what mattered most was personal choice, not the maintenance of heritage and admission into a collective covenant. Of course, it would still take another 1,500 years before personal choice on matters of faith became, after the Reformation, a fundamental and unequivocal principle. But the foundations for this future development were laid here. And since the solidary community was constituted by autonomous and voluntary individuals, the notion of society as founded on a "social contract" between individuals was also rooted here. After all, Christian believers had all reached this community of the faithful without preceding faith and had chosen independently to join it, accepting the terms of the new covenant of their own volition. This covenant was a contract with God, but the model of a voluntary contract could, when conditions ripened, become a secular, social, and political construct.

Here also lay the first separation between the religious and the political, which over 1,700 years later would be translated into a separation between religion and state. After all, it was Christ who said, "Render therefore to Caesar the things that are Caesar's, and to God the things that are God's" (Matthew 22:21), one of the most consequential decrees ever to be given, drawing a distinction between political and religious authority.[46] Unlike in the Kingdom of Israel, where the king followed Torah law and subordinated his realm to this same code of law, Christianity emphasized from the outset (usually more in theory than in practice) the clear division between these two domains. The bearers of religious and political authority—the pope and the emperor—were different figures. Thus Christians are bound by two sets of obligations: state law and religious law. The tensions between these two sets of laws would fuel battles and wars, and also new cultural developments and sensitivities. This distinction, as a theological paradigm and positive social order, would be articulated in the seventeenth century as the modern model of the separation of church and state. Yet long before this, the fact that the Church was distinct from the Roman imperial regime, argues the leading historian Jacob Burckhardt, fostered the evolution of the individual.[47]

The separation of the religious from the political, moreover, made it possible for the first time to insist on the freedom of religious conscience. Of course, in earlier eras, there were people who refused to convert or to violate the norms dictated by their faith—for example, the Hasmoneans, some 200 years before Paul wrote his epistles. The Hasmoneans revolted against the oppressive religious decrees of their Hellenistic overlords. Yet even the Hasmoneans did not dispute the logic of religious coercion, as the Idumeans, whom they forcibly converted to Judaism when they had power, would attest. Religious coercion was an accepted and understandable procedure. By demanding religious loyalty, a regime—be it Seleucid or Hasmonean—subordinated its subjects to its political sovereignty. Worship took place in the confines of a state religion, and obedience to this religion meant obedience to the emperor or to the laws of the realm.

Christianity changed this. It separated the religious and political domains. It proposed a new religious framework, unbound by and independent of the civil, legal, and political domains. Since Christianity was elective and internal, for Christians religious coercion went from being understandable to absurd. It was thus that Tertullian, one of the leading early Christian theologians, could write at the beginning of the third century that

> it is a basic human right (*humani iuris*) that everyone should be free to worship according to his own convictions. No one is either harmed or helped by another man's religion (*religio*). It is no part of the practice of religion to compel others to the practice of religion. Religion must be practiced freely, not by coercion; even animals for sacrifice must be offered with a willing heart. So even if you compel us to sacrifice, you will not be providing your gods with any worthwhile service. They will not want sacrifices from unwilling offerers—unless they are perverse, which God is not.[48]

Tertullian's argument sounds quite reasonable and even intuitive to us, but in his day, it was a sensational novelty. Tertullian was the first to insist that all must enjoy freedom of religion. As the historian Peter Garnsey writes, this was "a breakthrough that only a Christian could make, because the Christian, notoriously, had abandoned his ancestral tradition and embraced a supranational universal religion."[49] Christians were in a social and psychological position from which they could criticize religious coercion in the world around them. They also had a clear interest in insisting on freedom of worship.

But this was not the only reason for Tertullian's insistence. The modern concept of human rights was of course not familiar to Tertullian, but his use of the term *humani iuris* is significant. We can translate it as ascribing freedom of worship "by right" to "mankind." Some manuscripts have Tertullian insisting on both a *humani iuris* and a *naturalis potestatis*, i.e., a "natural capacity" or "privilege of nature" for the same freedom of worship.[50] These phrases hint at a conception of humans as having been inherently endowed from birth with a capacity for rational choice. Several times in his writings, Tertullian quotes verses from Genesis 1 about man's creation in God's image, employing them in the context of reason and free will.[51] It is humanity's creation in God's image that constitutes their right to freedom of religion.

Tertullian's assertion that the gods did not care for sacrifices offered under coercion called into question the ancient religious-political order, in which coercing others to offer sacrifices to a particular god was a means of subordinating them to this order and was not seen as religiously problematic. External gestures were deemed more important than internal intentions, and sacrifices offered under duress were considered perfectly valid in every respect.

This point can be understood from a well-known story from the period of the Maccabean revolt: the story of a Jewish woman (popularly called Hannah) whose seven sons were serially massacred for their refusal to bow to a Greek idol.[52] The Hellenistic rulers of Israel saw no problem in coercing people to prostrate themselves in front of idols; it is clear that the Jews also attached religious validity to such acts, and precisely for this reason they refused to comply. In the story, the Seleucid soldiers try to spare the seventh and youngest son, giving him an opportunity to save himself. They throw a signet ring on the ground, so that by picking it up he can appear to be bowing before the idol, thus saving his life. The boy refuses and is executed, but the Greeks' willingness to accept such a solution shows that they attach no importance to internal intentions: even if the boy bends over to pick up the ring, and everyone involved knows perfectly well that this is all that he is doing, the ritual gesture would have been performed; what matters, at least for purposes of asserting domination, is his obedience to religious-political law and physical performance of a ritual act. The boy, of course, refuses—because he too attaches no importance to intentions, only to practical deeds.

For Tertullian, following Paul, the logic of religion changed, and the validity of a religious act came to depend on intentions, not acts. Rituals performed involuntarily had no religious validity, and "religious coercion" was therefore an oxymoron. Religion had to be a voluntary matter. When Emperor Constantine proclaimed the Edict of Milan in 313, for the first time legitimizing Christian worship across the Roman Empire, he did so in language that reverberated Tertullian's teachings: "We thought . . . that we might grant to the Christians and others full authority to observe that religion which each preferred . . . so that the Supreme Deity, to whose worship we freely yield our hearts, may show in all things His usual favor and benevolence."[53]

Like other principles, this paradigm would only come to be taken for granted over 1,500 years later. Christianity certainly had no compunctions about imposing itself on other lands and peoples. But when Thomas Jefferson, who authored the U.S. Declaration of Independence, wrote in his *Notes on the State of Virginia* around 1782 that "rights of conscience" were beyond the government's control and that "it does me no injury for my neighbor to say there are twenty Gods, or no God," he scrawled in his personal copy of his book the abovementioned statement by Tertullian, in the original Latin. Among the books in Jefferson's bequest was a copy of Tertullian's writings, and the only marking inside was Jefferson's own underlining of this specific paragraph.[54]

The roots of freedom of religion and conscience lie here, in the belief that each and every human possesses reason and a capacity for choice by virtue of their creation in God's image, in the conviction that only by applying these qualities in worship is worship meaningful, and in this transition from collective to private religion.[55]

The Transformation of Women into Legal Subjects

The undermining of the status of the family and the beginning of a separation between the religious and the political also heralded the undermining of traditional social hierarchies. Paul internalized the principle of the image of God, elevating all members of humanity into individual humans. The notion that everyone was created in God's image, that everyone—including women, foreigners, and slaves—possessed an equal and eternal soul, and that *this soul* would be judged by God and could achieve personal redemption and liberty, became widespread with the spread of Christianity. As we have seen, when people formed a private relationship with God, they did so at the expense of prior religious attachments. The family was no longer the religious subject, and neither was the ethnic community. At the same time, other social distinctions—concerning ethnicity, class, or sex—were also devalued.

Thus, for example, women could declare independence by devoting their lives to God. Monks challenged the social framework by living outside it. And female monasticism, whereby nuns abstained from marriage and dedicated their lives to their relationship with God, afforded women relative independence, cutting themselves from patriarchal families and allowing them to lead individual lives. None of this would have been possible unless women's internal lives—their personal, religious experiences and decisions about themselves—had received the importance that it had previously lacked.[56]

Women, who also possessed an internal image of God as immortal souls answerable directly to God, were no longer defined by their relationships with men (their fathers or husbands), but as individuals exercising relative autonomy. Paul, as we have seen, transformed adultery into a sin committed by a man against a woman, not only vice versa. Women became legal subjects by being rendered religious subjects. They established personal relationships with God, and therefore also with their societies. They were responsible for themselves, and others had responsibilities toward them. The narrative around personhood changed, and therefore so did the law—at least incipiently.

"Christianity did not give political emancipation to either women or slaves," writes Henry Chadwick, a historian of the early Church, "but it did much to elevate their domestic status by its doctrine that all men are created in God's image and all alike redeemed in Christ." Creation in God's image, combined with the notion of personal redemption, rendered all humans individuals and all individuals, humans. As Chadwick explains, "they must therefore be treated with sovereign respect."[57]

Deprivation of Liberty: Slavery

Sometimes this treatment involved more than respect. In this section of our discussion about liberty, we shall explore the subject by means of the most extreme example of the deprivation of human liberty: slavery. We shall explore how people sought to justify slavery—and how this institution was ultimately undermined.

Slavery was a fact of life in antiquity, and in the Near East, as in Greece and Rome, enslaved people were considered their masters' private property. Slavery was established as one of society's most natural institutions, and answered a range of social and economic needs. Most people in the ancient world would presumably have struggled to imagine a human society without slaves, and in any case, they did not regard slavery as an institution that could be separated from society or conceivably abolished.[58]

The ancient Hebrews also held slaves, both from among their own people and from surrounding nations. The Essenes, an ascetic Jewish sect, who renounced slavery entirely, were the exception to the rule. According to Philo and Josephus, they did so out of a principled belief in human equality, solidarity, and the injustice of slavery.[59] Nevertheless, we must remember that the Essenes lived in small, collectivist communities that appear to have renounced private property altogether. Moreover, their fierce emphasis on ritual purity and perpetual fear of impurity hardly encouraged the integration into their community of people who did not totally subscribe to their worldview. This, more than theoretical attitudes about slavery, appears to have underpinned their shunning of slavery.

None of these factors existed in wider society, where slavery was seen as a natural social institution, an economic necessity embedded in the logic of society. But if the institution itself had a certain social and economic logic, justifications for slavery had various motives. First and foremost, people generally seek to justify the injustices that they inflict on others, or at least to explain to themselves why their world, in which some are fortunate and others are miserable, some are blessed and others are wretched, is a just world. It's a basic human need. Slavery, therefore, also required legitimation and justification.

For the Israelites, it was fairly easy to justify slavery: their laws about slavery were divinely ordained. Other societies required alternative reasoning. As in later periods, slavery in antiquity was linked to ethnicity. The Spartans had their own slave nation, the Helots, a different ethnic group whose members they enslaved for agriculture and other tasks they considered beneath them. The Israelites were also enslaved, as a nation, in Egypt (according to the biblical narrative), and Jewish law distinguished between Hebrew and "Canaanite," i.e. non-Jewish, slaves.[60] Thus, for societies that were not based on divine law, ethnicity provided a basis for racial justifications for slavery. The assumption was that enslaved ethnic groups were *substantively* destined for slavery: that their members were not free because they were different in some essential sense and inferior to their masters. This apparently logical resolution was also consistent with the teleological disposition of the ancient world: the belief that everything had a function and a purpose, which it had to fulfill. Some people were simply born to be slaves.

It was Aristotle who articulated this teleological paradigm most fully, and he also addressed slavery. For Aristotle, slaves were "living tools" in the hands of their masters,[61] while slavery itself was a natural essence with which one was born: "From the hour of their birth, some are marked out for subjection, others for rule."[62] Slaves had different bodies: "Nature would like to distinguish between the bodies of freemen and slaves," wrote Aristotle, "making the one strong for servile labor, the other upright, and although useless for such services, useful for political life."[63]

The ethnic distinction between slaves and masters was distilled into a matter of physical difference, and this provided a universal explanation for slavery. But Aristotle, like his contemporary readers, knew that there existed upright and weak slaves and strong and deformed freemen. It was also known that many slaves had entered their condition by chance and were not born into it, because it was possible to be enslaved by being captured in war, or simply by being unable to pay one's debts. Aristotle therefore needed to add that "the opposite often happens—that some have the souls and others have the bodies of freemen."[64] There therefore existed slaves with the bodies of freemen, and freemen with the souls of slaves—and in any case, whoever found himself enslaved would somehow be fulfilling his purpose. There was a justification for turning people into slaves.

The Body-Soul Dichotomy and the Justification for Slavery

Without expanding on criticism of Aristotle's unsuccessful attempt to justify slavery,[65] it is clear that the Hellenistic body-soul dichotomy did not encourage him—or the Greeks, more generally—to adopt the Pauline view that all humans are equal (at least in the eyes of God). Although Aristotle's body-soul dichotomy was not dualistic in the Christian sense—he did not consider the soul a distinct entity, existing independently of the body—subsequent Hellenistic philosophers in late antiquity, who *did* subscribe to a form of dualism similar to Christianity's, did not use the body-soul dichotomy in order dispute the logic underpinning slavery, and none of them protested its existence.[66]

In the Roman world, as in Greece, slavery was regarded as equally natural. Gaius, the famous second-century Roman jurist, divided the objects of law into three categories: people (*personae*), objects (*res*), and actions (*actiones*).[67] Slaves, at least until their manumission, were considered objects.[68] The Stoic philosophers accepted this premise and refined it, thanks to the body-soul dichotomy. For them, the soul was the true locus of personhood, and since, in their view, the soul was eternally free, there was no way to truly enslave somebody. It was not so terrible, therefore, to enslave folks, as one could enslave only their bodies.

Thus Epictetus (c.55–135), a former slave himself, opened his *Enchiridion* ("Handbook") with a division of the world into things under his control—"everything which is our own doing"—and things beyond his control, among them his body and fate.[69] We should care only about what is under our control, Epictetus argues, and the rest must simply be accepted with stoic sanguinity. Seneca (c.4–65), a famous Stoic thinker and statesman, wrote that:

> It is a mistake to think that slavery goes all the way down into a man. The better part of him remains outside it. The body belongs to the master and is subject to him, but the soul is autonomous, and is so free that it cannot be held by any prison. . . . It is the body that luck has given over to the master; this he buys and sells; that interior part cannot be handed over as property.[70]

As Bernard Williams explains, like Aristotle, the Stoics also considered it important to justify slavery in a manner that would explain how, despite the existence of this institution, life was not inherently unjust.[71] Accordingly, Stoic philosophers used the dichotomy between the eternally-free soul and the trappable body as a means of adapting the institution of slavery to their conception of justice, not disputing it.[72] Seneca himself owned slaves.

Thus, while the ancient Hebrews (besides the Essenes) understood slavery as part of divine law, and while Aristotle would explain that people were differentiated by their nature and that all slaves were meant to be slaves, the Stoics would have said that while nobody was *born* to be a slave, and while anyone could, with enough bad luck or according to malignant fate, find himself or herself enslaved and thus objectified, this did not mean that the world in general and their societies were bad or unjust, because in any case one's soul was eternally free, and that was what mattered.

Disputing Slavery

The fundamental change in relation to the institution of slavery began with Christianity. Alexis de Tocqueville briefly addressed the beginnings of this upheaval in his discussion of slavery in the United States. "The most profound geniuses of Greece and Rome," concluded de Tocqueville,

> never hit upon the very general yet at the same time very simple idea that all men are alike and that each is born with an equal right to liberty. They did their utmost to prove that slavery was inscribed in nature and would always exist. . . .
>
> All the great writers of Antiquity belonged to the slave-owning aristocracy, or, at any rate, saw that aristocracy as society's undisputed master. They stretched their minds in many directions, but in this one respect they proved limited, and it took the coming of Jesus Christ to make people understand that all members of the human race are by nature similar and equal.[73]

According to de Tocqueville, it was the advent of Jesus Christ, or rather the spread and establishment of Christianity across the Roman Empire, that engendered the notion that all humans were born equal—an idea obviously adopted from the Hebrew Bible and Jewish tradition, and that was nourished by the principle of the image of God.

The Jewish Sages, like Americans in the southern states in de Tocqueville's time, had no qualms about slavery, despite their devotion to the story of the Exodus, in which their ancestors were delivered from slavery. As we know, there are laws in the Hebrew Bible and Talmudic Halakha concerning and approving of slavery. From the Patriarchs to such rabbinic figures as Rabban Gamaliel, Jews owned slaves, and this fact does not appear to have cost them any sleep. Nevertheless, thanks to the principle of the image of God, the ancient Hebrew tradition and the Talmud treated enslaved people relatively benignly. Slaves received a weekly day of rest, on which their masters could not employ them; it was forbidden to cause them physical injury; and Jews were mandated to protect runaway slaves instead of handing them back to their masters, as every other code of law in the ancient Near East required. Moreover, masters who killed their slaves were put to death (Exodus 21:20), in accordance with the law about the killing of anyone else (Exodus 21:12). It is clear that enslaved people were considered human beings and not private property, tools, or instruments at the disposal of their masters.

With Christianity's transformation into a major, widespread religion, the principle of the image of God gained acceptance across the Mediterranean Basin. When Constantine began Christianizing the Roman Empire at the dawn of the fourth century, imperial law was shaped by this principle. Eager to express Christian ideals in the legal code, the emperor instituted preliminary protections for such weak sections of society as children, slaves, peasants, and prisoners. Thus, for example, an edict proclaimed in 316 made it illegal to sear a mark on the face of a convict "because man is made in God's image," no less.[74] The law changes when the story we tell about ourselves changes.

The Church disseminated the tenets of its new faith, which had implications also for slaves. The Church did not abolish slavery, and in fact there were many clergymen, until as late as the nineteenth century, who supported slave ownership and used various theological arguments in an attempt to justify their positions. Yet as early as the period of the Church Fathers, in the third and fourth centuries CE, there were pioneering voices of principled opposition to slavery, predicated on the principle of the image of God. Thus wrote Gregory of Nyssa:

> God said, let us make man in our image, after our likeness. If he is in the likeness of God, and rules the whole earth, and has been granted authority over everything on earth from God, who is his buyer, tell me? Who is his seller? To God alone belongs this power; or rather, not even to God himself. For his gracious gifts, it says, are irrevocable [Rom. 11:29]. . . . But has the scrap of paper, and the written contract, and the counting out of obols deceived you into thinking yourself the master of the image of God? What folly! . . . Your origin is from the same ancestors, your life is of the same kind. . . . Are not the two [slave and master] dust after death? Is there not one judgement for them? A common Kingdom, and a common Gehenna?[75]

Humankind's creation in the image of God, according to Gregory, not only gave them supreme value but also made them, in the fullest sense of the word, *subjects*. In this respect, no human could ever be deprived of their personhood and considered an object that could be bought and sold. Nobody could become the "master of the image of God." Humans, as the image of God, were their own masters. Gregory's words are the first principled articulation completely invalidating the institution of slavery.

Gregory of Nyssa buttressed his assault on slavery with another two arguments: first, all humans are descended from the same primordial parents and therefore are all equal; second, all humans are judged by the same law. These two arguments are important. The first refers to the myth of Adam and Eve, which unlike other myths about the origin of humanity, as we have seen, points to a single source for the entire human family.[76] His second argument is more nuanced and concerns God's judgment of humanity: all humans are judged equally by God, and nobody may claim a higher status anyone else in the same trial before the supreme justice in the heavens.

This latter argument draws on the dualistic body-soul dichotomy, but unlike in the case of the Stoics, here the soul is also a locus of inter-subjective relationships, as each and every soul subsists in a personal relationship with God. Gregory argued that even if people are physically different—as they are from different ethnicities or are of different sexes, as some are stronger and better suited for manual labor, while others are upright and ill-suited for menial work—their souls are identical. More-over, all souls have value in their own right, and every soul is judged by God on its own merits.

Furthermore, the value of the human soul finds expression precisely in the fact that it is directly judged by God, because this attests to its importance, to its power to choose between good and evil, and to its divinely-mandated obligation to avoid evil and do good. Through a personal relationship with God, the individual is subordinated to God—and is therefore liberated from subordination to anyone else. Every soul is a legal subject in its own right, an autonomous entity, by virtue of which it enjoys its special value, its status also compelling an appropriate standard of behavior from others toward it.

Augustine, a Church Father and one of the great formulators of Christian theology, also addressed slavery (in his book *The City of God*) and argued that God had never wanted anyone to be enslaved by anyone else:

He did not intend that His rational creature, made in His own image, should have lordship over any but irrational creatures: not man over man, but man over the beasts. . . . The first cause of servitude . . . is sin, by which man was placed under man in a condition of bondage. . . . By nature, then, in the condition in which God first created man, no man is the slave either of another man or of sin.[77]

According to Augustine, if it were not for the original sin, there would have been no slavery. But humanity fell into sin, which enslaved it, and therefore—by analogy, and as a punishment—each person could also be enslaved by another. Nevertheless, the image of God, which for Augustine meant the human power of reason, which set humans apart from other animals, was a reminder that this was not the desired state of affairs. For Augustine, humanity's descent into sin corrupted the image of God in a manner that facilitated slavery, but future redemption would involve the abolition of both sin and slavery. Augustine did not call for the abolition of slavery—the punishment was justified, in his mind—but his attitudes toward it were decidedly negative. Although the Church also contained supporters of slavery, as we have seen, Augustine's position was the dominant view throughout the Middle Ages and made its way from canon law into the thinking of feudal jurists across Europe.[78]

Subjects, Not Living Tools

Gregory's and Augustine's teachings demonstrate how profoundly conceptions of the individual changed with the rise of Christianity. The perception of the soul as the locus of redemption, under God's gaze, which determined a person's fate—in other words, the transformation of the soul into the focal point of religious life—made the individual the centerpiece of the religious drama. But this new focus on the soul, or on people's inner lives in general, could not have instigated this revolution by itself. As we have seen, the Stoics solved the problem of slavery by focusing on the eternally-free soul. For them, the existence of the soul legitimized, rather than challenged, the prevailing state of affairs. Unlike the Stoics, Christian thinkers insisted that the person, in his or her entirety, must be free. The human person, body and soul together, merited liberty. This was not because physical freedom was a condition for redemption: slaves could also receive Christ's gospels, cleanse themselves of original sin, and gain admission to heaven. Instead, humans were entitled to physical liberty because, as subjects, they were obligated by God's law and it was therefore *improper* for them to be exclusively and absolutely subordinated to manmade law, let alone other people's wills and whims.

According to Aristotle, "the slave is a living tool and the tool a lifeless slave"; and according to Varro, a Roman educator from the first century BCE, slaves were "articulate instruments."[79] Jews and Christians could not have accepted such definitions, because these definitions deprived slaves of their humanity. They held a different narrative, which produced a different nomos. They found it inconceivable that slaves be analogized to instruments, because to do so denied their existence as creations in God's image. "Being in the image of God," affirms the *Catechism of the Catholic Church* (1992), "the human individual possesses the dignity of a person, who is not just something, but someone."[80] The individual was a subject and could not be turned into an object. Humans had won a modicum of autonomy, which could not be retracted. God's generous gifts were irrevocable.

Created in God's image, all humans had a special relationship with their Creator. Created in God's image, they also bore a duty to worship God and possessed the ability to turn their backs on him; that is, to sin. Unlike crime, sin was a category that existed only because of a human's special relationship with God, bound in a covenant with him. This covenant was possible in virtue of humanity's intimate relationship with God and its capacity to choose it. This was humanity's distinguishing feature: men and women were created in God's image, and it was God's image that enabled them, uniquely among God's creations, "to share, through knowledge and love, in his own divine life."[81] In other words, the human being was a subject—not an object.

Human individuals therefore possessed supreme value. Endowed with God's image, they stood before God and faced both his judgment and his love. It would therefore be absurd to enslave and sell them as if they were chattel. Humans possessed a special, inalienable value, and even if they could redeem their souls while still enslaved, slavery was impermissible because it was incompatible with the presence of God's image in humanity.

The guiding logic of these Christian luminaries would accompany Western civilization all the way to the total abolition of slavery. In the late eighteenth century, the famous abolitionist William Wilberforce would still cry that all humans were created in God's image and that slavery was therefore utterly illegitimate. The original French version of the popular Christmas carol *O Holy Night*, written in French by Placide Cappeau as *Minuit, Crétiens* in 1847, proclaims that Jesus "has broken all the shackles / The earth is free and heaven open / He sees a brother where there was once but a slave." Less than a decade later, writing in dissent of the majority verdict in the infamous case of Dred Scott v. Sanford (1856), Justice John McLean insisted in defiance of his colleagues on the United States Supreme Court that "A slave is not a mere chattel. He bears the impress of his Maker."[82]

But the ramifications of this would be felt far beyond slavery. The abolitionist struggle, which anchored itself on the principle of the image of God, proclaimed an ancient idea that would yet give rise to a discourse of protections for all humans in virtue of their basic human dignity and innate rights.

The Individual as a Legal Subject

The period between the fifth and ninth centuries witnessed the desuetude of slavery in central Europe. Instead of slavery, in its ancient form, emerged the institution of serfdom. Serfs were not the private property of their feudal lords, but they were chained to their land and worked it for them. There were several reasons for this transition, linked to various agricultural arrangements, but the changing intellectual and ethical climate inescapably played an important role. The decline of a millennia-old institution such as slavery cannot be explained without the rise of new social paradigms. In this period, Christianity had gradually conquered Europe. It was initially adopted in the major towns, and later in villages and by the peasantry. Together with Christianity, another notion took root: that all Christians formed a single religious community. This community, which spanned boundaries of class, ethnicity, and jurisdiction, transformed enslaved people into Christians: it elevated their identity as Christians above their identity as slaves. This process inevitably augmented their stature and validated demands that they be treated with respect. Their status had changed.[83]

The fate of slaves was but one example of the far-reaching shifts in conceptions of human beings in Europe. The Christian perspective, which held that all individuals were personally accountable to God, also influenced secular law. Christianity transformed individuals into private legal subjects, even if this was initially only in the eyes of God. All humans, be they slaves or masters, men or women, faced the divine judge in heaven in virtue of their individual possession of an eternal soul. This raised the question: if all were judged individually by God, should they not be judged individually by mortal kings? If all people were equal legal subjects in the eyes of the heavens, was it not proper for them to be considered the same on earth?

Thus, when Charlemagne sought his subjects' loyalty in the year 792, he forced all men to swear an oath of fealty to him. Not only freemen were forced to swear this oath: so were their slaves, something that would have been inconceivable in the Hellenistic world—after all, nobody demands allegiance from an instrument. Instead, this paradigm continued the biblical tradition, which held that slaves were equally obligated by God's commandments, now channeled through the universalist prism of Pauline theology. Since slaves, like everyone else, were subjects, and bound by divine law, it suddenly made sense for them to swear oaths before the supreme authority of law on earth: the king.

In the year 800, Charlemagne was crowned emperor by Pope Leo III, and went from being King of the Franks to the first emperor of the Holy Roman Empire, that shaky religious polity that claimed to have succeeded the Roman Empire. Two years later, he demanded another oath of fealty, this time from "every Christian person"—including women. Everyone was now required to swear to obey the emperor "with all my will and with what understanding God has given me."[84] The quotient of living beings considered fully human had expanded. Now, women were also legal subjects. For Charlemagne, *everyone* was bound by the law as creatures possessing free will, including those who were not free men. After all, everyone had the same soul, and therefore everyone, at least in this respect, was equal before the law.

Note that loyalty to the law, part of the ancient Jewish tradition, suddenly received the Christian emphasis on internality: those subordinate to the law were required to follow it with their "will and understanding." In other words, they had to *mean* it. In consequence, opposition to religious coercion started growing. The English theologian Alcuin, one of Charlemagne's courtiers, opposed—in the name of free will—the emperor's policy of forced conversions. He insisted that only faith undertaken freely could be genuine.[85] As we shall soon see, this view, which in the ninth century was held by very few, would become widespread and quite obvious in the seventeenth century, when internecine wars within Christendom in Europe would end, not only because of exhaustion, but also out of a newfound respect for the inner life of the individual.

In the meanwhile, Carolingian Europe was in the grips of a hugely significant development: there gradually emerged a private, inner sphere within which individuals had autonomy, and within which they were supposed to be *guaranteed* autonomy. Individuals became the sole masters of their own will. This was not because more powerful forces—namely political authorities and the Church—cared too much about granting them more freedom, but because of a growing perception that acts undertaken under compulsion were not genuine and were therefore unsatisfactory. In parallel, and complementing this shift, the notion that the same law should be applied uniformly to all subjects of the empire took hold. After all, said private sphere of autonomy was none other than the eternal soul, a person's most fundamental essence. Just as all souls were equal, and just as all souls were judged equally by God in accordance with their obedience to his divine law, so too it made sense that all souls would be judged equally by humans and by earthly law.

Indeed, this was how the matter was understood by Agobard (779–840), archbishop of Leon, who during the reign of Charlemagne's son, Louis the Pious, called on the masses to obey the law out of Pauline individualism:

> There is now neither Gentile nor Jew, Scythian nor Aquitanian, nor Lombard, nor Burgundian, nor Alaman, nor bond, nor free. All are one in Christ. . . . Can it be accepted that, opposed to this unity which is the work of God, there should be an obstacle in the diversity of laws [used] in one and the same country, in one and the same city, and in one and the same house? It constantly happens that of five men walking or sitting

side by side, no two have the same terrestrial law, although at root—on the eternal plan—they belong to Christ.[86]

Agobard, echoing Saint Paul, believed that all humans were "one": equal, under the one God and his only son. From this premise, he inferred directly that they must also be bound by the same laws—that is, equal—on earth. He deduced his insights from within the principle of the image of God, translated into its Christian form. For Agobard, only God's son, Christ, bore the divine image in its perfection, and by belonging to Christ, all other humans could reclaim God's image.[87]

In his book on the Italian Renaissance, Jacob Burckhardt concludes that in the Middle Ages, "man was conscious of himself only as member of a race, people, party, family or corporation—only through some general category."[88] Burckhardt's statement became famous, establishing the view that the Renaissance (in his understanding) marked the birth of the individual. We have indeed seen that in antiquity, people were not individuals as we understand ourselves today, and self-identified as parts, or extensions, of a greater collective. Yet it would be difficult to say that by the Middle Ages, the situation was still the same. Before us is evidence of a somewhat more nuanced picture. The individual did not suddenly emerge, complete, in the Renaissance, and it was not nonexistent before. People indeed saw themselves chiefly through various general categories before the modern era, yet even before the Renaissance, some conceived of humans as individual and autonomous beings, possessing will, the power of reason, and personal agency—and bearing the image of God, which gave them all these.

As we shall soon see, the complete, "possessive" individual would only begin to emerge in seventeenth-century England, and it would become a mass phenomenon only in the nineteenth-century United States. Yet there is no denying the existence of its roots much earlier, in the Middle Ages (such as with Agobard), and even in antiquity (with Paul), and earlier still—with the emergence of the notion of the image of God in the ancient Hebrew tradition.

Who Is the King?

Pope Gregory VII (1015–1075) spearheaded and witnessed several polit-ical and religious upheavals during his papacy. He was considered a great reformer, who sought to bring the clergy under his authority while also insisting on the independence and liberty of the Church—an insis-tence that placed him at loggerheads with the political establishment in Europe.[89] Gregory also spared no criticism for Europe's kings. He believed that all individuals were rulers unto themselves and placed a firm emphasis on equality between all people:

> All good Christians, whosoever they may be, are more properly to be called kings than are evil princes; for the former, seeking the glory of God, rule themselves rigorously; but the latter, seeking their own rather than the things that are of God, being enemies to themselves, oppress others tyrannically. . . . He who tries to rule over men—who are by nature equal to him—acts with intolerable pride.[90]

Princes who lacked self-control did not deserve the title "kings" more than good Christians, because the latter were capable of self-control. What seems to us like an unremarkable elucidation was for medieval people a profound change in conceptions of kingship. In a world in which monarchy was hereditary and considered an essentialist quality (royals were chosen by God and had "blue blood"), a prince's mental state had no bearing on his suitability for the throne. Caligula and Nero became emperors even though they were clearly mentally unfit, and they were joined by many medieval rulers.

As we have seen, after Paul, social institutions such as the family and class were weakened in the face of the inner life of the individual. The institution of monarchy was similarly destabilized. Honest Christians, contemplating their relationship with God and subordinate to his law, were kings unto themselves, by force of their free will and religious and moral choices. They were sovereign over their own private realms and were therefore better deserving of the title "king" than natural-born rul-ers. In contrast, royals who lacked true self-control were undeserving of the title. Rulers who acted like little children were not true rulers. The spiritual, internal, volitional dimension came to be seen as more important than the external, traditional, and social.

From this position, Pope Gregory reached another significant conclusion: since the internal was more important than the external, and since everyone possessed an eternal soul accountable to the same divine justice—all humans were equal. Whether a certain individual was the scion of a royal dynasty mattered less than the fact that he and neighboring peasants possessed the same, equal, eternal soul. Yet if this was so, then rulership over others was suddenly problematic. In the Middle Ages, it was commonly thought that the first man had bequeathed his mastery over the earth not to all humanity, but only to a specific dynasty, to which the kings of Europe belonged.[91] Pope Gregory thought otherwise. It would take centuries for the institution of monarchy to lose power, but Gregory VII was already signaling that this was in the cards.

There were political reasons for the pontiff's position. Gregory VII clashed with the political rulers of Europe in a colossal struggle for power and influence. He was the pope who in 1077 forced Holy Roman Emperor Henry VII to go to Canossa and beg him for absolution. By emphasizing humanity's relationship with divine law, he weakened the authority of the king while empowering the papacy, so this philosophical shift served him well. But it also served to foster the development of the individual, whom it similarly empowered. The existence of two parallel systems of law—one social and political, the other religious and spiritual—became increasingly apparent. Religious law was determined by the pope, and therefore presumed to bring all Christians in Europe under his command, but 500 years later the leaders of the Reformation would protest that a Christian's loyalty to his own conscience must *precede* his loyalty to the Church. Only then would conscience become a source of authority, and every individual—a king. As Larry Siedentop writes:

> The papal claim of sovereignty initiated the translation of a moral status into an organizing social role. . . . This required the definition of a primary or meta-role ("the individual") shared equally by all persons. Other social roles became secondary in relation to that primary role. To that primary role, an infinite number of other roles might be added as attributes of the subject. But they no longer exhausted the subject's identity.

Being a "seigneur," "serf," or "burgher" might be added to or subtracted from an individual's identity, but the individual or "soul" remained. That had not been the case in ancient societies.[92]

The Church sought control, and it could only impose its control on the souls of Christians. Luckily for the Church, all Christians had souls. But by defining Christians *through* their souls, the Church transformed them into private individuals, into subjects personally answerable to God. Individual identity, and indeed one can say individual *personhood*, therefore came to be located in the individual soul or psyche. It was the immortal soul, the image of God, that positioned men and women in the minds of European Christians as facing God as individuals, equal to all other men and women, who also existed as eternal souls facing God as individuals. Any other identity, significant and permanent as it may have been (and in the Middle Ages, social identities were extremely significant and decidedly permanent), existed only *in addition* to the soul from the outside and never replaced it as the most profound, basic, and central core of anyone's identity.

The result was nothing less than the reconstruction of personhood. European societies became communities of individuals, voluntary associations of persons, rather than what would traditionally and naturally have been tribes or feudal estates. Europeans became subjects. The road to such ideas as the social contract and democracy was slowly being paved. So was the road to the formulation of human rights and demands for their protection.

The Birth of Human Rights

Celebratory declarations of individual rights, from the U.S. Declaration of Independence in 1776 to the Universal Declaration of Human Rights in 1948, are commonly imagined nowadays as moments of creation, small big-bangs of human triumph, out of which the human rights that we cherish so dearly today shot out—life, liberty, speech, religion, the pursuit of happiness, and so forth. But like genesis myths of divine creation, the truth is somewhat more complicated.

The discourse of human rights did not descend from the heavens in one piece, but rather developed gradually. Even after it emerged and claimed successes, there were periods in which it gained greater acceptance and periods in which it was rejected in favor of rival conceptions of the common good. In the late nineteenth and early twentieth centuries, human rights suffered setbacks in the form of Marxism (Marx dismissed them as a bourgeois fiction that encouraged alienated individualism), historicism (which rejected universalism in deference to historical context), utilitarianism (with Jeremy Bentham's famous pronouncement that rights were "nonsense on stilts"), and of course fascism. These theoretical frameworks were extremely popular, and their adherents certainly did not believe that everyone on earth possessed "self-evident" and inalienable rights. As Samuel Moyn writes, the concept of human rights as an ethical system with universal ambitions became a popular ideal only in the 1960s, rising from the ruins of the grand ideologies that proposed rival visions of universal utopia.[93]

The idea of human rights presumes the existence of a certain universal set of human qualities that must enjoy permanent, basic protections. These dimensions might manifest themselves as powers or abilities (speech, movement) or as dimensions of the psyche where individual liberty must be protected (choice, faith). Thus, rights are not simply things that humans are allowed to do, but have the power of shaping reality, of commanding. They can require others or the government to act in a certain way or to place a demand to refrain from a certain action. For example, the right to property does not only allow an individual to own objects, but asserts that another person or the government cannot deprive them of their property without justification. In other words, rights presuppose a situation in which the individual has permission to do or not to do an act, and at the same time require all others, and all state institutions, to allow that choice, and to refrain from any action that would frustrate it. Sometimes human rights also involve an active duty on the part of others to support the exercise of these rights. In short, human rights emerge from within humans and compel those around them (at the very least) not to impede the exercise thereof.

Where did this idea come from? How were human beings granted "rights"? Who "bestowed" them, or recognized their existence, and why? When did human societies start respecting what would become an elaborate discourse on "human rights"? A lively and productive debate exists on these questions, and it would be no exaggeration to say that hundreds of books have been written on the subject. Some believe that this idea owes its genesis to Thomas Hobbes, others credit its origins to Hugo Grotius, and yet others attribute it to William of Ockham's philosophy of nominalism. Sometimes, as in the case of conservative thinkers such as Leo Strauss, who find the idea of human rights deficient, we observe an insistence that modern notions of human rights were born out of atheism (Hobbes) and therefore represent a break with prior religious traditions. Other thinkers find evidence of continuity, not discontinuity, between religious tradition and the notion of human rights.

This book places emphasis on the latter position. We shall demonstrate, taking our cue from the groundbreaking research of medieval historian Brian Tierney, that the critical turning point in the evolution of the idea of human rights came in the twelfth century, out of debates between Catholic scholastics and canon law experts, about the concept of *ius naturale* (natural law), as well as from the concurrent expansion and reinforcement of the idea of the image of God.

The twelfth century witnessed a kind of pre-Renaissance renaissance. Urbanization, growing trade, and relative agricultural abundance facilitated higher levels of literacy and cultural development along several planes. This was the era that witnessed the construction of Europe's first universities and great Gothic cathedrals, and as we shall see, also the beginnings of the comprehension of the study of nature as a legitimate human, and indeed religious, enterprise. Trends that had begun much earlier, turning the inner life of the individual into the core of individual identity, intensified. This was the era in which the perception of individuality claimed a greater presence.

We are not yet encountering the development of modern individuality, of course, not even the "possessive individualism" that we will engage in seventeenth century England. But we do encounter an empowerment of the individual and their agency, along with an increased awareness of the boundary between one's self and the other, and correspondingly an interiority, a "depth" inside one which was to be acknowledged and indeed respected. As Caroline Walker Bynum writes, in the twelfth century

> we find a keener awareness than in the immediately preceding centuries
> both of the complexity of the individual's inner life and of the boundary
> that separates that varied and fascinating inner being from other equally

fascinating and complex selves. . . . the twelfth century regarded the discovery of *homo interior*, or *seipsum*, as the discovery within oneself of human nature made in the image of God—an *imago Dei* that is the same for all human beings.[94]

This new sensitivity changed the way people thought and acted. Thus, for example, in the twelfth century marriage through the Church became possible only by force of the consent of both parties, not the ceremony itself; in other words, it was subjective will, not ecclesiastical ritual or tradition, that established a binding partnership. It was during this period that criminal law attached greater importance to the intentions of the accused. Peter Abelard, one of the great theologians of the age (who also gained renown because of his bracing love letters to his forbidden paramour, Héloïse), wrote that an action's morality depended only on the intentions behind it. This was a radically new way of thinking. This was also when the Church started allowing, and later demanding, private sacramental confessions in the presence of priests, which naturally placed significant weight on individuals' subjectivity.[95] These developments clearly emphasized people's internal worlds. The prevailing conception of the human person, of the subject, had changed, and with it, so did the law.

Rights, Universalized

The Magna Carta would be signed at the beginning of the following century, in 1215, guaranteeing the protection of various rights—of the nobility, of the Church, of merchants, of all free English subjects, and even of serfs. Nobody was yet speaking of "human rights" as we understand them today, but of legal rights that accrued to different social classes and role-bearers, on a case-by-case basis. Privileges, as we would call them today, and everybody checked their privileges. The Magna Carta would therefore represent the pinnacle of a lively debate that had raged throughout the Middle Ages, a debate in which rights were understood to be derivative of a certain status—unto each class, its own privileges.

This was the prevailing conception of rights in the Middle Ages. The great Jewish philosopher Maimonides, living in Egypt at the time, argued that justice was "the act of giving everyone their due."[96] As can be inferred from his language, he was not speaking about equal rights for everyone, but rather rights granted in accordance with each particular person's case. But when Maimonides wrote this in his *Guide for the Perplexed*, and when the Magna Carta was signed, there already existed the basis for the notion of permanent rights reserved for all human beings *qua* human beings: that is, rights reserved for *humans*, not for certain roles or classes. Centuries later, this idea would transform humans' conceptions of themselves and of their societies.

Where did this idea come from? As Tierney explains, it originated in an important codex of canon law known as the *Decretum Gratiani*. A *decretum* is a collection of laws and injunctions, and this particular decretum was the first attempt to provide a comprehensive, coordinated compendium of canon law. It was composed by Gratian, an expert on canon law from Bologna, and was published around 1140. The codex contained an extensive collection of Church laws and customs, featuring more or less all canon law published in the preceding millennium, and achieved widespread influence. It was studied by scholars from all around Christendom, and hundreds of commentaries were written on it.[97] The *Decretum Gratiani* therefore served as an excellent springboard for many ideas that then spread across the whole of Europe.

In the first chapters, Gratian explains the meaning of a core concept: *ius naturale*, or natural law. Legislators had used "natural law" since Roman times to denote the basic, objective law to which all humans were naturally bound. It referred to the most primordial law that existed before various groups or rulers started promulgating laws of their own, because it represented the most obvious of all laws. This was the law that anybody could deduce with barely a modicum of thought. Knowledge of *ius naturale* did not have to be discovered in books or acquired through special scholarship, because it could be understood through reason alone. Nor was there any need for divine revelation for this law to be binding. It was straightforwardly intelligible to all, for example, that one should not do to one's fellow that which is loathsome to oneself.[98]

Gratian understood natural law in this sense, but his successors took it one step further and reimagined it in a manner that was previously unprecedented. Their reading of ancient texts was shaped by the fact that they were already immersed in a culture that afforded much more room for the individual. As noted, the twelfth century heralded a (relatively) more individualistic culture, which attached much greater importance on the inner world of the individual.[99]

These cultural shifts encouraged interpretations of *ius naturale* as referring to some subjective quality—a power, skill, or ability—that existed naturally, and *internally*. In particular, they referred to one's ability to use their reason to discern, freely and independently, between good and evil.[100] But as soon as this concept was internalized and transformed from an objective description of *social law* to a subjective referent of a *human ability*, something dramatic happened: there suddenly emerged an opening for understanding "natural law" as a natural, universal, human *essence* that had to be allowed to operate naturally and universally: in other words, as an internal human essence that had to be protected.

Within the evolution of the notion of human rights, we can therefore see a pattern similar to Christianity's adoption of the principle of the image of God. Here too, an existing concept was internalized: a principle that had previously been considered *objective* was rendered a *subjective* reality. Nevertheless, it is noteworthy that Church scholars did not jettison the ancient meaning of *ius naturale* as objective universal law, and the synthesis between "natural law" as a natural social reality and "natural law" as an internal human ability enabled the latter to assume a universal social stature.

Natural Law as Wisdom and Free Choice

The transformation of general law into personal rights owed more than anything to the most preeminent commentator on Gratian, Huguccio (d. 1210). Huguccio studied in Bologna, Gratian's hometown, and from there life took him to the seat of the bishop of Ferrara in northern Italy. In his writings, Huguccio devoted serious attention to *ius naturale* and sought to elucidate its meaning. According to Huguccio:

> [T]he natural law is said to be reason insofar as it is a natural power of the soul by which the human person distinguishes between good and evil, choosing good and rejecting evil. . . . Now in the second place, the natural law is said to be a judgment of reason, namely, a motion proceeding from reason, directly or indirectly; that is, any work or operation to which one

is obliged by reason, as to discern, to choose, and to do good, to give alms, to love God, and those sorts of things.[101]

The second option that Huguccio presented was "natural law" in its social sense, which was understood as elementary back in Roman times, and to which Gratian also adhered. This is the law that reason instructs us to choose. Huguccio proceeded to list another two possible meanings of the term—animal instinct, and divine law—but it is clear that for him, "natural law" primarily carried the first meaning, i.e., natural law as human reason *itself* and as the human ability to choose between good and evil.[102] For the bishop of Ferrara, natural law was primarily an individual quality, a "natural power of the soul" associated with reason and choice.[103]

Huguccio's manner of understanding "natural law" became the accepted view in the twelfth and thirteenth centuries.[104] According to Tierney, this development was highly significant because it relegated the previously main meaning of "natural law" as a description of reasonable behavior (describing how people naturally *behaved*) in favor of a personal, internalized meaning, as reason and free will (describing how people naturally *considered how to behave*).

Note that reason and free will are exactly what underpin what we call agency, which stands at the core of what it means to be a subject or a person. Subjects, or persons, are beings that choose their own path autonomously and do so based on personal judgment and an understanding of their conditions.[105] Natural law, having been internalized, therefore became for medieval scholars of the *Decretum* a fundamental expression of humanity, of a sense of subjectivity that occupied a free and autonomous internal space.[106] From this point, writes Tierney, the road was short for this universal human power to be considered worthy of free expression and entitled to permanent protections.

But this distance could not be covered by leaping over it. Even if our powers of reason and free choice are natural and universal human abilities, there must be another, normative, reason to demand their free expression and social protections for them. The fact that "natural law" refers to my power for rational choice does not obligate others to respect this power, nor does it obligate the state to protect it. Though Aristotelian philosophy, through the prism of which Church scholastics thought, presented humans as a work in progress, fulfilling their potential and set goal through effort, there was no obvious reason why good Christians were obligated to let everyone, including heathens, do so. What Tierney neglects to discuss in his study is precisely this additional step, which emerged not out of a novel interpretation of an ancient concept, but out of a theological paradigm that *complemented* it and lent it normative force. This theological paradigm was the insistence that human reason and the capacity for free choice were nothing less than the image of God in each and every person.

Reason and Free Choice as the Image of God

In her study on the Thomist school of natural law, Jean Porter notes that Huguccio understood natural law as a power of rational and moral choice based on his understanding of human reason and free choice as the image of God within him.[107] Free choice was the core of humanity, and it was common both to the righteous and to the wicked (indeed, it had to be so—if we have no natural free choice, we cannot be blamed for sin or praised for benevolent conduct). Besides, the image of God for Huguccio meant not only reason and free choice, but rather a broader complex of "the human capacity for autonomous self-direction, mastery over one's own choices and acts, which is central to a conception of a subjective natural right."[108] The image of God was self-control, autonomy, and subjective personhood.

The notion that reason was the image of God was not an invention of Huguccio's. We have already seen that Philo of Alexandria understood the image of God as "the most important part of the soul, namely the mind." This interpretation entered Christianity quite naturally (such as through Augustine) because of the emphasis that the Christian tradition placed from the outset on the individual and their inner life, and the image of God was thus understood as reason, as intellect, as logos.[109] Nor was the view of the image of God as a matter of control novel.[110] Control (either self-control or control over others) was linked as far back as the Hebrew Bible to the principle of the image of God, because as soon as God creates man in his image, he orders him "fill the earth and master it; and rule the fish of the sea, the birds of the sky, and all the living things that creep on earth" (Genesis 1:28). Just as the benevolent God rules the world, so too must humanity, the image of God, rule over themselves, over all the animals, and in certain circumstances, over others. Pope Gregory VII's interpretation of kingship around a century earlier receives its proper context here. Humans—all humans—were rulers.[111]

In the twelfth century, these elements were interwoven and received the more substantial meaning of human subjectivity. Perceptions of the image of God placed greater emphasis on choice, moral decision-making, and free will. This period, as we have seen, was characterized by a growing emphasis on people's inner lives and the importance of individual will specifically. The encounter of Christian scholasticism with the teaching of Averroes (along with other Muslim philosophers such as Alfarabi and Avicenna) on the soul spurred a polemic on the meaning of individuation. Averroes's thoughts on the Aristotelian concept of the intellect and his view on individuation informed the views of Thomas Aquinas, who located the active intellect exclusively within the human soul (not transcendent to it) and contributed to the creation of a proto-modern conceptualization of the individual person as a rational being.[112] The nominalists proposed their own understanding, according to which entities exist as distinct without any universal shared form or essence—things come individuated from the beginning. In both cases, the image of God gained a deeper meaning of agency and autonomy.[113]

Aquinas (1225–1274) consolidated this interpretation of the image of God.[114] He was one of the most prominent theologians to have articulated a conception of the natural law in the sense of the various essences that God gave everything on earth, each according to its role. Humanity's essence was their rational part and included "understanding and will," i.e., reason and choice.[115] Aquinas regarded rational self-control as a supremely important virtue. For him, "reason" was the place where "God's image resides."[116] Human self-control was analogous to God's control of the whole world, and by virtue of this parallel, it constituted a dimension of the image of God in us. Humans alone, possessing God's image, were endowed with self-control, which all other animals lacked. Therefore only humans could act freely, while all other animals were pushed into action by necessity.[117]

The use of the image of God to distinguish between humans and animals establishes reason, free choice, and personal autonomy as the core of the human essence. Not only was the ideal of humanity, the proper form of human life, fundamentally linked to reason and free choice (as it was for Aquinas and other scholastics in his time),[118] but this was the most refined essence of humanity that rendered any living being *human*. Our autonomy, our ability to act freely according to our own choices, is the primary characteristic of our humanity.[119] Conversely, suppressing a person's reason and free will, trampling on their autonomy, means trampling natural law and denying their humanity.

The connection to natural law, revered since antiquity as a substantial element in the rule of law, made it possible to understand the image of God (in its extended version, as the core of subjective personhood) in legal terms and to draw the inevitable conclusions: just as the rights of various classes required protection (such as in the Magna Carta), so too were the inner qualities of every single person—not only nobles, indeed not only Christians—worthy of protection. Natural law was internalized, and so was the conception of rights. Rights were no longer derivative from a one's class or role but from one's inner essence, an essence that was universal and shared equally by all members of humanity.

Meanwhile, it also became clear that preventing others from thinking, choosing, and controlling themselves meant stifling the image of God within them, depriving them of the humanity endowed in them by their creator. Natural law, as an internal power, was none other than the image of God. Since no religious system could legitimize the suppression of the divine element in people, Christianity in Europe pivoted toward respecting the intellect, free choice, and autonomy of individuals—toward respecting their subjective personhood. Hence the beginning of the discourse that would take us from natural law to "natural rights."

The normative reason that compelled Christianity in Europe to turn reason and free choice into human virtues entitled to eternal protection was therefore the understanding of them as not only universal human skills, but the image of God itself. Natural law, having been internalized, came to be seen as the core of a subject's humanity, which was also the divine element within them. A person's reason, free choice, and autonomy were all sanctified. Subjective human personhood received both religious significance and a recognized legal status.

Let us recap: on the one hand, the concept of natural law was internalized and rendered equivalent to human reason and the capacity for choice. On the other hand, the principle of the image of God, which had already been internalized by Paul, was buttressed during this period and reinforced with elements of autonomy and subjective personhood. These two shifts intersected and were synthesized in Huguccio's writings, coming to place these qualities as the very essence of humanity. At this point, natural law, which was the same as the image of God, which was none other than human reason and freedom of choice, was elevated to supreme importance and simultaneously translated into the legal language of rights. In consequence, the following conclusion emerged: as expressions of the image of God, reason, free choice, and autonomy (and their derivatives) deserved protection as natural rights that inhered in each and every person.

"Not Only for Believers, but for All Rational Beings"

Based on these ideas, by the year 1200 scholars of canon law had created a language in which conceptions of natural rights could be articulated. By 1300, such rights were indeed proclaimed, including property rights, the right to the most basic material needs for survival, the right to self-defense, and various legal rights for people accused of crimes.[120] Every person, as a person, now had natural born rights that they were entitled to exercise and have protected. Nobody was entitled to interfere with these spaces of autonomous expression—of divine presence—without proper justification.

This was a dramatic development. Rights were no longer contingent on people's status or roles, but were rather universal and common to them all. They did not exist to protect privileges granted to specific groups, but rather served to protect the foundations of subjective personhood. They were not benefits that the state awarded in accordance with the laws that it dictated, but were rather derivative from a prior, self-explanatory natural law. They were not bestowed on people from the outside, but stemmed from deep within them. Natural rights were based on human beings' reason, free choice, and capacity for control (over themselves and property). They were based on the image of God inside them, which was now understood as the universal concept of natural law.

Of course, Europe did not suddenly turn liberal in the thirteenth century. These ideas were adopted by a small elite, and even for them as venerable ideals. Just as the biblical imperative that "Parents shall not be put to death for children, nor children be put to death for parents: a person shall be put to death only for his own crime" did not change the social reality in its day simply by being proclaimed (as we saw with the story of Achan), so too Europe was not going to quit the Crusades simply because its learned scholastics thought that each person's autonomy must be protected. A seed was planted, and it would take a few centuries of gestation before it came to fruition.

So the Crusades went on. And with them the inevitable question of the Church's treatment of heretics. What, indeed, about the wicked and the infidels? If human beings' reason and capacity for choice were the image of God within them, what happened when this power of reason failed them and their free will led them, purportedly, to sin? Would it still, even then, be impermissible to impose one's will on such people, even if one were certain that one's will expressed the will of God, the same God who created all human beings in his image in the first place?

Pope Innocent IV (who served from 1243 until his death in 1254) sank his teeth into this question. Church luminaries had previously believed that, since God had appointed the pope as his representative on earth, only those who recognized the pontiff's authority were entitled to rights to property and freedom. If God was the source of our basic rights, would rejecting his deputy not be tantamount to abdicating those rights? This position, of course, had obvious implications for the status of Jews and Muslims. Innocent fiercely defended papal authority but also saw no reason to expand it without limit.[121] In a composition penned around 1250, he addressed this matter explicitly:

> I maintain, therefore, that lordship, possession and jurisdiction can belong to infidels licitly and without sin, for these things were made not only for the faithful but for every rational creature as has been said: For he makes his sun to rise on the just and the wicked and he feeds the birds of the air, Matthew c.5, c.6. Accordingly we say that it is not licit for the pope or the faithful to take away from infidels their belongings or their lordships or jurisdictions because they possess them without sin.[122]

This was an amazing moment: the pope was limiting the power of the pope. The Church was restricting the Church. The privileged were narrowing their own privileges—out of their own free will. And so infidels—people who did not belong to the Catholic Church—were now taken to possess the rights to form their own governments, to own property, and to have jurisdiction over themselves. Nobody was entitled to deprive them of these rights. They possessed these rights *despite* being infidels, in virtue of the fact that they were rational creatures: human beings expressing the image of God. This paradigm now received formal papal approval. The law changed in accordance with the new narrative about humanity.[123]

"All Nations Are Children of Adam"

This statement by Pope Innocent was tremendously significant. It recognized the basic rights of all humans, including infidels. They too retained rights to property and self-governance. This papal statement attracted heightened interest some 300 years later, in the sixteenth century, when Spanish conquistadors needed to decide whether the indigenous peoples they encountered in the "New World" were entitled to the same protections for their rights. Were they even human? And if so, were they not so primitive that, as Aristotle taught, they were "marked out for subjection" from birth? The "infidels" who confronted Church scholars in the thirteenth century were mainly heterodox Christians, Jews, or Muslims. In the sixteenth century, in contrast, the Europeans who landed on the shores of the Americas discovered pagan tribes, at times majestically worshiping the Great Spirit, at times performing bloody human sacrifices. Did they too have rights?

John Major (or Mair, 1467–1550), a Scottish philosopher with considerable influence in his time, condemned slavery on the grounds that it was an abomination to buy and sell human beings, rational beings who were created to look up at the stars. But in the case of Native Americans, he had no qualms about declaring that they were "slaves by nature," just like Aristotle taught us, and so "the first to conquer them justly rules over them."[124] For Major they were barbarians, and barbarians were not rational beings. Others begged to disagree. In the first half of the sixteenth century a lively debate broke out on the matter in Spain, and one of Major's major detractors was Francisco de Vitoria (1483–1546), a jurist from Burgos who had studied in Paris (and whose writings would have considerable influence on the formulation of international law concerning shipping and commerce).

Vitoria approached the question of the Native Americans' status through Pope Innocent's categorization. He tried to understand whether they had enjoyed genuine dominion over anything before the arrival of the Spanish. According to Vitoria, there were only four possible grounds for the expropriation of the Native Americans' property: that they were sinful, heretical, irrational, or insane. As for the first two categories, Vitoria used an argument that Innocent had already deployed: the good God blessed the righteous with the same rain as the wicked. Besides, dominion was a consequence of the image of God, and all humans, as rational beings, were expression of the image of God and therefore had a right to property.[125]

But what if the Native Americans were irrational (as Major had thought) or insane? Vitoria opposed the notion that even things that lacked the capacity for reason, such as animals, and even inanimate objects such as stars and celestial bodies, possessed rights. In his view, the only thing that endowed rights was rationality.[126] For Vitoria and others, humans were thus unique in that they possessed rights. In any case, since animals and inanimate objects lacked a capacity for self-control, they could not have control over anything external to them. A lack of self-mastery entailed a lack of dominion in general, and a lack of control and dominion entailed a lack of rights.

But Vittoria insisted that it was incorrect to treat the Native Americans as non-rational beings. The "Indians," as he called them, were certainly rational and definitely not insane. "Even if we admit that the aborigines in question are as inept and stupid as is alleged, still dominion cannot be denied to them,"[127] because just as children, even though not yet holding the full capacity of reason, enjoy rights by virtue of being created in God's image, so do they. They retained a right to dominion, wrote Vitoria, and it would be wrong to treat them as "slaves by nature," without rights.[128] On the contrary, they were free people. As one of Vitoria's contemporaries, the Catholic scholar Bartolomé Las Casas (1484–1566), wrote:

All peoples of the world are humans and there is only one definition of all humans and of each one, that is that they are rational. . . . Thus all the races of humankind are one.[129]

Unlike Vitoria, Las Casas lived in the New World and personally bore witness to the Spaniards' horrendous treatment of the Native Americans. In time, he became the first bishop of the city of Chiapas in Mexico, and no less significantly, an important social reformer. In the abovementioned quotation, he insisted on the principle that reason is the core of human essence, the sine qua non that makes a living being human. As we have seen, reason was considered God's gift, and the image of God in all humans. Nobody could be deprived of it, therefore.

During the Valladolid debate (1550–1551), considered the first intellectual polemic in European history regarding the rights of indigenous peoples and the limits of colonialism, Las Casas debated the jurist and theologian Juan Ginés de Sepúlveda, defending the indigenous Americans' rights to self-rule and freedom. Against Sepúlveda, who (like Major and others) based his arguments on Aristotle's distinction and claimed the Americans were "barbarians" who should be treated as natural slaves by the Spaniards (who were in this scheme, of course, "civilized"), Las Casas argued that the people they met in the New World were fully capable of using the faculty of reason, having "long before they had heard the word Spaniard . . . had properly organized states, wisely ordered by excellent laws, religion, and custom," and that they should be converted to Christianity while respecting their basic rights.[130]

Las Casas marshaled in defense of the Native Americans' rights Pope Innocent IV's remarks about the rights of infidels and sinners to self-government, property, and autonomous jurisdiction. "Therefore all, both great and small, the whole people and individual persons, are to be summoned and their consent sought and obtained."[131] In his view, it was improper—and perhaps even impossible—to forcibly impose one's control on rational beings. They must remain free.

We are witnessing universal legal standards, articulated and applied for the first time as a coherent and systematic code within an encounter with a completely foreign civilization. "With Bartolomé de las Casas and Francisco de Vitoria we thus encounter the foundation of one of the most important tools for organizing international politics," writes Hartmut Behr.

Las Casas and de Vitoria are both linked with Latin American history and the effort to defend the indigenous peoples of Latin and South America against Spanish conquest and exploitation. Both did so by extending human rights to Indians and by introducing a body of legal restrictions and guidelines in international politics. The writings of both men established a strong legacy of modern legal thought.[132]

From Vitoria and Las Casas the baton passes to Roberto Bellarmine (1542–1621), an Italian cardinal who would become a Catholic saint and a "doctor" of the Church. Bellarmine reached a conclusion similar to them, and explicitly emphasized that:

> All men are equally made in the image of God with a mind and reason. [. . . Therefore] the infidels, who possess this nature [. . . must] without doubt be able to have true dominion.[133]

Natural law, the image of God, and the belief that all humans were created equal—these principles would all shape the development of human rights discourse in much later periods. The first paragraph of the Universal Declaration of Human Rights (1948) proclaims:

> All human beings are born free and equal in dignity and rights. They are endowed with reason and conscience and should act towards one another in a spirit of brotherhood.

The similarities between the two proclamations are clear, even as dignity replaces the image of God and the toleration of infidels is transformed into universal brotherhood. No direct influence should be assumed, but they are certainly links in a shared chain. The author of the first draft of the Universal Declaration of Human Rights, the Canadian jurist John Humphrey, wrote in his diary that "what we need is something like Christian morality without the tommyrot"—that is, without the theology, of course.[134] The concept of dignity replaced the image of God in this United Nations resolution, but the innate and substantive virtue of universal reason remained, together with free choice and conscience (which we shall get to soon), the gateway to basic equality of rights. Equal rights, in turn—for Vitoria and Las Casas, and especially in following centuries in Europe—led to demands for toleration and, in time, in democratic nation-states, correlated with social solidarity.[135]

"A Deadly War upon All Feelings of Reverence and Distance"

Vitoria and Las Casas were discussing an issue of burning importance in their time, which they cared about and about which they could not avoid expressing an opinion, but in their attempts to save the Native Americans from Spanish violence, they were further developing ideas that were born some 300 years earlier in the commentaries of Church scholars, chiefly Huguccio, on canon law. Their writings would be studied by future generations when they tried to confront similar problems and would evolve into the modern discourse of human rights some 300 years after their time.

The Europeans who discovered America found not only a new continent but also new people, and the question of their treatment demanded fresh thinking about the treatment of human beings in general. Christian clerics, including Las Casas, thought of course that they should try to convert the indigenous peoples to Christianity—but precisely for this reason they had to presuppose that they possessed human souls. It is now known that Christopher Columbus forbade the baptism of children in the region he governed (modern-day Dominican Republic and Puerto Rico) in order to be able to sell them as slaves.[136] The logic underpinning his atrocious behavior was clear: baptizing them would be an admission that they had souls, and if they had souls, they had rights. Conversely,

> the Spanish Dominicans [Vitoria, Las Casas, et al., ed.] were inevitably influenced by an underlying Christian attitude that animated all the scholastic disciplines, an attitude that attributed a unique value to individual persons as children of God, made "in his image." In this connection they often quoted scripture, especially the first chapter of Genesis.[137]

In the sixteenth century, this worldview protested (tragically, unsuccessfully) the deprivation of people's property and their systematic annihilation. As human beings bearing the image of God, the Native Americans had natural rights—human rights.

Not everybody was pleased, of course. Friedrich Nietzsche used the Christian roots of human rights as a dagger for his assault on Christianity:

The poisonous doctrine, "equal rights for all," has been propagated as a Christian principle: out of the secret nooks and crannies of bad instinct Christianity has waged a deadly war upon all feelings of reverence and distance between man and man[138]

Nietzsche was right about one thing: the notion of equal human rights undercut traditional hierarchies of class. It also made absolutist regimes untenable. The modern conception of liberal democracy evolved in part due to the inability of absolutist monarchy to accommodate private spheres of autonomy and self-worth.[139] And long before the emergence of democracies, ideas such as these were at the core of debates around demands for religious freedom. Vitoria and Las Casas were Catholics who lived and wrote soon after the eruption of the Reformation—the Protestant revolution, in and around Germany, which placed religious liberty and the freedom to interpret religious scripture center-stage. Later, after Europe fragmented along religious lines and spawned a multitude of Protestant denominations, the idea that just as Christians were entitled to religious liberty, so were all human beings, took hold. But we shall reach this dramatic shift only after studying the birth of the conscience as a source of supreme authority.

3

Conscience

A New Jerusalem

In the early 1530s, Anabaptists started gathering in Münster, in the region of Westphalia (modern-day northwestern Germany). The Anabaptists were among the first controversial offshoots of the Protestant Reformation, and one of the most striking examples of the "Radical Reformation": the movement of minor groups that turned dogmatic purism into a religious tenet in its own right and saw their small communities as having been elected for salvation. Münster, a medium-sized city that served as the region's trading hub, provided a safe haven for members of this new and controversial Christian sect, and they converged there from near and far—or basically from every place out of which they had been expelled. Within a few years, they became a major power and seized control of the city.

The Anabaptists were a stark example of that natural tendency among certain Christians to take the spirit of Luther's revolution to its logical extreme and demand a pristine and revolutionary form of Christianity, a Christianity purged of all and every sin and perfectly ready for the imminent second coming of Christ. Accordingly, they were interested in obsessively predicting the End of Days and holding assemblies of feverish religious awakenings. Between announcements of the end of the world and the ecstatic visions that gripped their most godly women, the Anabaptists whipped themselves into a frenzy, and many of their neighbors in Münster converted in festive baptisms. Sensing which way the winds were blowing, many Catholics and Lutherans left the city.

Under Jan Matthys, a chef-turned-prophet and religious revolutionary, Münster adopted a theocratic regime. Matthys's vision of establishing a "New Jerusalem, purified of all uncleanliness" included the confiscation and redistribution of property, the expulsion of the remaining Catholics and Lutherans, and the imposition of a violent regime of terror against anyone who refused to swear allegiance.[1] With the city transformed into a community of lovers of Christ under the direct rulership of God, there was no need for any books besides the Old Testament and New Testament, and all other literature was judiciously gathered up and burned. Correspondingly, the principalities around Münster placed it under siege. They could not allow these Anabaptist heretics to declare war on all that was holy. Having received a message from God to leave with a small band of soldiers and confront the armies besieging the city, Matthys followed orders, only to be ripped to shreds by the enemy.

Münster's new leader, a tailor and amateur actor by the name of Jan Bockelson, tightened its theocratic regime. The punishment for any sin—not just murder or theft, but also adultery, slander, enmity, avarice, or audacity—was death. In a perfect society, governed by a prophet, there was no reason (or excuse) for anyone to sin. Soon afterwards, Bockelson decided that the biblical injunction to "be fruitful and multiply" required every man to take multiple wives. The Anabaptists' fierce loyalty to scripture did not allow them to deny that polygamy had indeed been practiced by the ancient patriarchs and kings. The practice became a commandment, and anyone who resisted was put to death. Unmarried women, and those whose husbands remained outside the besieged city, were forced to marry local men. Domestic arguments between longtime wives and their husbands' new sweethearts quickly erupted, but since arguing was a sin, the result was a sharp spike in the execution rate.

When Münster's authorities permitted divorce in order to prevent such arguments and the ensuing bloodshed, marriage in the city became a brief and utilitarian affair: women married, then quickly divorced, and so forth, on a loop. As Norman Cohn writes in his book *The Pursuit of the Millennium*, thousands of Münster residents quickly experienced the full spectrum of sexuality, from stringent puritanism to almost total sexual licentiousness.[2]

The siege of Münster was ultimately successful, of course. The city was ravaged and its inhabitants slaughtered. But its story reflects not only the spirit of total revolution that the Reformation ushered into Europe, but also the theological dilemmas with which it had needed to grapple from its inception. In those formative days, Martin Luther, the standard-bearer of the Protestant revolution against the Catholic Church, found himself negotiating between the principle in the name of which he had charted a new course for Christianity, namely the right to interpret holy scripture privately and in accordance with one's conscience, and the basic social need for institutionalized religion, that is, for binding collective law. The tension between these two—spiritual and institutionalized, subjective and objective, particular and general, authenticity and order—nourishes and animates Protestantism to the present day.

At the heart of this tension was the conscience. As we shall soon see, Luther invoked the conscience in disputing the Church's exclusive authority to interpret scriptures, and he staked his incipient revolution on the cause of free, individual choice as an expression of loyalty to God's word. "We are interested in the pure and true course," declared Luther, "prescribed in holy Scripture, and are little concerned about usage or what the fathers have said or done in this matter. . . . Herein we neither ought, should, nor would be bound by human traditions, however sacred or highly regarded."[3] Revolutionary words, if ever were such spoken.

Luther advocated for what he called "Christian liberty," a form of individual liberty derivative from one's religious faith. Faith, according to Luther, was the only necessary condition for salvation—faith, and not good deeds or obedience to the law. It is faith that anchors us in God's word, liberating us from obedience to "numberless fathers, innumerable councils, the custom of ages, or a majority of all the world," as he pointedly put it.[4] As long as our internal capacity for choice is rooted in faith and the scriptures, it liberates us from tradition entirely. Loyalty to our inner convictions about God's will even compels us, if need be, to rebel against the Church's authority. By following the "pure and true course," we become individuals who are answerable only to their own conscience. It is easy to understand how enticing Luther's words were; it is also easy to understand their danger. After all, the Anabaptists raised the flag of that same commitment to truth and purity—and the same determination to manifest it in daily life, on earth.

Precisely in the context of its profound repercussions, it is worth noting that the Reformation, in terms of its guiding logic and intellectual structure, in both its mainstream (Lutheran and Calvinist) and more radical forms, was not a freak event in the Christian tradition. On the contrary, it was a natural and predictable continuation of it. This tradition, whose roots as we recall lay in a revolt against Jewish law, had fostered an ethos that *demanded* persistent rebellion against the establishment as a path towards heaven. Under the logic that claims proximity to God by turning inside (faith, psychological metamorphosis) and rejecting outer "forms" and "works," the arrow of revolution against the authority of heteronomous law and in the name of autonomous spirituality is drawn, an arrow the trajectory of which culminates in rejecting the authority of the Pope, indeed even of any Church. The use of the conscience as a tool of this revolt was but a translation of this ancient tradition to a proto-modern disposition.

The Jewish Conscience

The conscience is a fascinating human instrument. As an existential and ethical dimension of the individual condition, it combines certain moral premises with a call for internal integrity, or autonomy. We act in accordance with our conscience in order not to betray what we regard as appropriate, or as our proper self-image. We generally believe that if we fail to heed the call of our conscience, we will be neglecting the good and throwing ourselves into a state of cognitive dissonance and emotional distress. Understandably, the imperative to be faithful to our conscience is especially valid when one's conscience demands one to do something against convention, practice, or the law. It is precisely when one must summon the courage to heed one's inner voice, as opposed to the masses, tradition, or public decree demanding that we do otherwise, that one's courage, integrity, or authenticity is tested.

Heeding one's conscience, therefore, means deferring to an internal, subjective, and autonomous source of authority over an external, objective, and heteronomous one. When pacifists seek exemptions from mandatory military service out of respect for their conscientious refusal to engage in war, they are asking to prioritize the personal over the general, their own needs and values over those of others, and their conscience over the law. Freedom of religion and conscience, which is recognized nowadays as a fundamental right, is based on the premise that we must respect such requests: that we must afford a special and honored place for someone's conscience, even if this sometimes grants them privileges over other citizens.

The conscience is not an aspect of the human condition emphasized in Judaism's traditional texts. On the contrary, the story of the binding of Isaac (Genesis 22) seems to celebrate the ability to ignore one's conscience and to obey an external voice, even if it orders one to do something totally atrocious. The Israeli philosopher Yeshayahu Leibowitz advocated for this fiercely:

> The Torah and the prophets never appeal to the human conscience, which harbors idolatrous tendencies. . . . So long as a person's religiosity expresses only his personal awareness, his conscience, his morality, or his values, the religious act is merely for himself and, as such, is an act of rebellion against the Kingdom of Heaven.[5]

Leibowitz draws extreme conclusions from his legalistic and exceptionally restrictive interpretation of the Jewish tradition. Besides the binding of Isaac, as we know, the Hebrew Bible tells us the story of Abraham's argument with God over the fate of the city of Sodom, which leads, as Rabbi David Hartman emphasizes, to a dialogue-based Halakha, a covenant in which each party, human and God, has a voice.[6]

In the modern era, various Jewish thinkers would embrace the conscience as a legitimate source of authority; nevertheless, there is no doubt that the conscience does not claim a central place in the Jewish tradition. As a tradition that emphasizes the collective, together with unique moments of collective revelation, Judaism could not give a central place to the inner voice of the individual. The Hebrew word for conscience, *matzpun*, was coined only in the twelfth century, and then denoted concealed, or hidden, moral feelings. It was not until the twentieth century that it was brought into common currency.[7]

The Pauline Revolution and the Internal Logic of Christianity

Conversely, if we recall the history of the evolution of Christianity, we will discover that for this tradition the inward turn, the search for sources of authority and religious meaning within oneself, was a natural development. As we have seen, as early as Paul's day, the relationship with God was rendered private and internal; in Paul's own lifetime, he juxtaposed this option against the Jewish tradition. Paul emphasized the conscience (*syneidēsis* in Greek, the language in which he wrote—and the idea itself also came to him from Hellenistic culture), and he made it central to his thinking. He privatized the dialogue between human and God, transforming it from a communal or national relationship into a personal, spiritual occurrence. As we have seen, individuals were called upon to undergo an internal transformation that would redeem them on an individual basis and establish a personal relationship with the true God. In order to instigate this theological revolution, Paul rejected the "flesh" in favor of the "spirit," or in other words, renounced obedience to religious law as a meaningful ritual act and clarified that the primary if not exclusive sphere in which the true religious drama unfolded was the soul—the internal life.

By turning inward, Paul rejected the notion that belonging to a specific ethnic group was a condition for an authentic relationship with God. There was no longer any importance, therefore, to such categories as Jew and Greek, slave and freeman, man and woman—at least when it came to worshiping the divine. Worship took place in one's soul (in the domain of the "spirit") and did not depend on the body (the "flesh") or belonging to any particular group or class. Religious law and ritual became even less important, because they were concerned with permission and prohibition, with physical movement and the spoken word, whereas true association with God was established inside, in the soul.

Paul's denunciation of the contemporary religious establishment was revolutionary. He dismantled Judaism's first principles and rebuilt a minimalistic, voluntaristic, and individualistic religious system. According to this paradigm, there seemed to be no need for a religious establishment at all, because every individual could establish a personal relationship with God (a problem that would come back to haunt Luther). It appears that at the outset of his journey, the Apostle to the Gentiles believed that the End of Days was nigh and that it would not be long before Christ returned to earth, such that all that was needed was to spread his good word, not to build a practical vessel to carry it forth. When it became clear that the second coming of Christ was running late by at least a few years, the first Christian communities were forced to organize themselves accordingly—that is, to institutionalize. Law and deed, custom and ritual were becoming part of the new Christian religion. For lack of choice, this rebellious and audacious movement became an organized and hierarchical Church; proto-Christian denominations of varying shades of anarchism were dismissed; and an orthodoxy was entrenched. The Catholic Church was born.

Nevertheless, the Pauline maneuver remained embedded in Christianity's genetic code, creating a recurring theme of challenges to the "fleshy" establishment in the name of the spirit. The Church embodied this theological irony at the heart of Christianity: it was skepticism of the law that enabled diverse streams and denominations in the Christian tradition to define themselves and their relationship with God in terms of their association—or dissociation—with the establishment. They understood their rejection of the latter as affinity for the former. The influence of this theology was striking: according to comparative research by Joseph Henrich and others, exploring hundreds of countries and peoples, the longer a particular country remained under the control of the Catholic Church, the less importance its inhabitants attached to tradition.[8] In other words, Catholicism was, throughout its history, an anti-traditional tradition. If we take religion as a collective traditional framework, the Church was a secularizing force.

The history of Christianity can thus be broadly understood as the history of recurrent attempts, cast in the model of Saint Paul, to promote a more authentic version of Christianity by making it more internal and more private. According to the internal logic of the Pauline revolution, any attempt to be "more Christian" inevitably pulls religion in the direction of being "more spiritual," in the sense of rejecting whatever is considered "fleshy." Thus, over the past two millennia, Christians repeatedly denounced the Church establishment and the formal laws of their religion and tried to promote a form of religiosity that was more internal, subjective, hostile to the body and to the establishment, and therefore "purer," "higher," and of course more "spiritual."

Some examples should clarify this principle. In the second century CE, the early Church was forced to contend with Montanism, a movement whose adherents specialized in ecstatic frenzies that they believed originated in the Holy Spirit and constituted the only true expression of Christianity. The Montanists, who called their sect the New Prophecy, emphasized both asceticism and direct experience of the Holy Spirit, claiming that the Church had been corrupted and had sunk into worldliness. It was no coincidence that Tertullian, the eminent thinker who was the first to write about freedom of religion as a right, embraced Montanism in his old age and observed that "the Church, it is true, will forgive sins: but (it will be) the Church of the Spirit, by means of a spiritual man; not the Church which consists of a number of bishops."[9] In other words: true spirit was opposed to the established Church.

Montanism eventually declined, but similar movements kept cropping up, especially when the material and social conditions encouraged their proliferation, most emphatically starting in the twelfth century. In his classic study *In Pursuit of the Millennium*, Norman Cohn provides myriad examples of the heretical spiritual temperament of Christian religious innovators in this period. Figures such as Tanchelm of Antwerp (d. 1115), Henry of Lausanne (active from 1116), Master Jacob of Hungary (of the Shepherds' Crusade of 1251), and Marguerite Porete (burned at the stake in 1310), some of whom were self-proclaimed prophets or messiahs, and movements such as the Brethren of the Free Spirit (between the thirteenth and fifteenth centuries), the Beghards, and their female, more significant counterparts, the Beguines (from the late thirteenth century), the Bohemian Adamites (fifteenth century), the Cantonists (sixteenth century), and many others all shared a dismissal of the Church's authority and a rejection of the efficacy of the sacraments. For the most part, these figures and movements rejected authority altogether and the validity of any aspect of religion besides personal prophecy and internal experience. Cohn cites the opening line of a prayer used by the Bohemian Adamites, which succinctly encapsulates this point: "Our father who art in us, illumine us, thy will be done."[10]

The emphasis on religion as an internal, emotional, and experiential phenomenon contradicted the authority of tradition and came at its expense, and also at the expense of the Church establishment and religious dogma. The focal point of religion was internal to the individual, and whatever was external to her or him (besides holy scripture and God himself, at least at this stage) was dismissed as irrelevant in the best case or as an obstacle to a personal relationship with God in the worst. The Christian tradition therefore presents us with an internal dynamic in which the aspiration to be a better Christian finds expression in the sidelining of law and ritual in favor of internal authority, experience, and a personal relationship with God.

The Source of the Conscience in Christian Tradition

Internal authority not only takes the form of spiritual experiences or transformations, of course. As early as Hellenistic culture, the conscience was understood as an inner voice instructing one how to act properly and rebuking one for negative conduct. Socrates, as we have seen, heard a divine voice (a *daimonion*) speaking to him from within and guiding his behavior, and Greek and Roman philosophers wrote extensively about the conscience (Cicero considered it a gift of the gods).[11] The conscience crossed over from Hellenistic civilization to Christianity, which emerged from within it. Paul uses the Greek word for "conscience" (*syneidēsis*) no fewer than fourteen times in the New Testament, counting only epistles that are conclusively authentic (the term is used another eight times in other letters attributed to him), and he presents it explicitly as an alternative to the law.[12] The Church Fathers and Doctors adopted the conscience in Paul's wake. Thus, for Origen, the conscience was the "educator of the soul"; for Augustine, it was a means of approaching the divine presence; for Aquinas, it was the "kingly" part of the soul; and for Bonaventure, it was the pinnacle of the intellect.[13] Practically every Christian thinker discussed the conscience.

As in Greece and Rome, Christian thinkers also thought of the conscience as a divine voice, albeit of course as the voice of the monotheistic God. The conscience had suffered from the original sin, but it was still capable of repairing itself through the Holy Spirit and God's grace. Since the conscience was identified mainly with the human capacity for reason, various thinkers, starting in Augustine's time, understood it as the image of God.[14] Nevertheless, the consensus among theologians was that the authority of the conscience was not to be accepted over the even higher authority of the Church or tradition. The conscience could err. "Conscience cannot break another law; that is why it cannot absolve us either from God's command or from the command of a superior to whom we have obligated ourselves by law of a vow," wrote Bonaventure.[15] One important exception in this regard was Thomas Aquinas, who believed that one should always follow one's conscience, in every situation. For Aquinas, the conscience served to reveal to us the explicit will of God.[16]

The evolving discourse of rights also addressed the conscience. William of Ockham, the early-fourteenth-century Franciscan friar who was one of the pioneers of Nominalism and gave his name to the famous philosophical "razor," an analytical tool for excising superfluous metaphysical entities, wrote emphatically that there was a difference between the liberty of the conscience and moral behavior. Ockham argued that our free choices deserve protection even if they are wrong. The conscience was an autonomous sphere in which a subject's capacity for free choice found expression. Since there was no value to choices unless they were made freely, the freedom of one's autonomy had to be protected even in cases where others considered one's choices to be poor.[17]

This process of individuation, with the growing importance of the inner world, meant that ultimately, with the end of the Middle Ages, the conscience became the supreme source of authority. At this stage, it was still connected to God: loyalty to one's conscience, as it guided one through matters of faith, was the same as loyalty to God's word. But this emphasis on the conscience, in the context of the fundamental Christian dynamic that we discussed earlier, rendered obedience to one's conscience a supreme moral ideal. Loyalty to God's voice, arising from within, became the greatest challenge of any religious person—the complete opposite, we must note, of the logic of Abraham's test in the story of the binding of Isaac. For Christians at the dawn of the modern era, believers were required to heed their conscience—even at the cost of their lives.

The most famous example of the price paid by Christians who adhered to this new ideal is that of Jan Hus, the Bohemian reformer who was tried for heresy in 1415. In his letters from prison, Hus wrote about the importance of following one's conscience, and on the day he was burned at the stake, when he was asked to recant, he said—according to tradition, "These bishops here urge me to recant. I fear to do this lest I be a liar in the sight of God, and offend against my conscience and God's truth."[18]

The conscience and divine truth were closely connected, and offending the conscience—despite the instructions of the religious establishment—was tantamount to offending God himself. Hus is particularly known for an anecdote about his execution, which states that while he was being burned at the stake, a pious old woman approached the flames and threw some straw into the fire. In response, Hus proclaimed, "*O sancta simplicitas!*" ("O, holy simplicity!"), observing the woman's act through the same inward looking lens: As he is meticulously heeding his conscience, she is her naïveté. Hus carved out a new ethos, one in which religious faith was measured by allegiance to one's conscience, even to the point of a martyr's death. A century after his death, as the Reformation took shape, Hus became the movement's most important martyr. In 1537, Martin Luther himself wrote the preface to an anthology of Hus's writings.

Martin Luther and the Point of Modernity's Conception

Protestantism's origin story places Martin Luther, an Augustinian monk and doctor of theology at the University of Wittenberg (in modern-day eastern Germany), in front of the city's church. Luther nailed his famous Ninety-Five Theses to the massive doors of the church on October 15, 1517, disputing the religious logic of the practice of granting indulgences, the permits that the Church issued to fee-paying adherents for the remission of their or their deceased relatives' sins. Luther was emerging out of a profound crisis of faith, convincing him that God wanted nothing more from us than faith and that nothing besides having faith in God could help one to achieve salvation. It was thus clear to him that the sale of indulgences was an outrageous blasphemy: it both robbed people of their money and filled them with futile hopes of atonement.

Luther's crisis of faith was rooted in his fear of God's judgment. Two years before he denounced the sale of indulgences, he sought respite for his tortured soul. The year was (probably) 1515, and Luther, then aged thirty-two, was already an Augustinian Catholic friar and Bible lecturer at the University of Wittenberg.[19] As a student of Gabriel Biel, a proud disciple of William of Ockham, Luther believed in the nominalist view of God as infinitely distant, such that humanity had no possible way of knowing how to please him. On the other hand, as an Augustinian friar, Luther was supposed to aspire to perfection in the service of God. The contradiction is clear. Luther felt alienated from God and alienated from himself, and he was terrified that he would be sent to Hell.

Luther sought relief in the holy scriptures. He repeatedly pored over the Gospels, praying constantly for relief, and in the Epistle to the Romans he came across the following verses:

I am a debtor both to Greeks and to barbarians, both to wise and to unwise. So, as much as is in me, I am ready to preach the gospel to you who are in Rome also. For I am not ashamed of the gospel of Christ, for it is the power of God to salvation for everyone who believes, for the Jew first and also for the Greek. For in it the righteousness of God is revealed from faith to faith; as it is written, "The just shall live by faith." (Romans 1:14–17)

Luther could not understand what in heaven's name God wanted from him. What did Paul mean when he spoke of the "righteousness of God"? How could a lowly sinner like him ever act in accordance with God's righteousness? After all, God made ultimate demands, while he, Luther, lived in a limited reality. God was in heaven and he was on earth—how could the two ever connect? And then suddenly—it happened when he went to the toilet—he was enveloped by a heavenly light. Luther described his personal miracle thus:

> I meditated night and day on those words until at last, by the mercy of God, I paid attention to their context: "The justice of God is revealed in it, as it is written: 'The just person lives by faith.'" I began to understand that in this verse the justice of God is that by which the just person lives by a gift of God, that is by faith. I began to understand that this verse means that the justice of God is revealed through the Gospel, but it is a passive justice, i.e. that by which the merciful God justifies us by faith, as it is written: "The just person lives by faith." All at once I felt that I had been born again and entered into paradise itself through open gates. Immediately I saw the whole of Scripture in a different light. I ran through the Scriptures from memory and found that other terms had analogous meanings, e.g., the work of God, that is, what God works in us; the power of God, by which he makes us powerful; the wisdom of God, by which he makes us wise; the strength of God, the salvation of God, the glory of God.[20]

The justice of God, Luther understood, was a "passive justice": justice that is not a result of any of our actions. On the contrary, passive justice exists when we do nothing besides believe in God, while God "justifies us." In other words, the meaning of "justice of God" is our *justification by God*. It is not a lofty ideal toward which we must aspire, but an internal occurrence that we must anticipate. God justifies us exactly as he empowers us or heals us; it is not something that we do *for* God's approval, but something that he does *in* us; it is not something that we are to perform, but something that happens to us.

Christian Liberty

Justification by God is a process that happens through perfect faith, and only through perfect faith. Paul used Habakkuk 2:4—"the just shall live by his faith"—to give preference to faith, which is individual and thus could be universal, over the particular covenant of the Jewish people. Luther gave complete supremacy to faith, because for him, it was the only thing that enabled our justification in the eyes of God. No longer would people have to fear that their deeds were insufficient to please God (in any case Luther believed that it was impossible to know what pleased God): all that they had to do was to *believe*. From then on, the process of justification by God would happen to them, *within* them. This notion transformed justice from a metaphysical, objective, abstract, and transcendent ideal into something that God does for us, within us, when he justifies us, individually, internally, and subjectively.

"Immediately I saw the whole of Scripture in a different light," wrote Luther. This is quite unsurprising, because Luther held up a mirror against it, producing a reverse replica. The work of God was now "what God works in us"; the power of God, that "by which he makes us powerful"; the wisdom of God, that "by which he makes us wise," and so forth. Luther initiated a great, Copernican revolution: he shifted the center of gravity of the relationship between humans and God from the outside to the inside, from the objective to the subjective, from the active to the passive, from the collective to the private, from the theocentric to the anthropocentric. Thus, writes Michael Allen Gillespie,

> Luther was able to transform the abstract and distant God of nominalism into an inward power that suffused individual human beings. The faith that arises from the encounter with God's word in Scripture thus works in us and transforms us. Through it we are reborn in God because God comes to dwell in us.[21]

The magnitude of this revolution cannot be understated: from that moment, God no longer resided in the heavens, but in the human heart. Once again, we see the same process of internalization and individuation at play. This was the starting point of Lutheran theology; this explained why salvation could only come through faith (*sola fide*), which in turn could only come through God's grace (*sola gratia*), not by any worthy deeds of ours. One could only achieve this by being anchored in personal readings and interpretations of scripture (*sola scriptura*), the only place where the truth was revealed in full. It is important to note that Luther himself experienced this redemptive discovery as a "rebirth": as an internal transformation, a spiritual experience that changed his understandings, existential condition, and whole life. This too, of course, was consistent with, and an elaboration of, the fundamental dynamic of the Christian tradition.

This exclusive emphasis on faith transformed the Christian journey into a private and internal matter, one between each person and their soul. The Church was no longer needed, and to that extent, it had no authority. The dismissal of good deeds as a metric or key for divine salvation heralded total liberty for individuals, because no longer could anyone demand that individuals adapt themselves to certain standards. Luther himself would make this point five years later, once he was already in the grips of his campaign against the highest echelons of the Catholic Church:

> It is clear then that to a Christian man his faith suffices for everything, and that he has no need of works for justification. But if he has no need of works, neither has he need of the law; and if he has no need of the law, he is certainly free from the law, and the saying is true, "The law is not made for a righteous man" (1 Timothy 1:9). This is that Christian liberty, our faith, the effect of which is, not that we should be careless or lead a bad life, but that no one should need the law or works for justification and salvation.[22]

Christian liberty, as Luther called it, liberated individuals from any heteronomous obligations. All that they had to do was to have faith, and they could receive faith, through God's grace, by reading the scriptures. Luther's idea was straightforward: every right-minded Christian could read and understand the scriptures by himself. Yet here too, Luther's idea was as revolutionary as it was simple, because it transferred the authority to interpret scripture from tradition to individuals. By conditioning salvation on individual faith, by turning individuals' inner workings into a necessary and sufficient condition for world salvation, and by entrusting interpretative authority for the holy scriptures to every layman, Luther laid the foundations for modern individualism, for resistance to the authority of institutions and traditions, and the veneration of our inner lives—or in short, for the world we know today. A central pillar in this enterprise was Luther's use of the conscience as a supreme source of authority.

I Can Do No Other

Luther wished not to bury the Church, but to reform it. His exposition of those Ninety-Five Theses in 1517 was a conventional way to initiate a theological debate. Yet soon enough, it became clear that this young friar was unwilling to accept authority. A series of debates with theologians who were sent to engage him failed to move him from his position, and whereas others might have buckled under the weight of the Church establishment, the intense pressure crystallized in Luther a great outburst of creativity. Luther wrote and wrote, and thanks to the printing press, invented by Gutenberg just fifty years earlier, his writings spread far and wide. In fact, Luther's writings became monumental bestsellers: Luther was singlehandedly responsible for one fifth of all publications printed in Germany in that decade. The public devoured his radical new teachings, and its appetite proved insatiable. The Church understood too late that it was dealing with something truly unprecedented.

Luther, for his part, gradually realized that the Catholic Church was beyond repair. In 1520, he announced that indulgences "were nothing but impostures of the Roman flatterers."[23] That same year, as we have seen, he also articulated for posterity the Lutheran concept of Christian liberty: "to a Christian man his faith suffices for everything, and that he has no need of works for justification." Works don't work. No good deed could secure one a place in heaven; in fact, people could be utterly depraved, and yet if God so wanted, the gates of heaven would still be open to them. The only thing that counted was pure faith, private and internal; the rest was commentary. Luther liberated religion from custom, ritual, tradition—and even morality. But by the same token, Luther also liberated morality from religion—he created the prospect that one do good not for the sake of one's own benefit, but simply because it is good. Think of Kant. Think of secular humanism.

Excluding divine providence, only luck and elaborate medieval political interests saved Luther from death at the stake. Wittenberg's prince, Friedrich III, wanted to keep his famous theologian safe and therefore protected him. In 1521, Luther was summoned to the Diet of Worms, in the presence of representatives of the Church and Holy Roman Emperor Charles V. His name already preceded him, and he was received in the city with acclaim. In front of the assembled dignitaries and the emperor himself, Luther was formally asked to recant, once and for all. Even if he personally believed that indulgences were invalid, he was told, he had to know that they had been approved by the Pope and official theological councils of the Church. If not for any other reason, then at least the authority of these mighty institutions were supposed to eliminate any doubt from his mind. What weight did the interpretation of a lone individual carry in the face of ancient traditions and the venerable authority of the Church? Who could dare raise doubts about the truths that Jesus Christ himself bequeathed, that the Apostles preached, that saintly blood had been shed for, that the Church Fathers had deepened, that Roman emperors had adopted, that illiterate masses had accepted, that councils had reaffirmed, and that the Pope himself believed in? Luther felt the gravity of the choice put before him and asked for a whole day to consider the matter.

The following day, Luther returned to the assembly hall, where everyone was standing and the Emperor alone was seated. Facing this congregation of churchmen, he launched into a well-reasoned speech, ending with these immortal words:

> Unless I am convinced by the testimony of the Scriptures or by clear reason (for I do not trust either in the pope or in councils alone, since it is well known that they have often erred and contradicted themselves), I am bound by the Scriptures I have quoted and my conscience is captive to the Word of God. I cannot and I will not retract anything, since it is neither safe nor right to go against my conscience. May God help me. Amen.[24]

There can be no overstating the significance of these lines. Luther was appealing to his conscience and positioning it as a higher source of authority than the word of the Pope, councils of the Church, and the whole of Christian tradition. No longer would they get to decide—*he* would.

Human Will as an Expression of the Image of God

Luther disputed other theologians who believed that the image of God had remained intact even after the original sin, and he also disagreed with those who understood the image of God as the human intellect. Both sets of opponents were completely wrong. The image of God, Luther believed, was one's ability to lead a life of perfect conformity with God's will. In the Garden of Eden, Adam's will was completely consistent with God's will, because he was God's image. The first man, therefore, lived a perfect life. But after the Fall, humanity was shorn of God's image and therefore lived in defiance of God's will—in sin.[25]

Luther was a dynamic and passionate man, and although by all accounts he possessed a brilliant mind, he did not think that reason was something to be admired, much less trusted. For Luther, the human *will* was the core of the image of God,[26] certainly before the original sin but also afterwards, because human will could be rendered consistent with God's will or at least aspire to be so. "We must examine our heart and conscience and act like a person who really desires to be right with God," wrote Luther.[27] One can understand, therefore, how important it was for Luther not to take lightly the instructions of his conscience, which was seeking God—the conscience that adhered to the word of God at Worms.

Note that Luther's conscience did not teach Luther about good and evil, but rather instructed him to consult God's word as he understood it from within the holy scriptures. Luther could not define good and evil, purity and impurity, justice and heresy as he wished—he was not a modern individual. Rather, their meanings came directly from God through revelation.[28] Luther considered it dangerous to liberate the conscience from God's word. Without a safety chain connecting it to the heavens, humankind was like "a ball which is kicked about the earth."[29] The conscience, Luther wrote, was like a woman's womb, barren if bereft of the two parts of the holy scriptures—the Hebrew Bible (the "Old Testament") and the New Testament—which were as a pair of testicles fertilizing it with sustainable seed.[30] Luther's writings, one might note, were full of lively metaphors.

The conscience, therefore, was not free to decide alone on the just path, but it *was* the supreme authority for anyone seeking to interpret what the scriptures had to say about it. The individual was not free to violate God's word, but only the individual could correctly interpret God's word. And this interpretation, based on the conscience, carried authority, at least with respect to that person, that far surpassed that of the Church, for all its popes and councils, and of all of canonical tradition to boot.

"Nothing in Christianity Will Remain Certain or Decided"

This was a dramatic shift. Whereas Augustine, in the fourth century, proclaimed, "I should not believe the gospel except as moved by the authority of the Church,"[31] Luther concluded that not only did he have no need for the Church's authority, but that it often actually impeded his path to the true and correct faith. "The pope's laws coerce consciences under statutes, rules, and orders,"[32] but conscience had to remain free. For Luther, it was conscience, focused on God's word in the gospel, that was (in addition to God's grace) the ultimate condition for faith—not the Church.[33]

Johann Eck, the theologian who was sent to debate Luther, understood the problem immediately:

> If it were granted that whoever contradicts the councils and the common understanding of the church must be overcome by Scripture passages [in order to convince the conscience of anyone who defies the church councils], we will have nothing in Christianity that is certain or decided.[34]

And indeed, nothing in Christianity remained certain or decided. If the ultimate authority over interpretations of the holy scriptures was individual conscience, then the gates to pluralism and the diversity of opinions were blown wide open. If even that which was already settled by tradition was open to debate, and if church councils had to prove that they were right by appealing to scripture instead of simply mandating obedience, the Church would fracture. And indeed, it did.

It bears emphasizing: Luther was not worried that people might differ in their interpretations of the scriptures. Faith, by the grace of God, was available to all, and the scriptures, Luther wrote, were simple, "easy and open," and would confuse only those who sought to make them complicated.[35] "The book is laid into your own bosom, and it is so clear that you do not need glasses. . . . Thus you are your own Bible, your own teacher, your own theologian, and your own preacher."[36]

As far as Luther was concerned, every right-minded Christian believer with a modicum of intelligence would read the holy scriptures and interpret them in the same way, the only correct way—that is to say, the Lutheran way. Soon enough, reality proved otherwise. Other reformers, such as Ulrich Zwingli, Thomas Müntzer, and Jean Calvin, as right-minded and intelligent as they were, differed in their understandings of the New Testament. Despite repeated attempts to pursue unity, the Protestant churches remained divided—for how could anyone be expected to compromise on the commands of their own conscience?

Meanwhile, the Catholic Church tried to secure its authority. At the Council of Trent, convened in 1545 in an effort to mount a response to the spread of the Reformation, the Church explicitly decreed that

> in order to restrain petulant spirits . . . no one, relying on his own skill, shall—in matters of faith, and of morals pertaining to the edification of Christian doctrine—wresting the sacred Scripture to his own senses, presume to interpret the said sacred Scripture contrary to that sense which holy mother Church—whose it is to judge of the true sense and interpretation of the holy Scriptures—hath held and doth hold.[37]

There were, it turned out, increasing numbers of petulant spirits who wanted to interpret the scriptures by themselves, out of loyalty to their own personal consciences. The Catholic Church was determined to nip this trend in the bud. But the Church failed to do so, and a whole panoply of interpretations of the scriptures spread far and wide. In fact, Luther's precedent, ironically enough, sparked a tradition of deviating from tradition.

According to Mika Ojakangas, who studied the development of the concept of the conscience in the West, "as a doctrinal source for the religious upheavals of sixteenth- and seventeenth-century Europe, this single doctrine [about the precedence of the authority of the conscience—T. P.] was perhaps more important than any of the theological doctrines introduced by Luther himself."[38]

Suddenly, every revolutionary who sought legitimacy for his own revelation needed nothing more than the voice of his own conscience. Yet even the question of the difference between liberty and anarchy is a matter of conscience. And if everyone possessed their own irrepressible internal voice, who could guarantee the existence of some common framework? Judaism and Catholicism, writes the sociologist of religion David Martin,

> have both controlled the logic of choice within a vigorous collective bond. They have switched the focus back to behavioral criteria specified in terms of externalities and have defined membership not so much by choice as by genetic or quasi-genetic inheritance. But once membership or belonging is focused on choice and on states of genuine inwardness a corrosive logic is set in motion which extends indiscriminately to every sector of activity. All structures of convenience, and all hierarchies of achievement, are undermined by the appeal to inwardness and choice.[39]

Against the backdrop of premodern Judaism and Catholic Christianity, Protestantism marked a shift toward a more intense stage of internalization and individuation. As the scholar of English culture and literature James Simpson writes, "Protestantism is best described as an anti-tradition tradition of permanent revolution."[40] Luther presented the conscience as a source of authority and thus strengthened the core logic of Christianity, which treats a person's spiritual life as a source of existential and religious truth and distrusts religious establishments as obstacles in the way of attaining such truth.

But how could a religious establishment be built in a tradition that was inherently skeptical of religious establishments? "The logic of Protestantism is clearly in favour of voluntary principle, to a degree that eventually makes it sociologically unrealistic," writes Martin.[41] In other words, Protestantism would lead to secularism. We shall turn to that later.

Freedom of Conscience, Liberation of Heresy

Luther's decisive step came as a link in a chain of similar steps, which as we have seen were but expressions of a fundamental internal pattern in the Christian tradition. His insistence on obeying his conscience was his own way of internalizing sources of authority and emboldening individual autonomy. This conception of religiosity was based quite clearly on the internalization of worship: if the focal point of the religious drama migrated inward, then one's feelings and conscience gained religious significance.

The roots of this conception, as we have seen, lie in the privatization and internalization of religion that Paul applied to Christianity in its infancy. The internalization and spiritualization of the image of God, and the transformation of the relationship with God from collective to private, made religion a voluntary matter and therefore religious coercion an absurdity. Individual will was elevated to a place of unprecedented importance. Together with the Pauline emphasis on faith and spiritual transformation, Christianity sowed the cultural seeds that would germinate 1,500 years later in the Reformation and would, mere centuries later, become axiomatic in the modern world. "This is the essence of the Reformation," wrote Hegel in his *Lectures on the History of Philosophy*. "Man is in his very nature destined to be free."[42]

The problem is that absolute freedom means absolute solitude. As we have seen, the Reformation fostered a stridently anti-social disposition. If everyone is free to disobey any law, then the individual becomes an agent of anarchy, threatening the wellbeing of society. "In the sixteenth century," writes the English historian Christopher Hill, "the most persistent and determined law-breakers were the godly, who—like twentieth-century conscientious objectors in wartime—claimed to be obeying a higher authority than that of the state."[43] Luther, it seems, had opened a Pandora's box of delinquency and anarchism in the name of obedience to conscience.

Take the Anabaptists, returning to our earlier case. They rejected the notion of infant baptism because they believed that it made no sense to baptize anyone who did not consciously want to be baptized. What religious significance could there be to a forced ritual? How could the transformative conversion and rebirth of an adult choosing to be baptized be compared to the act of wetting an oblivious baby? When individual will is the metric for judging a person's connection with God, one must truly desire to be a Lutheran (or a Catholic, etc.) in order for religious conversion to have any validity. Once excitement is understood as a positive thing from a religious perspective, it is suddenly a theological problem if a religion, forced from above, fails to excite.

The Anabaptists only took Luther's magnified focus on individual authority to its logical conclusions: a true Christian was only one who had personally decided to be baptized. As we shall soon see with the Puritans, the stress on voluntarism was, counterintuitively, common among the most radical of the Christian sects. Indeed it was precisely those who took faith and worship the most passionately who had to insist that these be voluntary. This brand of theology was therefore consistent with the logic of Luther's revolution, but it could have unexpected consequences. In the Anabaptist case, it cast the whole Christian world outside this particular sect as submerged in sin and doomed to damnation; these outsiders were not "true" Christians, after all, because they had been baptized as babies in religiously meaningless ceremonies. This stance, along with the Anabaptists' tendency to reject the authority of earthly rulers and to revel in their apocalyptic visions, hardly won them many admirers.

But what could be done about them? If the more moderate Protestants shunned the Anabaptists as heretics, then such Protestantism would be but another incarnation of the Catholic Church. Could Luther, who upheld Christian liberty as a supreme ideal, rebuff other Christians' independent interpretations of their faith?[44] On the other hand, the Anabaptists were, after all, insufferable. Luther said that everyone should be free to believe as he pleased, but this did not stop him from persecuting the Anabaptists on charges of blasphemy.[45] People were free to believe whatever nonsense they wanted—but not to desecrate God's great name. Incidentally, Luther was also a virulent antisemite and was maliciously hostile toward Jews. These paradoxes within the working logic of Protestantism were part of the excruciatingly painful birth pangs of religious tolerance. The world could not have moved from the rule of the Catholic Church to unlimited religious acceptance overnight. Luther juggled questions of faith and tradition, truth and heresy, liberty and restrictions as they came.

In fact, the mere willingness to let people believe whatever they wanted—to err on matters of faith—was a great stride forward. The principle of freedom of conscience became an ideal in the Protestant world, initially as an unreachable utopia, and eventually as an accepted and protected right. In Christendom, which in a few short years came to be split between rival churches, the imposition of faith on others quickly became socially unbearable and claimed far too many lives. But major change ensued with the understanding that religious coercion also made no *theological* sense. A developing cultural sensitivity, acknowledging that coercively imposed faith is not true faith, gained popularity, and freedom of conscience became a coveted ideal. Religious minorities would ultimately also benefit from this; less than a century after Luther's death, a Puritan Protestant by the name of Roger Williams would already seek to grant freedom of religion to the Jews and abandon hopes of converting them to Christianity.

The key was the transformed status of the conscience and the new insistence on its absolute liberty. "In the Reformation," writes the historian and economist Dierdre McCloskey, "political theories shifted away from disputes between popes and emperors, and toward disputes between governments and individual consciences."[46] The road there was paved by the English Puritans.

The Puritan Demand for Freedom of Religion and Conscience

Five hundred years ago the word "Puritan" was already a term of abuse. The English Puritans started to be known as such in the 1560s because of their exaggerated emphasis, in the view of their Anglican rivals, on the purity of Protestant ritual worship. The Puritans were unwilling to tolerate what they saw as an excess of Church hierarchy, ceremonial formality, and Anglican Church dogma. In other words, they accused the Anglicans of still being Catholic.

And to an extent, they were. The break with Rome, Henry VIII's decision that England would break away from the Holy See, was flimsy to begin with. In 1521, the King had received the title *Fidei Defensor*, Defender of the Faith, from the Pope for penning a rebuttal of Lutheran theology, but thirteen years later he broke with the Catholic Church after seeking to annul his marriage (divorce is forbidden according to Catholic dogma) and failing to secure the Pope's consent. Given the precedent of Protestantism, a battle over authority that would have been solved in earlier eras with theological obfuscations transformed the English into a distinct religious community. If those blokes on the Continent could break away from the Catholic Church, the King reasoned, so could he. As for his objectors, he referred them to his conscience. "Though the law of every man's conscience be but a private court," Henry VIII declared, "yet it is the highest and supreme court for judgment or justice."[47] His conscience had instructed him to seek a divorce, and it was neither safe nor right to go against one's conscience.

England therefore turned its back on Catholicism after embracing the Reformation. But the Anglican Church under its new head, King Henry VIII, remained essentially Catholic in nature. The break with Rome, after all, was not instigated by a theological rupture. Yet England had become a breeding ground for an array of Protestant groups and churches, which gradually devised their own philosophies; if the Pope's religious authority had been eviscerated, then why should the religious authority of the king remain unchallengeable? The Puritans stood out among these groups as stridently anti-establishment figures and there-fore, among other things, as political dissidents.[48] The Puritans followed the teachings of Jean Calvin, because they deemed the liturgy, church hierarchy, and the theology of Lutheranism too close to Catholicism for their liking. All the more so, they saw the Anglican Church as grossly Catholic in its character. When the Puritans became a significant pres-ence in the kingdom, they received their moniker. They then launched a struggle for the right to practice and express their faith freely.

For the Puritans, the conscience was the ultimate authority. The con-science was considered to be the voice of God, the part of the soul that facilitated a connection with the divine. And the conscience had to re-main free. Major theologians such as William Perkins (1558–1602) and William Ames (1576–1633) devoted whole tomes to the role of the con-science, marching forward on the trail blazed by Luther. Like Luther, for both of these theologians the image of God represented positive volition, the desire to worship God; and for both of them, the conscience was the human faculty connecting and binding humans to God's word.[49] Per-kins, one of the most influential figures of his day, wrote that the image of God was nothing but "the holiness of the will," i.e., the human will in a state of conformity with God's will,[50] and that it was the conscience that instructed one to bring one's will into conformity with God's. The conscience therefore enabled the realization of the image of God. This doctrine universalized Luther's position at Worms and stated—note the dramatic extent of the internalization here—that any act undertaken without the total conviction of the conscience, based on an interpretation of the scriptures, was a sin.[51] The conscience had become a pivotal religious institution. The Puritans demanded freedom of religion and conscience accordingly. "In the history of Western Europe," writes Michael Walzer, "the sixteenth and seventeenth centuries mark a crucial phase of the modernizing process . . . in which the Puritan saint is the central protagonist."[52]

A New Type of Social Agent

The Puritans, notes Walzer, represented a new type of social agent: the fanatical ideologue who was willing to burn down the old world in order to build a new one, purporting to be ushering in utopia by his own deeds. When Christianity was explicitly introduced into politics, it brought its revolutionary dynamic along with it. As the Scottish philosopher David Hume frames it one hundred years after their exploits, the Puritans'

> enthusiasm; bold, daring, and uncontrouled [sic]; strongly disposed their minds to adopt republican tenets; and inclined them to arrogate, in their actions and conduct, the same liberty, which they assumed, in their rapturous flights and ecstasies.[53]

The straightforward flow from religious passions to constitutional politics that Hume depicts is of course simplistic. Nevertheless, by focusing on their demand for freedom of conscience, the Puritans spurred the process of individualization and democratization, and set the stage for the establishment of England's revolutionary republic. Their success in shaping society, in Britain and on the shores of the New World, resonates till this day.

It must be said: no single individual or group "invented" or "discovered" the principle of freedom of conscience, and certainly none singlehandedly made it socially accepted or legitimate. The Puritans, owing to their theology and particular sociopolitical circumstances, spearheaded the struggle for freedom of conscience and gave it the clearest and most systematic articulation to date, but had conditions not ripened to allow the acceptance of these ideas, they would not have taken off.

And conditions had indeed ripened: the word "sincere" emerged in the early third of the sixteenth century, a testament to the growing tension between inner truth and falsehood, between integrity and hypocrisy.[54] The need to interrogate what went on inside the mind and heart, and the willingness to do so, intensified—and the conscience became more important than ever. During this period, Puritan groups published dozens of "confessions," quasi-constitutional documents with a historical snapshot of their particular denominations' religious tenets. An examination of these texts reveals that in addition to metaphysical dogma, they repeatedly emphasized freedom of conscience and the importance of a separation between divine worship and sovereign power.

Thus, for example, a confession written by a leading group headed by the preacher John Smyth in 1610 noted in one of its thirty-eight clauses that while worldly government was an institution rooted in God's will (that is to say, that monarchy was divinely mandated), God "hath not ordained in his spiritual kingdom, the church of the New Testament, nor adjoined to the offices of his church."[55] In other words, a ruler's authority, despite its divine provenance, did not extend to spiritual matters—one kingdom could not trespass on another's territory. Another confession written by the same group in 1612 stated explicitly that "the magistrate is not by virtue of his office to meddle with religion, or matters of conscience, to force or compel men to this or that form of religion, or doctrine; but to leave Christian religion free, to every man's conscience, and to handle only civil transgressions, injuries and wrongs of man against man."[56]

The principle of the separation of church and state is articulated here quite clearly. When John Locke would propose it in his writings seven decades later, he would draw on these traditions, as would Thomas Hobbes, who would incorporate them into his political theory. It would be hard to overstate their impact: these were none other than the cornerstones of such modern political concepts as the separation of religion and state and the right to freedom of religion and conscience. The law changed in accordance with changing conceptions of the human.

In 1616, Samuel Ward, the Puritan minister of Ipswich, argued that a person's conscience was "the principal part of God's image, and that by which he resembles most the autarchy and self-sufficiency of God." Note the correspondence between conscience, God's image, and autonomy. Ward was influenced by Perkins and influenced others in turn. He described the conscience as "a little god in us," subordinate only to the greater God outside and to no other authority.[57] God, the image of God, and the conscience—this was the new holy trinity that took shape in the early seventeenth century. It was in order to safeguard the absolute liberty of the last two persons of this trinity that the Puritans demanded the separation of church and state.[58]

Civil and Religious Wars in England

They didn't get it. In fact, King Charles I did almost everything he could to injure puritan religious sensibilities, while snubbing parliament and seemingly disregarding their cherished "rights of Englishmen." With the social and political arena heating up, some chose to sail off for the New World. Others chose to stay and fight.

Between 1637 and 1642, the English and the Scots revolted against their king, Charles I. The monarchy was seen by them, naturally, as a religiously conservative institution imposing an inauthentic form of Christianity on the populace, and radical forces had their sights on a more purist form of Christianity. King Henry VIII, as we recall, had split from the Catholic Church back in 1534 after seeking a divorce. A century later, the religious makeup of the kingdoms of England and Scotland was still unstable. The Puritans (those who remained in England while their brethren sailed to North America) publicly denounced King Charles, who had elevated the status of the established clergy: the priests and bishops who emphasized rituality and Catholic traditions. William Laud, the bishop of London (and future archbishop of Canterbury), spearheaded a kind of re-Catholicization of the Anglican Church, among other things by downplaying homilies and spontaneous outpourings of religious sentiment in favor of the standardized liturgy and uniform prayer. On top of that the king ruled that all churchgoers must use the Book of Common Prayer, the official prayer book of the Anglican Church. Spontaneous prayer was made illegal. Of course for the Puritans, this was quite unthinkable and indeed unconscionable.

This return to ritualism came at the expense of more personal and internal expressions of religiosity. Consistent with the fundamental logic of Christianity that we have observed, those who sought a purer form of Christianity, as the Puritans did, could not tolerate this trend. When these independent Christian forces sought to petition Parliament, the king dissolved it; in 1629, he started ruling alone with an iron fist.

The attempt to impose the Book of Common Prayer stoked a revolt in Scotland. The rebels professed allegiance to the King while vowing to "defend the true faith," namely Protestantism, from Catholicism.[59] King Charles failed to suppress the rebellion, and his attempts to do so left him militarily weakened and financially exhausted. He convened Parliament once more, in order to receive the support of the merchants and the aristocracy, but Parliament exploited his weakness and overturned his liturgical reforms. Archbishop Laud was jailed.

For the radical Puritans, however, this was not enough. There emerged a demand, including from young Puritan called John Milton, to banish all bishops. Who needed a religious hierarchy when every person could form a personal and internal relationship with God and his beloved son? At the same time, the King's vulnerability allowed the Irish Catholics, who were also under his rule, to revolt; in 1641, they seized the opportunity to cast off the yoke of the English crown. The Catholic revolt in Ireland only exacerbated the religious tensions and Protestant fervor in England, and since the Protestants could not trust King Charles to suppress the revolt (would a crypto-Catholic suppress Catholics?), there began a rebellion in England. Charles fled London. A civil war erupted.

It is worth pausing for a moment and reflecting on the extent to which reductionist accounts of history, of the sort that reduce every story about humans or societies to the pursuit of power and control, or that understand every political development as driven by some lust for "profit" or capital, have little explanatory value in the context of developments in seventeenth-century England. Some will surely still seek to explain that "in fact" or "below the surface," the main actors in this saga sought only power or gold, that they risked being tortured to death or burned at the stake only because they wanted more control or capital for themselves, and they will never understand how outlandish they sound. For better or worse, people are motivated by ideas, by values, by moral, ethical, ideological, and theological callings. The attempt to reduce every human endeavor to an egotistical instinct, which is often motivated by a conscious or unconscious desire to make the sacred profane and diminish the moral to the efficient, cannot withstand a minimal historical study, certainly not in the case of the history of religion.

Back to the seventeenth century. During the course of the English Civil War, the Puritans rushed to "cleanse" the Church. Rituals full of Catholic pomp were excised and made leaner and more austere, in the finest of Calvinist traditions. The bishops were sacked en masse, and Archbishop Laud was executed. In 1646, when King Charles finally surrendered, there were concerns that not only would Parliament replace his quasi-Catholic Anglican Church with a more Protestant (Presbyterian) institution, but that it would establish a single, compulsory state religion that would prevent more radical Christians from practicing their faith as they wished. And if this were so, what good would the revolution have brought?

The same John Milton, who would rise to become one of England's greatest poets (and was at the time a personal friend of Roger Williams, of whom we shall talk shortly), composed in the year of the king's surrender a special sonnet denouncing the Presbyterians, the victorious Protestants, whom he suspected of threatening "to force our Consciences that Christ set free."[60] Years later, in his most famous work, *Paradise Lost* (1667), Milton would describe how God placed the conscience in the human heart.[61] Freedom of religion, that is, of one's inner faith, therefore had to be preserved. "The pre-eminent and supreme authority is the authority of the Spirit, which is internal, and the individual possession of each man."[62] It is clear that to Milton's mind it was illegitimate to impose external religious authority, be it Protestant or Catholic, on anyone.

One's Internality Becomes One's Personality

With the King's defeat, confusion reigned in the Parliamentarian camp. Religiously and politically, they were divided over their next steps. The Levellers, for example, one of the first movements to push for full representative democracy, demanded biennial elections for Parliament, equality before the law, and freedom of religion. They too agreed that nobody had the power or authority to dictate or proscribe anyone's conscience. In their view, which drew on the evolving concept of the "social contract," political legitimacy was based on the transferal by citizens to the government, in free elections, of their preexisting powers. But as the Levellers argued, nobody had the power in the first place to force even their *own* conscience to think in any particular way—the conscience, after all, tells us what is right, whether or not we want it to—and therefore nobody could transfer such a power to government. In elections, individuals could decide who would govern their country on matters of taxation and security, because these realms were already under their own control. But nobody could control the conscience. *A fortiori*, it was inconceivable for the state to possess such control.[63]

One of the main Leveller leaders and thinkers was Richard Overton, who as early as 1615 penned a declaration of faith that emphasized freedom of conscience and equality between all people, created, as they all were, in God's image.[64] In 1645, he again underlined the importance of the "general and equal rights and liberties of the common people," and in 1646, in his most famous work, *An Arrow Against All Tyrants*, Overton stressed that:

> to every individual in nature is given an individual property by nature not to be invaded or usurped by any. For every one, as he is himself, so he has a self-propriety, else could he not be himself. . . . For by natural birth all men are equally and alike born to like propriety, liberty and freedom; and as we are delivered of God by the hand of nature into this world, every one with a natural, innate freedom and propriety—as it were writ in the table of every man's heart, never to be obliterated—even so are we to live, everyone equally and alike to enjoy his birthright and privilege.[65]

Overton argued that God had written "in the table of every man's heart" his most fundamental rights, which were no less than his selfhood: the ability to be a complete subject, and indeed one's own particular subject. The confluence here between the image of God and modern individuality, which considers itself autonomous and unique, is striking: liberty is the ability to control ourselves and that which is ours, and all these together constitute our independence and selfhood. Without them, we simply could not be who we are. One's *internality* becomes one's *personality*: the persona that each of us instantiates.

Modern liberalism and the framework of human rights are based on this equivalence between our inner worlds—our reason, conscience, will, and choice—and our selfhood. We would not be who we are if these qualities were repressed. Even if we no longer believe that these manifest the image of God within us, in order for us to be able to live a genuine and coherent existence, others must respect these depths or domains ("rights") of our personalities. Later, we shall see how the focus on the liberty of these domains would also lead to a rejection of belief in God.

Another Leveller leader, John Lilburne, wrote in 1647 that:

> God, the absolute sovereign lord and king of all things in heaven and earth . . . gave him, His mere creature, the sovereignty (under Himself) over all the rest of His creatures . . . and endued him with a rational soul, or understanding, and thereby created him after His own image. . . . [Adam and Eve were] the earthly, original fountain, as begetters and bringers-forth of all and every particular and individual man and woman that ever breathed in the world since; who are, and were by nature all equal and alike in power, dignity, authority, and majesty—none of them having (by nature) any authority, dominion, or magisterial power, one over or above another. Neither have they or can they exercise any but . . . by mutual agreement or consent.[66]

Once more, we see the same principles: human authority, that of each person over himself, is based on the image of God, conceived as reason, and on God's commandment to man in Genesis 1 to govern the earth. Human equality, in turn, is based on the fact that we all share the same primeval parents, on the fact that we share the same capacity for liberty and control, and on human equality of authority and dignity. Taken together, these dispel any claim to a divine or natural right of kings, while at the same time making possible governance based on consent. It was during this period that the principles of universal suffrage and complete representative democracy were first explicitly articulated.[67]

Treason against the Dignity of Mankind

John Milton also played his part in this articulation. In 1649, he wrote that "no man who knows ought, can be so stupid as to deny that all men naturally were borne free, being the image and resemblance of God himself."[68] But of course, some people could be so stupid. These ideas were extremely radical at the time. Charles I would insist until his dying day that "a Subject and a Sovereign are clean different things": i.e., entirely unequal. Royalist theologians also had to grapple with the anti-royalist rebels' egalitarian arguments and to provide tenuous theological justifications to attempt to demolish the case for equality between the king and his subjects. They explained that "the king hath that same remainder of the image of God that any private man hath, and something more: he hath a politic resemblance of the King of heavens, being a little god, and so is above any one man."[69] Everyone was equal, but some were more equal than others.

For Milton, this position constituted "treason against the dignity of mankind."[70] One's dignity, the dignity of any person, was based on the image of God inside her or him, and everyone possessed the same image of God. There were no more Jews or Greeks, slaves or freemen, men or women. All were equal.

In 1649, Levellers published a pamphlet arguing that women deserved equal rights, because they too were created "in the image of God, and of an interest in Christ, equal unto men."[71] The image of God, which inhered in everyone and in every place where reason was manifested, compels us to allow freedom of conscience and freedom of expression while also forcing us to recognize equality between all humans and the right of every person to property and liberty.

In the meanwhile, divisions multiplied within the anti-royalist camp, and Charles I seized the opportunity to escape from his captors. He rallied supporters, this time including Presbyterians who believed that the Puritans had gone too far in demanding the dissolution of the established church. The civil war resumed, and after the King's forces were finally subdued in 1648, he too was finally subdued and was beheaded in January 1649.

After a few years of instability and another war with Scotland, Oliver Cromwell was proclaimed the Lord Protector of the Commonwealth, which he would henceforth lead. Long before the French Revolution or the founding of the United States, a republic was born.[72] Cromwell, himself a Puritan, did not govern an established church and permitted freedom of (predominantly Christian) worship under his rule.[73]

He supported religious tolerance and allowed the Jews, banished from England in the late thirteenth century, to return. Cromwell died peacefully in 1658, and after another bout of instability, the crown returned, this time on the head of Charles I's son, Charles II, in 1660. But nothing could erase what had happened. England had greatly empowered its predilection for political and religious liberty. Modern liberalism itself was crafted out of the political maelstrom that rocked England and the battles between different stripes of Protestantism.[74]

Women's Speaking Justified

Following the restoration, Margaret Fell (1614–1702) came to London to petition King Charles II and his parliament for freedom of conscience in religious affairs. Fell was the wife of George Fox (1624–1691), the founder of the Children of the Light, or the Society of Friends, commonly known as the Quakers. The son of a weaver from a village in Leicestershire, Fox grew frustrated with religious authority of any kind, and during the war strode across the countryside, preaching to whoever would listen that not only all churches and bishops but even the Bible itself held less authority than one's own conscience, or inner light.

To this conclusion he came through his own spiritual journey, which initiated with a total rejection of all things "outwardly," while turning in and listening to the voice inside:

> [A]s I had forsaken the priests, so I left the separate preachers also, and those esteemed the most experienced people; for I saw there was none among them all that could speak to my condition. When all my hopes in them and in all men were gone, so that I had nothing outwardly to help me, nor could I tell what to do, then, oh, then, I heard a voice which said, "There is one, even Christ Jesus, that can speak to thy condition" . . . and *this I knew experimentally.*[75]

The Quakers (they were called thus because of their trembling during spiritual sessions) cast off any authority or hierarchy. They famously addressed strangers by the colloquial "thou" instead of the formal "you" and refused to take their hats off when engaging superiors. Fox maintained that God had made all humans equal by implanting all with an

Indwelling Spirit, which was their deepest self; as such, any sort of hierarchy among people is false, if not idolatrous. Like some of the Levellers they took the rejection of hierarchy and "outwardly" things to its logical conclusion and were among the rare groups that treated women as equals. Their egalitarian stance drew women to their cause, among them Fell, who became a seminal figure in the formative years of the movement and, after the death of her husband, married Fox in 1669.

Her most famous work is *Women's Speaking Justified*, a pioneering proto-feminist manifesto advocating for women's ministry. For Fell, the Indwelling Spirit was meant to speak not only through man, and she insisted that women be allowed to preach the gospel. Throughout her text she attributes the fundamental equality of the sexes to the creation in the image of God. As Fell explains,

> God joins them [i.e., men and women] together in his own image, and makes no such distinctions and differences as men do. . . . those that speak against the Power of the Lord and the Spirit of the Lord speaking in a woman, simply by reason of her sex or because she is a woman, not regarding the Seed, and Spirit, and Power that speaks in her, such speak against Christ and his Church.[76]

Fell presents a new kind of female Christian mystic: One that engages in political activism. From its inception, Christianity allowed a more egalitarian place for women than Judaism, by virtue of its emphasis on interiority. We saw that even the conception of adultery changes with Paul ("there is neither male nor female") and becomes reciprocal. In the varied sects that vied for representing the authentic voice of Jesus's gospel in the first centuries CE there were women leading movements and acting as prophets.[77] Gnostic groups, depreciating the body yet more than in the circles that would become the Catholic Church, offered several proto-feminist voices, some brought to popular fame by renditions such as Dan Brown's *The Da Vinci Code*'s portrayal of the Gnostic text, *The Gospel of Mary*.

Entering the Middle Ages, women in the Christian world were socially empowered by spiritual experiences, and at times gained tremendous cultural and spiritual influence. Earlier we briefly mentioned the Beguines, a groundbreaking religious and social phenomenon, in which urban expansion in the eleventh through thirteenth centuries, specifically in the Low Countries, saw groups of women who had decided to lead an unmarried life, devoted themselves to piety, and organized as lay monastic orders. The same pattern of rejecting institutional authority in favor of personal devotion made these groups both a challenge for the church and a new direction of action and meaning for women, with an added "republican" ethic, as these unaffiliated groups had to create and enforce their own terms of membership and rules of conduct.[78]

After 1200, the devotional gates open and out came a flood of writings by and on Christian women mystics, both autobiographical confessions and hagiographies written by male admirers.[79] Their reception is not always benign—Marguerite Porete, to name but one female mystic associated with the Beguines, was burned at the stake—but there can be no denying that through mysticism women acquired influence and social standing. Figures such as Mechthild of Magdeburg, Hildegard of Bingen, Julian of Norwich, Catherine of Siena, and Teresa of Avila made an immense impression on medieval Christianity and indeed contemporary European society.

The reformation enabled something more. If within the Catholic Church, women mystics had to fight for legitimacy and endure examinations meant to discern between true visions and the myriad ways in which the Prince of Darkness tried to lure impressionable women to his net, outside of the Church, legitimacy was in any case a matter for one's own community, and new paths could be broken. And if in the Catholic Church women mystics were circumscribed in monastic roles and to writing texts on visions and spiritual exercises, Protestantism allowed for social activism. Just as the Puritans exemplified a new type of religious revolutionary, so too women mystics could for the first time become active agents advocating for social change. In the seventeenth century, among radical Protestant groups, a demand for an equal place for women could be explicitly voiced.[80]

Thus Fell could pen a manifesto calling for equality for women in teaching the gospel, proving her case from scripture. She argued that God's Indwelling Spirit is the same for men and women, basing her claim on their mutual creation in the divine image and stating, "God hath put no such difference between the male and female as men would make."[81]

A hundred years after Fell, the same argument will be taken by pioneering feminist activists and, in time, suffragettes. Thus Mary Wollstonecraft (1759–1797) rejected the justification for discrimination against women on the basis of the presumption that "man was made to reason, woman to feel." In her *A Vindication of the Rights of Woman* she writes

> I discern not a trace of the image of God in either sensation or matter. Refined seventy times seven, they are still material; intellect dwells not there;[82]

Intellect dwells, of course, in the image of God, which is one and the same in all humanity. Such argumentation would pass as a shibboleth throughout the early feminist movement. Sarah Grimké (1792–1873) and Lucretia Mott (1793–1880), American suffragists (and abolitionists) deployed it, and it was naturally elaborated on in Elizabeth Cady Stanton's (1815–1902) project *The Woman's Bible*. This compendium of feminist theological texts, written in 1895 in collaboration with a committee of 26 other feminist activists, presents arguments such as, "Verse 27 declares the image of God male and female. How then is it possible to make woman an afterthought?". Stanton, along with Susan B. Anthony, Matilda Joslyn Gage, and Ida Husted Harper, also published the *History of Woman Suffrage* (the first volume came out in 1881), in which the same argument is recorded from a few supporters of the cause. Perhaps not by chance, Mott was a Quaker, and Anthony was sent to a Quaker boarding school.

Possessive Individualism

The seventeenth century was thus a significant period in the development of the modern conception of the individual and the emergence of the belief that all individuals possess basic rights. According to Marcel Mauss, the ideas of "the Puritans, the Wesleyans and the Pietists are those which form the basis on which is established the notion: the 'person' (*personne*) equals the 'self' (*moi*); the 'self' (*moi*) equals consciousness, and is its primordial category."[83] The journey toward establishing persons as fully-fledged individuals continued. After the internalization of the image of God as free choice and reason, volition and conscience, these were all unified and translated into a single, cohesive persona. Richard Overton's remarks about the self, arguing that it had to be free in order to be itself, began to resonate throughout Europe. The notion that all humans were "by nature all equal and alike in power, dignity, authority, and majesty," as John Lilburn wrote, received fuller articulation and preliminary recognition. Intellectual elites were already articulating new ideas based on the newfangled notion that all human beings were first and foremost autonomous individuals.

The Puritans on the British Isles brought to a head a process of intensifying individualism, which had developed in English culture over the preceding centuries, especially in terms of their intense focus on individual rights and the need to protect individuals from the power of their social surroundings.[84] "We cannot exaggerate the importance of sectarian movements throughout the seventeenth and eighteenth centuries for the formation of political and philosophical thought," writes Mauss.[85]

According to the historian of science and the modern era Margaret Jacob, late-seventeenth-century England witnessed the spread of "possessive individualism," which in C. B. Macpherson's classic definition denoted individuals' self-conception of themselves as owners of their own skills and as independent beings with no obligations toward society.[86] Indeed possessive individualism, which understands liberty to mean freedom from restrictions imposed by others, sees a virtue in independence, and treats one's talents as theirs alone without any duties toward their surroundings, developed especially in England.[87] After visiting England in 1729, Montesquieu wrote that the English "had progressed the farthest of all peoples of the world in three important things: in piety, in commerce, and in freedom."[88] These three were all interrelated, because Puritan piety empowered individuals and protected their rights—to property, and indeed to freedom of conscience. Economic and political liberalism were conjoined at birth. The Puritan worldview, as Max Weber writes in his famous study *The Protestant Ethic and the Spirit of Capitalism*, "stood at the cradle of the modern economic man," i.e., at the birth of the enterprising, systematic, rational, and autonomous individual.[89]

The shockwaves of these dramatic developments were keenly felt. In his poem *An Anatomy of the World*, the great English poet John Donne lamented the loss of the medieval world:

And new philosophy cals all in doubt, . . .
'Tis all in pieces, all coherence gone;
All iust supply; and all relation:
Prince, Subject, Father, Sonne, are things forgot,
For euery man alone thinkes he hath got
To be a Phœnix, and that then can bee
None of that kinde, of which he is, but hee.[90]

Donne composed this poem in 1611. The winds of change were already blowing and tearing through the old order: the class system was under pressure and the old patriarchal hierarchy was beginning to wobble. The idea that since all humans are equal before God, they must also be equal before the political authorities gained steam. The idea that the king's subjects had rights worthy of protection, and that the political authorities were obligated to protect them, took root. The idea that freedom of conscience and religion must be respected and protected was already spoken of publicly. These ideas were all intimately linked with the principle of the image of God, and they were all connected to the new status of the individual, who was morphing into the most basic building block of society (in place of the tribe, family, community, or congregation). The new philosophy suggested a new ideal to the minds of the peoples of Europe: that everyone "has got to be a phoenix"—unique, one of a kind, self-generating. But John Donne balked. For him, no man was an island, entire of itself.

Out of the fire and blood of the interreligious struggles of the seventeenth century, English culture brought forth the notion that every individual stands in his own right, free of prior associations, autonomous to determine the path of his own life—by themselves, for themselves, and from within themselves. This paradigm was still in gestation, but it would soon conquer the Western world. In less than 400 years, these assumptions would become axiomatic in Europe and North America. These individuals would see themselves as complete, possessive selves, would interpret autonomy as freedom, and would sincerely desire to be special and unique as individuals, for after all, there can be "None of that kind, of which he is, but he."

This was all fresh. In his magnum opus *Democracy in America*, Alexis de Tocqueville regaled his French readers with news of an American innovation: individualism. Tocqueville toured the United States in the early 1830s, and in his brilliant impressions, he mapped out the construction of the Western world. Here are his observations about the latest American invention:

> Individualism is a recent expression arising out of a new idea. Our fathers knew only the word egoism. Egoism is a passionate and exaggerated love of self that impels man to relate everything solely to himself and to prefer himself to everything else. Individualism is a reflective and tranquil sentiment that disposes each citizen to cut himself off from the mass of his fellow men and withdraw into the circle of family and friends, so that, having created a little society for his own use, he gladly leaves the larger society to take care of itself. Egoism is born of blind instinct; individualism proceeds from erroneous judgment rather than depraved sentiment. Its source lies as much in defects of the mind as in vices of the heart. Egoism shrivels the seed of all the virtues; individualism at first dries up only the source of the public virtues, but in the long run it attacks and destroys all the others and in the end will be subsumed in egoism. Egoism is a vice as old as the world. It is not to any great extent more characteristic of one form of society than another. Individualism is democratic in origin, and it threatens to develop as conditions equalize.[91]

This idea developed indeed. Our world today represents a direct outgrowth of these sources. What John Donne intuitively felt and balked at, what Tocqueville saw with his own eyes and sniffed at, is now completely taken for granted, to the point that we regard any other less individualistic and autonomous reality as the stuff of dystopian novels or horror movies. When film directors want their audiences to shudder at a lack of individualism and dearth of autonomy, they fill our screens with images of human beings trapped in the Matrix, with aliens that plot to harness and mechanize us (think of *Star Trek*'s Borg), with cyborgs, and with zombies.

The Puritans would fight to express these ideals in England, and they would also bring them to the New World. John Smyth, whom we met before, insisting, as a leader of one Puritan group, that a ruler's authority did not extend to spiritual matters, sailed with his followers aboard the Mayflower in 1620 to the shores of America. In the colonies of New

England, they would seek to discover and cultivate fertile and tolerant soil for their religious ideas; in time, they would become surrounded by more pioneering colonies, populated by Puritans fleeing England in search of the liberty to practice their faith and live their lives as they saw fit, as autonomous individuals. Tocqueville's famous statement that he saw "the entire destiny of America embodied in the first Puritan to land on its shores" reflects the extent to which the American political system and character is rooted in the mindsets and ideas brought over by the Puritans.[92] One of the most exceptional Puritans was Roger Williams, who founded the first colony to fully separate religion and state.

Roger Williams, and the New Religious World

Roger Williams was born in London in the early seventeenth century. While studying at Cambridge, he embraced Puritanism and came to believe that the Anglican Church had to purify itself of its residual Catholic influences. As we know, King Charles I thought otherwise. Remaining in England meant waging a constant battle, at great risk, against the authorities. Williams chose a different path. In 1630 he boarded a ship together with his new wife, Mary Barnard, and sailed to Boston, a Puritan colony at the time.

Having studied theology, Williams was received in Boston with open arms and was invited to be a full-time preacher at a church. Although the offer was respectable and he was destitute, Williams turned it down because Boston's church had not formally separated from the Anglican Church. He departed for Salem, a small colony north of Boston, but there too he found no respite. From Salem, he migrated to Plymouth, the colony founded by the Mayflower pioneers, which might have been expected to meet his hyper-Puritan standards, but to no avail. Two years later, Williams bade goodbye to Plymouth.

Williams was a theological pain in the backside, albeit usually on behalf of positive aspirations. He engaged in religious debates and defended the rights of the Native Americans, objecting to the theft of their lands, which were, in his view, lawfully theirs. He called into question the colonies' association with the English crown, called King Charles I a "friend of the Beast" who had committed "Fornication with the whore," and demanded that nobody be required to swear an oath by God ("So help me God"), because some people might not believe in God and they would therefore be taking his name in vain.

Unsurprisingly, Williams's opinions were initially considered eccentric and, after a while, dangerous. He was warned that absolute freedom of conscience and a full separation between political power and religious authority would lead to anarchy. He was dubbed an "Anabaptist" not only because of his opposition to infant baptism but also in order to brand him an extremist. He was an extremist, though as such all the more insistent on freedom of conscience. In July 1635, he was summoned to appear before a judge and told that his opinions were unacceptable. He was later asked to retract everything that he had previously written and preached. He refused to recant (his conscience was, of course, captive to the Word of God) and was thus sentenced to exile from Massachusetts.

Williams migrated westward. He founded the colony of Providence, which by 1640 was home to forty families, all religiously devout and pious. The government of this tiny colony was strictly separate from its religious establishment, and its residents were promised full freedom of conscience. This was the first time in history that people organized themselves around a system that enacted a full separation of religion and political rule.

None of Williams's sermons has survived to shed light on what he told his fellow believers. We know about his opinions from his books, and especially his polemics against John Cotton, Boston's prominent Puritan leader. Williams's most important work was *The Bloudy Tenent of Persecution for Cause of Conscience*, in which he articulated his thinking about the separation of church and state.[93] The book was published in England in July 1644. In August, Parliament ordered that all copies be burned.

Williams sought to dispel the residual theological arguments that favored religious coercion. The ancient Kingdom of Israel, he conceded, was indeed a theocracy, and anyone wishing to impose his religion on others could certainly cite precedents. But the mistake of supporters of religious coercion was that they failed to understand that there could be no legitimacy for such rule after the advent of Jesus Christ. Now, wrote Williams, humanity was in a new era. No longer could force of arms be used to impose religious dictates:

It is the will and command of God that, since the coming of his Son the Lord Jesus, a permission of the most Paganish, Jewish, Turkish [i.e. Muslim], or anti-Christian consciences and worships be granted to all men in all nations and countries. . . . God requireth not a uniformity of religion to be enacted and enforced in any civil state; which enforced unanimity, sooner or later, is the greatest occasion of civil war, ravishing of conscience, persecution of Christ Jesus in his servants, and of the hypocrisy and destruction of millions of souls.[94]

Williams believed that freedom of religion was a protected right not only for Christians, nor even only for believers in other monotheistic faiths, but even for "the most Paganish." The reason was not only that religious coercion entailed dire political consequences, but also that it would lead to the "ravishing of conscience" and hypocrisy—that is, it could not induce a valid form of religiosity. Religious coercion, according to Williams, was the "rape of the soul," and it was he who first used the famous metaphor "wall of separation" to describe what he wanted to stand between church and state.

Like Thomas Jefferson after him, Williams was directly influenced by Tertullian, the Christian theologian who, back in the early third century, had demanded that freedom of religion be honored and declared that without sincere desire, there was no point to religious worship.[95] Williams took Tertullian's thinking to its logical conclusions and even stated that "we must necessarily disclaim our desires and hopes of the Jews' conversion to Christ."[96]

When Williams wrote these lines, Jews were still discriminated against, persecuted, tortured, and murdered across most of Europe, and even in North America attitudes toward them were dubious, in the best case: they were completely barred from territories ruled by the French crown, and were harassed and threatened with expulsion in the Dutch colony of New Amsterdam (New York, as of 1664). In this context, Williams's outlook was revolutionary. He was not only exceptional for his time; he was also dismissing a long-standing theological tradition, as old as Christianity itself: the hope, and the efforts it inspired, for the ultimate conversion of the Jews to Christianity. Freedom of conscience had taken such a prominent place in his theological thinking that it lent him legitimacy to alter tradition.

The Separation of Church or State, and a Pioneering Call for Equal Rights

For Williams, Providence was an earthly expression of the transcendent ideals by which he lived. The foundation of this independent colony, unattached to any English royal writ or warrant, allowed Williams to hold extremely progressive views and to live by them in his daily life. Contrary to popular wisdom (and indeed to the beliefs of the Puritan founders of Plymouth), Williams believed that political power was not a divine right but rather based on the "voluntary agreement" of the governed.[97] Indeed, this was what happened in Providence: only those who wanted to live there settled there, and they were the ones who decided on its governing regime. Political rule was therefore human, whereas religion was divine—and they were very much distinct. If there was no divine right of kings, obviously no ruler had the religious authority to dictate his subjects' faith. One's conscience was a spiritual matter, and one alone could be responsible for it. On the other hand, in earthly matters, the ruler certainly possessed supreme authority. After all, this was the meaning of the social contract: all members of the political community had given their free consent and authorized their ruler to legislate.

Williams was making a vocal case for the principle of the separation of church and state and equality before the law, independent of religion. In his second composition, written as part of his public debate with John Cotton, *The Bloody Tenent Yet More Bloody* (1652), Williams articulated a distinction between civil authority and religious authority, and called for civil rulers not only to refrain from interfering in the religious domain, but also to maintain neutrality toward their subjects, irrespective of their religion. In other words, Williams was calling for equal rights for members of all religions.

> Yea, and there is a moral virtue, a moral fidelity, ability and honesty, which other men (besides Church members) are, by good nature and education, by good laws and good examples, nourished and trained up in, that civil places of truth and credit need not to be monopolized into the hands of church members (who sometimes are not fitted for them) and all others deprived and despoiled of their natural and civil rights and liberties.[98]

Public offices, Williams argued, could be given to individuals who were not members of his specific church. The reason was that everyone possessed a natural "moral virtue," by which he was referring, of course, to the conscience. Elsewhere in this book, he stated that "this conscience is found in all mankind, more or less, in Jews, Turks, Papists, Protestants, Pagans, etc."[99] Everyone has a conscience, and therefore everyone is fit for every role. Accordingly, Williams argued that civil government must defend members of all faiths: "If the magistrate be bound to defend his subjects . . . then he is bound . . . to defend the Jews, the Papists, and all several sorts of Protestants in their several and respective consciences."[100] The conscience constitutes a person's dignity, their point of meeting with the divine. It is therefore entitled to protection, and its capacity renders civil authority possible.

But Williams's argument that everyone must be afforded a share of political power was based not only on the universality of the conscience. For him, this was a matter of principle, related to his efforts to separate church and state:

> Christ Jesus was of another opinion [i.e., different from Cotton's] (who distinguisheth between God's due and Caesar's due and therefore with respect to God his cause and religion) it is not lawful to deprive Caesar the Civil Magistrate, nor any that belong to him of their civil and earthly rights. I say in this respect, although that a man is not Godly, a Christian, sincere, a Church member, yet to deprive him of any civil right or privilege due to him as a man, a subject, a citizen, is to take from Caesar that which is Caesar's, which God indures not though it be given to himself.[101]

Williams staked his claim for a separation of church and state on the famous verse in which Jesus said, "Render therefore to Caesar the things that are Caesar's, and to God the things that are God's" (Matthew 22:21). This ancient Christian tenet had evolved over 1,500 years to produce a desire for the separation of church and state. These two realms had to remain separate, Williams argued, and the subordination of the civil realm ("the things that are Caesar's") to the religious realm ("the things that are God's") deviated from the bounds of propriety. Therefore, even someone who did not believe in the Christian God (or in any god at all) was entitled to every civil right and privilege. This appears to have been the first explicit call for full equality of rights for all of humankind, without any religious distinctions.

The Jews in the New World

Roger Williams founded the state of Rhode Island around Providence, which provided a refuge for members of all religions and denominations seeking freedom of conscience. In 1652, the colony's legislature enacted "that all men of whatever nation soever they may be, that shall be received inhabitants of any of the towns, shall have the same privileges as Englishmen," and in the same year it also passed the first law in North America prohibiting slavery.[102] In 1664, the legislature anchored the principle of freedom of religion in the colony's bill of rights, which stated that "no person . . . shall be any wise molested . . . for any difference in opinion in matters of religion."[103] In 1684, one year after Williams's death, this measure was tested when some Jews—still the closest principal "other" in the West—inquired whether they too could settle peacefully in the colony. "[W]e declare that they may expect as good protection here, as any stranger, being not of our nation, residing amongst us,"[104] declared the legislature, and in 1694 a Jewish community settled in the colony, in the town of Newport.

Rhode Island did not always live up to its founders' ideals. Jews were not afforded full equality, but they did enjoy toleration. In the mid-eighteenth century, Newport's Jewish community, which numbered around one hundred souls, was the second largest in North America after New York[105] (where Jews achieved full equality in 1718),[106] and after the thirteen colonies' War of Independence, in 1790, it was the Jewish community of Newport that received the (now-famous) letter from George Washington promising that all citizens of the United States would

> possess alike liberty of conscience and immunities of citizenship. It is now no more that toleration is spoken of, as if it was by the indulgence of one class of people that another enjoyed the exercise of their inherent natural rights. For happily the Government of the United States, which gives to bigotry no sanction, to persecution no assistance requires only that they who live under its protection should demean themselves as good citizens, in giving it on all occasions their effectual support.[107]

Washington was echoing Williams and of course John Locke (whom we shall touch upon soon): the government of the United States was demanding that its citizens be good citizens, not good Christians. The government's authority was limited to the civil realm. Washington was therefore not talking about toleration but about full equality in the exercise of every person's natural and fundamental rights. Williams's vision had come true.

This understanding was reflected also in the U.S. Declaration of Independence (1776), and the U.S. Constitution, which entered force one year before Washington wrote his letter, provided that "no religious Test shall ever be required as a Qualification to any Office or public Trust under the United States." In 1791, the First Amendment was enacted, guaranteeing the separation of religion and state.

In the seventeenth century, the peoples of western Europe, and all the more so the colonists in North America, were gradually convinced that without faith in one's heart, there was no value to declarations or acts of faith. As for Luther in Worms, the measure of true faith ceased to depend on external gestures and came to be based on an individual's spiritual disposition. In virtue of the notion of the image of God as the internal foundation of human will and freedom of choice, the conscience evolved into a religious institution of supreme importance, and the demand for freedom of conscience became widespread.

A few years after Roger Williams died, John Locke published his *Letter Concerning Toleration* (1689), one of the most formative texts of modern politics. Even earlier, in 1648, the Peace of Westphalia was signed in Münster (yes, the same Münster), putting an end to the Thirty Years' War, advancing the cause of religious toleration between kingdoms, and laying the foundations for the modern conception of the nation-state. A new era was born, after painful and long labor. It offered Christians and Jews a new, unprecedented world: a world of acceptance and sometimes even equal rights. Nevertheless, as George Washington wrote, the condition for this was good citizenship. And the foundations of good citizenship, as would soon become clear, also included a new and updated formulation of religion itself.

4

Equality

Netanel Posner, Rebellious Jew

Netanel Posner was a prosperous Jewish stockbroker, clean-shaven and adorned with a wig in the finest of European fashions. An avowed theater-lover and avid consumer of culture, Posner fervently despised the religious establishment. In 1781, he expressed his stark opinions in synagogue, standing above the Torah scroll and telling the congregation, "Torah, you are good, but you have fallen into the hands of thieves, deceivers, and scoundrels, and now you are in the hands of false interpreters who have distorted you."[1] A scandal ensued.

Posner, who came from the town of Altona (near Hamburg, then under the control of the Kingdom of Denmark), was echoing the Deism that captivated educated European society at the time. The Deists believed that God was good and created the world in order to benefit humankind. Thus, contrary to received wisdom in the Middle Ages, pleasure was positive and asceticism was pointless. The Deists also argued that the only true religion was the natural religion, which was none other than the religion of Reason, intelligible to every thinking individual. There were no miracles, no saints, and no *deus ex machina* moments of divine revelation. The giving of the Torah at Mount Sinai? The crucifixion and resurrection? The angel Jibril's epiphany to Mohammed? Those were all myths.

In fact, Deists believed God did not intervene at all in the lives of humans, certainly not in the form of a top-down, once-and-forever imposition of supranatural law. On the contrary, the attempt to argue that a tradition's veracity depended on miracles, and the attempt to build on the basis of this argument an exclusive and sectarian institutional hierarchy of religious clerics who wielded supreme authority, was a distortion of the most natural, rational, and universal religion and a malicious subversion of every individual's innate right to religious liberty, independent thought, and freedom of conscience.

By his remarks, Netanel Posner therefore meant that without the intervention of religious clerics over the ages, the Jews would have worshiped their Creator in the natural, rational, and healthy form that God had originally intended. But Posner's audience thought otherwise, and they rushed to the *beit din*, the Jewish religious court, in shock. The judges manned their battle positions.

Posner, who in his business dealings with non-Jews went by the name Samuel Marcus, could not yet leave the ghetto—the Jews were still forced to live in closed communities—but the ghetto had already left him. He moved freely within contemporary European culture and had a fraught relationship with the rabbinic establishment in his city. When he fell into a dispute with his brother-in-law over his father's bequest, Posner appealed to the civil courts in Hamburg instead of the rabbinic courts, enraging the community's rabbi and president of the rabbinic court, Rabbi Raphael Cohen. When he was called to appear before the beit din on a financial matter, Posner ripped the summons and denied the rabbis' authority to judge him. Unfortunately for him, however, he was firmly within their jurisdiction. According to the law in Altona at the time, "all Ashkenazi [i.e., German] Jews residing within our principalities and lands are commanded . . . to obey the rabbi and *parnassim* [communal lay leaders] of Altona."[2]

Rabbi Raphael Cohen did indeed convict and sentence Posner over his earlier transgression. He was subjected to a limited excommunication: he was ordered to abstain from cutting his hair or shaving, and the community was instructed to exclude him from prayer services. But Posner could not imagine growing a beard: he already was, after all, a gentleman. For many members of the community, it was equally unthinkable to ostracize him, and they let him continue participating in their prayers. The fact that Posner prayed regularly tells us that despite his refusal to accept the rabbis' authority any longer, he still considered himself a Jew. And the fact that he continued praying with his community tells us that others, even if they were a minority, had also started questioning the rabbis' authority. The rabbis were no longer as powerful as they once were, certainly not as they had been a century earlier, when Baruch Spinoza was excommunicated by his community in Amsterdam and formally ostracized till his dying day.

This new scandal compelled Rabbi Cohen to denounce Posner once more, and this time to seek his full excommunication. Three witnesses testified to having heard him uttering the above-quoted blasphemy, and someone also recalled that a while back, when members of the community had tried to wake Posner up for an early-morning *Selichot* service ahead of the High Holy Days, he had rudely rebuffed them and said, "Yesterday I went to a comedy and then to a ball, and today you are waking me from my sleep for such nonsense."[3]

Together with another eight rabbis—an excommunication was a grave matter—Rabbi Cohen issued a ruling barring Jews from doing business with Posner or sitting anywhere near him. This was already a serious form of excommunication, and Posner found himself in trouble. On the one hand, he certainly had no interest in being totally ostracized by most of the Jews around him. On the other, the conditions for reversing his excommunication—a public statement of remorse, fasting every Monday and Thursday for a year, studying a certain fourteenth-century work of rabbinic literature every day, promising not to attend a ball for the rest of his life, removing his wig, and growing a beard—were to his mind utterly intolerable.

Fortunately for Posner, he found himself in conflict with the rabbis exactly as a lively debate emerged around him about religious tolerance. The same year, Christian Wilhelm von Dohm, a senior Prussian government official, published his *Über die bürgerliche Verbesserung der Juden* ("Concerning the Amelioration of the Civil Status of the Jews"), which sparked great interest. In his work, he sought to extend the principles of the Enlightenment to the Jews and to allow them to receive citizenship in their countries of residence. The polemic around the "Jewish Question," that is, about the Jews' status in the countries of Europe and their relation to both political and religious authorities, was in full swing. A liberal public sphere was beginning to take shape, and Europe's first secularists—the Enlightenment *philosophes*, Christian Deists, and the Jews of the *Haskalah* movement (the Jewish Enlightenment)—wished to break the authority of religious establishments, and the conflict in Altona was all that they needed to present Rabbi Cohen as a merciless inquisitionist and Posner as the victim of a capricious and overweening religious establishment.

Posner made a formal complaint to the Danish authorities, demanding that he be freed from the rabbi's authority. At the same time, he sent a copy of this complaint to Berlin for publication, in order to rally enlightened public opinion in his favor. Danish officials did indeed conclude that the rabbi was too powerful, but they could not simply revoke his authority, because in the governing system at the time, all Jews were obligated by the laws of their communities. The Jewish Emancipation, which would involve loosening the bonds of the community and making the Jews equal and individual citizens, had not yet dawned.

In the end, the rabbi's authority remained intact but the power of excommunication was made conditional on approval from the central government, effectively neutering it. The excommunication of Posner himself was overturned, and Rabbi Cohen found himself wielding formal authorities without any practical means of deploying his most serious weapon. "Freethinking" (*Freidenker*) Jews felt freer to express their opinions and live their lives as they saw fit. One more step had been taken toward the separation of religion and state in Europe.

Jews and the Inability to be Individuals

Netanel Posner's story was emblematic of his times. Freethinkers like him became increasingly common in the eighteenth century. Whereas in Posner's day, excommunication was a controversial but nevertheless effective means of deterrence and punishment, its efficacy would quickly begin to wane. When a large part of the Jewish population discarded the yoke of religious commandments, excommunication became futile; even if the rabbis wanted to, they could not ostracize half of their communities. The dam would burst open with the Jewish Emancipation, when Jewish communities were dismantled as juridical and political entities possessing relative autonomy. When Jews became citizens.

In Netanel Posner's case, the Danish authorities had no real means to help him. They could not remove him from his rabbi's jurisdiction, because there was no other authority that might take its place. There was no legal alternative to rabbinical rule over the Jews. This state of affairs changed when Jews became citizens, first in France and the Netherlands in the late eighteenth century and then during the nineteenth century in Belgium, parts of Germany, Britain, Norway, Sweden, and Austria-Hungary.

Many Jews must have wanted to leave their communities as individuals and begin new lives earlier, but were prevented by the law of the land and by their fear of the rabbis. These now seized the concrete opportunity to do so. As soon as they could embark on an independent path, they did so. This period witnessed the dramatic growth of *maskilim* (followers of the Haskalah), secular libertine Jews, and "assimilated Jews."[4] Contrary to the dictum of the famous nineteenth-century Jewish author Ahad Ha'am, it was not the Sabbath that kept the Jews together, but the lack of any legal or practical possibility to escape the bounds of their communities.[5] The moment that such a possibility emerged, many Jews embraced it.

But there was one caveat to all this. In order to leave their communities, Jews needed not only to be *able* to do so, but also to *want* to do so. They needed to want to discard, in whole or in part, their ancestral customs; to adopt new lifestyles, which they deemed preferable; and most importantly, to be independent. People do not acquire these desires out of nowhere, and they certainly do not do so "naturally." Such desires barely existed in the Middle Ages, however widespread and obvious we consider them today. In order for these desires to emerge, they had to be preceded by a sharp transformation in conceptions of the self and of society, of history and of the future. In other words: there would always be sinners, but in order for *even the notion of sin* to be dismissed, in order for Jews or Christians to live their lives as independent, "enlightened," and even secular individuals, they had to experience a profound and meaningful psychological shift.

Before the modern era, Jews remained distinct from the Christians around them, not only in rights, but also in appearance, language, and of course beliefs. Jews dressed differently, and unlike Christians, they grew beards (it was for a good reason that Rabbi Raphael Cohen insisted on this matter, punishing Nathaniel Posner for his clean-shaven appearance). In Europe, Jews spoke Yiddish as their main or only tongue (the same Rabbi Raphael Cohen, who came to Altona via Poland from Lithuania, did not bother to learn the local German language at all). Beyond these differences, Judaism and Christianity lived side by side in mutual hostility, often latent yet at times tragically externalized. From the Christian perspective, Jews had no right to live on European soil at all. They enjoyed this blessed opportunity by the grace of the local king or prince, but this privilege was neither permanent nor guaranteed. The

Jews were therefore severely limited and fenced off (sometimes literally) in their communities.

Moreover, Jews lived within a completely different religious and ethnic identity from the rest of society. They were connected to their communities not only through their families but also through faith and custom, the most basic building blocks of their personal and communal identity. For them, their faith was the whole truth, an indisputable certainty that they took for granted. Leaving this faith and joining the Christian world meant nothing less than defecting from the truth to a world of lies, and furthermore erasing their personal identity in the most fundamental sense. We can understand how important this identity was to its bearers if we recall that many Jews throughout history preferred to die than to convert. Their stories were cases not only of loyalty to God and self-sacrifice, but also of the immense difficulties involved in erasing one's identity—and their entire existence.

This sociopsychological reality was dismantled by a gradual social process in which the Jewish Emancipation played a central role. The Emancipation, as part of the flowering of Liberalism, not only straightforwardly provided an opportunity for individual Jews to leave the bounds of the ghetto and integrate into wider society. It went much further than that: *it transformed Jews into individuals.*

The Jewish Emancipation, drawing on the theoretical foundations laid by the Enlightenment and the liberal thought of John Locke (which we will get to soon), redefined the relationship between Jews and their communities in a way that allowed them to sever their links not only in a practical sense, but also psychologically. For the first time, Jews could define themselves as individuals, and not solely as members of a people, an ethnos, or a chain of generations devoted to a particular tradition. This required Jews to redefine their beliefs not only about themselves but also about their Judaism. In fact, they had to redefine Judaism itself, or rather their conceptions of the essence of the entity called "Judaism." We shall explore how this upheaval unfolded by examining the development of the Emancipation itself and the core texts that animated it.

The Creation of Religion

For Enlightenment philosophers in Europe, the Jews were the most obvious and accessible example of an "other." Most Romani (or Gypsy) people maintained their own brands of Christianity, and Muslims were the distant but threatening enemies across the lines of the Ottoman Empire. The Jews, however, were the perennial money-lenders, artisans, merchants and, from time to unfortunate time, victims of Christian Europe. As such, their fate was always also an immediate illustration of the continent's ideological and social developments.

As enlightened Europeans' view of the world changed, so too did they need to revise their attitudes toward the Jews. Indeed, many defined and examined their own embrace of humanism, pursuit of democracy, call for tolerance, and attack on the religious establishment in terms of their relationship with their ever-near yet ever-different neighbors. The "Jewish Question," the question of the fate of European Jewry, was therefore critical for them.

If, as Kant wrote, the Enlightenment was the moment we departed from our cognitive childhood and bravely insisted on exercising our powers of reason, and if indeed this use of universal reason allowed for self-fulfillment anywhere and at any time, regardless of one's class or religious tradition, then non-Christians were surely also potential partners in the Enlightenment. Reason, after all, was common to all humans.

On the other hand, Judaism was also sufficiently distinct from Christianity as to elicit doubts about whether what was good and well for Christians was necessarily relevant—or even possible—for Jews. Kant could speak in messianic terms about the transition from the traditional Christian church to the "Church of Reason," but were Jews capable of making the same shift? Synagogues, after all, were strikingly different institutions from churches, and surrounded Jews with a web of communal, ethnic, ritual, and legalistic ties that simply did not exist for their Christian peers.

In practical terms, the question was whether Jews should be afforded equal rights. This was not only a matter of rights to property and self-rule, rights that were also retained, as we have seen, by the pagan Native Americans, at least according to some Christian thinkers. The Jews were already afforded these rights, more or less. They were allowed to amass property and wealth, and they lived in semi-autonomous communities in which they enjoyed fairly expansive self-rule. Netanel Posner, indeed, suffered from exactly this form of Jewish collective autonomy. Of course, not all professions were open to Jews, and in certain lands they lived under restrictions governing where they could settle and even transit. Jews were in Europe severely discriminated against. And yet, they were the only non-Christians afforded a place in the continent.

The major change occurred with the understanding that the state was duty bound to allow the free exercise of the image of God: reason and the capacity for free choice. Once it was widely recognized that the exercise of reason was part of the bundle of "natural rights," the demand to respect all citizens' freedom of conscience (that is, of religion) spread accordingly. If we must all respect liberty of conscience, and if religion is indeed a private affair, what justification could there be for discrimination between Christians and Jews? In other words, if is agreed that there may be no discrimination between Catholics and Protestants, and if faith is no longer a deciding factor in an individual's civil status—should society stop there and make freedom of religion conditional on that religion being, nevertheless, some form of Christianity?[6] Or alternatively, should the circle be widened to include anyone whose reason or conscience directs them to worship God, whoever that god might be? The otherness of the Jew created for Europeans an unavoidable need to define, at the deepest and most principled level, their approach to the question of religion and state. Leo Strauss's insight that the "Jewish Question" was the quintessential expression of the human question receives validation here.

But even for those who wanted to provide a positive answer to the "Jewish Question" and give the Jews equal rights, this would not be simple. In order to agree that all believers, including non-Christians, were entitled to freedom of belief, one had to agree that all forms of faith were, first and foremost, *faiths*. In other words, that they were not fundamentally some other form of human expression such as heresy, sin, wickedness, Satanic temptation, and such. Recall that unlike polytheistic faiths, not only did monotheistic religions not recognize the legitimacy of other faiths; they also did not see them as alternative means, illegitimate as they may be, of worshiping the divine. Other faiths were not authentic expressions of the human heart, but rather temptations by the devil or conscious and malicious rebellions against God and truth.[7] Other forms of worship were simply *not worship*, but heresy. Augustine, the only pre-Renaissance Christian thinker to have devoted genuine attention to the Latin word *religio*, wrote a whole composition on the "true religion" (*De Vera Religione*).[8] One could certainly guess from the title that Augustine meant to praise Christianity and denigrate all other would-be religions as "false religions." But Augustine's thinking was altogether different. For him, the true religion was one's connection with God, and the Church existed only to *facilitate* this connection: that is, to make true religion possible.[9] Augustine made hardly any mention of "Christianity" as a belief system—in fact, the term appears only once in his book, in reference to the Church. "Religion," for Augustine, was not a system of faith, rituals, or institutions, but what we might nowadays call "spirituality" or "religiosity." In short, a genuine spiritual connection with God *was* the "true religion"; anything that did not involve such a connection with God was, understandably, idolatry.

As Talal Asad writes, for Christians in the past, "religion was not a universal phenomenon; religion was a site on which universal truth was produced, and it was clear to them that truth was not produced universally."[10] "Religion" was Christianity, and Christianity alone. It alone was born out of the revelation of God, whose only son was crucified and resurrected, and therefore it alone produced and gave expression to universal truth. All other forms of worship were particularistic expressions of lies. From within this mindset, it was impossible to see anyone who engaged in foreign forms of worship as "religious," because they lacked "religion" and practiced heresy disguised as such. They were not believers, but infidels, and these were two totally different categories.

For the collective category of "religion" to be created, a common denominator needed to be found between these diverse phenomena. In the twelfth century, Maimonides stated that Muslims were not idolaters after all, and that they were praying, albeit incorrectly, to the true God. Maimonides's solution was to augment, in an unprecedented manner, the principle of God's singularity and abstraction, that is, the notion that there existed only one God, about whom nothing could be said. Therefore, according to Maimonides, not only Judaism but Islam, which also professed the existence of one such God, was also a valid form of worship. But even for Maimonides, no other forms of worship qualified as religious; they were all heresies.

Another common denominator emerged from discussions about the "Peoples of the Book": the religions that believed in the divine revelations encoded in holy scriptures. The Prophet Mohammed famously attached this label to Jews, Christians, and Sabians;[11] later Muslims also added Zoroastrians to the list. But even this, of course, was not yet a universal definition of religiosity, but only an extension of the legitimacy of forms of worship beyond one specific tradition to encompass a few more (some of which were still considered erroneous). In this sense, for Mohammed and the first Muslims, Judaism and Christianity were "religions," whereas Hinduism and Buddhism were not.

"Religion" as a Universal Sentiment

The creation of the universal category of religion in Europe was rendered possible by the internalization of religious meaning in the Christian tradition.[12] We have already seen how the image of God, along with the focus of the religious experience, migrated inwards; and how faith, the conscience, sentiment, and experience were emphasized at the expense of ritual, tradition, the Church establishment, and religious dogma. Religion was internalized.

Indeed, one can say that over the past 2,000 years, the phenomenon of personalized, internalized religiosity became an increasingly powerful ideal in the West; in the last few centuries, the numbers of individuals who understand their relationship with the divine in such terms has proliferated as never before. This mentality, expressive of the archetypal Christian paradigm, would eventually lead to secularism, as we shall soon see; yet even before this, it shook Christian theology itself. If the most important thing was internal experience, then perhaps there was no need for the salvation of the messiah from Nazareth? Some Christians, such as Ralph Waldo Emerson, did indeed reach this conclusion in the nineteenth century. Yet even earlier, this paradigm would provide the basis for perceiving all the world's ritual traditions as belonging to the same family, the family of "religions." This paradigm would also allow Europeans to see Judaism as a "religion" and therefore the Jews as deserving freedom of religion and equal civil rights.

The first to speak about "religion" as a universal category were two late medieval thinkers, Nicholas of Cusa (1401–1464) and Marsilio Ficino (1433–1499). For Nicholas of Cusa, all "religions" (*religiones*) were based on an "internal impulse." This thinker, theologian, and Catholic priest sought to reconcile rival traditions by arguing that beneath different scriptures and faiths, "there is . . . but one religion," of which all other traditions are merely forms. They all shared the same supreme objective: our intellect—the image of God in us—aspired to conform with the divine intellect.[13] Traditions were but the external scaffolding concealing the same internal impulse, and therefore what was needed was for one to "walk according to his interior rather than exterior nature."[14]

Cusa's message was clearly resonant of Saint Paul's, but he went one step further: he did away with Paul's internal metamorphosis, the notion of accepting God's son and inviting him to act within us, as the starting point of authentically religious life. On the contrary: for him, this "internal impulse" was the starting point, and it was independent of any connection to Christianity, just as human reason, the image of God, was universal and independent of faith in Christ. This focus on internality led him to a perennialistic approach, which recognized a certain validity in all faiths. Non-Christian traditions were considered of lesser, yet comparable, importance; Christianity, for its part, became one more tradition in a long series of traditions.

Another essential thinker in this process was Marsilio Ficino, a key figure in the Renaissance and in the wider evolution of modern philosophy. He translated Plato's writings from Greek to Latin and made a critical contribution to the development of Western esotericism when he translated the ancient Hermetic texts. For Ficino the word *religio* denoted piety, a virtue involving mental intention. Yet unlike Augustine, Ficino thought that this mental intention was a universal phenomenon, vividly present in the spiritual life of every person and manifested as different traditions. The influence of Hellenistic philosophy and the culture of the Renaissance helped Ficino understand the human soul in a manner liberated from the shadow of original sin, which was a central tenet of Augustine's understanding of the human creature. Accordingly, different ritual traditions were but different expressions of the same pious impulse. "All opinions of men, all their responses, all their customs, change—except *religio*."[15] Since the rational soul, according to Ficino, was created in the image of God, it was naturally attracted to the divine. "Worshipping the divine is as natural to men almost as neighing to horses or barking to dogs," he wrote.[16]

Different philosophical traditions, taught Ficino, used different names to refer to the image of God, which had assumed physical form as Jesus Christ, but they all meant the same thing. There was only one universal truth, and it manifested itself as the image of God in the soul and as the image of God in revelation. All humans were naturally attracted to both forms of the image of God and sought to unite them. For Ficino, as for Cusa, traditions were but secondary and universally co-equivalent expressions of the same basic, human spiritual instinct. And that inner instinct was what mattered. Christianity was therefore one of many traditions, and non-Christian traditions were not necessarily heretical but rather other (albeit often inferior) means of attaining the same truth.

Cusa and Ficino's influence on European thought was immense, but it would be a mistake to credit the emergence of the idea that religion is an expression of universal internal impulses to them alone. On the contrary, my argument is that this was a natural and inevitable progression of the internal logic of the Christian tradition, combined with the principle of the image of God. Cusa and Ficino were simply the first to express this point clearly. The focus on what is *inside* a person, prioritized over any external dimension—the body, society, or a cultural context—in determining the validity of one's religious life, leads, given sufficient social diversity and the passage of time, to the rejection of the external dimension as having any relevance to religious life; indeed it often ultimately leads to the view that the external dimension is an *impediment* to religious life. Moreover, since rituals, dogmas, and religious establishments were considered of inferior value, and since all human beings were equal, this paradigm led to the conclusion that all humans could establish a genuine relationship with the "true" religion within them.

Finally, this focus on internal religiosity also subverted the notion of historical divine revelation as a singular event. Like ethnicity, law, and ritual, history was also undercut by immediate individual experience. If what matters most is what happens *inside* each and every person, does one really need the son of God? And why reserve this internal sentiment, or this internal transformation, only for Christians, or only for those who lived after a certain historical moment, namely the advent of Christ? Once more: on the one hand, this shift undermined the status of frameworks of all sorts (the Catholic Church, mass, faith in the virgin birth, the status of one-off divine revelations, etc.). But on the other, it attached the image of God to all humans, thereby endowing them all with a common inner realm of reason, volition, and sentiment. Since we are all human beings, we are all moved by the same "internal impulse" toward the divine, and different religions, Cusa and Ficino argue, are but different forms through which this universal impulse receives expression.

The Development of Freedom of Religion with the Rise of the Modern State

If all humans give expression to different forms of the same internal religious impulse, the source of which lies in the imprint that God himself made in them, should not everyone be allowed to express this impulse freely?

This idea gained acute importance with the dawn of the debate about the right to freedom of religion and the principle of the separation of church and state. The Protestant revolution that erupted in the early sixteenth century dragged Europe into a bloody era of religious wars.[17] For the first time, rival churches were at war with each other, each claiming ownership of the one and true form of Christianity. But the churches themselves did not have battalions. These interreligious wars were waged by kingdoms, each of which raised the banner of a particular Christian church. Interestingly, it was out of these religious wars that states began to coalesce. Just as, in the fifteenth century, the Catholic religion helped to unite the many principalities of the Iberian Peninsula into a single Spanish kingdom under Ferdinand and Isabella (at the expense of the Muslims and Jews), so too in the sixteenth century did a patchwork of churches become the glue binding the subjects of different kingdoms within their respective borders.

The modern state would emerge in a similar fashion, holding, in Max Weber's famous definition (which traces its roots back to Hobbes), a monopoly over the legitimate use of violence. The state, in other words, evolved as the mechanism subordinating a range of forces, within specific borders, to the authority of a single ruler. It did so, *inter alia*, by depriving churches of their ability to wage violent struggles against each other within particular kingdoms, and no less importantly, also by appropriating their power to decide what constituted legitimate and illegitimate force. The monarch became the sole authority over physical force and the legitimate use of such force.

The many attempts to end these religious wars, which claimed an intolerable price in blood, most notably the Peace of Augsburg (1555) and the Peace of Westphalia (1648), aligned Europe under the principle of *cuius regio eius religio* ("whose realm, their religion"): the principle that each ruler could determine their subjects' religion. This notion sat uncomfortably, of course, with the principle of freedom of religion, but it spurred the evolution of the modern state. Europe agreed on the principle of domestic religious homogeneity and the impermissibility of external intervention on matters of religion. There was to be no more religious conflict within states and no more meddling in affairs beyond one's own borders. The churches of one particular kingdom could no longer assist Catholics or Protestants of another. Each kingdom had its own sovereign territory, within which its ruler was the supreme and ultimate authority.

But at the same time that these principles were institutionalized, Europe also developed a certain sensitivity to religious coercion. As we have seen, the polemic around the idea of religious tolerance was central to the sixteenth and seventeenth centuries. For many, tolerance was a fool's errand: how could one believe wholeheartedly in a particular religious dogma and nevertheless tolerate contrary opinions? How could one tolerate heresy? Moreover, was letting one's neighbors err in their religious ways not an admission of indifference to the eternal fate of their souls? How could this be the Christian thing to do? While radical Protestants (chiefly the Puritans) and various other thinkers (most prominently Baruch Spinoza, Pierre Bayle, and John Locke) made their arguments for tolerance, others, including religious clerics, of course, rejected this principle as a practical and theoretical impossibility.

We have already seen how the conscience became a source of authority and how freedom of conscience became an ideal. This paradigm rested on the internalization of worship: if the focus of the religious drama now lay inside, then individuals' desires, feelings, and consciousness assumed religious significance. Once individual volition became a measure of the validity of a person's connection with God, people had to truly *want* to be Lutherans (or Catholics, and so forth) for their Lutheranism (or Catholicism) to count. We have also traced the evolution of the notion that everyone worships the same God, albeit in different ways, some better and some worse. As in the British colonies of North America, so too in Europe did these ideas, which were increasingly taking root, make their way into the new political ideas shaping the modern state.[18]

Evidence for this may be found as early as the sixteenth century, in the writings of Jean Bodin (1530–1596). Bodin, a French thinker and statesman who greatly influenced the modern conception of sovereignty, argued that the rulers of states were not subordinate to anyone else and held the exclusive authority to determine the laws of their realms. As we have seen, this was an important step on the road to the conception of the modern state. On the other hand, however, Bodin also argued that, although it was preferable for each kingdom to have a uniform religion, there were to be no forcible conversions.

> If the prince well assured of the truth of his religion would draw his subjects thereunto, divided into sects and factions, he must not, therein, use force. For that the minds of men, the more they are forced, the more forward and stubborn they are, and the greater punishment that shall be inflicted upon them the less good is to be done, the nature of man being commonly such as may of it selfe bee led to like of anything, but never enforced to do so.[19]

Bodin proffered a pragmatic reason for his recommendation against coercive conversions: they were simply ineffective. For Bodin, living in post-Reformation Europe, "religion" was already seen as a general category, and he could compare different religions and regard them as parallel belief systems. Religion was also an internal matter, and from his reasoning we can infer that he regarded externally imposed religion—rituals that people were forced to perform, prayers that they were forced to mumble, and tenets to which they were forced to swear belief—as lacking any religious validity. Simply put: we will never *like* any religion that is imposed on us, and since we do not *like* it, it cannot bring us any benefit. It cannot influence our sincerely held beliefs. For Bodin, the mechanical performance of rituals was not "true" worship, and religion depended on an internal disposition, and on the volition and faith of the individual. Bodin integrated this understanding into the architecture of the modern state.

Other philosophers presented similar arguments. Edward Herbert, the Baron of Cherbury (1583–1648), one of the most important early thinkers in the world of Deism, similarly understood religion as a "natural instinct" located in the human soul, although he preferred to define religion not as a sentiment but as a rational comprehension. For Cherbury, reason was the image of God, and therefore "the only Catholic and uniform Church is the doctrine of Common Notions which comprehends all places and all men."[20] He too sought to articulate these principles, and in any case he believed that individuals must look inside themselves to discover the true faith.

Thomas Hobbes (1588–1679) took a similar stance, albeit less clearly. There is a debate about Hobbes's views on religion, both personally, whether he had religious faith or was a total atheist, and publicly, concerning the role of religion in a state. Nevertheless, in his magnum opus *Leviathan*, Hobbes explained, in chapters 41–42, that Christianity had always supported the separation of the religious and the political, because while kings may impose their laws, a church may only seek to persuade others of the justness of its cause by non-violent means, because "Faith hath no relation to, nor dependence at all upon Compulsion or Commandment." Hobbes certainly had concerns about the anarchistic power of the conscience and sought to bring it under the authority of the sovereign, but in the 47th and final chapter of his book, he repeated his call that "there ought to be no Power over the Consciences of men, but of the Word it selfe."[21]

John Locke Comes Full Circle

The process of the creation of "religion," through the internalization of worship and derivation of the principles of tolerance from within it, reached its apogee with John Locke (1632–1704). As one of liberalism's founding fathers, Locke gave religious tolerance its most rigorous underpinning through his articulation of the principle of the separation of church and state. It was no coincidence that Locke was the first of a series of thinkers to explicitly support equal rights for Jews.

As we have seen with Roger Williams, religious tolerance, the separation of church and state, and the extension of civil rights to Jews were all based on the same interconnected principles: the definition of all ritual systems as "religious," based on the internalization of religious meaning, which in turn was connected to the notion that all humans were inherently equal and at their core carried the same image of God (be it reason, conscience, volition, or attraction to the divine). From here, we receive the inherent parallels between all "religions"; from here, we also receive the demand for tolerance between them, for besides the great practical cost of intolerance, there could be no meaning to coerced religion. And if all ritual systems are forms of religion, and if they must all be tolerant of each other, it necessarily follows that Jewish ritual worship is also worthy of tolerance. But more importantly: if Judaism was but another form of religious worship (and, significantly, not an ethnic group, nationality, or race), then Jews deserved the same rights as Christians. After all, they too were members of the same universal family of humans; they were one of many co-equal groups that together comprised humanity, each worshiping the divine according to its own particular manner.

This line of thought deserves our consideration, because it played a dramatic role in the shaping of the modern world. Just as the conception of a person's relationship with God as private emerged in tandem with a conception of the individual as maintaining this relationship first and foremost as a "person," i.e., as a universal human entity (Paul) possessing "faith" (Luther)—so too did the conception of diverse ritual systems as "religions" transform the communities holding these views into "human societies": into generic entities called "cultures" that built their own diverse systems of faith. No other civilization maintained a conception of human society existing in some abstract, primal, and independent sense, disconnected even in theory from its traditions or "religion." The theoretical separation of faith from society in western Europe rendered possible the development of the notion of universal human society.[22] Just as every person was deemed a legal subject before adopting a particular religious tradition, so too was every human collectivity a single community, encompassing all its members, whatever their diverse traditions. Every society, as a voluntary association of individuals, had its own creed or collection of creeds; but all societies without exception belonged to "humanity." In other words, they all possessed fundamentally equal worth.

Since this was so, concurrent with its own articles of faith, each society could also establish its own independent rule and in fact possessed a "right" to self-determination. The road to the establishment of the nation-state began to be paved. This development would have direct implications for the Jews (always the litmus test for any developments in Christendom): on the one hand, if the Jews were a nation, then they had a right to political self-determination. On the other hand, the Jews could also be thought of simply as another "church": as yet another religious denomination (as opposed to a distinct ethnic group, and certainly not an alien race), as yet more individuals who could join others in forming a multi-confessional nationality. The Jews, therefore, could become citizens just like all other Europeans, different only in their manner of worship.

This, of course, changed how the Jews saw themselves; indeed, it changed Judaism itself. Judaism, as Leora Batnitzky writes, became a religion.[23] This metamorphosis, however, would be worthwhile only if equal rights awaited on its other side, only at the realization of a liberal public sphere.

Locke and the Dawn of Liberalism

John Locke was born and raised in a Puritan family in southwestern England. In his youth, he worked as a lecturer in Greek and rhetoric before studying medicine. In 1683 he fled to Holland, famed for its religious tolerance, because he was mistakenly suspected of participating in a conspiracy to assassinate the king. He returned to England only after the Glorious Revolution of 1688. Locke's major writings—*An Essay Concerning Human Understanding, Two Treatises of Government*, and *A Letter Concerning Toleration*—were all published the following year.

Locke's philosophical world was shaped from within the Christian tradition and the events that engulfed his life. He was the heir not only of discussions about natural rights, but also of the notion that there exists a world of comparative "religions," of the basic assumption that religion finds its principal expression in the movements of the individual soul, and of the importance of freedom of conscience implied by all these. He also appears to have been familiar with the writings of Roger Williams. On the other hand, the protracted political instability during Locke's lifetime raised for him, as for others at the time, questions about the authority of government (in their case, of monarchy) and about relations between church and state. The confluence of these trends led Locke to demand religious liberty for all and religious tolerance between all social groups. To this, Locke added a further principle: human reason, with which humankind was endowed as part of the image of God inside them, was a source of authority—including on matters of religion.

As we have seen, the conception of religion as an internal disposition common to all of humanity necessarily came at the expense of the authority of divine revelation, and the same was true for Locke. In Book IV of his *Essay Concerning Human Understanding*, Locke touched on the differences between reason and revelation and the relationships between them. He averred that no revelation handed down by tradition (that is, not personally experienced) could carry more persuasive power than conclusions drawn independently by means of reason. Revelations experienced by others could therefore not overrule one's own independently drawn rational conclusions.

If revelation could subordinate reason, Locke argued, there would be no end to this process, and any conception, idea, or argument could be precluded by some other tradition: simply declare that you had experienced a revelation and expect everyone else to bow their heads in compliance. Locke limited revelation to realms beyond the capacity of reason, such as events in higher worlds or redemptive prophecies about the future. Yet here too, reason plays a role, which is to analyze and adjudicate whether a particular revelation is genuine. Locke underscored that:

> if the provinces of faith and reason are not kept distinct by these boundaries, there will, in matters of religion, be no room for reason at all; and those extravagant opinions and ceremonies, that are to be found in the several religions of the world, will not deserve to be blamed. . . . So that in effect, religion, which should most distinguish us from beasts, and ought most peculiarly to elevate us, as rational creatures, above brutes, is that wherein men often appear most irrational, and more senseless than beasts themselves.[24]

Locke beheld the "religions of the world"—a quintessentially modern expression, which of course denoted not only denominations of Christianity—and observed that they nearly all offered "extravagant practices" and "absurdities." He emphasized the importance of a rational critique of religion and the dangers that he identified in elevating traditional revelation over rational judgment. By ascribing supreme authority to reason—authority drawn from the fact that reason is the image of God and therefore the core factor explaining humanity's superiority over the animal world—Locke was able not only to analyze religion as a universal phenomenon, but at the same time and by implication, to draw comparisons between different religions.

Locke inherited the notion that all ritual systems in the world are "religions," or fundamentally human expressions of the same spiritual quality or internal disposition, from earlier thinkers. He could therefore write about the faults in these different religions and point to a common cause for failure, namely the absence of critical rationality.[25] We are witnessing here, among other things, the birth of the comparative study of religions.[26]

Locke's notion of "religions of the world"—his belief that there were many religions, and that they could all be rationally examined—was intimately connected to his conception of humans as a *tabula rasa*, or blank slate, at birth. If people are born as blank slates, then their religion is obviously external to them, an addition to them, something that *is not them*. Religion exists out there in the world: it is not a natural, essential part of us. Reason, however, *is* essential to us.

The possibility of separating a person from his religion was tied to the Christian conception of religion, the development of the modern understanding of the term "religion," and also the call for freedom of religion and equality of rights for "members" of different religions. Applying this way of thinking a century after Locke, figures such as the Count of Clermont-Tonnerre in France and Christian Wilhelm von Dohm in Prussia would insist that the Jews were not by their nature defective (as many claimed), but rather that their life circumstances had caused them to deteriorate to their present condition, and that if the state, as they proposed, granted them equality, they could in fact become model citizens.

Locke had articulated the grounds for this new understanding. The Jews were not by their nature flawed because by their nature they were *tabulae rasae*, like everyone else. They were human beings first, and only then Jews. Their Judaism was not a part of their nature. Reason most certainly was, because they were human beings, just like Christians.

With roots reaching Saint Paul's thoughts, this was a new, revolutionary, fundamentally liberal, and thoroughly modern articulation.

Life, Health, Liberty, Property—a Preliminary List of Rights

Locke also inherited, as we have seen, the discourse of natural rights from the philosophical tradition preceding him. In his *Two Treatises of Government*, Locke discussed at length conceptions of natural law and natural rights, as well as the idea of the social contract. Like others who considered natural rights before him, Locke emphasized that it was God who gave man the right to "dominion" by endowing him with the image of God:

> God makes him in his own Image after his own Likeness, makes him an intellectual Creature, and so capable of Dominion. For wherein soever else the Image of God consisted, the intellectual Nature was certainly part of it, and belong'd to the whole Species and enabled them to have Dominion over inferiour Creatures.[27]

Accordingly, natural law was entailed, in Locke's thinking, by the fact that humans were God's creation:

> The State of Nature has a Law of Nature to govern it, which obliges every one: And Reason, which is that Law, teaches all Mankind, who will but consult it, that being all equal and independent, no one ought to harm another in his Life, Health, Liberty, or Possessions. For Men being all the Workmanship of one Omnipotent, and infinitely wise Maker . . . And being furnished with like Faculties, sharing all in one Community of Nature, there cannot be supposed any such Subordination among us.[28]

The image of God, natural law, reason and rights—they are all here, all connected. This passage also holds one of the first lists of universal human rights in human history. According to Locke, natural rights such as life, bodily integrity, liberty, and property are entailed by the fact that all humans are in essence equal and rational. And humans are all equal and rational because they were all created by the same Creator (hence equality), who endowed them all with his image (reason). The words of

Richard Overton, Bartolomé de las Casas, Francisco de Vittoria, Roberto Bellarmine, Innocent IV, Huguccio, and many others writing from the twelfth century onward, and indeed the voices of opponents of slavery, such as Gregory of Nyssa and Augustine in the fourth and fifth centuries, received in Locke their most definitive expression.

From within the intellectual constructions that preceded him, Locke consolidated a set of ideas that would shape the political tradition of the whole of Western society. The liberalism that we are familiar with emerged out of the principle that all humans were created in God's image and were therefore all equal and entitled to liberty. This liberty was a consequence of human nature as a *tabula rasa* at birth, and it would be measured by the extent of an individual's autonomy to make voluntary and independent choices, in accordance with their conscience, first and foremost on matters of faith and worship. Freedom of religion and conscience—with "religion" judged mainly and most clearly in terms of movements of the conscience—was therefore part of every person's set of natural rights. As we shall see, Locke understood that the principle of the separation of church and state followed logically from this.

Nobody Is Born a Member of Any Church

In proposing a "state of nature" in which individuals were free to pursue their wants and acted in accordance with reason, Locke contributed his share to the formulation of the idea of the social contract. This idea, early versions of which could already be found in Greek and Roman thought, took shape in the seventeenth century as a form of political criticism and gained acceptance in the context of the Puritan worldview, which deemed voluntary agreement the highest possible form of human connection.[29] In an effort to terminate the terrible religious wars that were tearing Europe apart, various thinkers sought to criticize and reorder their societies, and to this end, they needed a new way of understanding how societies were formed. A removed perspective would allow them to analyze the shortcomings of the status quo.

Wishing to avoid recycling religious explanations for the creation of human society, several philosophers cultivated an alternative genealogical myth, which stated that communities were formed by virtue of the voluntary consent of individuals, who wished to defend themselves from a cruel state of nature in which might was right (Thomas Hobbes), establish a central government that would not only avoid injuring but would in fact protect their rights (John Locke), or promote their true liberty by forming a regime that would express their general will (Jean-Jacques Rousseau).

Note that each of these thinkers presented a genesis story for society that is consistent with the modern conception of humans as rational individuals endowed with a capacity for reason and free choice. They do not describe, as an alternative to a monarch ruling by divine right, the strongest man simply subordinating everyone else to his rule, but rather present a narrative about the voluntary, elective association of individuals, agreeing among themselves on a rational order. Society, in this conception, is but an aggregation of previously unassociated individuals who agree among themselves to come together. Indeed a fundamental element in the idea of the social contract is the articulation of a society built by individuals and maintained by them—by their will and consent—a society in which the individual comes first, both chronologically and ontologically. Every individual, of course, expresses their capacity for reason and choice, that is, the image of God inside them. Society, therefore, is built in the image and in the likeness of the individuals who constitute it, embodying the proper balance between reason, free choice, law, and order.[30]

As Locke argues in his *Two Treatises of Government*, in ratifying a "social contract" and constituting a society, people expect the government that they have formed to look out for their rights and to defend them. Any government that fails to defend these rights, violates them without a justified cause secured in the common good, or believes that it may deprive its subjects of these rights, is an illegitimate government. It would be entirely legitimate, in Locke's view, to revolt against such a government.

Locke devotes a separate treatise to the subject of faith and religion, his *Letter Concerning Toleration*. In this text, Locke presents an unequivocal case for the separation of the religious and political spheres:

> I esteem it above all things necessary to distinguish exactly the Business of Civil Government from that of Religion, and to settle the just Bounds that lie between the one and the other.

Locke then quickly reminds us what the business of civil government is:

> Civil Interests I call Life, Liberty, Health, and Indolency of Body; and the Possession of outward things, such as Money, Lands, Houses, Furniture, and the like.[31]

These are the aspects of its subjects' lives that the government must busy itself with defending. It need not concern itself with their chances of entering the golden gates of heaven; this is not its responsibility. The "Care of Souls," Locke writes, cannot and must not be included in a civil government's business. The reason, he explains, is that:

> All the Life and Power of true Religion consists in the inward and full persuasion of the mind. . . . Whatever outward Worship we conform, if we are not fully satisfied in our own mind that the one is true, and the other well pleasing unto God, such Profession and such Practice, far from being any furtherance, are indeed great Obstacles to our Salvation. For in this manner, instead of expiating other Sins by the exercise of Religion, I say in offering thus unto God Almighty such Worship as we esteem to be displeasing unto him, we add unto the number of our other sins, those also of Hypocrisie, and Contempt of his Divine Majesty.[32]

Notice a recurring theme: true religion is by definition voluntary, and it is an entirely internal matter. Its power lies exclusively in the soul's confidence in its truth. Our rituals and customs, even if performed with technical precision and panache, will, if disconnected from a belief that they are part of the religion of truth, not only fail to bring us any closer to spiritual salvation, but will in fact push us further away from it. Locke was adamant (repeating this point several times in this work) that unless rituals are performed out of a sense of deep internal conviction, God has no interest in them, because he has no interest in hypocrisy or in perfunctory ritualism that one does not believe possesses truth. And since it is impossible to forcibly convince anyone of the truth of a particular article of faith, or of the validity of certain rituals, civil government has no power, nor any authority, over the faith of any individual.

"No body [sic] is born a member of any Church," writes Locke, emphasizing the voluntary nature of religion, as shaped within the Christian tradition.[33] As noted earlier, according to Locke we are all born *tabulae rasae*—blank slates.[34] For Locke, one's *choice* of faith is important because it underpins his conception of religion as an internal, rational, and voluntary matter. For this reason, Locke emphasizes that there may be no discrimination against any citizens solely because they belong to another religion or because one disapproves of their faith. Under no condition may an individual's excommunication in the context of a particular religious tradition justify the violation of their civil rights. Locke also stated explicitly that nobody had the authority to punish Native Americans for failing to embrace Christianity.[35] This religious tolerance was rooted in the idea that religion depends on choice and that choice is the innate right of every individual.

Locke explained that no government has the authority to deprive its religious subjects of anything that their tradition demands of them, as long as it is within the bounds of the law. The state may not interfere with religious worship. Nevertheless, Locke was careful to stress that not everything is permissible. Child sacrifice, for example, would be forbidden because it violated the law of the land.[36] But as long as what the members of a particular religion wish to do is not illegal, the government may not prevent them from doing it.[37] Nor does the government have any authority to punish people for acts or habits that many consider sinful, such as avarice or laziness, because these do not prejudice the rights of others—and after all, the government's only role is to protect its subjects' rights, not to educate them.

Locke's conception of religion, therefore, is a quintessential product of the Christian tradition. For Locke, there is a clear distinction between the realms of politics and religion, and in his conception the latter is an individual affair. This line of reasoning was but a more emphatic articulation of the trend that Saint Paul set in motion in the first century CE. Locke took the Pauline revolution to its logical apex, at least in the context of the relationship between religion and state, and could therefore demand that no individual's freedom of religion be violated. For Locke, freedom of religion became another natural right, alongside the rights to life, bodily integrity, liberty, and property.

Judaism, Which Is Not Christianity

But if this was a Christian conception, what did it have to say about Judaism? Locke was completely aware that Judaism was another matter entirely:

> For the Commonwealth of the Jews, different in that from all others, was an absolute Theocracy; nor was there, or could there be, any difference between that Commonwealth and the Church. The Laws established there concerning the Worship of One Invisible Deity, were the Civil Laws of that People, and a part of their Political Government; in which God himself was the Legislator.[38]

In antiquity, the Jews operated a theocracy, because all their affairs of state were conducted in accordance with divine law. The Torah, as we recall, stipulates laws governing matters of agriculture, taxation, and war. These and other domains, which in a Christian state were considered separate from religion, were under the control of the state. More specifically, Judaism recognized no distinction at all between the "religious" and "secular" or "political" spheres, but rather viewed all aspects of life as subject to divine law. Indeed God was, in Locke's words, "in a peculiar manner the King of the Jews." Judaism, in short, was not a "religion" but an all-encompassing civilization, which contained laws about divine worship together with laws about the punishment of thieves, tax collection, agriculture, and support for the needy, along with laws instructing one how to check whether one's wife has committed adultery, or how, on what grounds, and why a nation should go to war.

Locke acknowledges that Judaism proposed a different model of religion and state relations. Unlike Christianity, the laws of the Jewish religion were also "the Civil Laws of that People." The reason was that Judaism *was* "that People": the religious framework *was* the political framework; they were both the same, single reality. The Jews were, simply put, an ethnic group. A clear illustration of this can be found in the process of Jewish conversion: the convert is understood to be joining the Jewish people, not simply accepting a certain faith. The first question that a candidate for conversion is asked, according to the Talmud, is: "Why do you want to become a convert? Do you not see that this people are debased, oppressed and degraded more than all other peoples?" (Mishnah Gerim 1:1). A fair warning, concurrently indicating that converting to Judaism means joining a *people*.[39]

The obvious differences between Judaism and Christianity had preoccupied the earliest advocates of the principle of the separation of church and state. They had needed to grapple with Christianity's Jewish roots and to explain why Judaism's rival model was problematic. Even before Locke, Spinoza had discussed the difference between the structure of the Jewish and Christian traditions. Whereas Christians recognized a distinction between the authority of the Church and that of the king, he wrote, Jews thought otherwise:

> Their church began at the same time as their state, and Moses, who held absolute power, taught the people religion, organized the sacred ministries and selected the ministers. Thus, it came about among them that it was the royal authority, by contrast, that had most influence with the people and that in the main kings exercised authority in sacred matters.[40]

Locke's account of history was the more accurate, but the message is the same. Indeed, Judaism was different. The Jews, or really the ancient Hebrews, were an ethnic group distinguished by their specific customs and laws. They did not recognize a distinction between ritual matters and political affairs, nor could they: the king was chosen by the prophet and was commanded to write a Torah scroll for himself to study and obey. A "righteous" king was one who worked to stamp out idolatry in his kingdom. Religion and state were one and the same.

Locke, however, was incorrect in his observation that the Jewish kingdom was "different . . . from all others." The ancient Jewish kingdom was different from the Christian Roman Empire but actually very similar to other polities at its time. Religion and state were not separate in the kingdoms of Babylonia or Assyria, nor even in ancient Greece or Rome. In the ancient world, the ruler possessed supreme religious status and sometimes was considered an actual god. Moreover, many other groups embody the same unity of ethnicity and religion, from the Druze to the Romani and from various Native American tribes to the manifold Hindu denominations. None of these are political groups that profess a particular religion, but rather ethnic units for which worship, culture, custom, and civil law are all organically and primordially interwoven. The Jews were simply another such group. Christianity is the exception to the rule in drawing an *a priori* distinction between religious authority (the pope) and political authority (the emperor). In his writings, Locke was the progenitor of a long tradition, which in the modern day has become dominant, of seeing Christianity as the most common, accepted, and "normal" model of religion, but Christianity is in fact the odd one out.

Christianity proposed a new conception of religion and state relations. Locke acknowledged this, arguing that Jesus Christ "prescribed unto his Followers no new and peculiar Form of Government, nor put he the sword into any magistrate's hand, with commission to make use of it."[41] Christ, as it were, wished for a government that would maintain a clear distinction between these two realms, in which one would render unto Caesar that which is Caesar's and unto God that which is God's; a government in which the political would not transgress the boundaries of the religious. Whether or not this Christian vision was a positive development, it was certainly not a universal and obvious model. It was Christianity that constituted a model of religion and politics that was "different from all the others."

Yet entering the modern era, the Jews had much to gain from the new Christian order. Locke argued that in a proper system of government, following the Christian model, nobody could be deprived of the civil rights reserved for them by natural law. The Jews, therefore, also deserved equal rights:

> If we may openly speak the Truth, and as becomes one Man to another, neither Pagan, nor Mahumetan, nor Jew, ought to be excluded from the Civil Rights of the Commonwealth, because of his Religion.[42]

Locke took his conception of religion to its logical conclusions. One's religion is a private affair; why, then, should anyone be discriminated against on account of their religion? Jews, as well as Muslims and even pagans, were entitled to equal rights.

Locke did not connect the dots, however, between these remarks and his earlier observations about the different nature of Judaism. He failed to notice that since Judaism differed fundamentally from Christianity in terms of its internal logic and conception of the place and role of the divine, it could not easily become a "religion" in accordance with the Christian model. In demanding that no Jew be discriminated against "because of his Religion," he reimagined Judaism as a domain of faith and worship, a confessional matter, and the prerogative of the voluntary conscience. But for the Jews, certainly for those alive during Locke's lifetime, there was no meaningful distinction between Judaism's ritual dimension and any other domain, including the political. The extension of rights to the Jews according to the Christian model could therefore be conducted in one of two ways: either by changing the Christian model, or by changing Judaism. We shall see below how the extension of equality to the Jews transformed the face of Judaism.

Naturalizing Jews, Dismantling Judaism

The clash between Netanel Posner and Rabbi Raphael Cohen exemplified the distress of Jews who were fed up with the authority of the religious establishment. Few had any problem with their Jewish identity, nor did they have any intention of denying or shirking it, but they were unwilling to tolerate heavy penalties, from flagellations to excommunications, merely for not wanting to rise for early prayers or for resorting to civil courts. Their numbers swelled. In the latter third of the eighteenth century, many Jews in western and central Europe cast off the yoke of ritual observance. No longer were they a brave few, but a large swathe of the population, defined not by any organized ideology or revolt against the religious establishment, but rather by their desire to enjoy the pleasures of life and to revel in the *haute culture*, refinement, and sophistication of evolving European bourgeois life.[43]

At this point, they ran into resistance from the conservative establishment, precisely because their aspiration came in the context of a broader social and cultural movement. Europe was in the grips of an intensifying trend of secularization (a concept that we shall examine soon), which also affected Europe's Jews. Unlike the Judaism that we might call "traditional," which existed in Europe before the influence of secularism, and in which the occasional, unideological lax observance of ritual law was not only tolerated but a mundane part of Jewish life, now, with the rise of religious and philosophical ideas that explicitly encouraged dissent against the authority of the religious establishment, with the blurring of boundaries between Jewish and non-Jewish communities, and with increasing numbers casting off the yoke of religious observance—the rabbis could no longer countenance even minor deviations from Halakha. Both sides were gradually pushed into opposite, extreme positions, and ultimately, into distinct communities. Thus, ultra-Orthodox Judaism also emerged and took form in tandem with secularization and in response to it.

Certain thinkers, who are associated in retrospect with the Enlightenment movement, sought to extend equal rights to the Jews, but they also believed that Judaism as a whole had to be reformed and rendered "cultured," that is, modern. The *maskilim*, those Jews who identified with the Enlightenment, agreed with them and made their own efforts to adapt Judaism to the new zeitgeist of free thought, national patriotism, and growing individualism.

Of course, there were also those who opposed extending rights to the Jews. For many, the Jews could never become cultured because what impeded their development was not their petrified tradition but their basic nature. Such views, some of which reeked not only of antisemitism but also of biological racism, ran counter to the increasingly popular Enlightenment position that everyone was first and foremost a human being. The Jews, in the more conservative view, were not primarily human beings but primarily Jews. As such they were *substantively* different and therefore beyond repair. A battle of ideas raged between those who believed that Jews were people who practiced a Jewish "religion" (however much improvement it needed), those who maintained, correctly at the time, that Jews were a minority ethnic group, and those who saw the Jews as a distinct and inferior race with inherently negative traits.[44]

One of those who believed that the Jews were first and foremost human beings was Christian Wilhelm von Dohm, whom we mentioned earlier. Around the time of the eruption of the Posner scandal, in 1781, Dohm published his essay *Concerning the Amelioration of the Civil Status of the Jews.*[45] He argued that there was nothing in the Jews' traditional laws that might prevent them from discharging their civil duties if they were given the same status as other subjects of Prussia. On the contrary, he argued that if the Jews were given equal rights, they would become exemplary patriots and loyal citizens. The reason: "The Jew is even more man than Jew."[46]

Dohm saw the Jews as members of the "Mosaic faith." It was therefore clear to him that any negative traits that they possessed were not connected to their nature but rather to their terrible predicament: "This supposedly greater moral corruption of the Jews is a necessary and natural consequence of the oppressed condition in which they have been living for so many centuries."[47] Anyone subjected to oppression would sink into moral corruption, Dohm believed, and it was therefore obvious to him that if the oppression of the Jews were to vanish, their negative traits would vanish too. Jews therefore had to be naturalized and their rights equalized to those of non-Jews; it was also important to improve their schools, that is, to teach them a general curriculum. This would "do away with [their] clannish religious opinions," subjecting the Jewish religion to a serious process of reform. A new conception of the human, and a new conception of the Jew as human, was leading to demands for legal reform.

Dohm believed that as long as the Jews' laws did not contradict the laws of the state, they should be permitted to maintain their own judicial system with all its powers, including that of excommunication. This made Dohm an outlier. For the most part, supporters of the Jewish Emancipation demanded abolishing the rabbis' powers of adjudication and punishment, because if the Jews continued to enforce their own laws, they would exist as a kind of state within a state. This was the subject of a fierce debate, and opposition to Dohm came from within the Jewish community. Moses Mendelssohn, the most famous Jewish philosopher of the time, who was also a personal friend of Dohm's, disagreed with him—and made his position public.[48]

Moses Mendelssohn, Archetypal Modern Jew

Moses Mendelssohn (1729–1786) was an exemplary model of the new Jew: the enlightened Jew who succeeded in integrating fully into his country's high culture while nevertheless maintaining a Jewish life. This Jewish thinker impressed many with his mastery of both Jewish and general philosophical knowledge and became a major voice both within the Jewish community and within the republic of letters in the broader Enlightenment movement.[49]

Mendelssohn clung to both worlds and refused to let go. He wrote a commentary on the Torah to accompany his own full German translation of it and, like his contemporary Immanuel Kant, wrote an essay that sought to answer the question: "What Is Enlightenment?" He became the archetype of the enlightened Jew, although his opinions and approach differed from those of the *maskilim* who flourished around and after him, who were more socially active and frequently also more radical in their positions (such as Naphtali Hirz Wessely, whom we shall meet soon).[50] As the axis around which history of European Jewry revolved, Mendelssohn's life reflected the transition from one era to the next, not entirely belonging to either. Yet despite the ambivalence that Mendelssohn's life story reflected, his personal achievements were undeniable. As we shall see, he was the progenitor and pioneer of the idea that Judaism is, in fact, a religion.

Mendelssohn's retort to Dohm in 1782 was instructive of his thinking, which would find ultimate expression with his final work, *Jerusalem*. The book opens with words of thanks to "kind providence" for the fact that "the Rights of Man are beginning to be taken to heart."[51] Mendelssohn was vexed less about the fact of Jewish autonomy, detached from the general public, and more about the power of the rabbis, from whom he had already personally suffered when they tried to ban his commentary on the Bible. In the name of freedom of thought and expression, he believed that the rabbis could not be afforded the power to impose their beliefs on others. Mendelssohn was an observant Jew and argued that Jews should practice their ancestral traditions, but by the same token he believed that they should be permitted to do so of their own free will. In his view, the state should not be allowed to impose matters of religion, nor should Jewish communities be allowed to impose their religion on their members:

> Ecclesiastical jurisdiction, ecclesiastical authority and power! I must confess, these are phrases which convey to me no intelligible idea. . . . True divine religion arrogates no dominion over thought and opinion . . . it knows of no other force than that of winning by argument, of convincing

and rendering blessed by conviction. True divine religion needs neither arms nor fingers for its use; it is all spirit and heart.[52]

True religion was "all spirit and heart" and had neither any need nor any right to use force. Mendelssohn argued, therefore, that rabbis should not be granted the power to excommunicate members of their communities. It was a mistake for Dohm to leave this prerogative in their hands, he reasoned:

> As yet, there is not a clergy sufficiently enlightened, that such a right (if it exist at all) may be entrusted to them without any harm. Nay, the more enlightened they are, the less they will trust themselves in this; the more reluctant they will be, to take in their hands an avenging sword, which madness only thinks it can manage surely. I have that confidence in the more enlightened amongst the Rabbis, and elders of my nation, that they will be glad to relinquish so pernicious a prerogative, that they will cheerfully do away with all church and synagogue discipline, and let their flock enjoy, at their hands, even that kindness and forbearance, which they themselves have been so long panting for.[53]

In Mendelssohn's opinion, the rabbinic establishment in his time was still insufficiently enlightened to be entrusted with what it already possessed: the power to excommunicate individual community members. And if it ever became sufficiently enlightened, it would understand by itself that it was wrong to wield such an "avenging sword," which only the mad thought they could use safely. Mendelssohn's survey of the contemporary rabbinic establishment led him to the grim conclusion that most rabbis had not yet reached the level of progress that he was hoping for, and that they certainly had no intention of willingly forgoing the slightest opportunity for religious coercion.

Mendelssohn's reply to Dohm did its work, but as a consequence he shifted the debate to another subject: himself. In the wake of Mendelssohn's rebuttal to Dohm's essay, an anonymous pamphlet was published in Berlin in 1782 calling on Mendelssohn to convert to Christianity. If he admitted the shortcomings of the rabbis, and if he was indeed looking for the religion of love and tolerance, was this religion not already Christianity, rather than Judaism? With abysmal timing, this happened exactly as the power struggle between Netanel Posner and Rabbi Raphael Cohen reached public consciousness, seemingly proving for all to see the coercive nature of Judaism. The episode put Mendelssohn in an embarrassing bind.

Was Judaism Also Capable of Tolerance?

Earlier that same year, the Jewish world was rocked by the publication of Naphtali Hirz Wessely's book *Words of Peace and Truth*, in which he called on Jewish community leaders to establish a modern education system that would teach secular subjects in addition to religious studies. As the scholar of modern Judaism Shmuel Feiner writes, Wessely was effectively proclaiming a new era in Jewish history, one in which Jews would naturally embrace the non-Jewish cultural world.[54] Influential rabbis, including Rabbi Yechezkel Landau of Prague and Rabbi David Tevele of Leszno, lashed out against Wessely's proposal. Rabbi Hirschel Levin of Berlin, who had Wessely under his jurisdiction, was pressured to punish the miscreant author. Like the Posner episode, this incident also dampened Mendelssohn's call for tolerance and the optimism of his rebuttal to Dohm. The rabbis still had power, and they knew how to wield that power in order to silence opinions that rankled them.

And then, in June 1782, that anonymous pamphlet was published.[55] Titled *Das Forschen nach Licht und Recht* ("The Search for Light and Right"), it demanded that Mendelssohn explain why he would not disavow his ancestral, intolerant faith. "The people are justly worthy of you providing them with a reason for the great disparity between you and the faith of your forefathers," it declared, "or that you announce the cause preventing you from publicly accepting Christianity."[56]

Mendelssohn was forced to fight on two fronts. On the one hand, he had to convince the rabbis not to excommunicate or impose other penalties on Jews who behaved or expressed themselves contrary to tradition. At the same time, he also had to fend off agents of the German Enlightenment, to whom he now needed to explain why, despite what they saw and despite the failure of his own attempts to cajole the rabbis, Judaism remained consistent with the values of the Enlightenment and was a model of rational religion. Mendelssohn's critics knew, of course, that the Christian establishment also used violence and coercion, of the most terrible sort indeed. But for German Enlightenment thinkers, "true Christianity" was nothing of the sort. True Christianity, they averred, was a tolerant religion and the most compatible with reason.

This, of course, was the same Deist conviction, which many, including Kant, had developed and embraced. In this view, the original, good form of Christianity had been corrupted by the Church and turned into a vessel for its own selfish interests, but it was now time to go back to pure basics. Granted, it was relatively easy to believe in this notion as it pertained to Christianity because of Christianity's traditional emphasis on private and internal redemption, its basic separation between religion and state, and its recurrent aversion to law and established authority. It was therefore only natural to identify the Christian "true religion" as a voluntary and private matter, unlike Judaism, which was founded on the collective covenant of an ethnos, binding on all its members and including political laws.

Despite this, as we shall see, Mendelssohn embraced the Deist outlook regarding Judaism. In *Jerusalem*, he painted a picture of what was purportedly the original form of Judaism, which he believed to have existed in the distant past. Indeed it was this Judaism, he argued, not Christianity, that could best be described as the "rational religion."

On Religious Power and Judaism

Jerusalem, or on Religious Power and Judaism, published in 1783, was Mendelssohn's longest and most important work. It was written out of necessity, in conditions that Mendelssohn would have preferred to avoid, but the moment he set his mind to writing this book, he threw himself into it and produced a work that became an immediate cornerstone in the history of the Jewish Enlightenment. No Jewish *maskil* who had ever wondered whether and how Judaism could be brought into modernity, and no Jewish reformer who hoped to fix or adapt Judaism to modern times, could avoid reading *Jerusalem* and being influenced by its ideas. This groundbreaking and visionary work also provided the first systematic articulation of Judaism's new status in the modern world: Judaism as a religion.

Mendelssohn's endeavor had two stages. In volume I, he drew a distinction between religion and state and argued that, just as it was illegitimate for the state to touch religion, so too was it illegitimate for religion, any religion, to touch politics. Neither realm, Mendelssohn argued, had the right to impose religious laws on the individual. In volume II, Mendelssohn sought to demonstrate that Judaism—that is, the Jewish "religion"—was perfectly compatible with this model. In order to do so, he needed not only to respond to the challenge posed by the anonymous pamphleteer, who pointed out that Jewish communities saw no problem in imposing religious laws on their members, but also to contend with the fact (which earlier thinkers, from Roger Williams to Spinoza and Locke, had discussed) that the ancient Jewish kingdom was certainly governed in accordance with religious law. It was a tall order.

Immediately in the first sentence of his work, Mendelssohn asked how these two realms, "state and church, civil and ecclesiastical government, secular and spiritual power" could operate in tandem without proving to be "burdens on social life." It was obvious to Mendelssohn, therefore, that the two had to be separated. The state, he reasoned, regulated a person's relations with his or her fellows; religion, with God. There arose a problem, Mendelssohn argued, not only when people fought but also when they *agreed* with each other, because they usually only reached consensus to suppress a third party, namely "the brightest jewel of human happiness . . . liberty of conscience."[57] Whenever the religious establishment joined forces with the political establishment, freedom of thought suffered.

Mendelssohn, of course, lived at a time when religion and state were not separate realms. He was concerned not that a secular state might undermine religious traditions, but that a monarchical regime might collaborate with the church to limit freedom of religion. He believed that liberty of opinion, or freedom of conscience, had to be protected. The state might force its citizens to obey its laws even against their will, but it had no right to force its religion on them, because religion "knows of no actions without persuasion, of no works without spirit. . . . Religious observances without religious thoughts, are idle boys' play, and no worship."[58]

Mendelssohn located the core of religion in the human heart. Without spiritual intent, religious acts were meaningless. In this sense, Mendelssohn was repeating an idea for which Tertullian had advocated in the early third century, and which had gained an increasing foothold in the Christian tradition in the Middle Ages before ultimately sweeping the whole Western world. Thomas Jefferson articulated the exact same idea at the same time in the United States, with the publication of his *Notes on the State of Virginia*, parts of which were influenced, as we have seen, directly by Tertullian. Jefferson used it to call for absolute liberty of inquiry and opinion on matters of religion and for a separation of religion and state in Virginia. In *Jerusalem*, Mendelssohn eloquently articulated the same ideas for Judaism.

Besides the state, the religious establishment also had no right to impose its positions on individuals. Religious acts that did not arise out of an individual's free will were "idle play and repugnant to the true spirit of religion."[59] If this were true for state institutions, the same held for religious ones. When forcibly imposed, religion was a self-defeating enterprise, subverting the "true spirit."

"The state," Mendelssohn concluded, "uses man as *the immortal Son of Earth*; religion as *the image of his Creator*."[60] The role of the state was to treat people as the "Son[s] of Earth" and thus govern their relations with other individuals and nature. But it was to have sufficient respect for them to refrain from trying to force them to think one way or another. The role of institutionalized religion, meanwhile, was to govern one's relations with God, but since all were created in God's image, the establishment was to remain conscious of their capacity for reason and free choice. In order to faithfully express the image of God, the individual had to be granted freedom of religion and conscience. For individuals to profess true, valid religion, the state could not impose beliefs or articles of faith on them.

Orthopraxy over Orthodoxy

In volume II of *Jerusalem*, Mendelssohn pivoted from principled questions about religion and state to an analysis of the Jewish tradition. He began with the question of excommunications. Dohm, perhaps confusing Christian excommunication, an essentially formal act, with Jewish excommunication, which meant social banishment, was content to leave Jews with the power to excommunicate fellow community members even after their naturalization. Mendelssohn disagreed. Just as religions had no right to impose their views, nor even to threaten punishments, they certainly had no right to excommunicate members. But was the institution of the *herem* (excommunication) not an integral part of the laws of the Jewish tradition? Was the Jewish tradition, Mendelssohn asked, putting the question in his sparring partner's mouth, not "but a system of religious government, of the power and right of religion"?[61] After all, did not the laws of Moses themselves mandate the death penalty for the offence of desecrating the Sabbath?

Mendelssohn acknowledged that such an impression had taken hold, even among Jews themselves, but he insisted that it was mistaken. This was not the true Judaism. Yes, Judaism did in fact contain "laws, judgments, statutes, rules of life, information of the will of God, and lessons how to conduct themselves in order to attain both temporal and spiritual happiness," but it contained "no dogmas, no saving truths, no general self-evident positions."[62] Judaism, Mendelssohn declared, had no concept of divine revelation in the sense of religious truths brought down from the heavens—it had no orthodoxy of *belief*. God had given the Jews the Torah, comprising practical laws, or *orthopraxis*, but he had not limited what they could believe, nor had he given anyone the authority to impose doctrines on them. The Jews, like everyone else created in God's image, would derive their faith through reason alone.

"I acknowledge no immutable truths, but such as not only may be made conceivable to the human understanding, but as also admit of being demonstrated and warranted by human faculties," wrote Mendelssohn.[63] The revelation to Moses at Mount Sinai did not present any articles of faith contrary to reason, nor was it even necessary in terms of the Jewish faith (inasmuch as it is a faith), because this faith was based on reason. Moses only delivered laws and commandments, and these were not intended to impose any particular article of faith on anyone, but merely to organize society in a manner that would contribute to its members' happiness. Unlike Christianity, in which divine revelation committed Christians to certain beliefs, Judaism, Mendelssohn argued, allowed for absolute freedom of conscience.

It is worth noting Mendelssohn's brilliant maneuver here, using the Christian emphasis on internal religion against Christianity itself. The Church, which maintained that faith, not practice, mattered most, sought to impose its own dogma on everyone, whether by volition or by coercion. But Mendelssohn was living in an age in which the coercion of another's conscience was already considered (at least by enlightened circles) an outrage and a fool's errand. From this position, he could rail against the Christian tradition as a form of tyranny. Judaism's emphasis on practical commandments, which in the past had rendered it "technical," "dry," "mechanical," or "flesh-like" in Christian eyes, now played into Mendelssohn's hands: the commandments were compulsory, as part of the covenant with God, but the same covenant left every individual free to decide on their own beliefs by themselves, using his reason.

In his perspective on reason, Mendelssohn adopted the Deist position, which, as noted above, stated that all religions ultimately shared the same principles of faith, and that these could be ascertained by means of reason alone. There was no need for revelation. The eternal truths of religion—which were generally understood to include faith in one God, good and benevolent, and the duty to worship him and to be kind to others—necessarily had to be available to everyone at every time, and it was therefore inconceivable that they might not be discoverable through rational inquiry. Given this, it also followed that these truths were necessarily shared by all religions, as Mendelssohn indeed argued.

The Separation of Political and Apolitical Judaism

But what about all the laws compelling observance of Judaism's ritual commandments? According to Mendelssohn, these laws were part of the political system of the ancient Jewish kingdom, and some of these laws were necessary. But as soon as the Jews no longer had their own independent kingdom, any coercion was uncalled for and improper.

In defining the laws revealed at Mount Sinai as fundamentally political, Mendelssohn continued Spinoza's line of thought, seeing the laws of the ancient Hebrew religion as the laws of the state founded by the Israelites. But contrary to Spinoza, who believed that all these laws were no longer in force as soon as this ancient state was destroyed, Mendelssohn argued that only the laws addressing Judaism's *national* dimension were no longer in effect (including the power to punish individuals, since the state had already acquired, in the seventeenth century, the monopoly on the use of force). Not only was Halakha still valid; it was also supremely important. Judaism's mission was to fly the flag of monotheism around the world, and the purpose of the commandments was to enable the

Jews to do so, because they gave form to monotheism and validated it, instituting a moral society. Law, as we know, informs and is informed by a narrative.

According to Mendelssohn, although the ancient Jewish kingdom practiced religious coercion, the laws that had regulated and legitimized it became invalid with the destruction of this kingdom. Jews in the modern world, after all, no longer formed an independent polity. All that they retained, therefore, was their apolitical Halakha: a corpus of liturgy, ritual, practice, dietary laws, and festivals. All that remained was Judaism's most essential and significant core: its *mitzvot*, or ritual commandments, and, naturally, the eternal truths of the rational religion. According to Mendelssohn, these two things were interrelated. Their commandments steered the Jews toward rational truths and morality. In fact, this was the reason why they were given in the first place.

Moses Mendelssohn depicted Judaism as the religion chosen to carry rational truths through the course of humanity's progress, as a tradition that encouraged its members, through its commandments, to face the truth and internalize its core principles. At the Sinaitic revelation, God gave the Jews commandments and laws but not articles of faith. The latter are for all to deduce freely, by themselves, using free choice and the capacity for reason, which is the image of God inside everyone. The commandments, in turn, simply point people toward these truths and safeguard their memory. The Jews, the people who observed these commandments, were surrounded all day and every day by these signposts directing them toward the truth, namely the existence of God, who is one, good, and benevolent, who must be worshipped, and who expects us to treat our fellows with kindness.[64] This, according to Mendelssohn, was the pure, rational monotheism that the Jews disseminated in the world.

How Judaism Became a Religion

As we have seen, according to Mendelssohn, what remained of Halakha after the Jews' dispersion was shorn of its national dimensions, the religious customs that the Jews had preserved without their political framework.[65] Mendelssohn thus separated, by force of historical circumstance, Judaism's political laws, which had been abrogated, from its ritual and moral laws, which were still in force. State was separated from religion, and what remained of Judaism was squarely on the religious end.

Like Roger Williams, Mendelssohn recalled Jesus's advice to the Jews of the first century: "Render therefore to Caesar the things that are Caesar's, and to God the things that are God's" (Matthew 22:21). He considered this sound advice. "And a more wholesome advice could not be given to the house of Jacob, even at this very day," he wrote. "Comply with the customs, and the civil constitution of the countries in which ye are transplanted, but, at the same time, be constant to the faith of your forefathers."[66] Halakha was worth maintaining because it was an expression of rational truths and steered Jews toward them. This was the Jews' covenant with their God, and Mendelssohn beseeched his fellow Jews to not loosen their observance. He also thought, however, that they were required to obey civil law and be patriotic citizens wherever they were.

Mendelssohn asked Christians to accept the Jews as they were, on the grounds that they were loyal to their consciences—and there was no value in having citizens living a lie. And as long as Jews were loyal subjects of the king, Christians were requested to be loyal subjects of God and to respect his creations' freedom of conscience, because this, as Mendelssohn wrote at the start of his book, was "the brightest jewel of human happiness." This was God's image, which God, in his benevolence, had implanted in every human being. It was this divine core that had to be respected, and therefore the Jews had to receive equality of rights.

This, therefore, was Mendelssohn's vision: to achieve the Jews' integration into modern Western society, securing agreement about the tenets of rational religion and demanding mutual tolerance for the diversity of symbols attached to these tenets, which varied between religious traditions.

It is worth dwelling on the dramatic implications of the Mendelssohnian vision for the Jewish tradition: it transformed Judaism into a *religious* tradition, that is, into a ceremonial system that accompanied individuals' relationships with God—a "faith," or religion in the modern sense of the word. Judaism had no implications for other spheres of a person's life, because reason dictated all educated people's beliefs, and Jewish political commandments were annulled with the exile from the land of Israel. Jews could therefore be proud citizens of Germany (or

France, and so forth) and fully integrate into the social and political life of their countries. Jews belonged to the Jewish "church," but not the Jewish nation. The national collectives to which they were loyal were the nations in which they dwelled. Judaism was only their religion.

Mendelssohn was therefore demanding equal rights for Jews as individuals, not as a nation. It was no coincidence that when, as early as January 1770, Mendelssohn was presented with a proposal to establish a Jewish state in the Land of Israel, he rejected it out of hand.[67] By insisting that the Jews had political rights as individuals, but not as a community, Mendelssohn brought Judaism into the modern world.[68] But its admission would come at a steep price.

In the words of Julius Guttman, *Jerusalem* was "the first attempt to justify Judaism before the cultural consciousness of modernity."[69] The Jews, for Mendelssohn, became enlightened individuals, who practiced their ancestral customs only to the extent that they did not conflict with civil law. They too believed in the same universal rational religion in which all enlightened individuals believed. The Jews became citizens; Judaism, a religion. Judaism's national dimension was downplayed if not entirely erased. Thus would it integrate into the developing modern nation-state. It was for a good reason that Heinrich Heine dubbed Mendelssohn the "Jewish Luther."[70]

Conditional Jewish Equality

Mendelssohn's questions and proposed solutions would continue to preoccupy western European society and culture for decades after he wrote *Jerusalem*. Democracy would spread across Europe, and the "Jewish Question" would become central to discussions of the human condition. Was Judaism indeed a religion, many Europeans would wonder, and even if so, was it of the sort that did not limit the conscience and was capable of integrating into the civilian life of the nation-states coalescing across the continent? Could Jews become equal citizens and true patriots, loyal to the nations of Europe rather than to the Jewish nation? Could Judaism, in other words, conform to the Christian model?

Only six years after *Jerusalem*'s publication in Germany, France marched into a new era with the outbreak of the French Revolution. The masses crying, "Liberté, égalité, fraternité!" had to grapple early on with the possibility of extending liberty, equality, and fraternity to their Jewish neighbors. Would the revolution remain faithful to its founding ideals? Would the revolutionaries' commitment to equal citizenship for all men (and indeed, we are talking about *men*) include Jews as well?

The answer seemed to be yes—under certain conditions. Article I of the Declaration of the Rights of Man and of the Citizen (*Déclaration des droits de l'homme et du citoyen*), adopted in August 1789 by France's National Constituent Assembly, the governing body of Revolutionary France, proclaimed that "men are born and remain free and equal in rights. Social distinctions may be founded only upon the general good."

Humans were universal, free, and abstract creatures. They were essentially free and removed from everything around them: from any distinctions of ethnicity, class, or sex. It was therefore also natural that religious characteristics would have no bearings on a person's legal status. The echoes of Paul's declaration that "there is neither Jew nor Greek" were loud and unmistakable.

Indeed, Article X of the declaration stated: "No one shall be disquieted on account of his opinions, including his religious views, provided their manifestation does not disturb the public order established by law." This formulation represented a logical continuation of Article I, echoing the thoughts of thinkers such as Locke, Dohm, and Mendelssohn. Religious opinions, or beliefs, were a private matter of conscience. They were none of the state's business. Nevertheless, religious commandments could not be allowed to contradict the law of the land. Mendelssohn's version of Judaism fits well into this model.

The Jews did not receive equal rights immediately, however. There were proposals to grant them what they deserved according to the logic of liberalism, and in response to one such proposal, Count de Clermont-Tonnerre delivered a speech in December 1791. His remarks encapsulated the Jews' problematic status, specifically the evident unsuitability of Judaism in its pre-modern form to the model demanded by the Enlightenment. Clermont-Tonnerre began with general remarks about relations between religion and state, echoing the writings of the liberal philosophers of his time:

> The law cannot affect the religion of man. It can take no hold over his soul. It can affect only his actions. . . . So leave man's conscience free,

that sentiments or thoughts guided in one manner or another towards the heavens will not be crimes that society punishes by the loss of social rights. . . . Every religion must prove one thing—that it is moral.[71]

Having clarified this, Clermont-Tonnerre reached the "Jewish Question":

> The Jews should be denied everything as a nation, but granted everything as individuals. . . . It is intolerable that the Jews should become a separate political formation or class in the country. Every one of them must individually become a citizen. If they do not want this, they must inform us and we shall then be compelled to expel them. The existence of a nation within a nation is unacceptable to our country.[72]

Clermont-Tonnerre made his problem with Judaism perfectly clear. The Jews were entitled to citizenship, with all its associated rights—they were, in fact, human beings like anyone else—but they were entitled to rights *as individuals alone*. They had no right or option to remain a separate community within the French nation. The Jews, like all other inhabitants of France, had to be *French*: members of the French nation, not of the so-called Jewish people. A "nation within a nation" could not be tolerated. The naturalization of the Jews would therefore have to come in tandem with the dismantling of Judaism as an ethnic or national collective and its transformation into a private affair. Judaism, in other words, had to become a religion.

For Clermont-Tonnerre, Judaism could only remain part of a Jew's life in this restricted sense. Judaism would have to become a matter of "sentiments or thoughts guided in one manner or another towards the heavens," existing only as an internal and private intellectual or confessional matter for the individual citizen. The Jews would not be permitted to continue thinking of themselves as a separate nation, perpetually expecting to abandon France and be swept away on eagles' wings to a land promised by God. They had to be fully part of the republic. The "égalité" part of the slogan could only be realized in association with complete "fraternité."

Jews as a Nation within a Nation

The motif of a "nation within a nation" would continue to haunt the Jews in Europe, resurfacing in every debate about them. As we recall, Dohm was exceptional in having no concerns about the collective character of Judaism, while it fell to Mendelssohn to explain that the Jews would receive citizenship as individuals, but not as a nation. It appears that he understood better than Dohm the meaning of modern citizenship.

Conceptions of modern citizenship served not only to advance the cause of Jewish naturalization but also to discourage it, specifically by highlighting the special—i.e., non-Christian—nature of Judaism. Nearly all opponents of citizenship rights for Jews argued, in effect, that it was not only a religion but also a nationality. Hence the accusation that the Jews formed a "nation within a nation," or in other versions, "a state within a state." This opinion was widespread among the enlightened classes in Germany. As both a factual distinction and an antisemitic sentiment, this position was used as a counterargument against the extension of equal rights to Jews or as the grounds for demands for the dissolution of a distinct Jewish identity as a precondition for the extension of rights. Early-nineteenth century thinkers such as Friedrich Rühs, Jakob Fries, H. E. G. Paulus, and Bruno Bauer all raised such arguments.

Yet even before all these, Johann Gottlieb Fichte, the renowned idealist philosopher and one of the fathers of German nationalism, addressed the same matter. In his essay *On the French Revolution* (1783), he wrote:

> Does this not recall to you the notion of a state within a state? Does the obvious idea not occur to you, that the Jews alone are citizens of a state which is more secure and powerful than any of yours? . . . I see absolutely no way of giving them civic rights; except perhaps, if one night we chop off all of their heads and replace them with new ones, in which there would not be one single Jewish idea. . . . I see no other way to protect ourselves from the Jews, except if we conquer their promised land for them and send all of them there.[73]

Fichte conceived of the Jews as a foreign and indeed rival nation, dwelling among the nations of Europe. The only way to contend with the Jews was to intellectually decapitate them or to send them to live in a land of their own: the natural state of affairs, Fichte maintained, for every nation. Leaving aside Fichte's blunt language and apparent antisemitism, it's worth noting that in giving a nationalist answer to the "Jewish Question" he presaged future Zionists' own conceptions. The Jews, they would argue, have two options only: to be fully assimilated in European culture, or to reclaim their true identity as a nation, and establish an independent state. For them, Jews were indeed an ethnic group, or in its modern rendering, a nation. Turning Judaism into a religion was an impossibility—it was either Judaism, or religion.

The Euthanasia of Judaism and Kant's Messianic Age

Immanuel Kant would hold the same position, though he would choose religion. Rational religion. The same year that Fichte published his defense of the French Revolution, Kant published *Religion within the Bounds of Bare Reason*. Kant knew Mendelssohn, admired his philosophy, and was influenced by his thinking about Judaism, but he utterly repudiated his view of Judaism as a religion. "The Jewish faith is, in terms of its original arrangement, a sum of merely statutory laws, on which a state constitution was based. . . . Judaism is properly not a religion at all," wrote the great philosopher.[74] Kant repeated Spinoza's and Mendelssohn's conviction that Judaism originated as a political state constitution, but rejected Mendelssohn's attempt to argue that times had changed. To Kant's mind, the legal-ritual nature of Judaism was sufficient to deny it the status of a religion. God was the king of the ancient Jewish kingdom, since God "is here being venerated merely as a secular regent who makes no claim at all concerning and upon conscience"—which, of course, was exactly Mendelssohn's point. For Kant, however, the meaning was antipodal: Judaism was not a religion but a theocratic regime.

Just as Mendelssohn leveraged Christianity's traits against it, Kant repaid the favor and did the same for Judaism. He supplies an extremely restrictive answer to the question "what is religion?" presenting it as a matter of conscience alone. The formula is strikingly simple: all religions address the conscience, and anything that does not address the conscience is not religion. And since religion is intimately tied to the conscience, in Kant's view all religions contain eternal truths about reason and morality. In *Jerusalem*, therefore, Mendelssohn did not establish Judaism as a religion but rather explained exactly why it was *not* a religion. According to Kant, religions were required to discard anything that interfered with, or was surplus to, proper moral and conscientious choice. These conscientious choices—the core of religion—would also be the last facets of religion to remain when all the world's religions ultimately united. For Kant, this was nothing less than a messianic process:

> There is, however, ground for saying "that the kingdom of God is come unto us," even if only the principle of the gradual transition of church faith to universal rational religion and thus to a (divine) ethical state on earth has taken root.[75]

In the Kantian kingdom of God, "church faith" (institutionalized religion) would crumble and give way to the universal rational religion: the church of reason. Only there would the perfect moral state—heaven on earth—finally exist.

If all denominations of Christianity were ultimately destined to merge into a single "rational religion," clearly there was no point preserving Judaism, which was an even more political, ceremonial, and practical framework than the churches. As Kant wrote in the last book that he published in his lifetime, *The Contest of Faculties* (*Der Streit der Fakultäten*, 1798): "The euthanasia of Judaism is pure moral religion, freed from all the ancient statutory teachings."[76] The transformation of Judaism into a pure moral religion, a metamorphosis that would ultimately unfold in the modern age, was its blessed euthanasia. Turning Judaism into a (rational) religion would be the soothing end of Judaism.

In Kant, the Pauline metamorphosis would reach full fruition with the Christianization or secularization of Judaism. But Kant also voided Christianity of its dogmatic and ritualistic elements. With the disappearance, over time, of the plethora of churches, humanity would reach "the conclusion of the great drama of religious change on earth (the restoration of all things), when there will be only one shepherd and one flock."[77] The "one shepherd" was the conscience, which for Kant was none other than reason. The secularization of God's image and the messianic ideal had never received more explicit expression.

Friedrich Schleiermacher Proposes a New Denomination of Judaism

Kant took the internal logic of the Enlightenment to its logical zenith, but the idea that Judaism had to change in order to enter the modern era was, as we have seen, quite widespread. In order to further understand its implications, let us consider the remarks of the tremendously influential German theologian Friedrich Schleiermacher, who presented an orderly, two-stage plan for the naturalization of German Jewry in a public letter published in 1799.[78]

Schleiermacher was no fan of Judaism. Unlike Kant, who called for the "euthanasia of Judaism," Schleiermacher declared in his most famous work, *On Religion: Speeches to its Cultured Despisers*, that Judaism was already deceased. The Jews professed a "dead religion," he argued, while simultaneously dismissing the "prejudice" that Jews were afflicted by an "internal rot" and therefore could not be naturalized. A dead religion was one thing; the people who professed it were another. The Jews, Schleiermacher insisted, were human beings and could therefore also be citizens.

Schleiermacher advocated for a position popular among the intelligentsia: the demand for a separation of religion and state. "Reason," argued Schleiermacher, "demands that all should be citizens, but it does not require that all must be Christians."[79] The way to transform Jews into citizens, however, passed through the refashioning of Judaism itself. Schleiermacher's remarks provide an apt summary of the intellectual framework that had developed over the preceding centuries, and it is worth quoting them at length:

> In brief, I demand that the Jews who are serious about becoming citizens do not completely reject ceremonial law [i.e., Halakha] but only subordinate it to the laws of the state so that they would declare that they didn't want to escape from any civic duty under the pretext that it conflicts with ceremonial law. No one should be forbidden on account of religion from doing or undertaking anything that is allowed by the state. Further, I demand that they officially and publicly renounce the hope for a messiah; I believe this is an important point where the state cannot yield to them.

. . . If French refugees publicly declared completely openly that it was certain that they—sooner or later—would return to their fatherland, would the state not be perfectly authorized to view them immediately as foreigners, to exclude them from owning property and from assuming state offices, or to limit their activities in some other manner during their interim sojourn?

The Jews clearly find themselves in the same situation, as long as the belief that at some time they will again be a proper nation still defines their relation to one another and towards their fellow citizens and the state in a wholly distinctive manner. It may be that this belief has few true followers any longer; but as long as it remains a public confession, the state cannot treat them other than by assuming that they believe in it, and thus it is not to be blamed if it does not wish to bestow full civil rights upon them. Just as one assumes that someone who leases a plot of land for a couple of years and then intends to leave will spend nothing on it and is apt to exhaust it, so it is also to be assumed that those who do not view the state as their fatherland and as their permanent home will also not concern themselves with putting forth their best effort but only wish to draw the best possible advantage from it, even if to its ruin.

. . . I demand that those who accept both points [i.e., subordinating Halakha to state law and renouncing hopes of the advent of the messiah] should constitute a special ecclesiastical society. The state must be sure that the change of religion that it declares necessary is always connected with the advantages that it bestows.

If those who have embraced this altered Judaism remain mingled with the rest and distinguish themselves through nothing but the provisional act of their confession, the state loses them from view and cannot know what kind of change occurs in their convictions, or at least those of their progeny, due to family circumstances or foreign education.

. . . So that the advantages will be acquired upon entrance into the same [ecclesiastical society] and forfeited with voluntary separation—for you can trust me not to institute the right of the ban. Be amused if you will, but I am completely serious about this new sect.[80]

Schleiermacher gives clear articulation to principles that had taken root before his time. He supported the extension of civil rights to all, whatever their religion. His first condition, which he applied to every religion, was that religious laws not contradict the laws of the state. No religion could permit anything that the state prohibited, nor could it coercively prohibit anything that the state permitted. We have already seen that Locke stipulated a similar condition in his *Letter Concerning Toleration*, and Mendelssohn also accepted it in *Jerusalem*. This notion, which seemed quite obvious, expressed at its core the principle of the separation of religion and state, while also making clear that this separation not only rendered religion and state two separate realms but also subordinated religion to the authority of the state.

The Citizen Is Born

Indeed the birth of "religion" as an intellectual category, as the part of human life in which the heart, conscience, and intellect are directed toward a particular faith out of free choice, happened in tandem with the birth of the nation-state.[81] The conception of religion as a personal matter belonging to the individual evolved parallel with the conception of the public realm as a space that belonged to the public (and not the king). Just as religion was a private matter, the state was the *res publica*: the public affair. Just as religion became what one does in private, the state developed as that thing all citizens do together. Moreover, as religion was increasingly pigeonholed into the individual psyche, the individual was transformed into part of a collective that was not religious but national. These processes developed together and complemented each other. "The ideas of liberalism, nationalism, secularism and self-determination of people were closely connected," writes C. A. Bayly, "in that they all presupposed the action of autonomous individuals singly or in groups."[82]

The citizen was born: the autonomous individual who was first and foremost a person, who made decisions about their religious beliefs by themselves and about their country's government together with fellow citizens. The public sphere was rendered void of religion and placed at the service of its citizens' decisions, in accordance with their ideological and pragmatic considerations and majority rule. Religious life became focused on the private sphere, and religion came to be considered the exclusive prerogative of individuals and their personal considerations. It became illegitimate for the state to meddle in an individual's faith or for individuals to seek to impose their religious convictions on others. The modern (liberal democratic) state, therefore, which was defined in parallel and complementary to the modern definition of religion, grew as part of the process of secularization.

If Schleiermacher's first principle was quite elementary, his later remarks revealed that inasmuch as it concerned Judaism, the situation was not so straightforward. Judaism represented an especially problematic case because the Jews conceived of themselves as a nation. According to Schleiermacher, some Jews failed to understand that they could not demand equal rights while at the same time maintaining that they were a separate people. The state quite simply could not grant equal rights to members of another nation, let alone ones who explicitly declared that in the not-so-distant future, they would leave and move to their true land. A citizen must be of one state only.

It was not only a theoretical issue. Obviously, Schleiermacher argued, people who did not intend to remain wherever they lived would not invest their energies and capital there in order to protect and ameliorate the place. For this reason, Schleiermacher demanded that the Jews "officially and publicly renounce the hope for a messiah"[83] and thus confirm to their neighbors and their government that they were not planning on an exodus, that they saw their European homelands as the places in which they would build their lives and their children's lives, and no less importantly, to which they would contribute as expected of every citizen.

A Reformed Judaism

Oh, and another small matter: Schleiermacher demanded that the Jews create a new religious framework. It would be a kind of an updated Judaism, a streamlined Judaism, a modernized Judaism. This Judaism would be bereft of commandments that conflicted with the law of the state and shorn of messianic expectations. It would be a reformed Judaism, adapted to the modern era: a Judaism that had cast off its national dimensions and that no longer conceived of itself as a nationality, but as a religion, and therefore as the private business of every Jewish citizen, just as Christianity was for Christian citizens. This was exactly the sort of Judaism that Rabbi Dr. Abraham Geiger (1810–1874), the founder of what would become the largest Jewish denomination in the U.S., Reform Judaism, would seek to forge less than fifty years later.

In many ways, Geiger related not only to Schleiermacher's thinking but also to Mendelssohn's. Like Mendelssohn, Geiger was also certain that Judaism was a religion; like Mendelssohn, Geiger also erased its political dimension; and like Mendelssohn, Geiger also believed that Judaism was founded on reason. The only difference between them was how they related to the halakhic tradition.

While Mendelssohn saw the traditional rituals and commandments as an essential framework, both for the preservation of the covenant with God and for shaping human character, Geiger regarded them as superfluous and often downright silly. If, for Mendelssohn, Halakha was a supra-historical Jewish reality given by God so that his people would better understand and keep the universal rational religion, for Geiger monotheism, morality, and rationality were the only supra-historical realities, and Halakha was a historically contingent, mostly irrelevant, external crutch. It was Judaism, Geiger claimed, that first adopted Monotheism, received the Ten Commandments, and had since advocated for them as its gift to humankind. Propagating them is still Judaism's essence and message, and what better way to do so then by integrating into society as equal, outstanding citizens?

Of course, to do so, Judaism would have to forfeit its national character. The American Reform Movement's declaration of principles, the Pittsburgh Platform of 1885, would give this explicit articulation:

> We consider ourselves no longer a nation, but a religious community, and therefore expect neither a return to Palestine, nor a sacrificial worship under the sons of Aaron, nor the restoration of any of the laws concerning the Jewish state.[84]

The metamorphosis is complete. What began with Mendelssohn ends with what Schleiermacher explicitly demanded: the creation of a new and improved Judaism: a Judaism that had become a modern religion. Such a Judaism would allow Jews to be Germans "of Mosaic faith," Frenchmen "of Mosaic faith," Englishmen "of Mosaic faith," etc.—no longer Jewish by nationality but solely by confession.

In 1866, in his poem "Awake, My People!," Judah Leib Gordon would echo this view precisely with the mantra "be a human at large and a Jew at home." The poem, which exalts the values of the Enlightenment and sings the praises of the new, enlightened Europe, became dominant in the consciousness of the Jewish *maskilim* and suited the vision that they aspired to promote. But the poem's title embodied the acutely painful Jewish paradox: Gordon was calling on Jews to keep their Judaism as a personal matter, in the privacy of their own homes, but still addressed the Jews as a whole—"Awake, My People!"—as possessing a collective public status, as a single community. As a nation.

Napoleon's Jews

In September 1791, France became the first country to grant its Jews full and equal rights. The Jew was simply another person, valuable, equal, autonomous, and abstract, like anyone made in God's image. The French Revolution had remained loyal to its values. But the idea of a "nation within a nation" continued to haunt the Jews. Napoleon, who seized control of France in 1804, had concerns about Judaism's national character. He restricted the Jews' rights, and in 1806 he convened the "Parisian Sanhedrin," an assembly of seventy-one rabbis and Jewish notables, so that its representatives could declare for the record that Judaism's laws did not contradict French law (such as on matters of marriage or usury) and that Judaism itself did not contradict French nationalism.

One of the questions posed to the rabbis in this assembly was: "Do the Jews born in France, and treated by the law as French citizens, consider France as their country?"[85] Napoleon wished to force the Jews to forswear their aspiration to return to the Land of Israel during the messianic era and instead to swear allegiance to France as their only homeland. In their response, the Jewish representatives indeed swore allegiance to France and cited the meager rate of Jewish return to Israel after the Edict of Cyrus (539 BCE) as evidence that Jews had always reserved their love for their adoptive lands, wherever they may be. Babylonian Jewry's refusal to return to the Land of Israel, which caused the biblical leaders Ezra and Nehemiah such anguish, became for the rabbis of France a positive model, that they were happy to share with Napoleon. Later on, the rabbis hinted that liturgy about

the return of the exiles was purely ceremonial. The Parisian Sanhedrin also decided that:

> Divine Law, the precious heritage of our ancestors, contains within itself
> dispositions which are political and dispositions which are religious. . . .
> These political dispositions are no longer applicable, since Israel no lon-
> ger forms a nation.[86]

Once again, as with Mendelssohn, Judaism's political laws were struck
down as antiquated, leaving only the religious laws. The ethnonational
dimension of Judaism is erased and Judaism becomes a religion.

Napoleon could feel reassured. In 1812, Prussia, the country of Kant
and Schleiermacher, gave the Jews equal rights, only as individuals of
course. Netanel Posner did not live to become an equal citizen in his native Denmark, which only gave Jews equal rights in 1849. He and other
Jews like him lived in the liminal period between the rise of modern
liberal conceptions, which treated people, including Jews, as individuals
with a free conscience, and the translation of this new paradigm into law
and politics. They would thus continue to be buffeted between the rabbis' powers and the temptations of enlightened society.

During this period, Napoleon conquered expansive swathes of Europe. Unlike earlier conquerors, Napoleon marched under the banner
of the French Revolution and purported to bring liberty, equality, and
fraternity to the lands and peoples he conquered. Rabbi Shneur Zalman,
a resident of the town of Liadi on the border of modern-day Russia and
Belarus, the founder of the Chabad Hasidic court, and one of the greatest Jewish spiritual leaders, was anxious about the possibility that Napoleon, who invaded Russia in 1812, might conquer the tsardom and its
Jews. He was not concerned for the Jews' physical wellbeing (they were
already suffering greatly under the tsar) but for their religious fate. The
elderly rebbe believed that if Napoleon conquered Russia, the situation
of the Jews would improve materially but deteriorate spiritually:

> If BP [Bonaparte] is victorious, the horn of Israel will be raised, and
> wealth will be abundant among the Jews, but the heart of Israel will be
> separated and divided from their Father in heaven. And if A.A. [our Lord
> Alexander] is victorious, even if the horn of Israel is brought down and

poverty increases among the Jews, their heart will join and cleave to their Father in heaven.[87]

The elderly rebbe was concerned about the improvement of the Jewish people's dignity and the growth of their wealth. He feared their acceptance into non-Jewish society and naturalization as equal citizens, which was indeed the French Republic's vision. If the Jews became equal citizens, Rabbi Shneur Zalman believed, they would drift away from God, but as long as they remained poor and despised, they would remain close to him.

As we have seen, the transformation of Jews into citizens included the transformation of Judaism into a religion. It enabled Jews to become conscious of their Judaism as a matter of faith and worship, to redefine Judaism as their confession, and since they enjoyed religious liberty, to adapt this religion to their personal preferences, or to drop it altogether and adopt new identities as non-believing citizens of modern nation-states. This was secularization, and although not all Jews, at least as they saw it, drifted away from God, this was undoubtedly the disintegration of Judaism as Rabbi Shneur Zalman had known it. From his perspective, his fears were certainly justified, and his projection came true.

5

Meaning

Atheism as an Ethos

> At a certain point on his path the absurd man is tempted. History is not lacking in either religions or prophets, even without gods. He is asked to leap. . . . Hence, what he demands of himself is to live *solely* with what he knows, to accommodate himself to what is, and to bring in nothing that is not certain. . . . The revolt gives life its value. Spread out over the whole length of a life, it restores its majesty to that life. . . . The absurd man thus catches sight of a burning and frigid, transparent and limited universe in which nothing is possible but everything is given, and beyond which all is collapse and nothingness. He can then decide to accept such a universe and draw from it his strength, his refusal to hope, and the unyielding evidence of a life without consolation.[1]

With these words, Albert Camus (1913–1960) described the absurdity of human life, absurdity that is created in the tragic junction between the human need for meaning and the world that is void of it. There is no meaning to life. The most basic human condition involves the recognition of this fact. At a certain point in our lives, Camus tells us, we face a temptation. This temptation, which arrives under the guise of religious and ideological systems, is to make a mental leap into the realm of faith. Faith endows life with meaning; in this, it provides its primary consolation. Faith also endows life with order and justice, its second consolation. Faith promises that the wicked, no matter how happy and successful they appear, will be punished; and that the good, no matter their travails, will be rewarded. Faith also lessens our fear of death: it promises that just as life contains meaning, death is not its ultimate end. In heaven, or in a national hall of fame, life continues after death. This is faith's third consolation.

The absurd man, Camus declares, rebuffs this temptation and the consolation it offers. He pushes himself to live *only* by what he knows. This is his rebellion. And this rebellion, according to Camus, gives life its value. That is to say, life *does* have value, but this value comes not from meaning discovered in the world, nor from any system of faith that frames reality for us, but rather from the repudiation of such systems: in the refusal to succumb to the temptation that they offer, in the rejection of the false comfort they provide, and in the insistence on living only with what one knows. Only with what exists and with what does *not* exist. A meaningful life is carved out of a cold refusal to fill the void with empty verbiage. The rejection of imagined meaning is itself meaningful. It is the very decision to live in a world of "collapse and nothingness" that endows the absurd man with his strength.

Camus summarizes the cycle of existential human development: first, the encounter with the absurd, fully exposed; then comes an escape to false comforts, to deceptive consolations; and finally, a rejection of those and a return to the absurd, this time out of free choice. It is this bold resolution that gives life its meaning.

Camus's proposed successive model—natural truth, inauthenticity out of human weakness, realizing the truth through an awakening— contains echoes of Deism. For the Deists, the natural state of affairs was rational monotheism, whereas for Camus it was the fundamental lack of meaning; for the Deists, the greatest offense was idolatry and established religion, and for Camus it was idolatry and established religion; for the Deists, change comes through the use of reason and courage, and for Camus too, change depends on the use of reason and courage. In both cases, we see a return to the source. In both cases that return bestows dignity upon us; and in both cases, we return to the source by using the essence of our humanity: our capacity for reason and free choice.

The difference between Camus and the Deists is that for the latter, God's existence could be logically deduced through the intelligent use of one's reason, whereas for Camus, reason suggests that there are no grounds for thinking that God might exist. Camus rejects faith in God. He does not deny the possibility that God might exist, but he is unwilling to make the leap of faith that would confirm God's existence for him. Such a leap, in Camus's view, would mean embracing an illusion for the sake of the comfort it offered. Rejecting faith is an act of loyalty to truth and of courage. The rebellious man, Camus writes in *The Rebel*, "defies more than he denies" the existence of God.

Camus's position is not foreign to us. Indeed, it is quite familiar. His thought process is easily recognizable, even if not in the French thinker's dramatic language. For us, the association between atheism and courage seems quite straightforward. The rejection of imaginary consolations is something that we consider a virtue. We are encountering, ultimately, a specific ethos that is not alien to anyone living in the modern West. Camus did not invent it, even if in the twentieth century he gave it one of its most popular articulations.

The first figures to raise the banner of atheism as they stormed into the intellectual battles of the Enlightenment era, such as Baron d'Holbach (1723–1789), whom we shall meet shortly, spoke of the courage and sacrifice that they believed was necessary to deny God's existence. Back in the eighteenth century, these Enlightenment figures were already emphasizing the importance of a critical examination of reality and of loyalty to the facts that such an examination revealed. Among the most militant atheists of the twenty-first century, we find the very same ethos. Richard Dawkins, for example, writes that:

> the atheist view is correspondingly life-affirming and life-enhancing, while at the same time never being tainted with self-delusion, wishful thinking, or the whingeing self-pity of those who feel that life owes them something.[2]

Same idea. While we certainly cannot say that atheism has conquered Western society—most people, even in the West, are not atheists—we can say that atheism is perceived by large sections of Western society as a valid, reasonable, and respectable existential position: we do not regard atheists as madmen or empty-headed hedonists. Atheism is considered legitimate—and this is a historical sea change.

The Historical Fear of Atheism

It is hard to appreciate nowadays the extent to which the denial of God's existence was not only a rare but a terrifying prospect until a few centuries ago. Atheists, for our ancestors, were what pedophiles are for us:

not only repulsive but also profoundly incomprehensible. How could anyone deny God's existence? How could anyone repudiate something so obvious and necessary for the continued functioning of life as we know it? And how could anyone lead a healthy, not to mention upright, life without God? The atheist threatened not only faith in God but also the whole sociocultural framework. The terror that atheists inspired was rooted in fear not simply for the future of religion, but for the basic cornerstones of morality and culture and for the social order itself.

In his book *The Great Cat Massacre*, the American historian Robert Darnton reviews the diary of the inspector Joseph d'Hémery, who recorded his experiences trailing intellectuals in mid-eighteenth century Paris. Darnton reveals that d'Hémery was appalled by atheism and made sure to monitor and imprison suspected atheists. "D'Hémery did not separate impiety from politics. Although he had no interest in theological arguments, he believed that atheism undercut the authority of the crown."[3] He was right. D'Hémery was not a theologian, and he objected to atheism not because it contravened his own faith. Rather, atheism was dangerous because it was socially destabilizing. It denied the existence of the king of kings, and in doing so disputed the authority of the king. It was an affront to the natural view of the world as based on a clear chain of hierarchy.

Police officers, responsible for the maintenance of public order, considered it their duty to thwart atheism. And indeed, atheists, at least those who were brave or foolish enough to come out publicly as such, were jailed, tortured, and executed. This was not a pathology of the Ancien Régime alone. Well into the French Revolution, as the whole fabric of French society disintegrated and a new social order was forged, Robespierre believed that atheism was dangerous and "aristocratic" (the ultimate condemnation in his eyes).[4] Even in the modern world's first and most veteran democracy, the United States of America, atheists were considered dangerous. The Constitution of the State of Tennessee, ratified in 1796, recognized freedom of conscience but nevertheless barred from public office anyone who "denies the being of God or a future state of rewards and punishments."[5] Abraham Lincoln also declared in the nineteenth century that if not for the Bible, "we would not know right from wrong."[6] If not for faith, there be would chaos. Even today, many Americans would consider avowed atheists a danger to the public.

Yet atheism presented an even greater threat. The denial of God's existence called into question the foundations of European civilization, but such heresy was also considered subversive of the rational framework of human thought. God's existence was an essential precondition not only for morality but also for reason. Without God, not only would there be no way to tell right from wrong; there would also be no way of being rational. How could anyone think without the source of all thought? How could one articulate an argument without the force that constituted and preserved the logical order? As we recall, many in the Christian West understood the image of God as the human intellect and capacity for free will. It was therefore obvious that these were received from God. Without God, how could rational thought even be possible?

For Augustine, the fact that we all agree on the laws of mathematics and logic proves that we did not invent them, but rather that they originate beyond our consciousness and therefore in a source higher than us. This was one of Augustine's proofs of God's existence. Different iterations of the same reasoning could be found in the writings of Anselm of Canterbury (1033–1109), the influential theologian who declared that "unless I believed, I should not understand"[7] (since God's existence was a condition for understanding), of Thomas Aquinas, and of Descartes, for whom only God's existence saves us from perpetual uncertainty about what we know, including about supposedly obvious and necessary logical and mathematical truths. This conception of God as underwriting reason is interwoven into the history of the West. For almost all educated individuals in the West until the eighteenth century, the truth of God's existence was simply taken for granted.

Atheism elicited anxiety, therefore, because until around 300 years ago, it was obvious to most heirs of the monotheistic traditions that their capacity for rational thought, and the fact that they were motivated to act not only by desires but also by "higher" moral and spiritual aspirations, pointed to the existence of the divine. The divine was the source of both reason and morality, of the infinite horizons that propelled them forward, and of the transcendent to which they aspired and without which there would be nothing aspire towards.[8]

A world without God seemed to them like a chaotic wilderness in which organized thought was impossible and human beings, like animals, were fated to chase their basest urges and confront each other with malice. It was no coincidence that the first modern philosophers devoted so much attention in their writings to God. Descartes's variety of proofs for God's existence, Spinoza's equivalence between the material world and God, and Leibniz's perfect divine order—none of these were clichés used solely for rhetorical embellishment. Nor was this lip service intended to appease church authorities (as is taught sometimes, incorrectly and anachronistically, at university philosophy departments). For these thinkers, God's existence was not only an obvious fact but also a necessary condition for all understanding. God was the foundation of the whole world order (Spinoza, Leibniz), of the possibility of organized thought (Descartes), or of the very condition for the existence of the world (of mind only) in toto (Berkeley).

Tolerance for All—Except for Atheists

An examination of these philosophers' attitudes to atheism will suffice to demonstrate how appalled they were by the idea. Baruch Spinoza provides a good example, because he had no problems attacking the core religious principles of Judaism and Christianity but nevertheless devoted considerable energies to refuting suspicions that he was an atheist. In 1665, Spinoza briefly stopped writing his *Ethics* and started working on his *Theological-Political Treatise*, in which he would effectively inaugurate biblical criticism and argue that, according to the "natural light" (i.e. reason), the Torah was written by somebody other than Moses, many years after his lifetime.

That year, he wrote to Henry Oldenburg, a member of the Royal Society of London, to explain that he was setting about this new endeavor for different reasons, among these to refute "the opinion which the common people have of me, who do not cease to accuse me falsely of atheism; I am also obliged to avert this accusation as far as it is possible to do so."[9] Spinoza wished to refute accusations that he was an atheist. He had no qualms about being labeled a "heretic." He had already been excommunicated and banished by his Jewish community. He was lonely, poor, and had no fixed abode. It was clear to him and to everyone around him that his thinking about God was very different from that of the monotheistic traditions, and for this reason he was shunned by wider society. The question, therefore, was not whether Spinoza denied the Torah or the tenets of the Christian faith: he plainly did. The question was whether he denied the existence of God. And it was this suspicion, despite everything that he had endured, that Spinoza was eager to dispel.

Similarly, Spinoza wrote to the physician and Protestant preacher Jacob Ostens, a fan of his, that charges of atheism against him were based on "perverse" interpretations of his remarks "whether . . . from malice or from ignorance." Atheists, he continued, "are wont to desire inordinately honours and riches, which I have always despised, as all those who know me are aware."[10] Spinoza was making the case to Ostens that atheists had a corrupted sense of morality and were obsessed with the pursuit of honors and riches. Obviously, he wasn't. Atheism, he implied, was not only a theological position (however problematic or faulty), but also a moral defect. The problem with denying God's existence, for people in this period, was not only heresy against core religious tenets, but the moral degeneracy that it implied.

We encounter the same sentiment in the writings of John Locke. As we recall, in 1689 Locke published his *Letter Concerning Toleration*, in which he called for the toleration of members of other religions. He argued that individuals' basic rights should not be prejudiced on account of their different beliefs and ways of worshiping God, as long as they did not violate the law of the state. But Locke was unwilling to extend the same toleration to all traditions. The boundaries of Lockean toleration stopped at the point of total heresy against God's existence:

> Those are not at all to be tolerated who deny the Being of a God. Promises, Covenants, and Oaths, which are the Bonds of Humane Society, can have no hold upon an Atheist. The taking away of God, tho but even in thought, dissolves all.[11]

For Locke, as for his contemporaries, if God doesn't exist—anything goes. The atheist could not be trusted, because he recognized no source of morality. The atheist would not keep his promises, because without God, there was nothing compelling him to do so. The removal of God, Locke argued, "dissolves all." Atheism was a danger to society. While other religions should be treated with toleration, therefore, there could be no toleration for atheists.[12]

Spinoza and Locke were neither churchmen nor conservative theologians. On the contrary, they were two of the most liberal minds in seventeenth-century Europe. Yet even for them, atheists were beyond the pale. For generation after generation, atheism had inspired terror in the hearts of Europeans.[13] How, therefore, less than 400 years later, have we entered a world in which atheism is seen as legitimate and, in the minds of many in the West, even as the only realistic, rational, and respectable position to take?

The Myth of the Enlightenment

Considering how atheism has been embraced, it would be easy to invoke the well-worn argument about the Scientific Revolution and its discoveries. It would be tempting to explain that after it was understood that the earth revolved around the sun and did not lie in the center of the cosmos, and after humanity obtained evidence that the universe had existed for billions of years and was not five millennia old, and after the Five Books of Moses were discovered to have been composed by multiple authors and not Moses himself (let alone God), and after it was shown that humans had emerged from a process of evolution and were not created in a wink by the divine, there began a pan-European "disenchantment," at the end of which religion was cast aside and Europeans embraced the absence of faith. But this explanation for the emergence of atheism would be a dodge. This story, which is nothing more than the Enlightenment's own myth of divine revelation ("I once was blind, but now I see"), contains some truth, but not all of it, and it cannot fully explain the dissipation of the notion that God was essential for a rational and moral life.

Examining the narrative adopted by the heirs of the Enlightenment, we find that they imagine a process of rational evolution over time: they possess a historical conception of secularization, fundamentally, as a protracted developmental process in which humanity came to its senses. Disbelief in God and acknowledgment of divine non-existence entered the world gradually, as Western cultures became increasingly "rational." According to this story, the Age of Enlightenment effectively marked humanity's adolescence: its escape from the chains of childish myth and legend and its elevation to reason. After Kant called on people to "dare to know" (*sapere aude*) in his famous essay "What Is Enlightenment?"—or so the story went—they rose to his challenge and truly dared to know. They accumulated knowledge, and this knowledge in turn liberated them from "immaturity" (per Kant) and made them secular. The most knowledgeable of all, of course, became atheists.

According to this narrative, secularization was a linear and deterministic process. Exposure to the truth delivers us to liberty, and the greater humanity's exposure to the principles of modernity, the more secular it became. Communities or individuals who do not embrace secularism are willingly closing their eyes to the light. They are motivated, understandably, by a fear of relinquishing the known and confronting a cruel reality. Understandably, but regrettably. Those who embark on this journey and then return to religion are, of course, pitiable would-be secularists who simply lack the courage to stand their ground and refuse the allurement of the warm and inclusive framework of faith, snapping and finding consolation in the convenient lies of tradition. People of faith, in short, according to this narrative, are those who have succumbed to the temptations that Camus had described above.

It takes considerable naïveté to believe this narrative. The notion that knowledge is what invalidates faith is superficial even according to the assumptions of those who make it, because they would be the first to acknowledge that human beings are capable of believing in all sorts of nonsense, whatever they know or do not know. If new information were sufficient to disrupt long-held beliefs, we would be changing our views constantly, be they religious, political, aesthetic, etc. It would similarly be futile to assume that only confirmed and authoritative information changes our positions about the world, because such knowledge has already been offered to humanity on many occasions. Aristotelianism, Kabbalah, and Buddhism presented "official" knowledge about the world, but needless to say, not everyone who was introduced to them was convinced to adopt them. We require something else to revise our established assumptions about reality: a good reason to relinquish our former premises and adopt new ones. And this reason cannot be based on those new premises themselves.

I am referring not to the pragmatic level, where it is clear that the scientific method, built over previous centuries in Europe, has been successful not only in explaining a whole range of phenomena but also in providing the foundations for technology that has made truly revolutionary changes to our lives. This is certainly true. But this has no bearing on the level of principles. Even if we were to successfully convince a citizen of Athens in the second century BCE that lightning bolts are created by static electricity and are not hurled down to earth by Zeus, our Athenian would not stop believing that Zeus existed (and was frequently irate). It is true that certain scientific findings indeed dispute various religious beliefs, yet even nowadays it is not rare to find believers—Jews, Christians, Muslims, Hindus, and so forth—who would not deny scientific achievements but would still express fervent and complete religious faith. One could also always become a Deist, rejecting the possibility of wonders and miracles while maintaining that faith in God remains entirely logical.

The Scientific Revolution certainly contributed to the process of secularization, but the refutation of certain religious beliefs by means of scientific discoveries constituted only a minor part of this contribution. Much more significant was the destruction of religion's monopoly over knowledge, followed by the creation of a whole field of non-religious knowledge: a domain about which religion had nothing to say. The first scientists were all religious believers, but the scientific method—a method of observation, experimentation, and logical causality—allowed them to create a world that operated independently of traditional frameworks. From the seventeenth century onward, the phrase "Book of Nature" came to mean not only that just as God had given us the holy scriptures, he had also given us the natural world, which could likewise be read. It meant that "reading" nature was an alternative way to redemption, one that at first was still religious, but in time, with scientific visions of perfecting humanity, secular. "Reading" the book of nature also meant learning a new language, the language of the scientific method, a language that was alien to scholars of the holy scriptures and offered a different way of understanding reality. An independent field of thought was thus created, one that would make the religious establishment's stamp of epistemological validation redundant.

The separation of knowledge from religious tradition was the greatest achievement of the Scientific Revolution, and this achievement indeed contributed to secularization. Yet by itself it was insufficient. Change would require the independence of another field. In addition to knowledge, *ethics* would also need to be extricated from religious control. It was the development of an ethics independent of religious tradition that underpinned the transition away from the seventeenth-century world in which the notion of God's non-existence elicited horror and toward the twentieth- and twenty-first-century world in which faith in God's existence is frequently belittled and denigrated.

In what follows, we shall explore this process.

The Scientific Revolution, the Fall, and the Image

The foundations of the Enlightenment lie in the rejection of the authority of tradition and the empowerment of humankind as the supreme authority over every matter. Even before Western individuals turned to other systems of meaning (such as science), their previously natural sense of piety and obedience to tradition was undermined significantly by the Reformation. As noted earlier, while Augustine wrote at the end of the fourth century that "I should not believe the gospel except as moved by the authority of the Catholic Church,"[14] by the start of the sixteenth century, Martin Luther was already in a position to insist that faith in the Gospel (the New Testament) was valid not because of the authority of the Church, but rather only out of fidelity to one's own personal interpretation of scripture. The emphasis on an individual duty to read and understand God's word alone was revolutionary, inasmuch as it repudiated many generations' natural acceptance of ecclesiastical authority. The individual was empowered and given a direct, unmediated line of communication to God—that is, to the good and the true. Luther launched the journey through which modern, autonomous, and independent individualism would receive its contours and validity.

Luther's call for personal interpretations of scripture laid the logical base for the Scientific Revolution. As Menachem Fisch notes, reading scripture without prior assumptions, adopting skepticism about prior metaphysical theories and with one's own understanding empowered might suggest to some that nature can be read the same way. The inductive, not deductive, method received legitimacy from this approach.[15] Thus the Protestant revolution branched into the scientific revolution by the creation of a separation between knowledge and religion. Such a separation, however, inescapably demands the empowerment of humans and their facilities of knowing (not their conscience, as for Luther), thus liberating them from dependence on the presumptive authority of tradition also in the field of reason. The first step there begins in the twelfth century, when the ideal of *imitatio dei* acquired a new meaning: not becoming loving or merciful, but becoming knowledgeable.

As Peter Harrison writes, since early in the history of the Church, patristic writers held that the first man, Adam, had incredible intellectual capabilities.[16] He would either know all there is to know about nature intuitively, or his faculty of reason was such that such knowledge came to him with ease. The Fall changed that, and left humanity wandering blind. Or almost blind, as humans were still endowed with the image of God. A distorted image, perhaps, due to original sin, but a source of efficacy yet. Church Fathers and eminent theologians from the first centuries like Origen, Irenaeus, Tertullian, Athanasius, and Augustine agreed that the Fall damaged the once sublime image of God, but none thought that it was completely erased. Since human minds were designed originally to know the truth, the question was not whether knowledge was possible, but how hard its attainment would be. In other words, how far have we fallen?

For many, certainly for Luther and Calvin, the Fall had irrevocably warped God's image, and thus destroyed the credibility of reason. Faith and grace alone could save us. But others thought there might still be hope. Thinkers such as Descartes held the view that God's image enabled every human to attain, in Descartes's words, "perfect knowledge," and that through the operations of mind alone, comprehending the truth by logic and deduction. Others, raised in Calvinist climates, were weary of relying only on reason, though they would not give up on it entirely, either. These, like Francis Bacon (1561–1626) and Robert Boyle (1627–1691), would develop an experimental approach, and held that knowledge was accumulated gradually, would never be absolutely certain, but could still offer great improvements to humanity.[17]

This was particularly so in England, where Calvinism was joined by Puritan millenarism, which inspired revolutions not only in politics but also in science.[18] As Harrison shows, most major works in the experimental cultivation of knowledge developed there because of a spirit of dissent and inquisitiveness, on one hand, and a deep-seated Calvinist suspicion in unaided reason on the other. Descartes's confidence in the "natural light" of reason providing "clear and distinct ideas" was thus, ironically, not conducive to knowledge. Empiricism was a more reliable way to read the book of nature.

And yet without any confidence in humanity's ability to understand nature, nothing could be gained. Blaise Pascal (1623–1662) held that the ancients could not fully know the world because they were either too vain, having not learned of the Fall, or too sunk in despair, knowing not of the image of God in us all.[19] Even before him Philipp Melanchthon (1497–1560), Luther's colleague in the university of Wittenberg and a central figure in the Reformation, wrote about "traces of the divine image on it [i.e., the human soul], and the remains of the heavenly gifts," which for him explained humanity's mathematical abilities.[20] Johannes Kepler (1571–1630) thought the same, and held that only "the correspondences between the persisting divine image in the mind, and the triune images of the creator in the cosmos thus made possible an a priori knowledge of the mathematical ordering of the cosmos."[21]

The image of God gave humanity the capacity to know the natural world. Indeed, for some thinkers in the late Middle Ages, the image of God was not only the precondition for knowledge, but also its beneficiary. The damage done by the Fall could actually be rectified by the accumulation of true knowledge, the stain on our soul removed by the cleansing light of truth—natural truth, that is. This was to be accomplished by the informed reading of the Book of Nature.

Reading the Book of Nature, Not Contemplating It

Perceiving nature as a "book" written by God was nothing new. Gregory of Nyssa, Augustine, and John Chrysostom all referred to the physical world as God's writing, to be "read" by us.[22] For them, however, the natural world was an object worthy of contemplative awareness, a source of divine inspiration, not knowledge. That changed beginning in the twelfth century, in two dramatic ways. First, "reading" nature was to become acquiring knowledge of the world; second, the act of accumulating knowledge would be redemptive.

For theologians like Hugh of St. Victor (~1096–1141) or Honorius Augustodunensis (1080–1151), humans not only had the potential to discover truth by examining creation, but that very act of discovery had salvific significance. If the Fall diminished humanity's capacity for reason, supporting reason and uplifting it would reverse the damage done. According to that logic, the results would be redemptive. Just as Christ came to rectify the image of God by faith, gaining knowledge of nature's secrets would work as a means of restoring the divine likeness.[23]

As we have seen, for Paul the restoration of the original likeness involved contemplation of God and inner transformation. When he instructs Christians to behold, "with unveiled face" the "glory of the Lord," he promises being "transformed into the same image," i.e., the image of God (2 Corinthians 3:17–18). This charge was taken to heart through more than a millennium of Christian existence. We noted Bernard McGinn's observation that "The linking of contemplation and the perfecting of the image of God made this passage one of the most important in the history of Christian mysticism."[24] In the twelfth century these same words were infused with new meaning. Our "unveiled face" became a clear mind capable of examining the world, and the promise of a renewal of the image came not from contemplation but from the acquisition of knowledge.

> This would take place in two ways: first, by knowing the world, the human mind would restore things to the original unity which they had possessed in the divine mind; second, by controlling and subduing the world, human beings would be restored to their original position as God's viceroy on earth, and harmony would be restored between those creatures within their constituency. The restoration of a lost likeness to God was thus to take place through imitation of God: of his power, by manipulating the world; of his wisdom, through coming to know it. To know God, to become like God, to possess the knowledge of the mind of God, these were synonyms for the process of redemption. Redemption, in short, did not entail as it did for Augustine, flight from the material world, a mastery of the beasts within, and a mystical absorption into divine reality, but rather an ordered knowledge of the natural world.[25]

Knowledge of God was still crucial for redemption, but gaining that knowledge did not entail a withdrawal from the world, but an engagement with it; not a rejection of material reality, but its examination and control. If for Augustine, as for multiple Christian mystics through the ages, the path to redemption called for an inward turn, away from the temporary and fallen world and into the eternal and perfect reality of the spirit, for Christian thinkers beginning in the twelfth century redemption could be gained by venturing out, by examination of that same temporary and fallen world, by gaining knowledge of it, and moreover by controlling it. That would indeed imitate divine knowledge and power, be a form of *imitatio Dei*, and a restoration of the divine image that was tarnished in the Fall.

This line of thought would be taken in earnest in the late sixteenth and into the seventeenth century by figures such as Bacon, Boyle, and other "natural philosophers." For Bacon, reading the book of nature was critical for understanding God. For Boyle, natural philosophy was "a reasonable worship of God."[26] These were expressions of a common sentiment among pioneering scientists. The Royal Society (named in full The Royal Society of London for Improving Natural Knowledge), the oldest continuously operating scientific academy in the world, was founded in November 1660 by a royal charter from king Charles II, just half a year after the restoration. One of its prominent members, Robert Hooke, declared in his *Micrographia*, published in 1665 as the first major publication of the Royal Society, that

> [A]s at first, mankind fell by tasting of the forbidden Tree of Knowledge, so we, their Posterity, may be in part restor'd by the same way, not only by beholding and contemplating, but by tasting too those fruits of Natural Knowledge, that were never yet forbidden.[27]

Not by "beholding and contemplating" will we be restored, but by natural knowledge. "This new, *ergetic* ideal of knowing stood squarely against the old, *contemplative* ideal"[28]—and it was a knowing of a new sort. Working in the wake of the Protestant Reformation, not to mention the English Revolution, these thinkers were all influenced by the severe crisis of authority that shook the world they lived in. Unlike their twelfth-century predecessors, they had much more freedom—both psychologically and politically—to depart from the Aristotelian and scholastic worldview, as well as from the comprehension of the natural world as a veritable jigsaw puzzle of correspondences and symbolic references. Empowered by their understanding of reason as the image of God, with humanity's potency (in line with Renaissance humanism) and place in creation, but with the added temperance of Calvinist pessimism, they would embark on a journey of discovery that used empirical knowledge and induction to paint a new picture of the world. As Amos Funkenstein put it, "The world turned into God's temple, and the layman into its priests."[29]

An Alternative Path to Knowledge

An alternative way of gaining knowledge had developed, one that was not only out of the Church's control but that replaced traditional faith as a central ethos and as a path to redemption. In short order, it challenged church and faith directly. As the scientific method developed there was no evading the discrepancies between it, its findings, and church dogmatics. Allowing the existence of miracles, for example, was in direct contradiction to an understanding of nature as a unified field adhering to consistent and unbroken laws. The tension was real, and presented a challenge of authority: to whom was it prudent to adhere, nature or scripture? The crux of the conflict between Galileo and the Church was not whether the sun revolved around the earth or vice versa, but whether Galileo's telescope and mathematical equations could supersede the pope's authority. We have already seen how Locke positioned reason above revelation in his discussion of religion. He was joined by other thinkers in the seventeenth century, who took the book of nature, studied rationally, as a religious authority superior to that of particular revelations.

This was the road to Deism. Indeed Edward, Lord Herbert of Cherbury, proclaimed that from reason and nature alone a religion could be derived that was both universal and sufficient.[30] The universal religion, discovered simply, demanded the beliefs, or rather the rational comprehensions, of God as good, of his wish that we too be good, and of future rewards and punishments. Out went revelation, miracles, spirituality, sacred things and times, ritual and the church. From humanity's imitation of God by venturing out to discover the world rationally, we have come to God's imitation of rational humans. From an alternative path to religious redemption we have come to an alternative redemption, sans religion.

By the seventeenth century the study of nature, while still a religious duty, was already treating it not as a speculum of symbols pregnant with divine meaning, but as a dynamic material continuum adhering to laws—the understanding of which will allow humans to control and manipulate it for their own purposes. God's infinite wisdom could still be inferred through a thorough examination of the world, but that God was now the Deistic passive and rational infinite, not the biblical loving and angry king whose mighty hand smote sinners. "Theological concerns were expressed in terms of secular knowledge," writes Funkenstein.[31] The allegorical reading of the natural world was dead, and a utilitarian attitude replaced it. Leading it were men for whom the divine image stood for detached reason and control, not for a microcosm reflecting and complementing the macrocosm.

With the secularization of the scientific endeavor, witnessed already at the beginning of the eighteenth century (as we shall see with the works of Baron d'Holbach below), "No longer was salvation considered to be a process in which the divine image in mankind was restored. Instead, the impulse to restore the divine likeness within was redirected outwards into the natural world, and scientific activity became an increasingly material means of obtaining secular salvation."[32] The deep significance of the scientific revolution was thus in offering an alternative path to (secular) redemption, which demanded an alternative way of thinking, and which finally called for adhering to an alternative authority.

Lastly, nature was stripped not only of symbolic meaning, but also of moral meaning. David Hume (1711–1776) would present a persuasive case for the separation of values and facts, arguing that factual claims could not provide imperatives from moral actions. He simply articulated an understanding that followed the treatment of the natural world as a realm of laws and forces, not goals and wills. As the last remnants of Aristotelean thought were uprooted from European thought, a new source of morality had to be formed, to replace both scripture and nature. That source would be the human self.

Secularization Demands More than Knowledge

By the end of the seventeenth century, the famed Deist thinker John Toland (1670–1722) could already declare that "there is nothing in the

Gospel contrary to reason, nor above it."[33] Toland, who shared certain ideas and conceptions with Locke (they both read each other's works), drew a full equivalence between divine revelation and reason. God reveals to us that which is rational, and that which is irrational is *a priori* not divine revelation (even if it happens to appear in the Bible). Toland's position effectively gave reason supreme authority on matters of religion and dismissed the realistic value of biblical narratives about miracles and such dogmatic principles as the existence of the Holy Trinity or the Virgin Birth. Moreover, it also made divine revelation redundant, inasmuch as anyone could use their reason to discover the fundamental truths of all world religions. The Church, or organized religion more widely, no longer had any role to play.[34]

Three important Christian thinkers discussed here—Augustine, Luther, and Toland—took God's existence as an obvious and established fact, and none of them could have imagined being an atheist. But each of them built his religious world out of fidelity to a different source of authority. For Augustine, tradition not only gave form and content to faith; it also gave it its validity. We discover within ourselves the most basic truths of the Gospel, but the Church's chain of transmission and its insistence that it was the sole legitimate heir of the testaments of Jesus's earliest disciples guaranteed the truthfulness of its interpretation of this Gospel. Martin Luther, who argued that faith alone (*sola fide*) was the key to salvation, believed that one must be loyal to one's own conscience's interpretation of scripture. For Luther, our own conscience was a higher source of authority than the authorized interpreters of tradition; and therefore conscience, in interpreting scripture, could dismiss the Church's interpretations of scripture. Nevertheless, Luther did not dispute the sanctity and authority of the Bible. The individual was free to interpret it alone, but they would interpret *it*, and not any other text or entity. For Toland, not only were commentators on tradition irrelevant; tradition itself was irrelevant. The Bible was irrelevant. Religion was dictated solely by reason, understood to be innate and universal. One did not need to believe or read scripture; one needed only to think in an orderly fashion. The Church's pronouncements about various articles of belief had no *a priori* validity. The Church itself was redundant.

The preference for reason came before the loss of faith. Deism, which swept educated elites in Europe and North America in the eighteenth century, disavowed tradition and ecclesiastical authority but not faith in God. "I believe! I believe in you! Powerful God, I believe!" cried Voltaire, champion of the French Enlightenment, before making sure to add: "As for monsieur the Son, and madame His Mother, that's a different story."[35] Once reason was a source of authority, one could dispute tradition, and only after reason was established as a source of authority could God's existence be called into question. Yet even this, it is important to understand, was not a "natural" process, purportedly just another obvious step on the path trodden by all those faithful to reason. As we have seen, for the Deists, reason *demonstrated* God's existence. "It is perfectly evident to my mind that there exists a necessary, eternal, supreme and intelligent being," wrote Voltaire. "This is no matter of faith, but of reason."[36] In order to move from certainty in God's existence to a denial of it, there needed to be another maneuver, in which reason was used *against* God: against what was considered, not long earlier, the source of reason itself and the very condition for its existence.

This development is hinted at in the language used by Camus (and Dawkins). Camus's glorification of atheism does not describe a straightforward process of learning, as if believers in God came across new facts that shed light on reality and caused them to jettison religious faith. As we have seen, Camus glorified atheism as an *ethical* position. The atheist was brave and clung to the truth even though it was uncomfortable and unpopular. It was this conception of atheism as an ethos, as a moral calling, that underpinned the deep process of secularization that coalesced in Western culture over the past few centuries. Secularization is not limited to a lack of faith in God, but included, first and foremost as we saw, the diminishing power and authority of institutionalized religion. We shall, however, examine the process that led to atheism, in order to gain a better understanding of secularization in its entirety.

Descartes and the Idea of the Perfect Being

We shall point to a crucial moment: the shift from faith in God as a precondition for reason, toward the notion that reason *discounts* faith in God. Focusing on that moment, we will examine the writings of three philosophers: René Descartes, Matthew Tindal, and Baron Paul-Henri Thiry d'Holbach. These philosophers enjoy no particular status, besides the fact that they clearly reflected the thinking among progressive intellectual elites in their times. It bears emphasizing again: the ideas that they articulated did not shape European discourse and thereby influence modern culture: no person alone can shape a whole civilization. These ideas were *born out of* European discourse, and the fact that they influenced modern culture is merely evidence that the societies surrounding these philosophers were *ready* to adopt these new ethical paradigms and directions of thought—and perhaps even *needed to* adopt them. Descartes, Tindal, and d'Holbach won their fame not only because they were supremely talented (although of course they were), but because each in his writings articulated an intellectual and ethical system that European society was ripe to accept.

René Descartes (1596–1650), considered the first philosopher of the modern era, in addition to being a brilliant mathematician and an important scholar of optics, devised a comprehensive system to explain the functioning of the universe. Nowadays, Descartes is known primarily for his method of skepticism, with which he cast doubt on everything he knew until he could reconstruct the world based on his knowledge of God's existence and benevolence. Indeed, God's existence, and its reflection in the human consciousness, was the axis around which he built his entire intellectual world.

For Descartes, reason was the image of God: it was God-given, and God, therefore, was a prior condition for any rational thought. One of Descartes's proofs for God's existence (in his *Meditations on First Philosophy*, published in Amsterdam in 1641) was the existence of the idea of "supremely perfect being," i.e., the divine, in the human mind. This idea originated, of course, with God himself:

> And certainly it is no wonder if God, when he created me, inscribed this idea within me, to serve, so to speak, as the mark by which the craftsman makes himself known in his handiwork. This mark does not have to be something distinct from the object itself. But, given this one basic fact that God created me, it is highly credible that I was in some way created in his image and likeness, and that the likeness, in which the idea of God is contained, is perceived by me by the same faculty by which I myself am perceived by myself. . . . I recognize that it cannot be that I should exist, with the nature I possess (that is, having the idea of

God within myself), unless in reality God also exists—the same God whose idea is within me.[37]

God created us in his own image and likeness ("in some way," since the similarity was obviously imperfect), and we are all, for Descartes, first and foremost thinking beings. For Descartes, the image of God found expression through reason. Humankind's similarity to God, that is, God's image, was also revealed by reason, which reflected on itself precisely as it discovered the mental idea of the perfect being, namely God, by itself.[38] This idea, like an artist's seal on his own work, pointed definitively to God's existence. If God did not exist, then this idea could not exist in the human mind. Besides, if God did not exist, then humans could not be thinking beings. Descartes created a self-reinforcing closed loop: God created humans in his image, namely reason, and reason reveals from within itself the idea of infinity, understood as God's signature, which pointed to God's existence, the same existence that rendered rational introspection possible in the first place.

It is this capacity for rational meditation that allows us to exercise control over nature. Discussing the Scientific Revolution, we mentioned above how Descartes's optimistic perception of reason led him to construct his entire edifice for studying reality on its base.[39] No less importantly, reason enables us to control ourselves: "The true function of reason, then, in the conduct of life is to examine and consider without passion the value of all perfections of body and soul that can be acquired by our conduct."[40] Reason is the means through which humans may dispassionately and unemotionally examine their conduct, making it an excellent tool. We look at ourselves coolly and calmly, and we make rational decisions about how best to act. Out of this notion, an ethos emerged in the nineteenth century that maintained that the rational examination of one's own conduct is a condition for the maintenance of self-esteem and dignity.[41]

Tindal and the Dignity of the Image of God

Writing nearly a century after Descartes, Matthew Tindal (1657–1733) looked at human reason and self-esteem from a different perspective. Tindal, an English Deist, was one of the eighteenth century's most influential philosophers. His most important work, *Christianity as Old as the Creation* (London, 1730), in which he explored the principles of the "natural religion" and explained how "true" Christianity was a framework of pure reason, practically became Deist holy scripture. The book presented the fundamental tenets of the Deist faith: natural religion was universal and rational, and therefore it was as old as humanity itself, because any individual could deduce it by exercising their powers of reason alone.

It followed that the natural religion did not depend on any form of religious revelation, whether at Mount Sinai or in Jerusalem. Its principles were entirely logical and included the existence of the benevolent Creator, who wants our well-being and happiness and who gives us no commands besides the rational laws of morality, which center on the promotion of our happiness and the happiness of others. Miracles, visions, divine revelations, bodies of water split into two, and pregnant virgins—anything, in short, beyond the natural order—were fantasies or forgeries that contravened the true religion. Reason was the metric for everything. As the English churchman John Standish complained in a sermon before the king in 1675, there were those who "would supplant Christian Religion with Natural Theologie; and turn the Grace of God into a wanton Notion of Morality." They "impiously deny both the Lord . . . and his Holy Spirit . . . making Reason, Reason, Reason, their only Trinity."[42] And, we might add, creating God in the image of reason, or reasonable man.

Like other Deists, according to Tindal, the role of (Deist) Christianity, as the perfect rational religion, was to liberate humanity from superstitions: from all other religions, including traditional Christian beliefs about miracles and other irrationalities. This was the end to which he and others, like John Toland, whom we met earlier, wrote their works, explaining clearly how reason revealed to humanity everything that there was to know about God, humans, and the world.

Tindal's book sparked an extensive debate in Europe, and over one hundred essays were written in an attempt to refute his conclusions. Needless to say, the Church, which of course Tindal considered a model for corruption of "true religion," denounced him. But for all his resistance to the monotheistic tradition, Tindal did not relinquish several of the core tenets that it handed down, chiefly the principle of the image of God. According to Tindal,

Hence we may contemplate the great Dignity of our *Rational* Nature, since our Reason for Kind, tho' not for Degree, is of the same Nature with That of God's; nay, 'tis our Reason which makes us the Image of God himself, and is the common Bond which unites Heaven and Earth.[43]

The image of God was our capacity for reason. It was reason that allowed for connection between humans and God, because it was reason (and not scripture, prophets, or authorized interpreters of tradition) that elucidated God's will. Even the ignorant and illiterate, "if they have but Courage and Honesty to make use of their Reason,"[44] could discover God's Gospel by themselves, without any need for tradition or the Church, because they too possessed the same universal and rational image of God.

It is worth noting what exactly Tindal was doing: in a dramatic sleight, he transformed the image of God from an important element in the religious tradition to a tool that *bypassed* the religious tradition. According to Tindal, it was precisely because God created us in his image that we can understand him by ourselves and therefore have no need of the traditions that purport to speak in his name.

Tindal introduced another important development: he argued that since our "rational Nature" is divine in origin, it endows us with a special dignity. As a positive value, dignity played an important role in Tindal's thought, and it bears noting its appearance as an ideal in the battles over the Enlightenment and secularism that still lay ahead. According to Tindal, our reason *is* our dignity, both because it is the point of resemblance between us and God and because it is the channel through which we can independently establish a relationship with God:

> If you allow, that Men by their reasoning Faculties are made like unto God, and fram'd after His Image, and that Reason is the most excellent Gift God can bestow; do they not destroy this Likeness, deface this Image, and give up the Dignity of human Nature, when they give up their Reason to any Person whatever? . . . Indeed, a blind Submission is so far from doing Credit to True Religion.[45]

Submission to any external authority, person, or tradition is a violation of our dignity and an affront to the true religion. Our image of God instructs us to use our reason as the ultimate authority on every matter. Any other avenue would be sacrilege. Once again, we see the same dramatic shift: it turns out that fidelity to the true, natural religion compels us to reject the authority of traditional religion. The image of God not only enables us to do so; it actively demands this of us, if not for the sake of the truth, then at least for the sake of the dignity of our image, the dignity of our human nature, and the dignity of God.

Tindal further developed the Cartesian conception and took it in a different direction. For Descartes, reason—the image of God—both teaches us about God's existence and enables us to examine ourselves and choose good over evil. Human dignity is preserved when we act appropriately, as rational, civilized individuals. Tindal agreed that reason was the image of God, but in order to maintain this dignity, it is not enough to behave appropriately; one must also defend reason itself, by rejecting anything that contravenes it. Tindal's proposed ethos stated that one's dignity is preserved when one thinks and acts exclusively according to reason. Reason, for Tindal, became not only the supreme but also the exclusive authority, and the preservation of reason's autonomy and independent capacity for choice became an ideal. In his writings, Tindal repeatedly emphasized that "external Revelation" was unnecessary for knowledge of the true religion. We need only examine matters with the aid of reason. And conversely: without rational inquiry, reliance on divine revelation will lead to faith in all sorts of nonsense and the debasement of the image of God inside us:

> Without this precedent Enquiry, our Belief would become unlawful; for to obviate the Rules of Conduct, prescrib'd to our Understanding, were to overthrow all the Laws of Nature, to debase the Dignity of Mankind, and to efface the Image of God implanted in us.[46]

For Tindal, the "true religion" was the rational approach to the world, to ourselves, and to each other. Anything else, any irrational belief (in miracles, revelations, etc.) or contingent faith (in a particular tradition or event), had nothing to do with authentic divine worship, and moreover, debases us. Tindal argued that God wants nothing more from us than our happiness and that he endowed us with all we need to be happy, specifically the use of our reason.[47] By means of our reason, we can deduce the sum of our duties toward God, toward ourselves, and toward humanity. "True religion" involved nothing beyond this.

Tindal reduced religion to reason alone. God, belief in whose existence was to his mind entirely logical, remained a distant source of light, a shining star on the horizon, who had illuminated our minds and had given us reason but had since receded into complete passivity, leaving us—and our reason—to fend for ourselves.

D'Holbach and the Human Machine

Tindal, who died in 1733, believed that reason points unequivocally to God's existence and also protects our dignity when we allow it to reject false beliefs. The next stage in our journey begins with the rejection of belief in God, as false, and indeed as an affront to reason and therefore also to human dignity. A clear articulation of this position can be found in the writings of Baron Paul-Henri Thiry D'Holbach (1723–1789).

D'Holbach, one of the preeminent figures of the French Enlightenment, dedicated his life to the fight against religious faith and for the dissemination of atheist thought. He funded the translation of enlightenment literature, wrote over fifty volumes (most of which were published anonymously), supported young artists and philosophers (among them Rousseau), and hosted a regular salon for the Parisian intellectual elite at his home from 1750 until his death, which became one of the most important social institutions of Enlightenment France.

D'Holbach was known among the Enlightenment thinkers of his time as an atheist. Among French Enlightenment circles in the latter half of the eighteenth century, "atheist" was not necessarily a derogatory term, but atheist beliefs could still not be voiced in public, and even the intellectual salons of Paris exercised self-censorship, out of both caution and good manners (the custom of being considerate of religious sensitivities is nothing new).[48] D'Holbach's intellectual salon was in fact extraordinary in its audacity and defiance against the social conventions of the day.

D'Holbach's magnum opus, Système de la Nature, was published in 1770 in Amsterdam under the name of Jean-Baptiste de Mirabaud, the perpetual secretary of the Académie Française. It included, besides a broad assault against religion, also a comprehensive defense of atheism.

Writing under Mirabaud's name was the surest way for d'Holbach to ensure that nobody got hurt, because he could not be personally identified as promoting atheism, and Mirabaud had died ten years earlier. The book, which as expected aroused the ire of the religious authorities, became one of the most popular texts of the Enlightenment and, in an unprecedented manner, reached a diverse array of social classes in western Europe, including, if Voltaire's reports may be trusted, not only the scholars but also women and artisans.[49] As a Deist, Voltaire despised d'Holbach's book and believed that his atheist agenda was dangerous. To his mind, d'Holbach's book pushed European thought over the brink and gave Enlightenment thinkers a bad name. In a letter in 1770 to the Marquis de Condorcet (1743–1794), another prominent French Enlightenment thinker, Voltaire warned that the ideas presented in d'Holbach's book would lead to a "great revolution."[50]

The French Revolution, which erupted nineteen years later, can evidently *not* be attributed to the publication of this book, but d'Holbach's work made a significant contribution to another revolution: a philosophical and ethical one. D'Holbach used his book to promote quintessentially materialistic positions: it stated that humans are but natural machines operating in a deterministic fashion, that there is no God, that free will is an illusion, and of course that there is no such thing as an eternal soul. The universe is nothing but a material field of laws and forces, and humanity is simply another natural phenomenon.

A young Goethe read d'Holbach's book soon after its publication and believed that with his "dreary, atheistic half-night," he was obscuring "the earth with all its formations, heaven with all its stars."[51] But according to d'Holbach's Epicurean philosophy, the positions expressed in his book were not supposed to depress anyone, because knowledge of the truth will enable us to reconcile ourselves with our condition, stop fearing death, and be happy. D'Holbach certainly presented his materialistic atheism as a path toward knowledge of the truth, but in order to know the truth, one must first disavow illusions. This requires courage:

> If man possessed the courage, if he had the requisite industry to recur to the source of those opinions which are most deeply engraven on his brain; if he rendered to himself a faithful account of the reasons which make him hold these opinions as sacred; if he coolly examined the ba-

sis of his hopes, the foundation of his fears, he would find that it very frequently happens, those objects, or those ideas which move him most powerfully, either have no real existence, or are words devoid of meaning, which terror has conjured up to explain some sudden disaster; that they are often phantoms engendered by a disordered imagination, modified by ignorance; the effect of an ardent mind distracted by contending passions, which prevent him from either reasoning justly, or consulting experience in his judgment; that this mind often labours with a precipitancy that throws his intellectual faculties into confusion; that bewilders his ideas; that consequently he gives a substance and a form to chimeras, to airy nothings, which he afterwards idolizes from sloth, reverences from prejudice.[52]

The baron's picture of the state of humanity is quite depressing: our hearts pursue fantasies, jealously hold onto illusions, are animated by fear, and are enslaved to ignorance. Religion, according to Baron d'Holbach, is the devil. It is "chimeras and airy nothings," which out of laziness, anxiety, and distraction devolve into idolatry. This, in turn, becomes entrenched as part of our lives; it was already part of our ancestors' lives, and it will continue to be part of our children's lives. And it paralyzes us, unless we cut off this cursed chain and put an end to it all. This can be done, of course, by means of courage, inner might, and cold reason.

Significantly, D'Holbach was presenting not only a historical analysis, but also a moral calling. Humanity's condition was miserable, he explained, but if only we mustered the courage, if only we examined reality as it was—we could then lift ourselves out of this predicament. D'Holbach's ethos was rich and enticing: courage, inner strength, cool and rational examinations—these were the virtues that were required to be liberated from the illusions of religion. And why do we cling on to these illusions? The answer is obvious: fear, confusion, ignorance.

"Materialism as it appears in the eighteenth century, as it is justified and defended, is no mere scientific or metaphysical dogma; it is rather an imperative," wrote Ernst Cassirer aptly.[53] This is evident in d'Holbach's case. We find in his writings the Cartesian call to examine reality objectively and rationally, alongside Tindal's injunction to preserve human dignity. D'Holbach amplified these arguments and added a demand for courage and strength. He repeatedly underscored the need for resolution in order to cast off the yoke of religion. Atheism, he argued, was based on nature and reason, no more and no less.[54] It is logical. One must look straight at the facts. But this simple condition is all that is needed to prevent most people from becoming atheists, because they lack the courage to do so. They can't handle the truth. Even the most educated, d'Holbach wrote, betray signs of a hesitancy and reluctance to face up to reality. Indeed, d'Holbach went out of his way to mock Deists. As far as he was concerned, they were only going halfway, failing to take the use of reason for the examination of religion to its logical conclusions:

> The principles of atheism are not formed for the mass of the people, who are commonly under the tutelage of their priests; they are not calculated for those frivolous capacities, not suited to those dissipated minds, who fill society with their vices. . . .
>
> Much less are they made for a great number of persons, who, enlightened in other respects, have not sufficient courage to divorce themselves from the received prejudices. So many causes unite themselves to confirm man in those errors which he draws in with his mother's milk, that every step that removes him from these endeared fallacies, costs him uncommon pain. Those persons who are most enlightened, frequently cling on some side to the general prepossession. By giving up these revered ideas, we feel ourselves, as it were, isolated in society. . . .
>
> We are apt to fancy ourselves placed on a barren, desert island, in sight of a populous, fruitful country, which we can never reach: it therefore requires great courage to adopt a mode of thinking that has but few approvers. In those countries where human knowledge has made some progress; where, besides, a certain freedom of thinking is enjoyed, may easily be found a great number of deicolists, theists, or incredulous beings, who, contented with having trampled under foot the grosser prejudices of the illiterate, have not dared to go back to the source—to cite the more subtle systems before the tribunal of reason.[55]

D'Holbach had no doubts that the masses could not be made into atheists. They are a flock willingly under the watch of their shepherds. Nor was atheism intended for the mentally challenged, or for hedonists, known only for their wanton licentiousness. The reason was that adopting atheism demanded not only knowledge but also courage. Atheism was unsuitable for the weak of mind and frail of heart. But alas, even the wisest and best educated, d'Holbach discovered, were mostly incapable of admitting atheism's truths. Even "the most enlightened" still clung to their superstitions, the disavowal of which would cause them pain. For this reason, one might encounter Deists and theists who take pride in having jettisoned superstitions and express satisfaction in their achievements, but nevertheless, in d'Holbach's argument, have not abandoned the ultimate superstition, the source of all superstitions: faith in God's existence.

D'Holbach was aiming his remarks at Tindal and his ilk. In fact, he was using Tindal's ethos against him. D'Holbach also wished to exalt reason and preserve its dignity (and thus to preserve our dignity as human beings) by rejecting anything that contravened it, but he believed that not only faith in miracles or the Holy Trinity was contrary to reason; so was faith in God. D'Holbach was therefore calling for the repudiation of faith in God's existence. For him, this was the next logical step, and whoever failed to take it was clearly lacking the same "courage and honesty" that Tindal himself spoke of in the context of the ignorant souls who clung on to their belief in miracles.

Another Step on the Path

Witness, therefore, the three-staged process that we have watched unfolding. Reason, which for Descartes was the means of discovering truth, of proving God's existence, and thus of proving the existence of reality; reason, which for Tindal was the means of understanding religious truth beyond tradition, without the illogical excesses of custom; reason, this same reason, now became for d'Holbach the tool with which humanity would do away not only with tradition but also with faith. Of any sort. This would happen, of course, only if humankind could muster the requisite courage.

Moreover, for Descartes, reason, the image of God in us, teaches how to achieve maximal control over the world and over ourselves. For Tindal, reason leads us to an understanding of the truth and to the preservation of our dignity, for there can be no dignity without the proper use of reason, which is the image of God. For d'Holbach, reason may be necessary for the maintenance of our dignity, but this dignity demands that we reject belief in God and more generally also the belief that God is the source of reason. Humans, after all, are but machines. There is no God, and *obviously* there is no such thing as the image of God.

Writing half a century after d'Holbach, Alexis de Tocqueville could already reflect on the shift in human thought over preceding centuries:

> In the sixteenth century reformers submitted to the judgment of individual reason some of the dogmas of the ancient faith but continued to bar discussion of all others. In the seventeenth century, Bacon in the natural sciences and Descartes in philosophy rejected received formulations, destroyed the empire of tradition, and overthrew the authority of the master. . . . The philosophers of the eighteenth century set out to subject all beliefs to the scrutiny of each individual.[56]

Whereas in the sixteenth century, the first Protestants submitted the tenets of Christian dogma to individual judgment tied to scripture, by the start of the seventeenth century, Francis Bacon and René Descartes were working to create the scientific method and modern philosophy, which would rely on reason. By the eighteenth century, philosophers such as d'Holbach could already apply these principles to all faiths and even call into question the very belief in God's existence. "Who does not see that Luther, Descartes, and Voltaire all employed the same method and differed only as to the breadth of applicability they claimed for it?"[57] asks de Tocqueville. And who does not see that d'Holbach is but another step on the path following Voltaire? In no other civilization, writes C. A. Bayly, "did a significant number of thinkers render the idea of god's saving intervention so thoroughly redundant as in eighteenth century Europe."[58]

Beyond Liberty and Dignity

By the end of the eighteenth century, God was no longer a source of political law, nor even of moral law. Just as the state is seen nowadays as a mechanism that follows a rational system of laws rather than a random aggregation of tribes, is constituted by a voluntary social contract and not by a king ruling by divine right—so too for d'Holbach, humans were neither God's creation, bearing his image, nor souls reaching upward toward their source, but sophisticated, earthly, and material machines.[59] Relating to the Scientific Revolution, D'Holbach and others took Newton's systematic theory of nature and turned it on its head. For Newton, as for pioneering astronomers such as Kepler and Galileo, the world operated in accordance with fixed laws, but these laws were determined by God's infinite wisdom and for the sake of his glory.[60] Indeed, the fact that the world was planned so perfectly was unambiguous evidence of God's existence, and God himself, as Newton colorfully described him, had to be "very well skilled in mechanics and geometry."[61] D'Holbach adopted this mechanical conception of the world and of humankind but erased God's presence, which had thus far hovered over it. All that remained was a machine, fully material and all alone.

But this human machine possessed a capacity for reason and the dignity that this entailed. In the concluding lines of his *System of Nature*, d'Holbach made a call "to inspire the intelligent being with courage; infuse energy into his system, that, at length, he may feel his own dignity."[62] For d'Holbach, as for the Deists, only the use of reason would lead to a happy life; but whereas for the Deists, reason was the gift of a loving God who cared for his creations, for d'Holbach, reason was a natural and organic development.

On the face of it, d'Holbach's philosophy presents remnants of a theological structure that had been secularized: unconnected fragments, like disarrayed columns left standing after the building they once supported had collapsed. Humans were nothing but machines, but they were required to maintain their dignity and not believe in falsehoods. But why would doing so endow a machine with dignity? Because doing so requires the machine to transcend itself—to be courageous, to resist false comfort—and because doing so brings about the internal perfection of this machine, integrity in its loyalty to itself. But how could a machine possibly transcend itself? And why should the internal perfection of a machine be something that endows it with dignity?

In 1971, the psychologist B. F. Skinner, one of the founding fathers of behaviorism, wrote a book in which he sought to establish that humans had no free will or moral autonomy, and that their actions were always determined by their preceding conditions. Its poignant title was *Beyond Freedom and Dignity*. As far as Skinner was concerned, the transformation of humans into machines shifted the discourse about them away from such terms as "freedom" and "dignity." Machines, after all, had no freedom, and without freedom there could be no dignity. Once the image of God had been discarded, it was choice (moral, difficult, self-transcendent choice, if we recall Camus) that gave a person their dignity. But now, without even choice, there was nothing left that might endow humans with dignity. D'Holbach was an absolute determinist and did not believe that people possessed free will. Nevertheless, he took a different approach and avoided taking his position to its logical conclusions, as Skinner did. One wonders whether he would ascribe this to lack of courage.

As we have seen, for d'Holbach, dignity and freedom were certainly possible—at least the freedom from illusions. Our dignity comes not from realizing the image of God inside us, but from denying its very existence. Human dignity follows from one's devotion to reason, from one's conscious choice not to succumb to comforting illusions, and from one's discovery of the courage needed for this. Dignity follows from loyalty to the truth and from the internal perfection that this implies: reason shows us the truth, and we are faithful to it, resisting the temptation to embrace beliefs that will give us solace. It is by standing for the truth that one earns one's dignity. The only difference between this and Camus's "absurd man," who draws his power from acknowledging the "collapse and nothingness" of the world is the loss of the happy optimism that still defined d'Holbach's perspective.

How God Went from Being a Condition for Morality to a Threat to It

What led d'Holbach to take this additional step beyond Deism? It would be easy to accept his version of events: the Deists, as educated as they were, lacked sufficient courage, while he and his fellow atheists were unafraid to attract social opprobrium—and, in that era, real risks to their wellbeing—and to make the heart-wrenching decision to abandon the illusions to which they had become accustomed. Yet this answer, which is presently in vogue, misses a crucial element in the transition from faith to its absence. This element, which was also critical to the evolution of secularism, was the ethical element.

Charles Taylor offers a brilliant description of the process that allowed reason to be turned against God, and the forthcoming discussion is based on his thinking.[63] In his book *Sources of the Self*, Taylor describes how the creation of sources of morality alternative to God ultimately underpinned the rejection of his existence. Significantly, the creation of these new sources of morality was a necessary step for people to relinquish God, who until then had been considered the source of all morality. The godless were deemed corrupt (recall Spinoza's words) or simply untrustworthy (recall Locke's intolerance). And in truth, allowing for the era's presuppositions, how could they be otherwise? After all, they had no reason to do good, and moreover, had no possibility of even knowing what the good was.

In order to live without God, there first needed to exist the conditions to enable The Good Life without God. Most people cannot live without a moral compass. As human beings, we define our lives, *inter alia*, by our position along and within normative coordinates. If these are not imposed from above, we must create them by ourselves. And only after we create them by ourselves can we relinquish those imposed from above. God's existence is therefore connected to morality not only theoretically but chronologically: just as believers maintain that only after God can there be morality, for unbelievers only once it is possible to be good *without* God is it possible to renounce his existence.

Taylor explores two sources of morality alternative to God, which "begin to emerge in the eighteenth century, and which define our contemporary situation."[64] These sources are humankind's rational faculties and the perfect natural order (to which we can also gain access from within our emotional complex). The first source, the only one we shall address here, lies in the human intellect.[65] This ability, conceived of, as we saw, as the image of God inside us, became in Cartesian philosophy an internal capacity, removed from the "external" world.

The concept of reason before Descartes—from Plato, through the Stoics and Augustine, to Thomas Aquinas and Maimonides—was based on a cosmological paradigm, according to which reason was a reflection of the cosmic or divine order (*logos*, God's laws, divine wisdom). According to this conception, in order to lead a good life, an individual had to conform with and connect to this order by means of their reason. Descartes transformed this general paradigm, turning reason into a private and procedural affair: a mode of thought. As we have seen, for Descartes, being rational means thinking in accordance with certain standards as opposed to operating in accordance with a rationality somehow embedded in the cosmos. In other words, reason was internalized and became the exclusive prerogative of an individual's inner life.

Autonomy as a Moral Ideal

This paradigm was augmented after Descartes, running through Deism and reaching its epitome with Kant. Reason was indeed universal, but it was no more than a mode of thought, a means of accurately seeing these "clear and distinct" ideas in our minds and using them to draw valid conclusions. The modern individual learns to see himself or herself as a disparate, "rational" subject, as a "consciousness" or "pure thought," facing the phenomenal world, including the body, yet detached from it. This represents a refinement of the notion of the "buffered self," which exists aloof from the world. Reason migrated inward, and we began to see ourselves as possessing a subjective and autonomous life inside ourselves, shielded from the outside world.

For Descartes, the capacity for reason was God's image and gift to humanity, and as such it was necessarily and fundamentally linked to God's existence. But almost immediately afterwards, as could already be seen with Descartes himself, rational autonomy was suffused with moral value, and it came to be believed that this autonomy must be safeguarded for the sake of our dignity as "mature," i.e. rational and level-headed, individuals. Not only do we exist as rational consciousnesses observing the phenomenal world, but this state of existence carries positive moral force. We must protect our independent thought and not allow it to be distorted by feelings or external coercion.

We are all familiar with the ethos instructing us to think "with our heads" rather than our "guts," to be "in control" and remain level-headed, to analyze situations "rationally" and not to let extraneous considerations interfere with our judgment. Descartes wrote about the importance of controlling nature and ourselves. Following him, the European Enlightenment developed a dominant cultural theme of detached introspection and rigorous examination of the self. From this position, it came to be understood that logically analyzing statements and claims in one's mind and then forcing one's body to act in accordance with the rational judgments of the correctly informed will was a *moral* act, and even *the highest moral* act: an act of courage, of autonomy, and of dignity. In the twentieth century, this conception would contribute to the adulation of "coolness": an aesthetic and social ideal that valorizes the same revered psychological and existential condition of equanimity of mind and calm contentment.

This is not the end of the story, however. At first, rational thought was considered God-given, an expression of his image. This, as we have seen, was the case with Descartes and Tindal. Submission to the dictates of reason was thus the worthy, divinely sanctioned thing to do. But in the next stage, autonomous thought itself was given moral force and came to be seen as a good in itself. Autonomous thought did not point us to the good—it *was* the good.

In the course of the eighteenth century, reason gradually drifted away from divinity and became an exclusively human capacity. One's conception of oneself as autonomous and separate from one's surroundings led to autonomy gaining a moral dimension. Our rational autonomy became a value and an ideal, conjoined with the "dignity" that was acquired by realizing it. The ability to think independently, in a clear, unbiased, and accurate way, had become *a virtue in its own right*, one that required preservation and cultivation. Autonomous thought was a moral activity. Kant was the leading philosopher to advocate this moral position. "We shall not look upon actions as [morally] binding on us, because they are the commands of God," explained Kant, "but we shall regard them as divine commands, because we are internally bound by them."[66] Internal, rational commands were prior to any divine commands, and they were binding on us. Moreover, these commands *necessarily* had to be prior to divine commands because acting purely out of external compulsion, even in the form of God's commands, could not be considered a moral act. Morality depended on autonomy, and autonomy itself was rendered a moral ideal.[67]

The next, critical stage came when the connection with God went from being a necessary condition for morality to an obstacle to it. This happened when dependence on God, or even God's existence as the highest authority, came to threaten human autonomy and the capacity for moral choice. Not only was it now considered important to obey one's internal commands; it was also impossible to accept a reality in which these internal commands might be influenced or overruled by some external authority. If autonomy were a condition for morality and a value in itself, then anything that might manipulate or sway it, and anything that might revoke it, was a moral injustice—or even a violation of the moral order itself.

How can we autonomously resolve to take a certain moral course if the promise of heaven or the fear of hell hang above us? How can we consequently exercise our nonpartial and independent reason? And how can we trust in our continued existence as moral agents if a superior being can at any time command us to do this or that, or even proclaim a different set of morals? The answer is: we can't. This was the moment at which God went from being a necessary condition for any moral system to nothing less than the greatest threat to morality itself.

The individuals created by the Enlightenment see themselves as moral subjects only on condition that their decisions are autonomous and free, both of a desire for benefits and of a moral dependence on God. Nor is the Enlightenment subject willing to accept any moral authority that threatens their autonomy or purports to be higher than it. The problem with such a situation is not only that it would wound one's pride or violate one's dignity; the problem is that it would impair one's *moral capacity*, one's capability for being moral. Out of the loftiest motivations, our subject has therefore reached a state in which it is not only possible but also *morally required* to live without God.

The Human Struggle for Dignity

Let us explore this process from another angle. We can track the transition between these stages by examining the different conceptions of self-esteem and dignity that emerged in the West. We have already seen how dignity, as an ideal, provides an illuminating example of the transition from dependence on God to a disconnection from him or rejection of him altogether. Human dignity, for Enlightenment thinkers, was substantively connected to the proper use of reason, to one's loyalty to the writ of reason and conscience, and correspondingly to autonomy. Voltaire, who could distill the spirit of the Enlightenment like no other, implored humanity to be faithful to the inherent good within them: "Remember thy dignity as a man!"[68] As we shall see, the sources of human dignity and means of exercising this dignity evolved over the course of the last few centuries, and these changes had fateful implications.

The intellectual pedigree that idealized human dignity began with Giovanni Pico della Mirandola (1443–1494), one of the most important Renaissance philosophers. Pico, an Italian nobleman whose writings shaped the humanism of the era (and who also began the Christian interest in Kabbalah), wrote perhaps the most important text of Renaissance Italy: the *Oration on the Dignity of Man*. This work, from 1486, was written as a speech, which Pico intended to deliver as part of a public debate over one of his other writings. It soon became his most famous work. In the speech, Pico exalted the human as the crowning jewel of creation and argued that humans held a loftier status than all other creations by virtue of their ability to become whatever they wanted. A person's identity and life depended entirely on their will, and their will was the essence of their dignity.

According to Pico, after God had given unique virtues to all his other creations—to plants, animals, and assorted angels—he had nothing specific left that he could give to humans. He therefore made them boundless creatures:

> At last, the Supreme Maker decreed that this creature, to whom He could give nothing wholly his own, should have a share in the particular endowment of every other creature. Taking man, therefore, this creature of indeterminate image, He set him in the middle of the world and thus spoke to him. . . . The nature of all other creatures is defined and restricted within laws which We have laid down; you, by contrast, impeded by no such restrictions, may, by your own free will, to whose custody We have assigned you, trace for yourself the lineaments of your own nature.[69]

Humanity is at the center of Creation, not only physically but also substantively. Humans have no specific character or trait, and are limitless in principle (a note heralding the liberal abstract individual). Humanity can autonomously create itself. The human is a "creature of indeterminate image" and therefore free to be whatever it wants to be. "Image" in this translation was *imago* in the original Latin. And indeed, according to Pico della Mirandola, it was God's image in humanity that allowed them to be whatever they wanted. In a later composition, *Heptaplus* (1489), in which he explored the six days of Creation, Pico wrote that:

> We seek something peculiar to man in which we may ascertain both the dignity proper to him and the image of the divine substance which he shares with no other creature. What can it be but the substance of man which (as some Greek commentators intimate) encompasses by its very essence the substances of all natures and the fullness of the whole universe? I say by its very essence, moreover, because not only the angels, but any intelligent creatures whatever include all things in themselves in some degree when, filled with their forms and reasons, they know them.[70]

Human beings' image is their distinctive essence, which enables them to embody everything at once. According to Pico, when one knows something, one holds it, in some sense, inside oneself. One is a party to it. This is unlike angels, who also possess reason, but when they know something, they do not hold it inside themselves. Here we see not only an emphasis on humanity's uniqueness but also the glorification of humans as beings who are capable of some degree of infinity, who embody everything, and who therefore can, in theory, do anything.

In Pico's account, the fact that each person shares their essence with the whole of Creation and is capable of free choice defines the image of God inside them.[71] Obviously for Pico, these virtues were handed down directly from God and were also dependent on him. The human is nothing without God. Humans are dependent on God because God created them, because God gave them his image, and because they need God's grace in order to be able to act appropriately. But it is important to note: the roots of the emphasis on human autonomy, on understanding human dignity as an ability, as *agency*, lie here.

The Honest Desire for Truth

Forward to the seventeenth century: we have seen how for Descartes, one was required to exercise reasoned introspection in order to know good from bad. With the aid of reason, we inspect ourselves and decide how best to act. Descartes understood the human subject as disembodied reason, capable of observing the world of matter and therefore of controlling it. The rational human essence marshals its autonomy against the body and against the outside world. Descartes did not use the language of dignity to describe humankind, but Taylor identifies him as the start of the tradition that we discussed earlier, in which one's personal sense of dignity is judged by one's ability to coolly and rationally analyze the world and then derive one's next steps in accordance with this analysis:

> A great shift has taken place. If rational control is a matter of mind dominating a disenchanted world of matter, then the sense of the superiority of the good life, and the inspiration to attain it, must come from the agent's sense of his own dignity as a rational being. . . . The ethic of rational control, finding its sources in a sense of dignity and self-esteem, transposes inward something of the spirit of the honour ethic.[72]

For Descartes, human beings are distinguished from mere matter by virtue of their consciousness, and correspondingly distinguish themselves from matter by examining it rationally and investigating it responsibly—this is why they were endowed with a consciousness, after all. The most fitting form of life is one of rational examination of ourselves and of the world; safeguarding our rational sovereignty therefore means safeguarding our own sense of dignity. We must remain constantly lucid, level-headed, calm and responsible. It was out of this ethos that modern culture constructed, for example, its disdain for people who use even the mildest mind-altering substances. Drug users, the thinking goes, do not maintain their own sense of dignity. As previously noted, it was also out of this ethos that we received the ideal of the "cool" icon: someone who is not necessarily a great intellectual but does not get carried away with his feelings, remaining in full control. Yet for Descartes, all this was true only on the condition that God gives us wisdom and the world a coherent existence. In time, God's existence would become redundant—and then intolerable.

For Tindal, in the late seventeenth and early eighteenth centuries, one's sense of dignity came to be dependent on their ability to rebuff superstitions, which debase their capacity for reason, this being the image of God. We receive our dignity, like our capacity for reason, from God, but we must protect them both. For Descartes, a person protects their dignity by engaging in rational inquiry about the world and not letting their emotions affect their judgment. Tindal insisted that one must reject irrational beliefs, and unlike Descartes, he had the audacity to attack religious tradition itself.

Notice the extraordinary turn of events: whereas in the past, one sustained one's image of God by not sinning, or by obeying God's word, or by having faith in Christ, for Tindal sustaining the image of God meant repudiating superstitions, which to his mind included what had previously been considered the most sacred articles of faith. For Tindal, it was the rejection of nonsense, even nonsense anchored in the authority of tradition (in fact, *especially* nonsense anchored in the authority of tradition), that expressed our rational autonomy and give us our personal sense of dignity.

"The attitude of deism," wrote Ernst Cassirer, "the honest desire for truth and the moral seriousness with which it undertook its criticism of dogma, were more effective than all those [theological] deductions."[73] In other words, the ethos of pursuing the truth and rejecting lies contributed much more to the Enlightenment project than Deist theology itself, which indeed has today been completely forgotten. Tindal no longer needed God to hold the cosmos together and guarantee its intelligible existence. God created the world and gave us our capacity for reason, but then left us alone. We must now act independently, and we are fortunate to have been equipped with appropriate skills by the Almighty. In order to live worthy lives we must steadfastly exercise our rational faculties—God's image in us—and repudiate irrationality. We must reject falsehoods—and for Tindal, most of religious tradition was falsehoods.

Then came d'Holbach. For d'Holbach, in the latter half of the eighteenth century, the picture shifts again. Dignity is no longer derivative from some divine gift. Humans, after all, were but an organic machine. But the fact that each of us is a machine, d'Holbach emphasized, does not entail that we have no dignity:

> Let it not then be said, that it is degrading man to reduce his functions to a pure mechanism . . . the true dignity of man [. . . in] the honest man,

when he has talents, when he possesses virtue, is, for the beings of his species, a tree that furnishes them with delicious fruit, that affords them refreshing shelter.[74]

Human dignity lies in human virtues. D'Holbach ignored the fact that in his account, people lacked free will, and insisted that they could still be moral. A talented and moral person was one who contributed to the world. But one's dignity was preserved not only through one's morality and the utilitarian gain that one brought others; it was they who always resisted the temptations of illusory beliefs who would maintain their own sense of dignity. Even if a good and honest person's lot is wretched, d'Holbach wrote, even if they remained mired in suffering, poverty, loneliness, sickness, and injustice,

in the midst of all his misfortunes, in the very bosom of his sorrows, in the extremity of his vexation, he finds support in himself; he is contented with his own conduct; he respects himself; he feels his own dignity.[75]

A person finds their dignity within themselves. A human being's dignity follows from their upstanding life, their honesty, their integrity. They know that they have not lied or deceived themselves or others. They have not succumbed to the temptation to believe in falsehoods, and have even courageously rejected their most basic faith in God (even in the distant and passive Deist God). They have been morally fair to their fellows and rationally fair to themselves, and it is based on this conduct, conscious of this situation, that they muster their own sense of dignity. They are at peace with themselves because they possess integrity, are rational, and hold steadfast to their rationality. They possess an un-impeached autonomy faithful to the principles that they summon from within themselves.

The Atheist's Dignity

D'Holbach was articulating a modern conception of a person's own sense of dignity, a dignity rooted in the person himself and measured by human criteria. No longer is one's dignity bestowed upon them by God, nor does it depend on their obedience to divine commands. On the contrary, human dignity depends on the preservation of one's intellectual and practical independence, and on one's fidelity to its principles. Human dignity depends on one's autonomy and integrity. The modern conception of a person's "authenticity" is developing, in which one is charged with loyalty to their own principles or emotions. Man and woman are no longer the image of God; humans are not divine or spiritual at all. Yet even as biological machines, they can maintain their own sense of dignity. They do so, argues d'Holbach, by acting in accordance with the dictates of morality and reason, which emerge from within them.

What we have before us is a complete ethical system: the source of morality has been internalized and placed within the individual's power of reason. This power of reason allows us to act appropriately, both toward others and toward ourselves. Toward others, our reason instructs us to act with decency and fairness (Kant would articulate the principles of rational morality one way, Bentham and Mill another). Regarding ourselves, our reason instructs us not to accept the assorted beliefs of religious traditions, including faith in God. This, d'Holbach argues, is a socially and psychologically difficult process. It condemns us to solitude and demands great courage. It is therefore unsuitable for the masses, and even the most educated individuals are fearful to take it to completion. But precisely because it is so difficult, its moral value is clear. According to d'Holbach, this is the only way to live a laudable life.

Tindal and his contemporaries believed that reason necessitates God's existence—in fact, that God's existence is a necessary condition for reason. Reason, they believed, is the image of God. Humans, created by God, were endowed with reason because God imbued them with his image; to their minds, there was no other explanation for the fact that we are thinking beings. D'Holbach proposed another explanation: reason developed organically. He did not explain, of course, exactly how this happened (admittedly, neither did Tindal explain the mechanism by which God gave us his image). Rather than historical or genealogical accounts, these were different normative frameworks.

The growing adulation for d'Holbach's interpretation, beginning in the eighteenth century, undoubtedly owed a sizeable debt to the Scientific Revolution, to the proven ability of the scientific method to explain nature and invent new technologies on the basis of these explanations, and to the creation of a whole field of knowledge independent of religion. But these developments in themselves, even if they were permissive factors, did not *compel* d'Holbach (or anyone else) to reject God's existence or to assume that our powers of reason are natural rather than divine in origin. What compelled d'Holbach to take this path was the moral imperative that he erected, which involved the inward migration of the source of human morality and dignity, and a corresponding rejection of any outer source thereof.

D'Holbach rejected God's existence not because he had evidence of God's non-existence, nor because he lacked evidence of his existence; neither did Tindal have evidence of God's existence, but he took it for granted because he was incapable of imagining a rational life without God. D'Holbach rejected God's existence because he could imagine a rational life without God, and because for him faith in God's existence was a violation of human dignity. Belief in God, or in any other religious dogma, meant forfeiting an essential part of what makes us human and grants us our dignity. According to d'Holbach, and according to increasing numbers of the eighteenth-century intellectual elite, religious believers were surrendering their powers of reason and free choice. More than any specific scientific finding, it was this belief that most profoundly crushed religious faith.

Indeed, not only was faith in God's existence a threat to human dignity for d'Holbach; so was *God's mere existence*. Of course, on a superficial level, d'Holbach's whole enterprise, in which he conceived of the human as a machine that had developed by entirely materialistic means, was threatened by God's existence, inasmuch as this would render each human a purposeful creation in possession of a soul. This much is clear. But God's existence threatened d'Holbach not only technically, but also normatively—and this was the thrust of the matter. God's existence would detract from human dignity, to d'Holbach's mind, because human dignity depended on autonomy and courage, and these two traits depended on the fact of human *solitude*. God, for d'Holbach, threatens our autonomy while also making our world easier and more tolerable. In both of these senses, God's existence erodes our own sense of dignity. The logical endpoint of d'Holbach's mechanical man is Camus's absurd man, the subject that *draws his strength* from the merciless and brutally honest recognition of his own absurd condition. Introduce God to Sisyphus's world, and it would no longer be absurd.

The Ethos of Atheism

This recurring discussion of courage as a condition for atheism, and of the atheistic life as a life of heroism, might remind readers of the discussion at the start of this book, about heroism as an ancient ideal. In order to be brave in antiquity, we may recall, people needed deities to suffuse their chests with courage. In order to be courageous in the modern era, people would need to reject belief in deities altogether. Not only does courage stem from within us; it does so by means of our explicit denial of the possibility that such courage might be curtailed or otherwise influenced by some higher force. In the ancient world, the "porous self" required external, heteronomous assistance in order to stand on its own two feet. In the modern world, the "buffered," autonomous self takes pride in his rejection of any external authorities, based on the perception that only thus can it truly stand on its own two feet.

Accordingly, d'Holbach sought to establish human life on its own terms, independent of any external factors. The source of human dignity was life itself, morality, and inner integrity. These emerge from within us and were not handed down by a deity or written in any holy texts. This, ultimately, was the radical project of the Enlightenment: establishing human life on its own terms.

The Enlightenment sought to enable and promote humanity's control over itself and over the world. Out of this self-control came knowledge of, and control over, human consciousness. The next stage, however, had to be control over control itself. Enlightened individuals sought to entrench and reinforce their control and were therefore ultimately fated to reject God's existence, because nothing threatened their control more than an eternal father figure with infinite powers. "The first revolt," wrote the anarchist philosopher Mikhail Bakunin in 1871, "is against the supreme tyranny of theology, of the phantom of God. As long as we have a master in heaven, we will lie slaves on earth."[76] In order to be delivered from slavery to freedom, humanity must reject God's existence. This is the modern subject's exodus from Egypt.

The philosophers we have discussed represent an illustration of a wider cultural development, in which the Western individual turned against God's existence and did so *for ethical reasons*. The image of God, internalized and reimagined as reason and free will, became a rival source of authority to God himself. Reason became an autono-mous ethical framework, independent of God. In time, reason, which already made possible the rich normative system of autonomy and dig-nity, would have to reject God's existence on ethical, normative grounds: God's existence is immoral because it impairs morality; it sabotages our capacity for independence and self-esteem. It frustrates our standing as self-conquering entities.

Articulating the dynamic we have charted above, Friedrich Nietzsche wrote that what "really triumphed over the Christian god" was:

> Christian morality itself, the concept of truthfulness that was understood ever more rigorously, the father confessor's refinement of the Christian conscience, translated and sublimated into a scientific conscience, into intellectual cleanliness at any price. Looking at nature as if it were proof of the goodness and governance of a god; interpreting history in honor of some divine reason, as a continual testimony of a moral world order and ultimate moral purposes; interpreting one's own experiences as pious people have long enough interpreted theirs, as if everything were provi-dential, a hint, designed and ordained for the sake of the salvation of the soul—that is *all over now*, that has man's conscience against it, that is considered indecent and dishonest by every more refined conscience—mendaciousness, feminism, weakness, and cowardice. In this severity, if anywhere, we are *good* Europeans and heirs of Europe's longest and most courageous self-overcoming.[77]

Europe has courageously overcome itself. Christianity has bravely re-jected Christ. Behold, such self-crucifixion in the name of humanity. *Ecce homo.* Atheism is an ethos.

The U.S. Declaration of Independence (1776) would still proclaim that people are "endowed by their Creator with certain unalienable Rights." In the French Declaration of the Rights of Man and of the Citizen (1789), God is only hinted at, and our rights are considered "sacred." In the Universal Declaration of Human Rights (1948), not even this appears. According to the protocols of the committees that drafted the UDHR, the representatives omitted any mention of human creation in God's image because they hoped to reach a consensus among all U.N. member states.[78] One may assume that members of the Communist bloc objected to this because they believed that religion was the "opium of the masses" and that a proper, free, and unalienated human life was only possible by rejecting God's existence.

The process of secularization was therefore profoundly connected to the process by which the Western subject was transformed into an autonomous individual. No less importantly, it was connected to the discovery or creation of sources of morality alternative to God, sources that gradually came to be seen as necessitating God's *non-existence*—on moral grounds. More than the inventions of the Scientific Revolution or the corruption and oppressiveness of the religious establishment, it was these ideals of autonomy, morality, and self-esteem that led Westerns to reject not only faith in God as a dangerous falsehood, but also the proposition of God's existence at all.

After the image of God, as an idea, was internalized, God himself, this time as a source of morality, was also internalized. And if God was internalized, then there was no longer any room for God outside, in the objective sphere. The world could not possibly be shared between two gods; such is the nature of monotheism. Loyalty to one's own moral voice demanded the repudiation of any external moral voice; such is the nature of secularism.

The Secularization Process

When we talk about "the secularization process," we usually mean that people are less religious nowadays than in the past, citing statistics that point to declining levels of faith in God. This definition of secularization is misleading, for two reasons. First, the loss of faith was at most a secondary dimension in the process of secularization. It is not the fact that we believe less nowadays that makes our world a secular world. Second, there are secular countries in which levels of faith in God are quite high. According to Pew Research Center polling data from December 2017, 90 percent of Americans believe in some higher power, 80 percent believe in God, and 56 percent believe in the biblical God. According to the same poll, 75 percent of Americans speak with God and 28 percent report that God also answers them.[79] In Europe belief levels are lower, but still significant. 27% of Christian Europeans believe in the biblical God. 38% believe in another form of higher power, and only 26% do not believe in any higher power.[80]

Are these not secular states? Have they not undergone secularization? Or does the power of secularism lie in that 10 to 30 percent of the population's abstention from religion? These possibilities must be discounted, because it is abundantly clear that relations between humanity and religion, and between the community and religion, have changed dramatically over the past centuries, and religion nowadays wields much less power. Secularization happened, and it was deeply significant. The vast majority of the U.S. and European populations are not religious in the sense that this term had until a few centuries ago. Religious tradition plays a much more minor role in their societies, and the religious establishment has much less power. Something dramatic has changed.

So what *did* happen? Scholars of the process of secularization usually point to trends in rates of membership of particular religious denominations and of church attendance (or synagogue, mosque, and temple attendance). We have relevant data for some Western countries beginning in the eighteenth century, and it points to a gradual decline of religious activity in most of them (the exceptions, although not according to all metrics and at all times, are the United States, Poland, and Ireland).[81] Thus, for example, the data points to declining church attendance among all Christian denominations in Britain starting in the 1880s. In Germany, the trend began in the mid-nineteenth century, and the same was true in France.[82] These are interesting findings, and they coincide, more or less, with the popularization of Enlightenment ideals. Yet we should be wary of drawing far-reaching conclusions from this. There are always sociological reasons that affect people's belonging to religious denominations and their participation in organized worship, as can indeed be discerned from the exceptions to the rule in the Western world (not to mention the non-Western world).[83] In the end, these trends reflect only symptoms of secularization, not its essence. The thrust of the process of secularization was changing attitudes toward tradition, especially concerning its status as a source of authority.

The study of secularization has been riven by disagreement since the 1970s. If until then, starting in the nineteenth century, there was a consensus among thinkers and scholars about the future of religion—that it was fated to disappear, at least as a social institution of any public significance—in recent decades many have cast doubt on this assumption, to varying degrees. In the past, Nietzsche announced that God was dead, Marx opined that religion was the "opium of the masses," from which they would be weaned by the revolution, Freud saw religion as an "illusion" that would dissipate, and Max Weber predicted a disenchanted world that was but an "iron cage" of "mechanized petrification." Yet nowadays one would be hard-pressed to find any atheist scholars or thinkers with such confidence or pride. Key events in the late 1970s—chiefly the fundamentalist revolution in Iran and the rise of the "Moral Majority" in the United States—led to the recognition that religion, even in its most institutionalized and conservative forms, was not dying; it was alive and doing surprisingly well.[84]

One of the major problems with predictions about religion's demise since the Enlightenment era is that they are more a matter of ideology than theory. The thinkers who promoted these forecasts were in fact advancing the Enlightenment movement's conception of itself: the assumption that more reason, education, democracy, and prosperity would translate into less religion, and that as these forces progressed, religion would gradually retreat before disappearing altogether. Philosophers such as Auguste Comte, Herbert Spencer, and Karl Marx presented their own historical flowcharts, showing how religion would naturally wither as humanity developed in what they considered the right direction—which in their theories was also the only possible direction. The passage of time has proven that this is not happening.

One simple example comes from Russia, where membership of the Russian Orthodox Church has risen since the fall of Communism. Whereas in 1991, 31 percent of Russians defined themselves as Orthodox Christians, by 1998 that number had risen to 54 percent, and by 2008, Orthodox Christians were already 72 percent of the population. And whereas in 1991, only 38 percent of Russians believed in God, by 2008, 56 percent did.[85] There are various reasons for this phenomenon, perhaps the main reason being the rise of Russian nationalism and the connection between it and the Russian Church. But since we are dealing with people raised in a strictly atheist environment, who have since, at least between 1991 and 2008, experienced economic prosperity and democracy, it is impossible to keep adhering to the Enlightenment's simplistic narrative.

Most popular discussions about secularization attach great importance to the Scientific Revolution and "rationality." We have already explained why scientific discoveries were less significant as catalysts of secularization than the discovery of a source of information other than tradition, and indeed the rise of an ethos that saw adherence to empirically verified knowledge as an ideal associated with human dignity. The term "rationality," which means little more than prudent conduct, is used in this context as a popular alternative to the older term "naturalism." This referred to a "natural" conception of the world: an attempt to understand the world as operating according to fixed laws that follow a causal logic, which usually (but not always) governs the material world. Such naturalism stood in contrast to premodern conceptions of the world as a battlefield for the supranatural *wills* of gods and demons capable of intervening with the regular and "natural" operation of things, or as operating according to magical correspondences, according to which a physical or substantive similarity between two things points to a connection between them.

Naturalism was indeed connected to secularization, especially as it deprived religious institutions of their authority to interpret God's will, which was no longer relevant to most aspects of life. One famous anecdote describes the astronomer and mathematician Pierre-Simon Laplace in 1802 presenting to the French Emperor, Napoleon Bonaparte, the structure and operation of the solar system. When Napoleon asked him how God fitted into his theory, Laplace replied, "I had no need of that hypothesis." The acceptance of naturalism as a first principle removed any possibility of the interference of external agencies in the world, including the will of God. More than revealing previously hidden knowledge, the Scientific Revolution facilitated a different way of thinking about the world and nullified tradition as a source of epistemological authority.

It was always all about authority. One of the most fundamental distinctions in the study of religion is between religion as a social institution and religion as a private, personal affair. Both phenomena have always existed, albeit to different extents. On the one hand, religion as a system of customs and commands, of holy sites and rituals, of class hierarchies and of festivals; on the other hand, religion as sentiment, experience, a spiritual journey, an inner transformation and a personal endeavor, connected to but not necessarily dependent on religion as an institution.

The Jewish tradition, as we have seen, has always emphasized the collective at the expense of the individual, seeking to establish a society, a people, a "kingdom of priests and a holy nation." It therefore afforded limited space to personal spirituality. Conversely, the Hindu tradition, as early as the period of the Upanishads (around the mid-first millennium BCE) emphasized, in addition to society, the individual's journey to personal spiritual liberation. This distinction is important, because it gives us a key to understanding the interplay between secularization in the public sphere and the private faith of the individual. It is possible to live in a secular society and be religious; it is also possible to be an atheist and live in a religious society. The faith of the former, as a private and internal affair, represents a different model of religiosity from that of the society in which the latter lives, where it is collective and public. My argument in what follows is that Western individuals nowadays inhabit a profoundly secular society, despite the presence of many religious believers.

What Is Secularization? Religion as a Single Domain

The great historiosophical thinkers we mentioned earlier—Kant, Spencer, Marx—spoke of and imagined the secularization of the world, but they did not use the term "secularization" and therefore made no attempt to define it. The early twentieth-century founders of sociology, such as Weber and Durkheim, discussed religion and its disappearance at length, but they too neglected to define secularization.[86] Only in the 1960s, shortly before these forecasts of the world's secularization were called into question, did scholars begin to formulate definitions of secularization and to subject it to formal research.

The American sociologist and theologian Peter Berger was a pioneer in this field. He encapsulated the matter in his 1967 classic *The Sacred Canopy*, arguing that secularization is "the process by which sectors of society and culture are removed from the domination of religious institutions and symbols."[87] Berger was alluding to the shrinking space occupied by the church (and other religious establishments). Whereas in the pre-modern past, these religious systems were responsible for education (ideological or practical), healthcare, tax collection, and war, and whereas religion once narrated history, answered questions about the world's origins and development, gave life its meaning, and of course distinguished good from evil—nowadays, other institutions and entities are responsible for all of the above. The modern state has assumed responsibility for most practical aspects of its citizens' lives; science is responsible for knowledge; and meaning and morality now fall under the responsibility of each individual's private reason and conscience. "Put simply," concludes Berger, "this means that the modern West has produced an increasing number of individuals who look upon the world and their own lives without the benefit of religious interpretations."[88] This is secularization.

In his influential book *Public Religions in the Modern World* (1994), the sociologist of religion José Casanova presents a complementary definition, which takes account, from another angle, of social changes that reflect secularization. According to Casanova,

> in reference to an actual historical process, the term "secularization" was first used to signify the massive expropriation and appropriation, usually by the state, of monasteries, landholdings, and the mortmain wealth of the church after the Protestant Reformation and the ensuing religious wars. Since then, secularization has come to designate the "passage," transfer, or relocation of persons, things, functions, meanings, and so forth, from their traditional location in the religious sphere to the secular spheres.[89]

The dualist system that Casanova describes is the separation, both temporal and spatial, of the "religious" and "secular" spheres. We have a religious sphere (churches and anything under them, such as knowledge and morality), and there is a secular sphere. There is secular time (the present) and there is religious time (the past, and the world to come). This distinction, as we have seen, was built into the Christian tradition, but in the modern era it was expanded, dismantled, and rebuilt—the other way around. The boundaries between the sacred and the profane were challenged and then erased, and the whole world became secular.[90] Religion still exists, but it now must find its place not as a superstructure encompassing the whole world, touching every aspect of life, shaping its every dimension, subordinating the world to its affairs, and designating parts of it as "secular" and other parts as "religious." Nowadays, religion is but another sphere, one of many, *within* the framework of the profane: within a multifaceted secular reality. "If before, it was the religious realm which appeared to be the all-encompassing reality within which the secular realm found its proper place, now the secular sphere will be the all-encompassing reality, to which the religious sphere will have to adapt."[91]

Religion, simply put, has been transformed from being the natural horizon of all of our actions in the world into a single sphere of life, one that exists alongside other spheres, such as education, culture, and leisure. One may be a lawyer, a mother, a political right-winger, a collector of antique clocks—and religious. Or not. Modern society, which breaks reality down according to a functionalist logic, gives religion a place alongside other social functions (politics, education, economics, etc.)—not above them. This was an extremely significant shift, inasmuch as it transformed religion from the obvious framework within which life was conducted into just another "interest" that could become a part of one's life—or that one could easily live without.

This situation led to a radical transformation. In the past, people understood both spheres, the religious and the secular, the sacred and the profane, as necessary sides of reality (like up and down, north and south, good and bad); they saw these dimensions as existing in a close and mutually beneficial relationship, as a vital partnership, and as structures in their own relations (physical and social) with the world around them. Yet nowadays it is possible to contemplate an entirely secular world, one without any tension with the religious realm—because the religious realm is not considered necessary. The distinction between religious and secular has become a cultural, elective, and consciously social matter. In modern democracies, the "religious" is restricted to the private realm (that is, it is a voluntary matter), and the secular becomes the obvious reality of the public sphere.[92]

Soccer as a Religion

The process of secularization made the world a religiously neutral space. History no longer has any transcendental meaning, and neither does anyone's choice of profession. We might pray to God to make our favorite soccer team win, but its victory or defeat would carry no religious significance for us. The world keeps spinning, and it spins naturally. Moreover: we too act naturally. Not only do many not believe that a particular deity takes an interest in their lives; they would also not consider asking any deity for permission for their actions, nor would they judge their own deeds by the writ of some transcendental authority. Even those who live a life of faith operate in a secular world, in which their basic assumptions about the working of systems—economics, politics, research, even romance—leave no room for the supranatural. A naturalistic paradigm guides us in all these. Not only do we expect things to happen naturally and predictably, but we also judge things that happen by naturalistic standards. Charles Taylor calls this conception of the world the "immanent frame": an understanding of the world from within itself, without any need for appeals to authority or meaning beyond it.

At this point, it is worth noting the weakness of analogies between modern institutions—the nation-state, psychoanalysis, fascism—and religion. This rhetorical trick, beloved of scholars and journalists alike, that seeks to describe soccer, for example, as a religion, carries extremely limited force. It is true that sometimes there are similarities to religion in terms of the form of an individual's devotion to these institutions, and one can certainly claim that they play social roles that religion played in the past. But as institutions located within the secular world, they bear a resemblance to religion as we know it *after* the process of secularization: that is, to a reduced form of religion, shorn of overall authority. In the case of professions (such as psychoanalysis or hockey, for example), these are human institutions that form part of a wider array; they are not comprehensive frameworks that encompass all others within them. Clifford Geertz encapsulates the matter in his classic essay on religion: "A man can indeed be said to be 'religious' about golf, but not merely if he pursues it with passion and plays it on Sundays: he must also see it as symbolic of some transcendent truths."[93]

There is greater similarity between the nation-state and religion, inasmuch as both are ideational structures that purport to be all-encompassing, yet here too we must ask whether this is a framework that draws its authority from humanity or from something beyond it. The democratic nation-state differs from premodern religion in that its authority comes from its citizens, not from some metaphysical entity above them. It would appear that only totalitarian ideologies—Bolshevism, Nazism—offer such a transcendental worldview, because they promise an equivalent framework to a transcendental order, whether in the form of dialectical materialism or a master race with its own unique destiny. These might be considered metaphysical entities that constitute supreme and undeniable sources of authority, bringing these ideologies very close to the definition of religion.

Even though scholars nowadays tend to omit deities from their definitions of religion, belief or worship connected to metaphysical entities remain important to its proper definition. Not because these are "irrational" and therefore suit religion as "primitive," but because they endow a particular social framework with a transcendental dimension. Faith in metaphysical entities removes the source of authority from this world and imagines a higher, supreme reality that both encompasses our physical reality and subordinates it. In such a system, the good life—and life in general, on every level—depends on something that is not here with us. That is completely other. The same is not true of soccer.

Modernization, Religious Dogma, and the Social Class Structure

How did all this happen? How did these great shifts occur? One answer is connected to the word "modern," which we have used at length in this book. "Modern" is a catch-all term for certain processes, of which we have only addressed a few aspects, specifically its intellectual and private aspects. In practice, modernity has included immense social changes, including urbanization, industrialization, the creation of an economic middle class, soaring living standards, rising life expectancy, and the consolidation of the nation-state as a social experience and a political reality. These changes made the units of society larger and more diverse. Feudal estates became towns and then cities. Our neighbors were no longer like us; they came to hold different beliefs, and we became obligated, both by the ethos of the conscience and by the political and economic needs of the state, to tolerate these beliefs.

Modernization is closely linked to the establishment of the liberal order, which is based on heightened individuality and a conception of the person as an abstract individual, equal to all others, whose different dimensions' autonomy ("rights") is to be protected, developments that themselves owe much, as we have seen, to the idea that all humans were created in the image of God. As Ernest Gellner demonstrated in his writings about the evolution of nationalism, modernization reinforces an ethos of equality.[94] If we are all citizens of the same republic, then we might presume to have similar interests and needs. Labor mobility disrupts preexisting class systems. In a privatized, profit-seeking market in which people are judged by their talents, religious discrimination becomes economically illogical long before it is banned for moral reasons. We learn to recognize, and then like, people from other faiths. Religion becomes one aspect among others in the life of each individual. One's beliefs become one's private matter, meaning we come to see others first and foremost as human beings, human beings who hold particular beliefs. Which beliefs? That matters less.

We have already cited de Tocqueville, who outlined the evolution of skepticism in early modernity ("Who does not see that Luther, Descartes, and Voltaire all employed the same method and differed only as to the breadth of applicability they claimed for it?"). Later in the same passage, he sought to understand why the widespread, popular adoption of skepticism regarding the traditional dogma had not occurred at an earlier date:

> The philosophical method we are discussing was born in the sixteenth century and developed and generalized in the seventeenth. But it could not be widely adopted in either. The political laws, the social state, the habits of mind that derive from these two primary causes worked against it. It was discovered in an epoch when men were beginning to be more equal and more alike. It could be generally followed only in centuries when conditions had finally become all but identical and men almost the same.[95]

De Tocqueville understood that only with the demolition of the social hierarchy ("political laws, the social state"), once taken for granted, could faith in traditional frameworks, equally taken for granted, be broken as well. These two shifts were interrelated: they both relied on the transition to a paradigm in which the individual was an abstract and universal entity, possessing inside itself its sources of knowledge and morality—contrary to the conception of each person as a necessarily contextualized entity, firmly rooted in and growing out of a particular setting, as a self belonging to and living as part of a social matrix, and as an individual subordinate to external, traditional sources of knowledge and morality.

In other words, only after the image of God, following a prolonged process of internalization, following its transformation into an inner virtue and its conception as a general human capacity, is detached from its divine origins, and only after our powers of reason and free choice became part of our universal human "nature," could simple doubt concerning the truths of tradition and the traditional structures of society emerge and gain wider traction.

"Seventeenth-century nobles [in France]," wrote the historian Jonathan Dewald,

> became preoccupied with the nature of selfhood . . . and they came at the same time to doubt many of the ethical underpinnings of their society. They came, in other words, to see the isolated self as real, important, and complicated, and they correspondingly doubted the value, even the reality, of the social conventions that surrounded it. This combination of sensibilities seems to me distinctively modern.[96]

The conception of the self as isolated and abstract, sustaining and defining itself as autonomous, arrived in tandem with the emergence of doubts about the validity of the social conventions that surrounded and had previously defined it. Indeed the second development was dependent on the first. This shift, which began with Paul the Apostle, matured in the modern era with the growing separation of the self not only from society but also from God. The image of God was internalized, then severed from its divine origins, and finally wielded against God and used to reject any deity's existence altogether.

These developments made the medieval form of religion, which was all-encompassing and imposed on the population by the Church and the king, an impossibility.[97] Religion was privatized and became a series of different "denominations," all living side by side. Different models of religion and state relations developed, sharing a conception of religion and state as separate entities, and an understanding that in their interactions, the state possessed public power and religion was pigeonholed into the private sphere. Religion found its place as a "sphere," one of many in life.

The internalization of sources of authority and meaning, the conception of the self as autonomous, and the elevation of this autonomy into a religious and moral ideal (dignity), along with the heterogeneity of society, led to the diversification of religion, its privatization, and for some, ultimately, its total rejection.

This process intensified with time. Whereas in the eighteenth and nineteenth centuries, individuals no longer needed to identify themselves with their ruler's religion but could associate with other denominations, in time, by the latter half of the twentieth century, they could quit denominations altogether or embark on their own personal spiritual journey, devising their own idiosyncratic beliefs. In fact, they were *required* to do so by the rising ethos of the day, because passive membership in an established denomination now seemed to many to be spurious, a compromise of one's authenticity, a limp concession that did not "truly" grapple with the question of religion and forfeited "true" religious meaning, which could, in this view, derive only from conscious individual choice.[98]

This is the meaning of the secular society: a society in which religion is yet another function, an "interest" that the individual must choose, and then within it, choose from a diverse supply. The transition to secularism, writes Charles Taylor, is a transition

> from a society where belief in God is unchallenged and indeed, unproblematic, to one in which it is understood to be one option among others, and frequently not the easiest to embrace. In this meaning, as against sense 2 [participation in religious activity], at least many milieux in the United States are secularized, and I would argue that the United States as a whole is. Clear contrast cases today would be the majority of Muslim societies, or the milieux in which the vast majority of Indians live.[99]

Taylor's last sentence here is significant. He signals that the sweeping processes that we described earlier—urbanization, industrialization, the rise of the middle class, and the creation of the nation-state—do not provide the full answer to the question of secularization. They are significant, of course: in India, a more economically and technologically advanced state than most countries in the Muslim world, certain classes of society, the more educated and financially established ones, are indeed more secular and less inclined to see religion as a source of authority. But they are not quite secular in the same way as equivalent classes in Europe or the United States are secular. It would also be a mistake to assume that the astronomical wealth of Muslims in Saudi Arabia or the Gulf emirates (or their use of advanced technologies) predicts that they are secular. These conditions, as we have seen, do not provide a full answer to the question of secularization. Such an answer will require an examination of our sense of selfhood—and an examination of the ethos animating it.

Secularization as Autonomous Individualism

Let us now try to understand secularization from another, complementary angle, which will allow us to elucidate the differences in conceptions of religion and secularism in different societies, such as India and the United States. This perspective, following the course that this book has described thus far, will present secularization as the intensification of individualism, or in other words, as the long process in which human beings learned to see themselves as autonomous individuals, learned to interpret autonomy as liberty, and learned to conceive of their psychological lives as sources of authority, meaning, morality, and identity.

Secularization, in this sense, includes the following points:

- The rise of people's self-conceptualization as individuals;
- The shift toward seeing the conscious and emotional dimensions as the focal points of the religious drama, a process that coincided with the devaluation and sometimes rejection of religious rituals and laws;
- The discovery and/or creation of personal, internal sources of authority, meaning, morality, and identity. These sources supplanted tradition as a source thereof;
- The consolidation of personal autonomy not only as a pragmatic possibility but as an ideal;
- The conception of autonomy as liberty, and the view that it is contrary to law and tradition, i.e., that these are obstacles to liberty.

If we proceed on the basis of these points, we will learn that the process of secularization was first and foremost a process by which individuals' conception of themselves changed. We have traced this change throughout this book. Beginning with the person who acted as a "porous self," susceptible to external influences, open to the penetration of the gods and demons that animated them. This was a person who did not conceive of their selfhood as residing inside them, but as a decentralized entity and multi-branched complex. One's selfhood included one's body but also the reality beyond one's body. Individuals were part of a clan, tied to a patriarch, an organ in a collective organism, and their thoughts, desires, and characters were also permanently susceptible to changes induced by the penetration of forces from beyond. Courage, creativity, fear, the urge to sin—all these could originate outside the body, penetrate the body, and become part of it. This was not a theory but part of people's lived experiences, a totally different set of experiences from how we conceive of ourselves nowadays.

The principle of the image of God began to change this. It transformed humans into unique individuals. Not in one go, of course: this was an ongoing process, which gained steam with time. Not by itself, either; Hellenistic culture obviously contributed to it. Yet in the ancient Jewish tradition, the life of the individual gained specific significance. With the rise of Christianity, the life of the individual also became a focal point of redemption. It was the individual, and no longer the collective, who attained freedom. The image of God was internalized and turned into a power of reason and free will. These were still associated with God, but they began a journey from being objective phenomena, connected to the cosmos, to being subjective dimensions of the individual self. Over time, reason and will as universal essences would become *my* reason and will.

The self became "buffered." The buffer between the subjective world "inside" and the objective world "outside" solidified. Later on, the self became a focused and eminently internal presence. The internal world therefore became increasingly important. The image of God, reimagined as an internal personality attribute (reason, control, conscience), gave slaves their right to liberty and "savages" or pagans their right to live their lives unmolested. These people were no longer primarily and essentially extensions of their communities, but rather unique and distinctive individuals. A whole discourse developed that saw the state and society as obligated to protect a person's internal life, now considered precious, to maintain their equal and universal "rights," i.e., the dimensions emerging from their integrity and autonomy. That which made us subjects or personas became our defining essence (as opposed to our relationship with a patriarch, for example, or with God). Our subjectivity became suffused with ethical and religious meaning. Our psychological worlds became critical components in our search for identity. We define ourselves by our choices, our desires, our dreams, our creativity, our authenticity, our autonomy—no longer only by our place in the social matrix, or the fact that we are the mothers of someone or sons of someone else, members of some tribe or some social class.

In time, our internally-sourced religious meaning, our inner relationship with the divine, is forgotten, as is the principle of the image of God itself. The moment that our reason and inner liberty assumed center stage, it became less important to find external sources or even external objectives for them. There was less of a need for dialogue, or for a horizon. Instead, there emerged another need: to protect our reason and liberty from external threats—threats from bad people, from political authorities, and also from the supreme authority of God. Our reason and liberty, according to the thinking that emerged in the eighteenth-century West, compel us to reject God's existence. Our autonomy has been sanctified, defined as freedom from external coercion, and thus as goading us to discard what was once defined as a necessary condition for its existence.

In brief, we became modern individuals. People began to conceive of themselves as independent and autonomous beings, and steadily came to regard their autonomy as possessing immense significance, as an ideal that it would be a violation of their dignity, of the essence of their humanity, to surrender. Since we are talking about Westerners, who emerged from within the Christian tradition and were animated by the internal dynamic of Christianity—by the Christian pattern of seeing proximity to truth as correlated with distance from formal authorities—they interpret their own autonomy as contrary to law and the establishment, to social institutions and tradition, and therefore attempt in various ways to reject or subvert all these. For the same reason, Western individuals also came to oppose God in his traditional monotheistic form—as a king or a supreme judge—and to commit themselves to resist him, reject him, and deny his very existence.

Secularism, therefore, is a state of affairs in which autonomy, as a personal ideal, is juxtaposed against law (and tradition, and rituality). It is the idea that any heteronomous constant is a barrier to freedom, because freedom means being unrestrained. This idea induced a dynamic that would culminate with a rejection of external authorities, such as deities or divine law, while those continuing to believe in God would practice their faith privately, keeping the authority over their religious lives to themselves. The proposition that law is inversely correlated with freedom is not necessarily true, but it is a notion that evolved within the Christian tradition.[100] Besides heightening individuality and sanctifying the inner life of the individual (its reason, freedom of choice, autonomy, conscience—in short, its image of God), this new conception also led to the secularization of the Western world.

Private Religion as Modern Religion

According to this interpretation, the process of secularization is profoundly connected to: 1) the process of individualization, and 2) the rise of a distinctive ethos of autonomy and liberty. We shall try to elucidate both of these aspects. Earlier, we invoked the basic distinction between religion as a social institution and private religiosity. This distinction is elementary, to the point that many scholars of religiosity define "religion" exclusively according to one or the other of these conceptualizations: that is, effectively proposing totally opposite definitions. Thus, for example, Emile Durkheim, one of the founding fathers of sociology, wrote in 1915 that

> religion is a unified system of beliefs and practices relative to sacred things, that is to say, things set apart and surrounded by prohibitions— beliefs and practices that unite its adherents in a single moral community called a church.[101]

Religion, according to Durkheim, is a social, communal system that concerns the public and shared separation of reality into the sacred and the profane.[102] It is a system that provides a moral framework for a community—religion's main role, *per* Durkheim. It is the notion "that God is not mad,"[103] that there is order to reality and that the source of this order is metaphysical, and it involves activities (rituals, law-based conduct) derived from this conception of order. Such a cosmic order is first and foremost social; without a community to be loyal to it, this sort of order could have no meaning.

Contrary to Durkheim, William James, a pioneering psychologist and American scholar of religions, writes in his classic 1902 work *The Varieties of Religious Experience* that

> Religion . . . shall mean for us the feelings, acts, and experiences of individual men in their solitude, so far as they apprehend themselves to stand in relation to whatever they may consider the divine.[104]

James, who is interested, as is clear from the title of his book, in religious *experience*, believes that experience is the core and essence of religion. The subjective experience of the individual is the most important part of religion, and all the rest—tradition, institutions, festivals, scriptures, modes of worship, dogma, beliefs—are but later developments, invented to safeguard, enhance, or explain experience, although sometimes, alas, they can also interfere with experience. In James's definition, there is no trace of a metaphysical order, nor do we find laws and customs that a community must adopt. Religion, *per* James, is a private affair.

Although many of us might identify with James's definition, it is important to note that it is thoroughly modern. In fact, the reason that we identify with it is that we ourselves are modern: our notions of the idea of religion, like James's, have been shaped by the modern Western world. The idea of religion as a private and internal matter is a modern idea. Earlier, we discussed how religion was transformed into the private business of the individual in tandem with the consolidation of the nation-state as the public business of the citizenry. For most of human history, the framework of religion, which, as we have seen, encompassed all aspects of life, was maintained and sustained by the community as a whole.

Worship in the ancient world was always a collective project. Making sacrifices to the gods or goddesses, allaying their fury, asking favors from them, receiving protection from them against natural forces—all these were always collective, communal activities. The religious system itself, which encompassed the whole of society, served to strengthen the bonds of society and reinforce social institutions, and as Durkheim writes, instill morality and unite believers into a single moral community.

The covenant between the Israelites and their God, for example, was eminently collective; its laws applied to the whole of the nation, with the purpose of creating a "kingdom of priests and a holy nation": a nation that would be good in God's eyes and an exemplar in the eyes of humanity. Expressions of personal religiosity in the Hebrew Bible, first and foremost in the form of prophecy, were also enlisted for the benefit of the collective: the prophet did not leave society in a quest for mystical ecstasy or spiritual liberation, but rather preached his message in public, criticizing the kingdom and acting as an intermediary between the people and God.

The Jewish Sages emphasized the entry into a collective covenant and greatly restricted the study of mysticism (Mishnah Hagigah 3:1). The *tzibbur*, or community, was central to rabbinical thinking and constituted the main building block of divine worship. Whoever "separated himself from the community" was relegated to an obvious position of inferiority, if not considered an absolutely lost cause. God's presence was also a collective matter: "When ten sit together and occupy themselves with Torah, the *Shekhinah* [Divine Presence] abides among them" (Avot 3:1). The study and interpretation of the Torah, and the development and refinement of Halakha—something that was always done together, in a study-pair—became the thrust of Judaism. The commandment to pray in a quorum also points to the importance of the community even in prayer, supposedly an intimate and subjective endeavor. Earlier, we also saw the difference between the collective conception of redemption of the Jewish tradition and the individualistic conception that evolved within Christianity.

The Hellenistic world also emphasized collectivity, in society as well as worship. "Man is by nature a social animal," wrote Aristotle, and the word "idiot" (ἰδιώτης, *idiōtēs*) referred to someone who was not involved in politics, prioritizing their private affairs. Hellenistic forms of worship, which provided the complementary social framework to politics, were mandatory and communal. Citizens of the city-states of Greece and Rome were obligated to take part in the religion of the polis or of the emperor: to participate in a series of rituals and festivals. "No one shall have gods to himself, either new gods or alien gods, unless recognized by the State," wrote the Roman statesman and philosopher Cicero, while the Roman jurist Marcian argued that "sacred things are those that have been consecrated publicly, not in private."[105] Religion was public and collective. It was "civil religion" in the most basic and non-metaphorical sense: religion whose meaning followed from its public character, in which the core was not the relationship with God but between members of the community. Participation in rituals, exactly like divine worship in ancient Israel, was less an expression of a particular faith than an oath of allegiance to a founding myth, and thus to the community constituted by it.[106] Law emerges from within a narrative; obedience to the law validates it.

Christianity, as we have seen, blazed a long path that at its outset emphasized internal faith and transformation: private religiosity. The Church has always elucidated its authority and role as the exclusive gatekeeper to the new covenant with God, insisting that without the chain of transmission that it held, there could be no salvation. Ecclesiastical authority also grounded the validity of revelation, but the seeds of individualism and the inward shift were already sown. They would germinate step by step, mostly among various mystics (who were frequently burned at the stake as heretics) and "spiritual" breakaway movements from the Catholic establishment. Martin Luther's insistence on the importance of the conscience for the interpretation of God's word reflected another watershed moment in the conception of *internal* religion, and the door that Luther unlocked was burst wide open with the plethora of Protestant denominations that flooded Europe and emphasized internal, private religion in a dizzying array of ways. This was also when the principle of freedom of conscience emerged and emphasis was placed on the right of the individual to believe as they saw fit. In time, this right would become an injunction and a moral calling: we must decide our own beliefs by ourselves, because faith that we have not chosen by ourselves degrades our dignity. Such an ethos would naturally peel religion away from institutions.

"The irony," writes the scholar of Christianity Steve Bruce, "is that Christianity dug its own grave":

> Innovations pressed to rejuvenate the Church undermined it. . . . The religion created by the Reformation was extremely vulnerable to frag-

mentation because it removed the institution of the church as a source of authority between God and man. . . . It inadvertently fragmented the dominant religious culture and created the competition which, in tolerant and egalitarian societies, would lead to relativism and perennialism. By insisting that all people had a responsibility for their own spiritual state, the Reformation also contributed directly to the growth of individualism.[107]

As soon as the authority over interpretations of God's will was privatized, religion was privatized too. Loyalty to one's conscience, as a religious ideal, led to an individualistic form of religion. Believers would be extremely faithful to their conscience and therefore to themselves (and as they understood it, to God), but this would come at the expense of dogmatic uniformity and the preservation of collective frameworks. In time, the erosion of social cohesion would also follow. The Reformation brought about the next stage: a "crucial transition to a new interior paradigm has been made," writes the sociologist of religion David Martin, "and it is radical enough to be sociologically unrealistic."[108] Believers would go their separate ways; religion would become private. Once another ideal emerged—such as the independence of human reason, or authentic integrity—it would be possible to completely let go of God.

Contemporary Spirituality as a Manifestation of Secularism

Whereas religious traditions in the pre-modern past operated along the Durkheimian model—arranging reality in line with a cosmic order and unifying individuals into cohesive moral-religious communities—we live today in a totally different world. The role of framing reality has been taken away from religion by the nation-state, scientific research, and our own emotive lives. Communal worship is commonly perceived as archaic, stale, technical, and phony. Religious establishments are commonly seen as corrupt and oppressive. For many, the hip fresh brand "spirituality" is replacing the moldy old "religion," and the numbers of spiritual seekers, or those who identify as "spiritual but not religious," are higher than ever before.

With the internalization of our sources of meaning and authority, we have started looking for God inside ourselves, and when traditional religious frameworks make a pretense of being the exclusive bearers of truth, we are liable to see it as astonishingly presumptuous. Our autonomy is a principal ideal for us. We see its preservation as a safeguard of our liberty, and we believe that an authentic relationship with God can only emerge from such liberty. Freedom of conscience has been expanded, and now not only facilitates a relationship with God but also constitutes a religious or spiritual tenet in its own right. The ability to choose, on the basis of nothing more than introspection, is part of how we worship. In our view, the conscientious and emotional dimensions of our lives are the places where "religion" unfolds and where a relationship with the divine is truly forged. Sometimes God himself is internalized, coming to reside entirely within ourselves. The image of God, to the extent that it still exists for us, is a DIY endeavor: it does not point toward some higher reality, outside ourselves, but rather toward our own nature, spontaneously emerging from our own most profound essence.

Spiritual seeking is coming to replace belonging to collective religious frameworks, which are often considered not only unnecessary, but as obstacles to a true, intimate connection with the divine. Grace Davie, a sociologist of religion from the University of Exeter in England, calls this phenomenon "believing without belonging": the persistence of faith in a private form, detached from any institutionalized religious denomination.[109] This has led to a situation in which unprecedented numbers of people are unaffiliated with any formal religious denomination and believe that they have full legitimacy (indeed a duty) to tailor their religious-spiritual suits according to their personal measurements, while turning their backs on institutionalized religion, creating a new and revolutionary form of religiosity.

"The modern extension of the Reformation," writes David Martin, "has become just a celebration of faith for which there is no object of faith."[110] In contemporary circles of spirituality, faith is applauded as an important spiritual expression even if unconnected to any external divinity. We believe primarily in ourselves. We are creative, or authentic, or we fulfill our full potential, and these for us are the highest possible spiritual and religious goals. This is nothing less than a historic and unprecedented sea change. Religion in our world undergoing a transfiguration.

One precondition for the transformation of religion from collective to private is, naturally, the elevation of the importance of the individual, or in historical terms, the rise of the modern individual. We can say that the modern process of individualization finds expression in the field of religion as secularization, exactly as it finds expression in economics as capitalism, and in politics as liberalism. It follows from our observations, therefore, that the extent of a given society's communality is positively correlated with its religiosity (in the sense of institutionalized, collective religion). In other words, societies with a greater sense of community are less secular. Societies in which the individual is considered as an integral part of a complex (be it familial, tribal, or communal) will display outsized devotion to tradition and will grant more authority to tradition. Conversely, more secular societies are those in which people perceive themselves as individuals who are unencumbered by any ties that might bind them and are independent of their surroundings. Religious traditionalism and social familiarity are interconnected phenomena.

The deeper our individualization reaches, the more we conceive of ourselves as autonomous monads and of our autonomy as freedom, the more secular our society becomes. This process has its advantages and disadvantages, but whatever they are, we must understand the process itself. We cannot ignore it, nor can we turn the clocks back. Protestant Christianity is not about to disappear, with all its adherents suddenly readopting Catholicism, just as the Jewish world is not about to collectively return to the religious fold. There is no going back. Attempts to do so—different forms of fundamentalism—to re-cloak us all in an all-encompassing Durkheimian religion, end up the way of Iran or ISIS. The only way to subordinate the modern conscience to religious homogeneity and totalistic heteronomous authority is by means of violence.

Let us return to Durkheim and James's definitions. From the foregoing discussion, it derives that if we define religion according to James, we will discover that very few people were religious 2,000 years ago. Applying James's definition, historically most people invested time and efforts performing rituals that had nothing to do with "religion," because these rituals failed to arouse, at least for many of them and at least most of the time, any special sentiments or experiences. Since this would be absurd, it is clear that as a comprehensive definition of religion, James's definition can apply only to modern religion and cannot be used as an effective definition of religiosity more widely. Durkheim's definition, in contrast, applies to religious frameworks throughout history, although the modern world appears to contain very limited room for Durkheimian religion. My argument is that this is a core manifestation of the process of secularization: the shift of the phenomenon of religion from being collective to being private. The thrust of secularization therefore finds expression not in declining levels of religious belief, but in the transformation of members of organized religions into religious freelancers.

An Ethos Is a Culturally Contingent Matter

> In the same way as Western secular modernity is fundamentally and inevitably post-Christian, the emerging multiple modernities in the different postaxial civilizational areas are likely to be post-Hindu, or post-Confucian, or post-Muslim; that is, they will also be particular and contingent refashionings and transformations of existing civilizational patterns and social imaginaries mixed with modern secular ones.[111]

In this passage, José Casanova puts his finger on an important principle: secularization will express itself as different cultural changes in the different societies it unfolds in, evolving in manifold ways. There is no reason to expect secularization in the Philippines to look like secularization in Germany. The reason has to do with the cultural patterns within which secularization develops and which it integrates into its development. Secularization in a post-Christian culture will therefore be different from secularization in a post-Confucian culture.

This is a simple but important distinction. The point that we shall now elucidate applies to the basic mechanism that distinguishes post-Christian cultures from other ones, in relation to secularization.

The repudiation of tradition and of faith in God's existence was connected, as we have seen, to an ethos that developed in the Western Christian tradition: an ethos of autonomy, reason, free will, and a refusal to accept external authority. This ethos eventually instructs us to reject God's existence, because it is an obstacle to independent, rational, free, or moral conduct. We are called upon to be free and rational, with these ideals juxtaposed within our ethical framework against tradition and religious faith. We are commanded, by ourselves, to be autonomous, to control ourselves, and even to control our own capacity for control, defending it from subordination to external authority. We are fearful of losing our liberty, our freedom of choice, and therefore also fear institutional frameworks that offer prepackaged templates for our lives and identities. We reject rituals and organized worship as inauthentic, "stale," "dead," or simply boring, and seek a personal, emotional, and experiential connection to the world around us—including with God, if we happen not be atheists. Moreover, we sanctify the originality, uniqueness, and authenticity that emerge from a revolt against the familiar and institutionalized, and from faithfulness to our own individual inner distinctiveness.

These are all patterns of the same individualistic ethos that evolved, as we have seen, out of the European Enlightenment (and also out of the Romantic backlash to the Enlightenment), on the basis of the internal dynamic of Christianity. This ethos does not exist in cultures that did not sprout forth the Enlightenment or Romanticism, which did not develop a brand of individualism that idealizes autonomy and uniqueness. Secularization was a product not only of academic or technological developments, rising living standards or urbanization, rising literacy rates or falling educational inequalities, of democracy or capitalism (or Marxism), but of a *particular ethos*: a specific moral calling that arose from within a particular culture, namely the humanism of European civilization, which drew on the ancient Jewish idea and Christian interpretation of the creation in the image of God. It should therefore be clear that in other cultures, secularization will manifest itself differently, to the extent that it does so at all.

Non-Western civilizations—be they East Asian, Indian, Muslim, or Jewish—that enter (or are dragged into) the modern, industrialized, and urbanized world, will not combine this entry into modernity with the same cultivation of an ethos of autonomous individualism and therefore will not turn their backs on tradition, or at least will not do so in the same way. Hindus will have no difficulty continuing to light incense every morning in front of images of their beloved deities before they set out to trade shares, and the Japanese will not feel that observing their Shinto traditions undermines in any way their status as modern, educated individuals. For them, the call to reject external authority and the connection between liberty and the repudiation of tradition are not obvious, to the extent that they are familiar to them at all. For Muslims, the demand to renounce tradition, including public expressions of tradition, is as an affront, because the adherence to tradition, rather than its rejection, is a fundamental element in many Muslims' personal and collective identity.

The image of God, the core principle that shaped the Western tradition and powerfully contributed to the rise of autonomous individualism in the modern world, does not exist in Eastern religious traditions, nor is it emphasized in Muslim tradition (it is not even mentioned in the Quran). Even if these cultures adopt the political, cultural, and technological fruits of the West, there is no reason to assume that they will also adopt the same ethos commanding them to reject tradition or divine authority. For the same reason, individualism, which receives extreme emphasis in the Western world, will not necessarily develop in non-Western cultures. Different forms of community will be preserved, sometimes even zealously, as a targeted and defiant response to the individualistic culture of the West. In fact, since Europe and the United States constitute, after all, only a minority of the global population, we can assume that most of humanity will exemplify a model of secularization *unlike* that in the West, which will not lead to the form and character of society that we have witnessed developing in Europe.

As we can see, these developments also take different forms between one non-Western civilization and the next. Whereas cultures such as Japan's have embraced individualism, other cultures, such various Arab cultures, have rejected it. Whereas China and other East Asian countries such as Vietnam and North Korea imported various forms of Marxism and promoted the forced secularization of their populations, India championed democratic socialism, which gradually gave way to capitalism, and Hindu traditions have maintained their central place. It appears that Asian cultures, for reasons beyond the scope of the present study, find it easier than Muslim cultures to adopt individualism, which is indeed spreading in South Asia.[112] Nevertheless, it would be a mistake to think that this individualism involves an inner imperative to repudiate faith or tradition. This is secularization, but it is different from its Western expression.

If, as we noted above, the modern process of individualization finds expression in the field of religion as secularization, just as it finds expression in economics as capitalism and in politics as liberalism, it is clear that the secular West is capitalist and liberal not by accident. The dynamic that we have tracked throughout this book—the Christian division between the political and the religious realms, the moral calling, emerging from the juxtaposition of liberty and law, commanding us to be delivered unto liberty by rejecting tradition and, eventually, God—leads inexorably to a society of individuals who cherish their autonomy, view it and certain dimensions of their inner life as "rights" (that is, as sacrosanct and worthy of protection), and make an effort to establish political regimes that facilitate the protection and agency thereof.

Over the past millennia, history has witnessed many changes, sometimes sweeping ones. But none of them represented a fundamental transformation in how human beings understand themselves, religion (as a general phenomenon), and the divine. None called into question the basic authority of tradition, nor did any of these changes subvert the authority of religious institutions or offer humanity new, internal, and personal sources of authority. None of these changes transformed people into equal individuals, and none dismantled their traditional communities. None of these historical shifts made them secular. It was modernity that did all of this, itself being the culmination of a millennia-long process of development, which began with the idea that all human beings were created in the image of God.

Afterword

Has anything truly significant happened over the past few centuries? It is hard to imagine a more significant shift in the history of humanity than that in which selfhood, liberty, conscience, equality, and meaning have come under the sole authority of the individual self. Our understanding of the world, including our conception of humanity, has fundamentally changed. The idea of the image of God, planted as a seed approximately 3,000 years ago as part of the genesis story of a small but singular tribal people in Mesopotamia, has grown into a sprawling orchard whose fruits—forbidden or sweet—have led to a total revolution in the way we understand ourselves and the world around us.

The Protestant, Anglo-American West understood the image of God as reason and free will, or as conscience, encouraged individualism and a perception of liberty as autonomy, developed a sophisticated discourse of rights, fostered entrepreneurialism and democratization, and pursued equality in defiance of hierarchies. Moreover, it did all this grounded in a conception of the human subject as a bright nucleus of will or reason, unencumbered by ethnicity, religion, familial ties, or gender. This state of affairs gave rise to unprecedented personal autonomy, extraordinary social diversity, and immense material abundance.

The idea of the image of God has led humanity to a society populated by individuals, and to those individuals being both possessive and abstract, as we referred to them earlier. It promotes values such as equality, dignity, and freedom, and lays the base for establishing an unparalleled standard of living. It also undercuts tradition and community to an unparalleled degree. Modernity's wager,[1] as it were, is that without these sources of heteronomous meaning we will still be able to understand ourselves and to lead not only functional, but meaningful lives. That we will be able to fashion our own identity by ourselves, from within ourselves.

Will we? It seems the current crisis in the liberal order is a collective attempt to answer that question. Western individuals, whose self-concept is based on a modern translation of the principle of the image of God, tend to oppose homogeneity and coercion, while regarding the transgression of boundaries, free expression, creativity, and originality as manifestations of truth and authenticity. These all explicitly undermine tradition and community. The idealization of autonomy in Western culture also encourages and cultivates human diversity, with the manifestation of one's independent identity becoming a lifelong personal project, as people seek to develop and define themselves in manifold ways. The only means of governing such a diverse and prosperous society without the use of violence is within the architecture of the liberal order—which further fosters autonomy, thus increasing diversity.

We find ourselves, therefore, in a self-reinforcing system in which diversity begets the expansion of a liberal social framework, which in turn facilitates and therefore supports greater social diversity. The result is a colorful, creative, and productive society whose members are only loosely linked to each other, and which lacks the sort of overall framework of meaning that might help individuals find their bearings in time and space. The liberal order, which not only does not repudiate modern individualism but empowers it, cannot provide individuals with identity or meaning. Nor does it wish to, because its declared aim is to allow individuals to choose their own path, by themselves. The problem, therefore, is that the same social and ideational structures that secure our position as individuals detached from our surroundings and protect our autonomy as a sacred ideal tend to thrust us toward an unending search for meaning while undercutting sources thereof, such as community, solidarity, and tradition.

The crisis of liberalism that we have been experiencing in the past decade should be understood, therefore, primarily as a crisis of identity. Liberal thought conceives of individuals as abstract, genderless beings unencumbered by a past, ethnic roots, or religious attachments, who sign their social contract behind a "veil of ignorance." This definition of the individual is essential to the constitution of a society that treats all its members equally (and, liberals would add, fairly), but it also works to encourage abstract individualism. We are, the theory goes, in essence identity-less human creatures, and any other dimension of belonging or meaning in our lives—from ethnicity to gender—is an addition to our core humanity. That addition, we are told, can be discarded or changed as another expression of our autonomy.

The benefits of this conception are undeniable, but we must be aware of its deficiencies. What were once robust, non-voluntary, and indispensable dimensions of our identity have been relegated to a more marginal, elected, and at times superfluous status. For many, this works great. For many others, it creates anxiety and demonstrates anomie. Finding a way to counter and ameliorate this crisis of identity will be the next major challenge of the liberal order.

Living in a world that promotes proclamations about how all people are created equal or that they hold certain unalienable rights is in itself nothing self-evident. Such a rare reality is the civilizational peak of a process that began with the idea of the creation of all humans in the image of God. If it is treated as obvious, it is only because we ourselves, not only our ideas, have been shaped by this principle, and are not only its beneficiaries but its artifacts. Our own self-conception affirms it and demands the political world we share, even while we struggle to find our place within it.

The image of God is inescapably meaningful to us. It is part of us, at least inasmuch as we belong to the long historical chain that began with the book of Genesis and culminated in the modern liberal world. The ideas associated with man and woman's creation in God's image and the ideals to which these have given rise are deeply impressed in us, and they animate us no less than they animated the heroes of that ancient epic. They had led us to embrace faith in God, and to reject it and him; they drew us closer to organized religion, and they drove us to embark on a personal spiritual mission, or toward atheism. But we were and are propelled in both directions by the same fundamental idea, the principle that constitutes humans as individuals, as possessing singular value and endowed with rare abilities of reason, free choice, control, and conscience.

The idea of the image of God obliges us even today to support freedom and democracy. It requires us to protect our autonomy and that of our neighbours, to respect the dignity and intrinsic value of all human beings, to fight for human and civil rights, and to struggle for the establishment of a just, egalitarian society. The image of God compels us to see the divine in another, their unique, irreplaceable value, which stems from their subjective exceptionality.

After the liberal order reached extreme fruition in the early 2000s, it was thrust into a crisis—a crisis connected first and foremost to its members' capacity to maintain meaningful and sustainable identities. The liberal world's emergence from this crisis will depend on its ability to articulate new ideals and conceptions of meaning for itself, or in other words, to reimagine, while being rooted in the idea of the image of God, its conception of the human subject, and to cultivate more complete and better-developed notions of what constitutes selfhood, liberty, conscience, equality, and meaning.

ACKNOWLEDGMENTS

Like the ideas that these pages bring to the reader, they themselves also stand at the end of a long chain of transmission. I could not have written this book without the work of countless scholars who spent many years collecting and studying the materials I used, and whom I noted in notes throughout the book. I am indebted and grateful to them.

I wrote while being a research fellow at the Shalom Hartman Institute, and I thank the institute and its presidents, Rabbi Dr. Daniel Hartman and Dr. Yehuda Kurtzer, for the institute's enriching hospitality. I owe gratitude also to UC Berkeley, where I spent three wonderful years as a visiting professor, and specifically to The Helen Diller Institute for Jewish Law and Israel Studies and to its heads, Prof. Kenneth Bamberger and Prof. Ron Hassner.

Many thanks to Moshe Halbertal, Yoav Ashkenazi, Yaki Menschenfreund, Aviad Markovitz, and Ishay Rosen Zvi, who read parts of the manuscript or the whole of it and made comments that helped me formulate it properly. Of course, everything written in the book is solely my responsibility. Special thanks also to Eylon Levy for a brilliant translation; to Jennifer Hammer and Valerie Zaborski, my wonderful editors at NYU; to James Michael Reilly for his excellent copyediting work; and to Micah Goodman, who made all this possible.

Finaly, I owe much to my wife, Yael Yechieli, with whom I learn every day how to fulfill the scripture "In the image of God He created him, male and female He created them."

NOTES

INTRODUCTION

1 Tom Holland, *Dominion: How the Christian Revolution Remade the World* (New York: Basic Books, 2019).

2 Kenneth Pomeranz, *The Great Divergence: China, Europe, and the Making of the Modern World Economy* (Princeton, NJ: Princeton University Press, 2000); Prasannan Parthasarathi, *Why Europe Grew Rich and Asia Did Not: Global Economic Divergence, 1600–1850* (Cambridge: Cambridge University Press, 2011).

3 Walter Russell Mead, *God and Gold: Britain, America, and the Making of the Modern World* (New York: Vintage, 2008).

4 C. B. Macpherson, *The Political Theory of Possessive Individualism: From Hobbes to Locke* (Oxford: Oxford University Press, 1972).

5 Dror Wahrman, *The Making of the Modern Self: Identity and Culture in Eighteenth-Century England* (New Haven, CT: Yale University Press, 2006).

1. SELFHOOD

1 Robert Cover, "Nomos and Narrative," *Harvard Law Review* 97, no. 4 (1983): 4–5.

2 *The Code of Hammurabi*, trans. L. W. King, paras. 209–214, available online at the Avalon Project of Yale Law School: https://avalon.law.yale.edu/ancient/hamframe.asp.

3 In that they can be likened to formal declarations and statements, in which the narrative plays no less a part then the legislative, much like the United States Declaration of Independence. As we know, citizens of the United States in the eighteenth century did not always live according to the ideals set forth in its Declaration of Independence. Indeed, even its authors did not. Yet it had a profound effect on that society and its ongoing history.

4 Morris Jastrow, "An Assyrian Law Code," *Journal of the American Oriental Society* 41 (1921): 48–49.

5 *The Code of Hammurabi*, paras. 229–32.

6 The patriarch is of course the head of the family. In the ancient world, the extended family was the basic unit of society, and family members were thought of as limbs of a single body. Till today, many cultures (including Jewish culture) commonly have patronymic surnames, identifying people by their connection with a father figure. Ugaritic texts (from the fifteenth to thirteenth centuries BCE) feature first names incorporating "son of" or "daughter of" and then a father's

name. Back then, people's only associations were patrilineal. See Joshua Berman, *Created Equal: How the Bible Broke with Ancient Political Thought* (Oxford: Oxford University Press, 2011).

7 Henry Sumner Maine, *Ancient Law: Its Connection with the Early History of Society and Its Relation to Modern Ideas* (London: John Murray, 1908), 229.

8 Homer, *The Iliad*, trans. Robert Fitzgerald (Oxford: Oxford University Press, 1998), 376 (Book XXI, lines 462–66).

9 Cited in Hugh Lloyd-Jones, *The Justice of Zeus* (Berkeley: University of California Press, 1971), 3.

10 Genesis Rabbah 38:13.

11 See also II Kings 11:18; Ezekiel 7:20; Ezekiel 16:17; Amos 5:26; Daniel 3:1; II Chronicles 23:17.

12 Genesis 5:3 tells us, using both words in parallel: "When Adam had lived 130 years, he begot a son in his likeness after his image, and he named him Seth."

13 See, for example, descriptions of seeing God sitting on his throne in the prophetic books of Isaiah and Ezekiel, or the narrative in Exodus 24, when Moses, Aaron and seventy elders "saw the God of Israel, and there was under his feet as it were a paved work of a sapphire stone . . . they saw God, and did eat and drink." For more on God's corporeality, see Benjamin Sommer, *The Bodies of God and the World of Ancient Israel* (Cambridge: Cambridge University Press, 2009).

14 Yair Lorberbaum, *In the Image of God: Myth, Theology, and Law in Classical Judaism* (New York: Cambridge University Press, 2015).

15 Genesis Rabbah 8:10, cited in Lorberbaum, *In the Image of God*, 22.

16 Babylonian Talmud, Sanhedrin 46.

17 See Sommer, *The Bodies of God and the World of Ancient Israel*, 21–22; P. J. Harland, *The Value of Human Life: A Study of the Story of the Flood (Genesis 6–9)* (Leiden: E. J. Brill, 1996), 181–83.

18 See Sommer, *The Bodies of God*, 33–36.

19 Harland, *The Value of Human Life: A Study of the Story of the Flood (Genesis 6–9)*, 197.

20 Avot d'Rabbi Natan, version 2, chap. 30. Translation available from Sefaria.org.

21 Hillel the Elder was the standard-bearer of the conception of humans as God's image, and this way of thinking, as Lorberbaum argues (following David Flusser), can also be discerned in a plethora of his statements about the importance of the self: "If I am here, everyone is here; and if I am not here, who is here?" (Babylonian Talmud, Sukkah 53a), "If I am not for myself, who will be for me?" (Ethics of the Fathers 1:14), etc.

22 Plato, *Republic*, trans. Robin Waterfield (Oxford: Oxford University Press, 2008), 119.

23 Aristotle, *The Politics and Constitution of Athens*, ed. Stephen Everson (Cambridge: Cambridge University Press, 1996), 16.

24 Hymn 90 in *Hymns of the Rigveda*, vol. 2, trans. Ralph T. H. Griffith (Benares: E. J. Lazarus, 1897), 517–18.

25 In fact, in Thomas Jefferson's first draft of the Declaration of Independence, he also attributed human beings' "inalienable rights" to the fact of their equal creation: "We hold these truths to be sacred & undeniable; that all men are created equal & independent, that *from that equal creation* they derive rights inherent & inalienable, among which are the preservation of life, & liberty, & the pursuit of happiness." (Emphasis mine).

26 See Moshe Barasch, *Icon: Studies in the History of an Idea* (New York: NYU Press, 1995).

27 D. J. A. Clines, "The Image of God in Man," *Tyndale Bulletin* 19 (1968): 7; and J. Maxwell Miller, "In the 'Image' and 'Likeness' of God," *Journal of Biblical Literature* 91, no. 3 (Sep. 1972): 289–304.

28 Ibid., 80.

29 Ibid.

30 Importantly, there is also a very ancient Egyptian myth that speaks of all humanity as having been created in the image of God. The twenty-second- or twenty-first-century BCE text *The Instruction for King Meri-Ka-Re* describes God as having "made heaven and earth according to their desire, and he repelled the water-monster. He made the breath of life (for) their nostrils. They who have issued from his body are his images. . . . He made for them plants, animals, fowl, and fish to feed them. . . . He makes the light of day." Cited in James B. Pritchard, ed., *Ancient Near Eastern Texts Relating to the Old Testament* (Princeton, NJ: Princeton University Press, 1969), 417.

    Here, humans are born rather than created, but they are born in the image of God. Weinfeld regards this as proof of Egyptian influence in the book of Genesis, and this is quite possible. Nevertheless, the religion of ancient Egypt did not develop this idea any further, and in the following centuries the image of God was attributed exclusively to kings. In contrast, the Jewish tradition elevated this notion into one of its most central and fundamental tenets, and from Judaism it spread to the whole Western world.

31 Robert H. Pfeiffer, *State Letters of Assyria* (New Haven, CT: American Oriental Society, 1935), 120.

32 Cited in Clines, "The Image of God in Man," 84–85. Moshe Weinfeld summarizes it thus: "Both in Egypt and in Mesopotamia, the king was described as having been made in the image and likeness of a god. The Babylonian and Assyrian kings were the *ṣalmu* and *muššulu* ('image') of god, while the Egyptian king was the *hntj* or *twt* of god." Weinfeld, "The Creator God in Genesis 1 and the Prophecies of Deutero-Isaiah," *Tarbiz* 37, no. 2 (Dec. 1967): 114 [Hebrew].

33 There is another version of this famous dictum, which states "anyone who destroys one soul *from the Jewish people*, it is as if he destroyed an entire world," but this is not the original. It is a later revision, which appears to have entered common currency because it was recited when witnesses were given instructions prior to delivering a testimony. See Ephraim E. Urbach, "'Kol Ha-meqayyem Nefesh Aḥat . . .'—Development of the Version, Vicissitudes of

Censorship, and Business Manipulations of Printers," *Tarbiz* 40, no. 3 (1971): 268–74 [Hebrew].

34 Alexander Altmann, *The Face of Judaism* (Tel Aviv: Am Oved, 1983), 17 [Hebrew].

35 Tablet 2b in Avraham Levanon, *Anthology of Laws of Ancient Near Eastern Nations* (Haifa: O. R., 1967), 131 [Hebrew].

36 It is hard to pinpoint exactly when these laws were first drafted. The Torah is not a uniform document, but rather contains a variety of texts, composed at different times and collated at a later period. While we can date with confidence the composition of large parts of the Torah, especially the narrative-based texts, the collections of laws are harder to date, because even if they received their final form and entered the canon at a certain time, they might have been formulated much earlier. See Alexander Rofe, *Introduction to the Literature of the Hebrew Bible* (Jerusalem: Simor, 2009).

37 See Greenberg, "Some Postulates of Biblical Criminal Law."

38 James L. Kugel, *The Great Shift: Encountering God in Biblical Times* (Boston: Houghton Mifflin Harcourt, 2017), 260.

39 Ibid, 264.

40 For the creation of this model of selfhood, see the monumental study in Thomas Metzinger, *Being No One: The Self-Model Theory of Subjectivity* (Cambridge, MA: MIT Press, 2004).

41 For Taylor, see the forgoing discussion. Kugel writes about this theory in his *The Great Shift*. Both draw on different studies and the books of Bruno Snell and Julian Jaynes, which are considered deficient for several reasons nowadays, but they were the first to propose this theoretical direction. See Bruno Snell, *The Discovery of the Mind in Greek Philosophy and Literature* (New York: Dover, 1982); Julian Jaynes, *The Origins of Consciousness in the Breakdown of the Bicameral Mind* (Boston: Houghton Mifflin Company, 1976).

42 Walter T. Anderson, *The Future of the Self: Inventing the Postmodern Person* (New York: J. P. Tarcher, 1997), 23.

43 Kugel quotes Godfrey Lienhardt, a twentieth-century anthropologist, who wrote about the conception of self among the Dinka people of South Sudan, who "have no conception which at all closely corresponds to our popular modern conception of the 'mind' as mediating and, as it were, storing up the experiences of the self. . . . There is, for them, no interior entity to . . . stand between the experiencing self at any given moment and what is or has been an exterior influence upon the self." Cited in Kugel, *The Great Shift*, 49.

44 Clifford Geertz, "From the Native's Point of View: On the Nature of Anthropological Understanding," *Bulletin of the American Academy of Arts and Sciences* 28, no. 1 (1974): 31. Charles Taylor devotes his book *Sources of the Self: The Making of Modern Identity*, which I have cited extensively in this book, to tracing the creation of this singular modern self.

45 As can be discerned, for example, in statements such as "thoughts of transgression are worse than transgression itself" in the Babylonian Talmud, Yoma 29a.

See Ayelet Hoffmann Libson, *Law and Self-Knowledge in the Talmud* (Cambridge: Cambridge University Press, 2018).

46 Benjamin Read Foster, ed. and trans., *The Epic of Gilgamesh* (New York: W. W. Norton, 2001), 107–8.

47 In fact, the literal translation of what Huwawa sends toward Gilgamesh, at least in the Akkadian version of the myth, is simply "fear." The monster simply throws fear at Gilgamesh, which enters him.

48 Homer, *The Iliad*, 315 (Book XVII, lines 567–74).

49 Not only in relation to courage was the psyche of an ancient Greek susceptible to external influences. Sleep was also caused by the gods (Morpheus, or even Athena, such as in Book V of *The Odyssey*, 464–93), as was creativity (remember that the *Iliad* begins, like the *Odyssey* after it, with an appeal to the divine Muse to allow the poet to sing, because without the Muse's inspiration, creativity isn't possible).

50 There is an interesting parallel here to another covenant, this time with God: male circumcision, the maiming of the male sex organ. Both covenants are entered into between a population and a king; both are covenants of servitude; and in both, this servitude is marked on the flesh.

51 In the *Iliad*, the gods are also able to instill people with evil spirits. Agamemnon excuses his poor behavior toward Achilles by saying, "But I am not to blame. Zeus and Fate and a nightmare Fury are, for putting savage Folly in my mind in the assembly that day" (Book XIX, lines 85–90, p. 340 in the Fitzgerald translation). Aharon Shabtai explains that this "Folly" was a destructive spirit called *atē* in Greek and was "the most extreme stage of hubris. It is a demonic divinity that plays the role of destructive illusions, confounding people's senses, a blind frenzy, bound up with disaster." Homer, *The Iliad*, trans. Aharon Shabtai (Tel Aviv: Schocken, 2016) [Hebrew]. Hubris is therefore a deity that enters a person and changes his character.

52 Rofe, *Introduction to the Literature of the Hebrew Bible*. For points of commonality in the ancient Greeks' and ancient Hebrews' conception of selfhood, see Kugel, *The Great Shift*.

53 Snell, *The Discovery of the Mind in Greek Philosophy and Literature*, 31.

54 James Kugel addresses the conception of the self in the *Testaments of the Twelve Patriarchs*, and I base my own argument on the discussion in his *The Great Shift*, 37–56.

55 *Testaments of the Twelve Patriarchs*, trans. R. H. Charles (1908), available online at Sefaria.org (The Testament of Reuben 3:2–7). See also Jubilees 1, which describes the "unclean demons" that led Noah's sons to sin. In other words, Noah's sons did not go astray; they were led astray. See also Kugel, *The Great Shift*, 39.

56 Charles Taylor, *A Secular Age* (Cambridge, MA: Harvard University Press, 2007), 37–41.

57 *The Testament of the Twelve Patriarchs*, Testament of Simeon 2:7, available online at Sefaria.org.

58 Taylor, *A Secular Age*, 41.

59 Ishay Rosen-Zvi, *Demonic Desires: Yetzer Hara and the Problem of Evil In Late Antiquity* (Philadelphia: University of Pennsylvania Press, 2011), 129. Rosen-Zvi outlines a process by which the *yetzer hara* was internalized, transforming it from an external demonic force into an inner force. It is worth noting, nevertheless, the fact that the existence of the *yetzer hara*, the "evil instinct," as an internal rather than external element still does not make it part of the self. Modern Western individuals experience their "sinful" or bad urges as part of themselves (and sometimes even as a part that must be recognized, given space, not repressed, and so forth), but as Rosen-Zvi emphasizes in his study, for the Sages of the Second Temple period and later, the *yetzer hara* was not part of the self, but still an internal element, one of many that formed a complex of forces operating inside all human beings.

60 When he faces a decision, Socrates finds himself "subject to a divine or supernatural experience. . . . It began in my early childhood—a sort of voice which comes to me; and when it comes it always dissuades me from what I am proposing to do." Plato, "Apology," in *The Last Days of Socrates*, ed. Harold Tarrant, trans. Hugh Tredennick and Harold Tarrant (London: Penguin, 1954), 89. Augustine, writing in the early fifth century (800 years after Socrates), still thinks of Socrates's *daimonion* as a foreign force speaking to him, and he devotes a chapter of his famous *The City of God* to disproving the position that this is God talking, and proving that it is a demon. See there, Book VIII.

61 E. R. Dodds, *Pagan and Christian in an Age of Anxiety* (Cambridge: Cambridge University Press, 2001).

62 See the discussion in Taylor, *A Secular Age*, 37.

63 Hippocrates, *Aphorisms*, Section 6, Aphorism 23.

64 Taylor, *A Secular Age*, 37.

65 Charles Taylor, *Hegel* (Cambridge: Cambridge University Press, 1999), 8–9.

66 Diderot, Denis, "Melancholia," in *The Encyclopedia of Diderot & d'Alembert Collaborative Translation Project*, trans. Matthew Chozick (Ann Arbor: University of Michigan Library, 2007). Originally published as "Melancholie," *Encyclopédie ou Dictionnaire raisonné des sciences, des arts et des métiers*, 10:308–11 (Paris, 1765).

67 Taylor, *A Secular Age*, chap. 2.

68 This is in contrast to the laws of the Babylonians and the Assyrians, for whom it is left to the discretion of the husband to pardon his wife and (sometimes with the permission of the king) the adulterer, or to punish them. The Hebrew husband of an adulteress cannot simply waive her punishment, because adultery in ancient Hebrew society was a sin not only against him as the husband, nor even just against the king, but also against the King of Kings: against God. The difference stems from the source of law. In Mesopotamia and the ancient Near East, the law was considered eternal, and the gods and the people empowered by the gods, namely the kings, were understood as defenders and enforcers of the law; in other words, it was not thought that the gods legislated these laws, only that they

enforced them. In contrast, Hebrew law was understood as coming directly from God. Consequently, violations of the law were considered not merely transgressions from proper norms, nor only interruptions of the cosmic order, but acts of rebellion against God's explicit will. In other words, violations of the law were not only mistakes, distortions, acts of blindness, or crimes—they were sins. This distinction is hugely significant. We may be responsible for our mistakes, but there is a limit to the guilt that can be ascribed to us because of them. In the case of crimes, guilt is clearly ascribed to their perpetrators, but they are guilty of crimes against individuals, not God. Sins, meanwhile, are crimes against God, and therefore the guilt that is incurred is much more severe. See the discussion in Moshe Greenberg, "Some Postulates of Hebrew Criminal Law," in his *Studies in the Bible and Jewish Thought* (Philadelphia: Jewish Publication Society, 1995), 25–41.

69 The word is translated from the Hebrew verb *ina* that suggests causing bodily damage or torture, and is used in the Bible to signify forced intercourse.

70 In Exodus 22:15–16, there is a law about a man who lies with a virgin of her own free will: "If a man seduces a virgin for whom the bride-price has not been paid, and lies with her, he must make her his wife by payment of a bride-price. If her father refuses to give her to him, he must still weigh out silver in accordance with the bride-price for virgins." A man who seduces an unbetrothed virgin to sleep with him must marry the woman. If her father refuses to give her to him (note, *she* is not asked what she wants), he must nevertheless pay her father a bride price for her virginity. Similarly, in the case at hand, the payout is apparently the bride price (see the *Mekhilta d'Rabbi Ishmael*, Mishpatim, Nezikin 17).

71 Israeli Penal Law 1977, para. 345. Unofficial translation from the OECD.

72 The offense caused to a jilted husband is not considered sufficiently important to classify adultery as a crime, and a woman is not considered "his" in a sufficiently serious manner to make him, her husband, an interested party.

73 Larry Siedentop, *Inventing the Individual: The Origins of Western Liberalism* (London: Penguin, 2015), 18.

74 In most ancient cultures, the family was the smallest religious unit, since each household had its own shrine, of which the patriarch—in the sense of the grandfather figure at the head of a multi-branched clan—served as the high priest. The building blocks of society and religion were therefore perfectly parallel. Ancestorworship is one of the oldest and most common forms of worship; "ancestral merit" is one of the most widespread means to accumulate religious and social capital; and relations with various divine entities were correspondingly conceived in familial terms ("our father in heaven," etc.). See Oswyn Murray and Simon Price, eds., *The Greek City: From Homer to Alexander* (Oxford: Clarendon Press, 2000); W. Robertson Smith, *The Religion of the Semites* (New York: Meridian, 1956).

75 Aron Gurevich, *The Worldview of Medieval People*, trans. Peter Kriksunov (Jerusalem: Academon, 1993), 70 [Hebrew].

76 Ibid., 234 [Hebrew].

2. FREEDOM

1 Cicero, *De Re Publica, Book I*, 43, in *The Republic and the Laws*, trans. Niall Rudd (Oxford: Oxford University Press, 2008), 20.

2 Livy, *The History of Rome, Books 1–5*, trans. Valerie M. Warrior (Indianapolis: Hackett Publishing Company, 2006), book 4, 260.

3 Ibid., Book I, 47, in *The Republic and the Laws*, 21. Cicero presents here the position of the *populares* movement, the populists of his day. He does not agree with them on various details (he was more conservative and wished to preserve more power for the elite, for fear that the masses would ultimately elect a demagogue, who would become a dictator), but he certainly agrees that genuine liberty means participation in political decision-making. See the (somewhat archaic but interesting) discussion on his quotation in Hans Kelsen, *The Essence and Value of Democracy*, trans. Brian Graf (Lanham, MD: Rowman and Littlefield, 2013), 27 onwards; and also in Annelien De Dijn, *Freedom: An Unruly History* (Cambridge, MA: Harvard University Press, 2020), 82–88.

4 Benjamin Constant, "The Liberty Of The Ancients Compared With That Of The Moderns," in *Political Writings*, ed. and trans. Biancamaria Fontana (Cambridge: Cambridge University Press, 1988), 316. The premodern conception of liberty remained resonant in the seventeenth century, as part of the struggle for democracy. See also De Dijn, *Freedom*, chap. 3.

5 Except, again, within the context of spiritual and philosophical sects. See below.

6 New Testament quotations herein are from the New King James Version.

7 Daniel Boyarin, *A Radical Jew: Paul and the Politics of Identity* (Berkeley: University of California Press, 1997).

8 Philippians 3:5: "[I was] circumcised the eighth day, of the stock of Israel, of the tribe of Benjamin, a Hebrew of the Hebrews; concerning the law, a Pharisee."

9 Of the thirteen epistles attributed to Paul, seven are consensually agreed upon as authentically his. These include Romans, 1 Corinthians, 2 Corinthians, Galatians, Philippians, 1 Thessalonians, and Philemon. Our discussion of Paul focuses on these letters, with the addition of Colossians, which some consider authentic and some as written by Paul's immediate follower—see James D. G. Dunn, *The Epistles to the Colossians and to Philemon: A Commentary on the Greek Text, New International Greek Testament Commentary* (Grand Rapids, MI: Eerdmans, 2014). In any case, Colossians has obviously been accepted by the church and Christian tradition as authentic, and the theology it presents has been part of Christianity since its founding.

10 Paul's conversion is described twice in the Acts of the Apostles, in chapters 9 and 22. On both occasions, Jesus's revelation to Paul is described as a great and sudden light ("a great light from heaven shone around me," Acts 22:6), and Jesus's invitation to Paul is described as a voice from the heavens ordering him to preach his gospel and to stop persecuting his followers.

11 Alan F. Segal, *Paul the Convert: The Apostolate and Apostasy of Saul the Pharisee* (New Haven, CT: Yale University Press, 1990), 22, 59–63.

12 See James D. G. Dunn, *The Theology of Paul the Apostle* (Grand Rapids, MI: William B. Eerdmans Publishing, 1998), 390–412. See also Segal, *Paul the Convert*; and Colleen Shanz, *Paul in Ecstasy: The Neurobiology of the Apostle's Life and Thought* (Cambridge: Cambridge University Press, 2009). The study of Paul's mystical experiences received attention from several prominent figures in the early twentieth century, most famously Albert Schweitzer ("Dying and rising with Christ is not [for Paul] . . . something merely metaphorical . . . but a simple reality. . . . For him the believer experiences the dying and rising again of Christ in actual fact, not in an imitative representation"). See Albert Schweitzer, *The Mysticism of Paul the Apostle*, trans. William Montgomery (Baltimore: Johns Hopkins University Press, 1998), 15–16. But after the Second World War, and especially with the postmodern "linguistic turn" in academia, Schweitzer was pushed aside and returned to relevance only decades later.

In my opinion, nothing is more important for an understanding of the Pauline religious revolution, because not only do Paul's mystical experiences stand at the core of his religious worldview, but also the emphasis on this inner, experiential, transformative dimension would remain with Christianity, and indeed with the whole Western world, into the present. But it is important to acknowledge that this is a particular view of Paul, that is still disputed within Pauline studies. For important alternative voices, see E. P. Sanders, *Paul and Palestinian Judaism* (Minneapolis: Fortress, 1977); Stanley K. Stowers, *A Rereading of Romans: Justice, Jews, and Gentiles* (New Haven, CT: Yale University Press, 1997); John G. Gager, *Reinventing Paul* (Oxford: Oxford University Press, 2000); Terence L. Donaldson, *Paul and the Gentiles: Remapping the Apostle's Convictional World* (Minneapolis: Fortress Press, 2006); E. P. Sanders, *Paul: The Apostle's Life, Letters, and Thought* (Minneapolis: Fortress, 2015); and Matthew Thiessen, *A Jewish Paul* (Grand Rapids, MI: Baker Academic, 2023).

13 1 Corinthians 1:2–8, 1:30; Romans 8:1–2. Deliverance from original sin is arguably the central tenet of Christian theology, and for Paul it is directly associated with living "in Christ" (2 Corinthians 5:21, Romans 3:24). As Albert Schweitzer wrote, "the doctrine of righteousness by faith is therefore a subsidiary crater, which has formed within the rim of the main-crater—the mystical doctrine of redemption through the being-in-Christ" (Schweitzer, *The Mysticism of Paul the Apostle*, 225). See also Dunn, *The Theology of Paul the Apostle*, 400–401.

14 Tom Stoppard, *Jumpers* (London: Faber, 1972), 79.

15 Jerusalem Talmud, Kilayim 8:3. An expanded version can be found in the Babylonian Talmud, Niddah 31a: "The Sages taught: There are three partners in the creation of a person: The Holy One, Blessed be He, and his father, and his mother. His father emits the white seed, from which the following body parts are formed: The bones, the sinews, the nails, the brain that is in its head, and the white of the eye. His mother emits red seed, from which are formed the skin, the flesh, the hair, and the black of the eye. And the Holy One, Blessed be He, inserts into him a spirit, a soul, his countenance [*kelaster*], eyesight, hearing of the ear, the capabil-

ity of speech of the mouth, the capability of walking with the legs, understanding, and wisdom. And when a person's time to depart from the world arrives, the Holy One, Blessed be He, retrieves His part, and He leaves the part of the person's father and mother before them."

16 Plato, *Laws*, trans. R. G. Bury (London: William Heinemann, 1926), 545.

17 Babylonian Talmud, Berakhot 70b.

18 Daniel Boyarin, *Carnal Israel: Reading Sex in Talmudic Culture* (Berkeley: University of California Press, 1993), 5–6.

19 Philo of Alexandria, "On the Creation," in *The Works of Philo: Complete and Unabridged*, trans. C. D. Yonge (Peabody, MA: Hendrickson, 1993), 10.

20 Only in the Mishnah do we first find a discussion about intentions in the course of performing religious commandments. The Hebrew Bible makes no mention of this, and scholars have indeed illuminated the Mishnah's novelty in this regard. But even in the Mishnah, little attention is paid to intentions. Most mitzvot, or commandments, can be performed without intention, simply through unconscious acts. Even in prayer Jews are required to be conscious of what they are saying only during the recitation of the Shema and the Birkat Avot (Blessing of the Ancestors). It is enough to mumble the rest in order to be considered to have discharged one's duties. From the strict perspective of Halakha, therefore, intentions are insufficiently significant to become a necessary condition.

21 Ishay Rosen-Zvi, "The Mishnaic Mental Revolution: A Reassessment," *Journal of Jewish Studies* 56, no. 1 (2015): 36–58, 51.

22 Ibid, 54. For a different opinion, see Ayelet Hoffmann Libson, *Law and Self-Knowledge in the Talmud.*

23 Note that Paul's new worldview had another foundation. As we have seen, since the days of Athenian democracy, there flourished in Hellenistic civilization various spiritual-philosophical schools that proposed ways of life that combined systematic ethics with soteriological promises that are realized as transformative experiences in the human psyche (recall the *metamorphosis* to which Paul alludes). As Pierre Hadot demonstrated in his groundbreaking study, Greek philosophy was interested not only in theory in its contemporary sense—i.e., with claims about the nature of existence—but also with theory in its *original* sense, as a form of contemplation, even meditation, that was itself part of a way of life and system of ethics. See Pierre Hadot, *What is Ancient Philosophy?* (Cambridge, MA: Harvard University Press, 2004).

The best-known Greek philosophical schools—the Epicureans, Cynics, Skeptics, Neoplatonists, and Stoics—led lives dictated by organized systems of ethics, in the hope of attaining some existential spiritual transformation as a result. Each school believed in a different path to spiritual wisdom, but they all shared the same end point, defined by a single, primary objective: equanimity and a sense of mental and psychological peace, usually called *ataraxia* (ἀταραξία). Ibid., 102–8.

Paul was likely familiar with these spiritual-philosophical methods, or at least understood their intellectual underpinnings. Yet he rejected them. The Christian framework that he developed and promoted did not involve spiritual control over one's own powers, but total dependence on transcendental salvation. No less important is the fact that it did not speak about *liberation from error*, but *redemption from sin*. For Paul, Christianity was not another philosophical school, but the one true faith. And the internal transformation that it heralded was more than the attainment of homeostasis or ataraxia—it was release from sin and true liberty (recall that unlike for the Hellenistic philosophers, for Paul, a Jew, "sin" was a live and thorny theological category).

See for example his coded remarks in 1 Corinthians 2:4: "My speech and my preaching were not with persuasive words of human wisdom, but in demonstration of the Spirit and of power." See also the discussion of Paul's rejection of philosophy in Alain Badiou, *Saint Paul: The Foundation of Universalism*, trans. Ray Brassier (Stanford, CA: Stanford University Press, 2003).

Nevertheless, inasmuch as he exemplifies a concerned individual's focus on his or her own spiritual life and the attainment of redemption through an internal transformation, Paul was consistent with Hellenistic philosophies.

24 Romans 9:32. As a Pharisee, Paul believed in the physical resurrection of the dead, and so, obviously, he could not completely reject the importance of the body. His renunciation of the "flesh," the internalization of the notion of the image of God and the spiritualization of the body, was for him a way to repair the image of God. For the difference between the "body" and the "flesh" in Paul's thinking and its ramifications, see Ishay Rosen-Zvi, *Body and Soul in Ancient Judaism* (Ben Shemen: Modan, 2012), 54–58 [Hebrew].

25 Paul's rejection of the contemporary religious establishment was revolutionary, and the "Apostle to the Gentiles" probably thought initially that the End of Days was nigh, and that Jesus would soon return to redeem the world. Indeed, some contemporaries interpreted Paul's resistance to Jewish law as a license to ignore law altogether, and throughout the second century, the Church had to underscore the need for moral behavior, that is, the need to restrict human conduct in accordance with clear norms. See Henry Chadwick, *The Early Church* (London: Penguin, 1993), 67–68.

When it became clear that the Second Coming of Christ was not immediately forthcoming, the first Christian communities had to reorganize accordingly, that is, to become a church. See Margaret Mitchell's discussion of the instructions given by the author of the Second Epistle to the Thessalonians, after Paul suggested in the first epistle that the final redemption was at hand: Margaret M. Mitchell, "1 and 2 Thessalonians," in *The Cambridge Companion to St. Paul*, ed. James D. G. Dunn (Cambridge: Cambridge University Press, 2003), 51–63.

In any case, law and practice became parts of the Christian religion. Moreover, the fact that the Church was institutionalized, instead of remaining simply one of many Gnostic cults (quite a few of which sanctified Jesus), shows that besides Paul's anti-institutional and antinomian ethos, there were also stridently pro-institutional and nomian forces in the Church. If the Catholic Church, for all its renunciation of the material (the world and the body), had not maintained some minimal necessary balance between calling for a departure from tradition and the embrace of a new tradition, it would have been incapable of enduring as a living religious framework, not to mention a world religion. Unlike the Gnostic sects, Christianity did not reject the Hebrew Bible but rather sanctified it (as the "Old Testament") and thus accepted the world as a positive creation of God. Unlike other Gnostic cults, Christianity was not elitist, did not create for itself a closed circle of chosen "sons of light," and did not purport to guard some esoteric knowledge hidden from the masses, but rather addressed the whole of humanity. In this, it received the legitimacy, not to mention a positive duty, to build and establish the Church in an institutionalized, and indeed hierarchical manner.

26 Siedentop, *Inventing the Individual*, 61–62.

27 Saint Augustine, *Confessions*, trans. Henry Chadwick (Oxford: Oxford University Press, 2008), 216.

28 Max Weber, *The Religion of China: Confucianism and Taoism*, trans. Hans H. Gerth (New York: Macmillan, 1964), 237.

29 In a fascinating and important book, Joseph Henrich, a Harvard professor of evolutionary biology, psychology, and economics, attributes the uniqueness of the Western world to the Catholic Church's dismantlement of the extended family. In brief, Henrich argues that in contrast to other civilizations, the Catholic Church forbade marriages between relatives of any sort in the areas under its jurisdiction. Whereas everywhere else, marriages were only forbidden within the nuclear family, in the Catholic (and later Protestant) West, marriages were also forbidden between cousins, all the way to sixth-degree relatives! The result over time was the breakdown of clan-based and tribal ties, which led to radical changes in how Western individuals saw the world. They adopted a more individualistic, universalistic, analytical, egalitarian mode of thinking, which was less conformist, communal, dogmatic, and holistic. Henrich's evidence is anchored in various psychological studies, and he presents compelling arguments.

What his book overlooks, however, are the theological reasons that led Christianity to focus on the individual and reject clan-based ties in the first place. What is attempted in this book is an examination of these reasons and their influence on the mentality of the West. See Joseph Henrich, *The Weirdest People in the World: How the West Became Psychologically Peculiar and Particularly Prosperous* (New York: Farrar, Straus and Giroux, 2020).

30 Augustine, *De Bono Coniugali, De Sancta Virginitate*, ed. Henry Chadwick, trans. P. G. Walsh (Oxford: Oxford University Press, 2001), 9.

31 Paul and the Church built their conception of monogamy not only on their conception of the person, but noticeably also on the basis of monogamy as it had

developed in ancient Rome, from which, through Christianity, the Western world inherited its own conception of monogamy. For the development of monogamy, see Walter Scheidel, "A peculiar institution? Greco-Roman monogamy in global context," *History of the Family* 14 (2009): 280–91.

32 Badiou, *Saint Paul.*

33 Marcel Mauss, "A Category of the Human Mind: The Notion of the Person, the Notion of Self," in *The Category of the Person: Anthropology, Philosophy, History,* ed. Michael Carrithers, Steven Collins, and Steven Lukes (Cambridge: Cambridge University Press, 1985), 19.

34 See Ishay Rosen-Zvi, "The Birth of the Goy in Rabbinic Literature," in Ishay Rosen-Zvi et al., *Myth, Mysticism and Ritual: Studies in the Relations between Jewish and Religious Studies* (Tel Aviv: Tel Aviv University, 2014), 361–438 [Hebrew]. Rosen-Zvi shows how the category of "Gentile," of generic non-Jews, who are distinguished from Jews simply by their non-Jewishness, evolved in rabbinic literature. This process heralded the beginning of a sharper distinction between Jews and non-Jews than existed in the pre-rabbinic Jewish world, and it should presumably be understood as a response to the development of Christianity and the Pauline pretense of turning "Israel" into a universal category. For more on the roots of Paul's universalism in Jewish tradition, see Boyarin, *A Radical Jew*; Terence L. Donaldson, *Paul and the Gentiles: Remapping the Apostle's Convictional World.*

35 In Tractate Rosh Hashanah, we read about a nightly protest organized by Yehuda ben Shammua against Roman imperial officials in the Land of Israel, decrying an oppressive decree that forbade Torah study, circumcision, and Sabbath observance. The protestors shout, "O Heavens! Are we Jews not your brothers; are we not children of one father; are we not children of one mother? How are we different from every other nation and tongue that you issue such harsh decrees against us?" (Babylonian Talmud, Rosh Hashanah 19a). Their petition to the Romans draws its force from basic human solidarity, rooted in the biblical myth of the birth of humanity from the same set of parents.

36 Babylonian Talmud, Yevamot 47b. It was the Jewish Sages who developed a ritual process of conversion, of becoming Jewish, away from the biblical conception of simple assimilation into the Jewish nation ("Your people shall be my people, and your God my God," Ruth 1:16) and toward a process of studying the Oral Law and ritual admission. See Shaye J. D. Cohen, *The Beginnings of Jewishness* (Berkeley: University of California Press, 1999).

37 Romans 2:29, Galatians 5:6, Galatians 6:12–15, and more.

38 Dunn, *The Theology of Paul the Apostle,* 53, 468.

39 Margaret M. Mitchell and Frances M. Young, eds., *The Cambridge History of Christianity,* vol. 1 (Cambridge: Cambridge University Press, 2008), 152.

40 Bernard McGinn, *The Foundations of Mysticism,* vol. 1 of *The Presence of God: A History of Western Christian Mysticism* (New York: Crossroads, 1991), 71.

41 (*Hom. on Gen.* 1.13), quotes in McGinn, *The Foundations of Mysticism,* vol. 1, 114.

42 Ibid., 243.

43 In terms of the metaphysics of the soul, Paul seems to have subscribed to the Stoic conception, whereby a person's essence was not an unambiguously internal matter. Later Church Fathers would subscribe to a Platonic view associating a person's essence with his soul, located inside the body. See Troels Engberg-Pedersen, *Cosmology and Self in the Apostle Paul: The Material Spirit* (Oxford: Oxford University Press, 2010), 8–38.

44 Siedentop, *Inventing the Individual*, 62.

45 Ibid., 61.

46 When asked whether one should pay taxes, Jesus asks whose image appears on coins. Since it is an image of Caesar, Jesus says: "Render therefore to Caesar the things that are Caesar's, and to God the things that are God's." It is not inconceivable that Jesus was familiar with an allegory that was put down in written form slightly after his time in the Mishnah, according to which the image of God was minted in humans just as the image of the emperor was minted in coins (Sanhedrin 4:5). For Jesus, just as we understand from the presence of God's image in humans that humans belongs to God, we may understand from the presence of the emperor's image on coins that politics and money belong to earthly forces. Versions of the story and this famous sentence appear also in Mark 12:17 and Luke 20:25.

47 Jacob Burckhardt, *The Civilization of the Renaissance in Italy*, trans. S. G. C. Middlemore (London: George Allen and Unwin, 1878).

48 Tertullian, "Ad Scapulam," cited in Maurice Wiles and Mark Santer, eds., *Documents in Early Christian Thought* (Cambridge: Cambridge University Press, 2005), 227.

49 Peter Garnsey, "Religious Toleration in Classical Antiquity," in *Studies in Church History* 21 (1984): 1–27.

50 See the translation by S. Thelwall in Allan Menzies, ed., *Latin Christianity: Its Founder, Tertullian*, vol. 3 of *Ante-Nicene Fathers* (Christian Classics Ethereal Library, Kindle Edition), location 4063.

51 Robert Louis Wilken, "The Christian Roots of Religious Freedom," in *Historical Perspectives*, vol. 1 of *Christianity and Freedom*, ed. Timothy Samuel Shah, and Allen D. Hertzke (New York: Cambridge University Press, 2016), 65.

52 The story appears in various forms in the Babylonian Talmud (Gittin 57b), Midrash Eichah Rabbah 1:50, 2 Maccabees 7:1–6, and 4 Maccabees 8–18.

53 Translation courtesy of the Internet Medieval Sourcebook: https://sourcebooks. fordham.edu/source/edict-milan.asp. See Timothy Samuel Shah, "The Roots of Religious Freedom in Early Christian Thought," in *Christianity and Freedom*, vol. 1, 56.

54 Shah, ibid.

55 Note that rabbinical Judaism, which took shape in the first centuries CE in parallel with Christianity, also developed a system of religion detached from the political realm. The Jews spoke about, learned about, and prayed for an indepen-

dent kingdom, but in practice they developed a religion that operated in parallel with a foreign political regime and created a corpus of religious law that existed beyond the political order. In fact, this had been the situation more or less since the fall of Jerusalem to the Babylonians in 586 BCE. The Babylonians gave way to the Persians, who gave way to the Greeks, who gave way to the Romans (after a brief interlude of independence under the Hasmoneans). Nevertheless, Judaism remained much less individualistic in its conception of worship and redemption, and it always attached significantly less importance to religious conscience.

56 Siedentop, *Inventing the Individual*, 116.

57 Chadwick, *The Early Church*, 59.

58 Ilaria Ramelli, *Social Justice and the Legitimacy of Slavery: The Role of Philosophical Asceticism from Ancient Judaism to Late Antiquity* (Oxford: Oxford University Press, 2016).

59 Ramelli, *Social Justice and the Legitimacy of Slavery*, 76–87.

60 According to Jewish law, a Jewish slave would have to be freed after six years in servitude (thus, on the seventh year, just as God rested on the seventh day), while a non-Jewish slave would not. This could be interpreted as a simple manifestation of ethnocentrism, though we can also ascribe it to the ancient understanding of liberty. As stated before, for the sages a free person is only one who deals with the Torah—studying and legislating the divine law. If so, a non-Jew cannot be free no matter whether they are enslaved or not, and so there is no real reason to release them, unless they convert to Judaism, and then are released after six years.

61 Aristotle, *The Nicomachean Ethics* (Oxford: Oxford University Press, 2009), 157.

62 Aristotle, *The Politics and Constitution of Athens*, 16.

63 Ibid., 17.

64 Ibid., 17.

65 For elaboration, see Bernard Williams, *Shame and Necessity* (Berkeley: University of California Press, 2008), 110–15.

66 There seem to have been Hellenistic philosophers before Aristotle's time, including some of the Sophists and perhaps even Socrates and Plato, who reached the conclusion that humans were fundamentally equal and that slavery was therefore arbitrary. Nevertheless, Socrates and Plato at least did not protest the institution of slavery itself and did not call for its abolition. Plato himself, according to Diogenes Laertius, owned slaves. See Ramelli, *Social Justice and the Legitimacy of Slavery*, chap. 1.

67 Gaius, *Institutes* 1.8.

68 Gaius, *Institutes* 2.13.

69 *The Manual [Enchiridion] of Epictetus*, trans. P. E. Matheson (1916), available online at https://www.sacred-texts.com/cla/dep/dep102.htm.

70 *De Beneficiis* 3.20, cited in Williams, *Shame and Necessity*, 116.

71 Williams, *Shame and Necessity*, 116.

72 We do not know of any Stoic philosopher or public figure who freed his slaves, or did not own slaves at all. Criticism of the institution of slavery never evolved

into active opposition. See Ramelli, *Social Justice and the Legitimacy of Slavery*, 76, according to which there existed one Stoic philosopher who, although we do not know whether he owned slaves, rejected slavery in principle: Dio Crystostom, a first-century Greek. But a perusal of his writings on slavery does not lead to the conclusion that he rejected the institution of slavery itself, only that he disputed the manner in which people became slaves and sought to show that there was no valid means of enslavement.

73 Alexis de Tocqueville, *Democracy in America*, trans. Arthur Goldhammer (New York: Literary Classics, 2004), 496.

74 Chadwick, *The Early Church*, 128.

75 *Homilies* IV on Eccl. 2:7, cited in Peter Garnsey, *Ideas of Slavery from Aristotle to Augustine* (Cambridge: University of Cambridge, 1999), 82–83.

76 One thousand years later, Gregory of Nyssa's words would be echoed by the French jurist Beaumanoir: "Although there now exist several estates of men, it is true that in the beginning all were free and of the same freedom; for everyone knows that we are all descended from one father and one mother." Cited in Norman Cohn, *The Pursuit of the Millennium: Revolutionary Messianism in Medieval and Reformation Europe* (New York: Harper, 1961), 224.

77 Augustine, *The City of God against the Pagans*, ed. R. W. Dyson (New York: Cambridge University Press, 1998), 977.

78 Ibid. Alongside Gregory of Nyssa and Augustine, we should also mention John Chrysostom, an important Christian thinker who also served as archbishop of Constantinople, who viewed slavery negatively, and advised people to buy slaves, teach them a profession, and then free them; we should also mention Gregory Nazianzus, another archbishop of Constantinople, who like Gregory of Nyssa argued that the image of God was the core of humanity's fundamental freedom and that slavery was therefore abominable. See Ramelli, *Social Justice and the Legitimacy of Slavery*, 166, 214–16.

79 Aristotle, *The Nicomachean Ethics*, 157; and Marcus Terentius Varro, *De Re Rustica* 1, 17.

80 *Catechism of the Catholic Church* (1992), part 1, section 2, chap. 1, paragraph 6, line 357. See *Compendium: Catechism of the Catholic Church* (Washington, DC: United States Conference of Catholic Bishops, 2006), 46.

81 Ibid.

82 John Witte Jr., *Christianity and Human Rights: An Introduction* (Cambridge: Cambridge University Press, 2010), 225.

83 Guy Bois, *The Transformation of the Year One Thousand: The Village of Lournand from Antiquity to Feudalism*, trans. Georges Duby (Manchester: Manchester University Press, 1992), 27–29.

84 Siedentop, *Inventing the Individual*, 153.

85 Ibid., 155.

86 Agobard, cited in R. H. C. Davis, *A History of Medieval Europe: From Constantine to Saint Louis*, ed. R. I. Moore (London: Longman, 1988), 171.

87 The prevailing conception in those days was that the soul was the image of God, a conception advanced by, among others, Pope Paschal I (817–24) and the Libellus published by the Paris synod of 825. See more on this in the context of the debate around iconoclasm and the worship of manmade images, in Thomas F. X. Noble, *Images, Iconoclasm, and the Carolingians* (Philadelphia: University of Pennsylvania Press, 2009).

This conception also pushed Agobard to reject trials by ordeal (a judicial practice of trial by extreme suffering). In Europe at the time, the accused were forced to hold white-hot irons, or alternatively to be dunked, while bound, into a container of water. The idea was to transfer judicial authority to God: if God interceded to save the accused's life (or sanity), he must have been innocent. If not, he was surely guilty. Between the eleventh and thirteenth centuries, there developed a system of trials based on witnesses and adjudication, which would eventually develop into modern Western law, and which transferred the authority for ascertaining guilt from God to humans.

Agobard was one of the pioneering opponents of trials by ordeal, and argued that whoever spilled the blood of humans was effectively spilling God's own blood, basing this on the creation in the image of God. See James Q. Whitman, *The Origins of Reasonable Doubt: Theological Roots of the Criminal Trial* (New Haven, CT: Yale University Press, 2008), 87.

88 Burckhardt, *The Civilization of the Renaissance in Italy*, 129.

89 Julia Barrow, "Ideas and Applications of Reform," in *The Cambridge History of Christianity*, vol. 3, ed. Thomas F. X. Noble and Julia M. H. Smith (Cambridge: Cambridge University Press, 2008), 345–62.

90 Cited in Siedentop, *Inventing the Individual*, 205–6.

91 John Locke sought to dispel this position when he wrote, in the late seventeenth century, his *Two Treatises of Government*. See Fania Oz-Salzberger, "The Jewish Roots of Western Freedom," *Azure* 13 (2002): 89–130. Oz-Salzberger emphasizes Locke's use of the Hebrew Bible to disprove this position. See also Eric Nelson, *The Hebrew Republic: Jewish Sources and the Transformation of European Political Thought* (Cambridge, MA: Harvard University Press, 2010). Early modern Hebraism undoubtedly played a key role in thinking about the modern state, but it was not the only factor underpinning the rejection of kings' "natural" or "divine" rule over their subjects.

92 Siedentop, *Inventing the Individual*, 219–20.

93 Samuel Moyn, *The Last Utopia: Human Rights in History* (Cambridge: Belknap, 2012).

94 Caroline Walker Bynum, *Jesus as Mother: Studies in the Spirituality of the High Middle Ages* (Berkeley: University of California Press, 1982), 86–87. See also John F. Benton, "Consciousness of Self and Perceptions of Individuality," in *Culture, Power and Personality in Medieval France* (London: The Humbledon Press, 1991), 327–56.

95 Brian Tierney, *The Idea of Natural Rights: Studies on Natural Rights, Natural Law, and Church Law 1150–1625* (Grand Rapids, MI: Eerdmans, 1997), 55–56.

96 Moses Maimonides, *Guide for the Perplexed*, trans. M. Friedländer (New York: Dover, 1956), 393.

97 Brian Tierney, "The Idea of Natural Rights: Origins and Persistence," *Northwestern Journal of International Human Rights* 2, no. 1 (2004), 5.

98 It is interesting to note that for the Romans, slavery was not part of *ius naturale* but rather of *ius gentium*, the law of nations. In other words, in a natural state, there would be no slaves. Slavery according to the Romans was a social institution, which originated with the enslavement of prisoners of war.

99 Brian Tierney, *The Idea of Natural Rights*, 55–56. This process continued into the thirteenth century. As Aron Gurevich states: "In every field of life, we find signs of a growing aspiration for recognition of individual personalities. In art, we find the increasing individualization of human representations and the earliest buds of portraits; in literature, we find evermore writing in vernacular languages, opening up possibilities for diverse expressions of human feelings, far broader than was possible in Latin." Gurevich, *The Worldview of Medieval People*, 240 [Hebrew].

100 Tierney, "The Idea of Natural Rights," 6.

101 Cited in Jean Porter, *Nature as Reason: A Thomistic Theory of the Natural Law* (Grand Rapids, MI: William B. Eerdmans, 2005), 14. Porter notes that the text was apparently written in 1188.

102 In effect, he was explicitly rejecting the second meaning, which Grotius had accepted as valid. See Tierney, *The Idea of Natural Rights*, 65.

103 Ibid. Tierney compares Huguccio's interpretation to conceptions of natural law held by Stoic thinkers in the Roman Empire, such as Cicero. For them, too, natural law was an inner force, albeit one that led people into conformity with the cosmic natural law outside. Therefore "Stoic authors, when they wrote of *ius naturale* [natural law], were thinking mainly in terms of cosmic determinism; the canonists [i.e., writers who interpreted canon law] were thinking more in terms of human free choice." Ibid., 79–80.

104 Porter, *Nature as Reason*, 15.

105 See a discussion of this in James Griffin, *On Human Rights* (Oxford: Oxford University Press, 2008), 33.

106 Tierney, *The Idea of Natural Rights*, 65–67.

107 Porter, *Nature as Reason*, 350–51. For Huguccio, reason and free will were not yet sufficiently distinguished from each other, but in time they would be, and as we shall see later, the conscience would emerge as an inner mechanism of intention and choice. Sometimes the conscience would be identified with reason (as with Kant), and at other times it would be distinguished even further and juxtaposed against it (as with Locke and Rousseau). For more, see Edward G. Andrew, *Conscience and Its Critics: Protestant Conscience, Enlightenment Reason, and Modern Subjectivity* (Toronto: University of Toronto Press, 2001).

108 Ibid., 351.

109 This was the case for the major ecclesiastical thinkers of the first centuries CE, such as Origen (185/6–253/5), Athanasius (296/8–373), Ambrose (337/340–397),

Gregory of Nyssa (c.335–395), and Augustine (354–430). For these theologians and others, the image of God was the intellect (νοῦς), the *logos* (reason), or the soul (understood as the power of reason).

110 This understanding appears in the writings of Cyril of Alexandria (376–444), Basil of Caesarea (c.330–379), and John Chrysostom (347–407).

111 In fact, here we discover another fairly straightforward and direct way in which the principle of the image of God contributed to the birth of the idea of human rights: since the image of God grants dominion (as we saw explicitly in Genesis 1:28), and since dominion is a right (dominion over property and over ourselves, i.e. autonomy—according to many scholars of natural law in this period and later), we may infer that the image of God is substantively linked to our rights. From here, it is easy to reach the conclusion that rights are granted and reserved to all living beings that express the image of God.

112 See Herbert A. Davidson, *Alfarabi, Avicenna, and Averroes, on Intellect: Their Cosmologies, Theories of the Active Intellect, and Theories on the Human Intellect* (New York: Oxford University Press, 1992); Stephen R. Ogden, *Averroes on Intellect: From Aristotelian Origins to Aquinas's Critique* (Oxford: Oxford University Press, 2022).

113 Porter, *Nature as Reason*, 351.

114 Maimonides, who lived in the same period but a different place (Egypt), writes in his *Guide for the Perplexed* that the image of God is the human capacity for reason, but he does not associate this with human will: "The term *ẓelem* . . . signifies the specific form, viz., that which constitutes the essence of a thing, whereby the thing is what it is; the reality of a thing in so far as it is that particular being. In humanity, the 'form' is that constituent which gives human perception: and on account of this intellectual perception the term *ẓelem* is employed in the sentence 'In the *ẓelem* of God he created him (Gen. 1: 27).'" Maimonides, *Guide for the Perplexed* (part 1, chap 1).

115 *Summa Theologia*, 1.93.7.

116 *Summa Theologia*, 2.2.66.1, cited in Tierney, *The Idea of Natural Rights*, 146.

117 Porter, *Nature as Reason*, 351.

118 Ibid., 230.

119 Ibid., 359.

120 Tierney, *The Idea of Natural Rights*, 69. Joseph Henrich credits the creation of human rights less to theological principles and more to general prosperity (which arrived, nevertheless, in the wake of certain theological ideas). See Henrich, *The Weirdest People in the World*, 397–98.

121 Tierney, "The Idea of Natural Rights: Origins and Persistence," 7.

122 Cited in Tierney, *The Crisis of Church and State, 1050–1300*, 155.

123 Note that all these rights concerned dominion, or ownership: human control over resources or other people. This was no coincidence. Mastery, as we know, was one of the core elements of the image of God according to medieval Church scholars.

124 Cited in Tierney, *The Idea of Natural Rights*, 254. On Major, Vittoria, and Las Casas, see also John Marenbon, *Pagans and Philosophers: The Problem of Pagan-*

ism from Augustine to Leibniz (Princeton, NJ: Princeton University Press, 2015), 147–258, 288.

125 *De Indis*, 1.1.21.

126 Tierney, *The Idea of Natural Rights*, 267–68.

127 *De Indis*, 1.1.24.

128 Tierney, *The Idea of Natural Rights*, 269.

129 Cited in ibid., 287.

130 Quoted in Hartmut Behr, *A History of International Political Theory: Ontologies of the International* (Basingstoke, England, and New York: Palgrave Macmillan, 2010), 84.

131 Tierney, *The Idea of Natural Rights*, 299.

132 Hartmut Behr, *A History of International Political Theory*, 77.

133 Cited in Quentin Skinner, *The Foundations of Modern Political Thought*, vol. 2 (Cambridge: Cambridge University Press, 1996), 168–69.

134 See Susan R. Holman, *Beholden: Religion, Global Health, and Human Rights* (Oxford: Oxford University Press, 2015), 93–94.

135 In *The Dawn of Everything: A New History of Humanity*, anthropologist David Graeber and archaeologist David Wengrow suggest that the idea of equality between all humans was adopted by Europeans, largely if not wholly, from Native Americans. As they put it, "many of those living in Europe who came to embrace principles of freedom and equality (principles barely existing in their countries a few generations before) claimed that accounts of these encounters [with indigenous Americans] had a profound influence on their thinking."—David Graeber and David Wengrow, *The Dawn of Everything: A New History of Humanity* (New York: Picador/ Farrar, Straus and Giroux, 2021), 30. It seems unlikely that Las Casas would learn about equality from the Mayans he met in Chiapas, nor that Vitoria and Bellarmine, never leaving Europe, would defend the equal rights of the indigenous peoples using indigenous ideas they had just heard about. Indeed, as is elaborated in the middle of chapter 3 when we recount the thought of the English Puritans, especially the Levellers, and the early liberals, the idea of equality between all humans has a long history in the West. The roots of which, we maintain, go back as far as the Bible.

136 Consuelo Varela, *La Caída de Cristóbal Colón: El Juicio de Bobadilla* (Madrid: Marcial Pons Ediciones de Historia, 2006).

137 Tierney, *The Idea of Natural Rights*, 287. Tierney continues and argues that since they were drawing on a conception of "natural law," they were demonstrating that Christian (or Jewish) revelation was totally unnecessary for the development of a discourse of natural rights. I disagree, as I have sought to demonstrate in these chapters.

138 Friedrich Nietzsche, *The Antichrist*, trans. H. L. Mencken (New York: Alfred A. Knopf, 1924), paragraph 43.

139 Tierney, *The Idea of Natural Rights*, 289.

3. CONSCIENCE

1 Cohn, *The Pursuit of the Millennium*, 308.

2 Ibid.

3 "Concerning the Ministry," cited in Jaroslav Pelikan, *Spirit Versus Structure: Luther and the Institutions of the Church* (New York: Harper & Row, 1968), 39.

4 Ibid.

5 Yeshayahu Leibowitz, "Religious Praxis," in *Judaism, Human Values, and the Jewish State*, ed. Eliezer Goldman (Cambridge, MA: Harvard University Press, 1992), 18–20.

6 David Hartman, *A Living Covenant: The Innovative Spirit in Traditional Judaism* (New York: Free Press, 1985).

7 Elon Gilad, "*Matzpun* (Conscience) and *Matzpen* (Compass)—No Connection, Actually," *Haaretz*, 31 December 2014. Other terms used in the Jewish tradition did not carry the same meaning. The *yetzer hara*, or evil inclination, is not the conscience but a negative internal tendency, whereas *musar kelayot* (literally "morality of the kidneys") denotes regret and pangs of conscience over one's own bad deeds. In any case, neither refers to an internal source of moral authority that should be obeyed.

8 Henrich and others explored the Catholic Church's control in various countries in the period 500–1500. The Protestant Church, which emerged in the sixteenth century, only exacerbated this skepticism toward tradition, of course. See Henrich, *The Weirdest People in the World*, 226–29.

9 Tertullian, *On Modesty (*De Pudicitia*)*, XXI. Translation by Rev. S. Thelwall, available at www.tertullian.org.

10 Cohn, *In Pursuit of the Millennium*, 255.

11 Mika Ojakangas, *The Voice of Conscience: A Political Genealogy of Western Ethical Experience* (New York: Bloomsbury, 2013), 35.

12 "When Gentiles, who do not have the law, by nature do the things in the law, these, although not having the law, are a law to themselves, who show the work of the law written in their hearts, their conscience also bearing witness, and between themselves their thoughts accusing or else excusing them" (Romans 2:14–15).

13 Ojakangas, *The Voice of Conscience*, 29.

14 Ibid., 42.

15 Bonaventure, "Conscience and Synderesis," in *Ethics and Political Philosophy*, vol. 2 of *The Cambridge Translations of Medieval Philosophical Texts*, ed. Arthur Stephen McGrade, John Kilcullen, and Matthew Kempshall (Cambridge: Cambridge University Press, 2012), 185. See also Ojakangas, *The Voice of Conscience*, 49.

16 Ibid., 50.

17 Siedentop, *Inventing the Individual*, 314–15. In virtue of his push for individuation, Luis Dumont calls Ockham "the spiritual father of English minds"—Luis Dumont, *Essays in Individualism: Modern Ideology in Anthropological Perspective* (Chicago: University of Chicago Press, 1986), 64, n. 6.

18 Herbert B. Workman, *The Letters of John Hus* (London: Hodder and Stoughton, 1904), 278.

19 There are several versions of the story, including some told by Luther himself. See Patrick Collinson, *The Reformation: A History* (New York: The Modern Library, 2003), 7–8.

20 Martin Luther, cited in Andrew Thornton, "Preface to the Complete Edition of Luther's Latin Works."

21 Michael Allen Gillespie, *The Theological Origins of Modernity* (Chicago: University of Chicago Press, 2008), 107.

22 Martin Luther, *Concerning Christian Liberty*, available online at Project Gutenberg, www.gutenberg.org.

23 Martin Luther, *Three Treatises* (Philadelphia: Fortress Press, 1978), 124.

24 Cited in Martin Brecht, *Martin Luther: His Road to Reformation 1483–1521* (Minneapolis: Fortress Press, 1985), 460.

25 Jaroslav Pelikan, *Lectures on Genesis*, vol. 1 of *Luther's Works* (St. Louis: Concordia, 1968), 61–63.

26 "Satan assaults the greatest strength of man and battles against the very likeness of God, namely, the will that was properly disposed toward God." Ibid., 150.

27 Jane E. Strohl, "Luther's Spiritual Journey," in *The Cambridge Companion to Martin Luther*, ed. Donald K. McKim (Cambridge: Cambridge University Press, 2003), 149–64, quote from p. 163.

28 "Until the mid-seventeenth century, the conscience was generally retrospective: it meant individual self-awareness conjoined either to divine law (in the case of Luther) or to custom (in the case of Montaigne); judging oneself in relation to existing norms to ascertain guilt or innocence; and not deliberating about the future and then crafting new rules appropriate to those deliberations." Andrew, *Conscience and Its Critics*, 4.

29 Ibid., 16.

30 Ibid., 16.

31 Augustine, "Against the Epistle of Manichaeus Called Fundamental," in *The Manichaean Heresy*, vol. 2, ed. Marcus Dods, trans. Richard Stothert (Edinburgh: T. & T. Clark, 1872), 101.

32 Cited in Andrew, *Conscience and Its Critics*, 20.

33 Note that Luther understood the holy scriptures as possessing a clear and uniform meaning, which could be grasped directly by its readers. Luther's literalism would be opposed by Catholics, such as the thinker, jurist, and statesman Thomas More (the author of *Utopia*), who would argue, invoking arguments reminiscent of postmodernist literary criticism, that no text could ever exist in isolation and that interpretations would always depend on its readers' circumstances and preconceptions, and that in any case this argument was mainly about the authority to interpret scripture. See James Simpson, *Burning to Read: English Fundamentalism and Its Reformation Opponents* (Cambridge: Belknap Press, 2010), chap. 7. More was right: this was ultimately a question

of authority—Luther's conscience, the Pope, church councils, or the whole of
Catholic tradition.

34 Alec Ryrie, *Protestants: The Faith that Made the Modern World* (New York: Viking, 2017), 28.

35 Cited in James Simpson, *Permanent Revolution: The Reformation and the Illiberal Roots of Liberalism* (Cambridge: Belknap Press, 2019), 275.

36 Cited in Andrew, *Conscience and its Critics*, 17.

37 Cited in Menachem Fisch, "Judaism and the Religious Crisis of Modern Science," in *Nature & Scripture in the Abrahamic Religions: 1700–Present*, vol. 2, ed. J. M. van der Meer and S. Mandelbrote (Leiden: Brill, 2008), 532. Ignatius of Loyola, the founder of the Jesuit order, wrote in his book *Spiritual Exercises* (1548) that "what I see as white, I will believe to be black if the hierarchical Church thus determines it." Ignatius of Loyola, *Ignatius of Loyola: The Spiritual Exercises and Selected Works* (New York: Paulist Press, 1991), 213.

38 Ojakangas, *The Voice of Conscience*, 177.

39 David Martin, *The Dilemmas of Contemporary Religion* (Oxford: Basil Blackwell, 1978), 35.

40 James Simpson, *Permanent Revolution: The Reformation and the Illiberal Roots of Liberalism* (Cambridge, MA: Harvard University Press, 2019), xi.

41 Martin, *The Dilemmas of Contemporary Religion*, 9.

42 Cited in Deirdre N. McCloskey, *Bourgeois Equality: How Ideas, Not Capital or Institutions, Enriched the World* (Chicago: University of Chicago Press, 2016), 369. One must ask, of course, how exactly "free" is understood here. We have addressed this previously: freedom here means autonomy, liberation from the chains placed on us by others. This is obviously a very specific interpretation of freedom: a Western, Christian, and modern one.

43 Christopher Hill, *Liberty Against the Law: Some Seventeenth-Century Controversies* (London: Allen Lane, 1996), 181.

44 Luther initially believed that all Christians could interpret the Bible independently. After the Peasants' Revolt, the popular economic and religious uprising that was brutally suppressed and led to the deaths of over 100,000 people, he backtracked from this position in practice, albeit not forcefully. The revolt was supported by the reformer Thomas Müntzer, whose religious thinking was based almost entirely on internal revelations. See Richard Gawthrop and Gerald Strauss, "Protestantism and Literacy in Early Modern Germany," *Past & Present* 104 (1984): 31–55.

45 Ryrie, *Protestants*, 96–98.

46 McCloskey, *Bourgeois Equality*, 371.

47 Abigail Firey, *A New History of Penance* (London: Brill, 2008), 181.

48 King James I lamented in 1604 that the Puritans were "ever discontented with the present government and impatient to suffer any superiority, which maketh their sect unable to be suffered in any well-governed commonwealth." Cited in Ralph Barton Perry, *Puritanism and Democracy* (New York: The Vanguard Press, 1944), 69.

49 For more on Ames, see William Ames, *Conscience with the Power and Cases Thereof* (London: n.p., 1639).

50 William Perkins, "A Treatise of God's Free Grace and Man's Free Will," in *The Workes of That Famous and Worthy Minister of Christ in the University of Cambridge, Mr. William Perkins*, vol. 1, ed. John Legate (London: John Legate, 1626), 727. See also "An Exposition Upon the Epistle of Jude," in ibid., vol. 3, 481 and 495.

51 William Perkins, *The Whole Treatise of the Cases of Conscience* (Cambridge: John Legate, Printer to the University of Cambridge, 1606), 46.

52 Michael Walzer, *The Revolution of the Saints: A Study in the Origins of Radical Politics* (New York: Atheneum, 1973), 19.

53 David Hume, *The History of England, From the Invasion of Julius Cæser to the Revolution in 1688*, vol. 5 (Indianapolis: Liberty Fund, 1983), chap. 48, note J, loc. 9828 in the Kindle edition. This quote was part of a text published in the first editions (this volume published first in 1754), but later omitted by Hume. It can be found in the Liberty Fund edition, also published on their internet site.

54 Simpson, *Permanent Revolution*, 112. The internalization of the source of religious authority was predominantly a Protestant and Anglo-Saxon phenomenon, but was not limited to England, nor even to Protestants. King Sigismund II Augustus, the Catholic monarch of Poland from 1548 to 1562, who reigned in a brief period of relative pluralism, was known for his statement that he wished to be "king of the people, not their consciences." See McCloskey, *Bourgeois Equality*, 347.

55 "A Short Confession of Faith," in William L. Lumpkin, *Baptist Confessions of Faith* (Valley Forge, PA: Hudson Press, 1980), 111.

56 "Propositions and Conclusions Concerning True Christian Religion, Containing a Confession of Faith of Certain English People, Living in Amsterdam," in Lumpkin, *Baptist Confessions of Faith*, 140.

57 Ojakangas, *The Voice of Conscience*, 87.

58 Note that in contrast to humanists (such as Erasmus and Montaigne), the Puritans pursued self-interrogation not in order to achieve some form of liberation but in order to criticize and *restrict* themselves even further. They took a pessimistic view of humanity and believed that divine justice, under which all of mankind operated, required one to be strict with oneself and eternally vigilant against temptations of the flesh and the spirit. But they also believed that nobody could do this work in lieu of any other individual, and that certainly nobody had the right to prevent others from examining their own conscience and acting in accordance with its dictates. See Sacvan Bercovitch, *The Puritan Origins of the American Self* (New Haven, CT: Yale University Press, 1975).

59 Ryrie, *Protestants*, 110.

60 In the sonnet "On the New Forcers of Conscience under the Long Parliament."

61 *Paradise Lost*, Book III, 194–95.

62 In *De Doctrina Christiana*, cited in Ojakangas, *The Voice of Conscience*, 88. Elsewhere, Milton would write that "Truth is compar'd in Scripture to a streaming fountain; if her waters flow not in a perpetuall progression, they sick'n into a

muddy pool of conformity and tradition. A man may be a heretick in the truth and if he believe things only because his Pastor says so, or the Assembly so determins, without knowing other reason, though his belief be true, yet the very truth he holds becomes his heresie." John Milton, *Areopagitica* (Oxford: Clarendon Press, 1894), 38–39 (first published 1644). Milton's emphasis on internal, personal persuasion is evident here, as is his rejection of all traditions *qua* traditions, even if they conform with the truth.

63 Rachel Foxley, "Freedom of Conscience and the Agreements of the People," in *The Agreements of the People, the Levellers, and the Constitutional Crisis of the English Revolution*, ed. Philip Baker and Elliot Vernon (Basingstoke: Palgrave Macmillan, 2012), 122–23.

64 For more on Overton, see Glen H. Stassen, *Just Peacemaking: Transforming Initiatives for Justice and Peace* (Louisville: Westminster/John Knox Press, 1992), 141–55.

65 Cited in Macpherson, *The Political Theory of Possessive Individualism*, 140. Emphasis mine.

66 In "The Freeman's Freedom Vindicated," reproduced in Andrew Sharp, ed., *The English Levellers* (New York: Cambridge University Press, 2004), 30.

67 Perhaps the most radical of the Levellers was Gerrard Winstanley, the leader of the "Diggers," who advocated in 1652 for sharing all the earth, for free education for boys and girls, and for a death penalty not only for murder but also for buying things, selling things, and for being a lawyer or parson—see Jonathan Healey, *The Blazing World: A New History of Revolutionary England, 1603–1689* (New York: Alfred A. Knopf, 2023), 265. One might quip that not only democracy but also Jacobinism and Bolshevism were envisioned in this period.

68 In *The Tenure of Kings and Magistrates*, cited in Andrew, *Conscience and Its Critics*, 61.

69 Samuel Rutherford, *Lex, Rex* (Colorado Springs: Portage Publications, 2009), 143 (first published 1644). Samuel Rutherford was a Scottish theologian and religious leader. He supported a monarchical republic and limitations on the king's power. In this quotation, he presents common presumptions that he wishes to challenge and refute.

70 Cited in McCloskey, *Bourgeois Equality*, 363.

71 "The Humble Petition of Divers Well-Affected Women." See Ryrie, *Protestants*, 123. In Shakespeare's play *Othello*, written in England just a few decades later, Emilia, Iago's wife, declares: "Let husbands know their wives have sense like them." (act IV, scene 3).

72 The civil war, understood as waged by "the people" against the king, cast as an endeavor to cast off the "Norman yoke" and restore "the rights of Englishman," championed by Protestants against what was considered foreign Catholicism, and ending with a republic (albeit short-lived), set the conditions for the development of modern nationalism in England. As Hans Kohn writes in his classic study of nationalism, "England could develop earlier than any other European country certain fundamental conditions for the growth of modem nationhood and thus

prepare the ground for the full development of modern nationalism in the seventeenth century."—Hans Kohn, *The Idea of Nationalism* (New York: The Macmillan Company, 1944), 156.

73 The constitution drafted under his rule (1653) stated: "That such as profess faith in God by Jesus Christ (though differing in judgment from the doctrine, worship or discipline publicly held forth) shall not be restrained from, but shall be protected in, the profession of the faith and exercise of their religion . . . provided this liberty not be extended to Popery [i.e., Catholicism] or Prelacy, nor to such as, under the profession of Christ, hold forth and practise licentiousness." See "The Instrument of Government," XXXVII, in *The Constitutional Documents of the Puritan Revolution 1625–1660*, ed. Samuel Rawson Gardiner (Oxford: Oxford University Press, 1906), 416.

74 In his book *The Hebrew Republic*, Harvard historian Eric Nelson proposes a similar thesis, though in a way contrary in essence, and focusing less on liberalism than on republicanism. Nelson attributes the development of republican thought to the Protestant study of Hebraic sources, though in his opinion what was seminal to the process was not the idea of the image of God, but the perception of the Israelite request for a king, according to rabbinical exegesis, as a sin of idolatry (trying to replace God with a human monarch). This led to the strengthening stance that monarchy is a religiously illegitimate constitutional structure, and that only republican constitutions can be acceptable. Thus not the wish to separate religion and state lies at the root of the modern republic, but the drive to align the state with a religious ideal. See Eric Nelson, *The Hebrew Republic* (Cambridge, MA: Harvard University Press, 2010).

75 George Fox, *An Autobiography* (Philadelphia: Ferris & Leach, 1919), 82. Emphasis in original.

76 Margaret Fell, *Women's Speaking Justified and Other Pamphlets*, ed. Jane Donawerth and Rebecca Lush (Toronto: Iter Press, 2018), 157, 160.

77 See Elaine Pagels, *The Gnostic Gospels* (New York: Vintage Books, 1979).

78 John Van Engen, *Sisters and Brothers of the Common Life: The Devotio Moderna and the World of the Later Middle Ages* (Philadelphia: University of Pennsylvania Press, 2008).

79 Bernard McGinn, *The Flowering of Mysticism: Men and Women in the New Mysticism (1200–1350)*, vol. 3 of *The Presence of God: A History of Western Christian Mysticism* (New York: Crossroads, 1998).

80 See Gerda Lerner, *The Creation of Feminist Consciousness: From the Middle Ages to Eighteen-seventy* (New York: Oxford University Press, 1993). Significantly, the elimination of monasticism in the Reformation also weakened the position of women in Protestant circles. Apart from the more radical fringes, most Protestant churches solidified patriarchal social structures and derided female mysticism, which beforehand within the Catholic church would have been (after an authentication process) celebrated. I thank Aviad Kleinberg for these insights.

81 Margaret Fell, *Women's Speaking Justified and Other Pamphlets*, 158.

82 Mary Wollstonecraft, *A Vindication of the Rights of Woman, With Strictures on Political and Moral Subjects* (London: J. Johnson, 1796), 135.

83 Marcel Mauss, "A Category of the Human Mind: The Notion of the Person, the Notion of Self," in *The Category of the Person: Anthropology, Philosophy, History*, ed. Michael Carrithers, Steven Collins, and Steven Lukes (Cambridge: Cambridge University Press, 1985), 1–25, quote on p.21.

The Wesleyan Methodist Church was founded by John Wesley in eighteenth-century England. The Pietists were Christian denominations originating in seventeenth-century Germany, who sought an even more radical Reformation and placed their emphasis on internal intention at the expense of the orthodoxies of Lutheran dogma. The Pietists had intellectual counterparts across Europe: the Quakers of England and Quietists in France, Spain, and Italy (the latter, active in Catholic realms, were banned by the Church and branded heretics).

84 Alan Macfarlane, *The Origins of English Individualism* (New York: Cambridge University Press, 1978).

85 Mauss, "A Category of the Human Mind," 21.

86 Margaret C. Jacob, *The Newtonians and the English Revolution, 1689–1720* (Ithaca, NY: Cornell University Press, 1976), 193–94.

87 C. B. Macpherson, *The Political Theory of Possessive Individualism.* See also the groundbreaking developments in conceptions of the self in late eighteenth-century England, in Dror Wahrman's impressive study. According to Wahrman, identity was considered coextensive with selfhood, and both were disassociated from their social context: "Together with these interiorizing and essentializing transformations, late eighteenth-century identity [in England] became synonymous with self. . . . Here was the crucial shift from identity as . . . the collective grouping highlighting whatever a person has in common with others to identity as that quintessential uniqueness that separates a person from all others." Dror Wahrman, *The Making of the Modern Self: Identity and Culture in Eighteenth-Century England*, 27. According to Wahrman, eighteenth-century England saw the articulation of a concept of selfhood that was characterized for the first time by psychological depth, or interiority that manifested an exclusive, expressive individual identity—that is, a modern notion of identity.

Joseph Henrich cites data showing that the distinctive climate in England (and northern Europe) explains part of the sharp tendency to individualism there. See Henrich, *The Weirdest People in the World*, 250. Mead suggests a culture suspicious of dogmatism and orthodoxy and that lauds initiative and change. See Mead, *God and Gold*, 170–86.

88 Cited in Max Weber, *The Protestant Ethic and the Spirit of Capitalism*, trans. Talcott Parsons (New York: Charles Scribner's Sons, 1958), 45. On the particularity of the Anglo-Saxon culture and its influence in the emergent Western order, see also Mead, *God and Gold.*

89 Ibid., 174.

90 John Donne, *The Complete English Poems* (London: Penguin Books, 1996), 276.

91 De Tocqueville, *Democracy in America*, 585.

92 Ibid., 332.

93 Roger Williams, *The Bloudy Tenent of Persecution for Cause of Conscience Discussed as a Conference between Truth and Peace* (London: Danserd Knolls Society, 1848) (first published 1644).

94 Ibid., 2.

95 Wilken, "The Christian Roots of Religious Freedom," 77. Tertullian's original text was a focus of dispute between Williams and Cotton, with the latter maintaining that the ancient Christian theologian was referring to freedom of religion only in the private sphere, not the public sphere.

96 Williams, *The Bloudy Tenent*, 2.

97 Roger Williams, *The Bloody Tenent Yet More Bloody* (London: Giles Calvert, 1652), 17. Between Williams's first and second books, his publisher decided that he should tweak the spelling of "bloudy" to "bloody."

98 Ibid., 216.

99 Ibid., 307.

100 Ibid., 156.

101 Ibid., 246.

102 Oscar Reiss, *The Jews in Colonial America* (Jefferson, NC: McFarland & Company, 2004), 46.

103 Cited in George Bancroft, *History of the United States*, vol. 1 (New York: Appleton and Company, 1888), 364.

104 Max J. Kohler, "The Jews in Newport," *Publications of the American Jewish Historical Society* 6 (1897): 61–80, quote from p. 66.

105 Sheldon J. Godfrey and Judith C. Godfrey, *Search Out the Land: The Jews and the Growth of Equality in British Colonial America, 1740–1867* (Montreal: McGill-Queen's University Press, 1995), 64.

106 David Sorkin, *Jewish Emancipation: A History Across Five Centuries* (Princeton, NJ: Princeton University Press, 2019), 33.

107 Cited in Paul R. Mendes-Flohr and Jehuda Reinharz, eds., *The Jew in the Modern World: A Documented History* (New York: Oxford University Press, 1980), 387.

4. EQUALITY

1 Details on Netanel Posner are from Shmuel Feiner, *The Origins of Jewish Secularization in Eighteenth-Century Europe*, trans. Chaya Naor (Philadelphia: University of Pennsylvania Press, 2011); and Jacob Katz, "Rabbi Raphael Cohen—Moses Mendelssohn's Opponent," *Tarbiz* 56, no. 2 (1987): 243–64 [Hebrew].

2 Katz, "Rabbi Raphael Cohen," 247 [Hebrew].

3 Feiner, *The Origins of Jewish Secularization in Eighteenth-Century Europe*, 167.

4 A significant background from which Jewish dissenters and freethinkers rose was the Jewish Marrano experience. In the Middle Ages, Iberian Jews were not only forced to convert to Christianity, but were subject to constant scrutiny and

discipline by the authorities of the Inquisition, both in the Kingdom of Spain and in the Kingdom of Portugal. Called "New Christians," "Conversos" (converts), or "Marranos" (pigs), some chose to continue practicing Judaism in secret, while other retained only a few traditions, setting them apart from their Christian neighbors. Learning to live clandestine lives involved initiative, ingenuity, and the daily questioning of religious and political authority. Following the expulsion of at least 100,000 Jews from Spain in 1492 and the gradual emigration from Portugal of tens of thousands of Jews and crypto-Jews, different parts of Europe, especially the Netherlands, now hosted whole communities that "loathed and rebelled against religious coercion [. . . and that] forged the world's first genuine intellectually grounded revolutionary framework."—Jonathan I. Israel, *Revolutionary Jews from Spinoza to Marx: The Fight for a Secular World of Universal and Equal Rights* (Seattle: University of Washington Press, 2021), 36. According to Israel, "Repression of crypto-Judaism in the Iberian Peninsula was so brutal and relentlessly oppressive from the late fifteenth century onwards as to massively help provoke the new species of underground, university-trained, Latin-reading Jewish militancy, searching for surreptitious ways to hit back at the oppressor, forging a quite new, more combative Jewish mentality rigorously examining the Christian West's theology and intellectual culture specifically looking for weaknesses, every path by which to chisel away at tyranny of conscience." (Ibid., 86).

These communities were social hotbeds for secular and revolutionary thought, most emblematically personified in Baruch (Benedict) Spinoza (1632–1677), whose family were Portuguese Marranos. See Jonathan I. Israel, ibid.; Yirmiyahu Yovel, *The Marrano of Reason*, vol. 1 of *Spinoza and Other Heretics* (Princeton, NJ: Princeton University Press, 1989); Yirmiyahu Yovel, *The Other Within: The Marranos: Split Identity and Emerging Modernity* (Princeton, NJ: Princeton University Press, 2009). Indeed, according to Israel, it was in the Netherlands that the germinal seeds of the Radical (secularizing, revolutionary) Enlightenment were planted: "[T]he Dutch Golden Age was the Radical Enlightenment's original seedbed in the sense that it was in late seventeenth-century Holland rather than England that democratic republicanism was first explicitly and systematically pitted against aristocratic republicanism, bringing out the innate antagonism between the two tendencies, more conspicuously than one then found among republicans elsewhere, or at any point prior to the American Revolution."—Jonathan I. Israel, *Revolutionary Jews from Spinoza to Marx*, 57. Here, thus, lies an alternative path to what this book is presenting: a road to the liberal order rooted not in the idea of the image of God, but in Dutch republicanism and Marrano contrarianism. Israel holds that, "For a more historically accurate and balanced picture of the role of the revolutionary consciousness in modern Jewish history, and the rise of secular, democratic 'modernity' more generally, the well-worn usual notions pivoting on English republicanism and Rousseau need some pretty brusque clipping back, and for Spinoza, as he deserves, to be allotted a more central role in the emergence of democratic, free speech modernity than Hobbes, Locke, Rousseau or Marx." (Ibid., 84). Yovel is more cautious, and talks only of "Marranos [serving] as catalysts in modernizing trends that had already begun without them, or joined the process as a contributing factor. . . ."—Yovel, *The Other Within*, 345. I try to show in this chapter that Locke is justified in receiving the central place he is usually allotted. Perhaps the breaking line between the thesis presented here and Israel's is the one between liberal and radical politics.

5 Antisemitism also impeded, quite obviously, the integration of Jews into wider society. Antisemitism in Europe came in peaks and troughs, but we shall not expand on this here.

6 The British Parliament passed a law in 1858 allowing any man to swear an oath, in order to assume public or political office, in accordance with his own faith. Previously, the standard formulation required one to swear by "the true faith of a Christian," thereby barring Jews from these offices.

7 This was related to the fact that for monotheistic religions, the true faith, and truth in general, was determined by unique moments of divine revelation. Whether at Mount Sinai, or in the life of his son in ancient Palestine, or in the angel Jibril's whisperings in a cave in the Arabian Desert—the one God revealed himself and communicated at one of these moments, and only at one of them, his final and ultimate word. There was simply no possibility of regarding different forms of worship as authentic expressions of the human heart, especially if practiced by those who had already heard God's authentic revelation. We may thus understand that when such a possibility did arise, when it became possible to conceive of the worship of a different god as *worship*, and as an (albeit erroneous) counterpart to the correct form of worship, this *ipso facto* meant that the status of revelation as the exclusive source of faith was weakened.

8 Wilfred Cantwell Smith, *The Meaning and End of Religion* (New York: Mentor, 1964), 30.

9 Ibid., 31.

10 Talal Asad, *Genealogies of Religion: Discipline and Reasons of Power in Christianity and Islam* (Baltimore: Johns Hopkins University Press, 1993), 45 n. 29.

11 Scholars are divided about the identity of the Sabians. The term might refer to the Mandeans or the Manicheans, two traditions (the former also denoting an ethnic group) that emerged out of the development of Gnostic sects in the first centuries of the Common Era.

12 Moreover, the Europeans' early interactions with new cultures on the continents beyond the seas in the sixteenth and seventeenth centuries supported the development of the idea of "religion" as a system that varied between cultures. The Europeans arriving in the New World, mainly the Spanish, needed to wrap their heads around what they were seeing among the indigenous peoples, and some chose not to dismiss their practices as "pagan" but rather were willing to countenance a positive assessment of them as "religious" elements worthy of protection.

This was done in the context of the general inquiry of the indigenous people's position of rights, by figures such as Bartolomé de Las Casas, among others. Thus, some of the first figures to speak about "religions" around the world were early sixteenth-century Catholics, who gained a new understanding of reality in the course of their missionary campaigns. See Guy G. Stroumsa, *A New Science: The Discovery of Religion in the Age of Reason* (Cambridge, MA: Harvard University Press, 2010).

13 *Idiota de Mente* (1450), in *Complete Philosophical and Theological Treatises of Nicholas of Cusa*, trans. Jasper Hopkins (Minneapolis: Banning, 2001).

14 Quotations from Nicholas de Cusa in this paragraph are taken from *De Pace Fidei*, cited in William T. Cavanaugh, *The Myth of Religious Violence: Secular Ideology and the Roots of Modern Conflict* (Oxford: Oxford University Press, 2009), 70. On the groundbreaking thought of Cusanus and Ficino, see also John Marenbon, *Pagans and Philosophers*, 238–47.

15 Cited in ibid., 71.

16 Cited in James Hankins, "Marsilio Ficino and the Religion of the Philosophers," *Rinascimento* 48 (2008): 109.

17 Europe was convulsed by religious wars for the 150 years after the Reformation: the German Peasants' War (1524–1525); the wars between Protestant and Catholic cantons in the Swiss Confederacy (1529–1531); the Schmalkaldic War between Holy Roman Emperor Charles V and the Protestant princes of the Schmalkaldic League (1546–1547); the Eighty Years War, at the core of which was the revolt of the Seventeen Provinces of what is now the Netherlands (1568–1648); the religious wars in France between the Catholic crown and the Calvinist Huguenots (1562–1598); the Thirty Years' War between the Protestant and Catholic kingdoms of modern-day Germany (1618–1648); and the English Civil War (1642–1651). These wars were also driven, of course, by mundane political factors: internecine violence is not a religious imperative. Nevertheless, the breakdown of Europe into rival churches undoubtedly encouraged this enmity and fostered violence.

18 In his *The Foundations of Modern Political Thought*, Quentin Skinner charts another path to the development of freedom of religion and the modern state. According to Skinner, thinkers in the late sixteenth century, specifically French Huguenots who were suffering from their Catholic king's persecution, turned to Roman law traditions in order to argue that the natural state of humans is liberty, and that the power the monarch has was entrusted to him by God to perform a specific function, "doing good works." Philippe de Mornay and Theodore Beza in France, and George Buchanan in Scotland, proposed that the role of a regime was to protect the freedom and well-being of its subjects. Thus a king that did not, could be considered illegitimate, while the obligation to protect freedom and well-being might develop into an understanding that religion must be separated from state, and indeed into the elements of liberalism. See Quentin Skinner, *The Age of Reformation*, vol. 2 of *The Foundations of Modern Political Thought* (Cambridge: Cambridge University Press, 1978).

19 Cited in Jean Bodin, *Colloquium of the Seven about Secrets of the Sublime*, trans. Marion Leathers Kuntz (University Park: Pennsylvania State University Press, 2008), xxiii–xxiv.

20 *De Veritate*, cited in Cavanaugh, *The Myth of Religious Violence*, 75.

21 Thomas Hobbes, *Leviathan* (London: Penguin, 2017), 581. Around the same time as Herbert and Hobbes, Baruch Spinoza also argued that the state must permit absolute liberty on matters of conscience and expression to every person. Spinoza, who articulated the tenets of his political thought in his *Theological-Political Treatise*, demanded that the kingdom permit absolute liberty of thought: "No one, therefore, can surrender their freedom to judge and to think as they wish and everyone, by the supreme right (*jure*) of nature, remains master of their own thoughts. It follows that a state can never succeed very far in attempting to force people to speak as the sovereign power commands." Baruch Spinoza, *Theological-Political Treatise*, ed. Jonathan Israel, trans. Michael Silverthorne and Jonathan Israel (Cambridge: Cambridge University Press, 2007), 251.

22 C. A. Bayly, *The Birth of the Modern World, 1780–1914* (Malden, MA: Blackwell, 2004), 292.

23 Leora Batnitzky, *How Judaism Became a Religion: An Introduction to Modern Jewish Thought* (Princeton, NJ: Princeton University Press, 2011).

24 John Locke, *An Essay Concerning Human Understanding* (London: n.p., 1836), 531–32 (first published 1689).

25 For Locke, reason proved and in fact necessitated God's existence and the truth of the basic tenets of Christianity, but for his successors in this critical line of inquiry, reason would undermine their faith to a greater and greater extent. In the late seventeenth century and eighteenth century, Deists such as John Toland and Matthew Tindall would promote what they regarded as a rational version of Christianity, which drew exclusively on reason. Reason would become the sole and ultimate source of authority. They would dismiss the virgin birth and the divinity of Jesus as superstitions that could not be critically reconciled with reality. For them, God's existence was consistent with reason, but the Christianity that they would propose was extremely thin on dogma and mythology. The next obvious stage would be to dispute God's existence itself as yet another superstition that every "sober good man" (Locke's characterization of the rational person a few sentences after the above-quoted section) would have to renounce.

26 See Stroumsa, *A New Science*.

27 John Locke, *Two Treatises of Government* (London: Cambridge University Press, 1967), 180 (first published 1689). The first treatise lays the groundwork, as Jeremy Waldron writes, for the second treatise. In the first treatise, Locke establishes his argument that all humans are equal, and he does so by appealing to the image of God. As we see from the quotation above, for Locke the essence of the image of God was reason. See Jeremy Waldron, *God, Locke, and Equality: Christian Foundations in Locke's Political Thought* (Cambridge: Cambridge University Press, 2002).

28 Ibid., 289.

29 Walzer, *The Revolution of the Saints*, 301.

30 N.B.: Law and order are conceived, at least by Locke and Hobbes, as contrary to liberty, and as forces that reduce individual liberty. Here we see once more the established Christian pattern counterposing spirituality against the establishment, liberty against law. The difference is that this time, this pattern has been translated into secular language.

31 John Locke, *A Letter Concerning Toleration*, ed. James H. Tully (London: Hackett Publishing, 1983), 26 (first published 1689). Note that in an earlier composition, the *First Tract on Government* (1660), Locke did not think that religion and state must be separated, but rather that a ruler must determine the state's religion. In other writings, he exhibited a certain intolerance for Catholics, whose religious disposition he did not regard as free in the first place and certainly not as deserving of liberty. In his later writings, however, freedom of conscience gained increased importance, coming before the (Hobbesian) importance that he had previously attached to the preservation of public order and suppression of such dangerous sects as Catholics and radical Protestants.

32 Ibid., 26–27.

33 Ibid., 28.

34 Yet we also know that Jews, like members of many other religious groups, are also born into their own specific religious traditions and do not require any particular ritual to become what they are already. Judaism's transformation into a religion had to contend with that, as we discuss in the latter part of chapter 4.

35 Ibid., 43.

36 Ibid., 41.

37 Legal limitations on freedom of religion are, in Locke's thinking, a pragmatic means of separating religion and state and not a normative critique of religion on the part of the state. Obviously, no state's statute book at any particular moment in time should be considered the final word about human morality. Laws change in accordance with shifting views on morality. Morality-based restrictions on religion, in Locke's opinion, exist not to educate those who observe a particular tradition but to set clear boundaries for conduct in a particular commonwealth.

38 Ibid., 43.

39 Yair Furstenberg explores and elaborates on these distinctions in the context of the development of conversion to Judaism in his article "Who Was a Jew in Antiquity?," *Segula* 96 (June 2018): 42–55 [Hebrew]. Thus, for example, Furstenberg notes that for the Hasmoneans, the conquest of territory necessitated the imposition of the laws of the kingdom on its new subjects, including male circumcision. In other words, conversion meant simply the forcible incorporation of conquered subjects into the conquering nation and their obedience to the laws of the kingdom. Ibid., 50.

40 Spinoza, *Theological-Political Treatise*, 248.

41 Locke, *A Letter Concerning Toleration*, 43–44.

42 Ibid., 54.

43 Feiner, *The Origins of Jewish Secularization in Eighteenth-Century Europe*.

44 Pointedly, Max Weber defined Jews as "a pariah people . . . a guest people who were ritually separated." Max Weber, *Ancient Judaism*, trans. and ed. Hans H. Gerth and Don Martindale (New York: Free Press, 1952), 3.

45 On Dohm and his writings, see Ritchie Robertson, *The "Jewish Question" in German Literature, 1749–1939: Emancipation and its Discontents* (Oxford: Oxford University Press, 1999). Between Locke and Dohm, another famous work was written calling for the extension of equality to the Jews. In 1714, the famous Irish Deist John Toland published the short manifesto *Reasons for Naturalizing the Jews in Great Britain and Ireland, On the Same Foot with All Other Nations*, in which he sought to persuade his British readers that Jews would only benefit their country economically, that they had suffered greatly without justification (Toland devoted no less than one third of his work to elaborating on the horrors that English Jewry had suffered at the hands of their neighbors between the eleventh and thirteenth centuries, when they were finally banished), and that ultimately they are "not otherwise to be regarded, than under the common circumstances of human nature"—that is, that Jews were first and foremost human beings. Toland refers to the different nature of the Jewish tradition and admits that the Jews established a "theocracy," but he explains that the Jews do not want to convert anyone, are content with the non-Jews observing the "law of nature" (that is, the natural religion, expressed in the Seven Laws of Noah), and are not committed to any country except that where they live (in doing so, he ignores the Jewish connection to the Land of Israel and deals neither with the possibility of the Jews' return there, nor with the "theocratic" characteristics of the Jewish tradition at the time). Another important document in this context is the law enacted by the British Parliament in 1740 allowing Jews to become subjects with equal rights in Britain's colonies in the Americas, specifically in New York, Pennsylvania, Maryland, South Carolina, and Jamaica ("The Plantation Act").

46 Christian Wilhelm von Dohm, "Concerning the Amelioration of the Civil Status of the Jews" ["Über die bürgerliche Verbesserung der Juden"], trans. Helen Lederer, in *The Jew in the Modern World*, ed. Mendes-Flohr and Reinharz, 28.

47 Ibid., 29.

48 Mendelssohn answered Dohm in his preface to the new German translation (1782) of Menasseh Ben Israel's *Vindiciæ Judæorum*. Ben Israel had written this work, in English, over a century earlier, in an attempt to persuade the English Parliament to permit the resettlement of Jews in England. Mendelssohn used his preface to the translation as an opportunity to attack Dohm's positions.

49 Mendelssohn was also a personal friend of Gotthold Ephraim Lessing, one of the preeminent figures of the German Enlightenment, who died in 1781, around half a year before Posner and Cohen exchanged theological blows. Two years earlier,

Lessing published what is now his most famous work, *Nathan the Wise*, a play that depicts an encounter between representatives of the three monotheistic religions. The centerpiece of the play is the "Ring Parable."

The script describes a father who owns a magic ring, which makes whoever wears it find grace in the eyes of God and people. Not wishing to overtly discriminate against any of his three sons, the father creates two exact replicas. On his deathbed, he bequeaths one ring to each son, each believing that he inherited the real and only heirloom, only to realize, after their father's death, that each of them received a ring. In their fury, they ask a judge to decide whose ring is the real one, but there is no way to tell them apart. The judge suggests judging the men on their merits and determining which brother owned the true ring based on who was most loved by the two others (as the ring, remember, was supposed to endear its owner to everyone). But when it becomes clear that all three hate each other, the judge decides that they are all deceivers and that the real ring must have been lost long ago. The judge proposes that, instead of quarreling, each brother should simply believe that he is in possession of the true ring and act accordingly. Whichever brother is most generous, gentle, benevolent, and tolerant toward his brothers, and whoever's descendants after many generations continued to exhibit these traits, owns the true ring. The meaning of the parable is clear: Christianity, Islam, and Judaism might believe that they possess the truth, but their behavior suggests their belief might be based on a lie. They are neither loving nor beloved.

In this play, Lessing presents the Deist notion that all religions share a common source, but that over the generations their traditions have been corrupted and have become fraudulent. Religion, like a ring that may be worn and removed, is not the most important thing; the most important thing is the person who believes in it, who has the power to fill it with sanctity—or sacrilege. In any case, there is no way of knowing which religion is correct, and it actually doesn't matter. There is one conclusion: one must be tolerant and respectful toward everyone.

50 Shmuel Feiner, *Moses Mendelssohn* (New Haven, CT: Yale University Press, 2010).

51 Moses Mendelssohn, "Mendelssohn's Preface to *Vindiciæ Judæorum*," in his *Jerusalem: A Treatise on Ecclesiastical Authority and Judaism: Volume 1*, trans. M. Samuels (London: Longman et al., 1838), 77.

52 Ibid., 103–4.

53 Ibid., 115.

54 Ibid.

55 It was in fact written by August Krantz, a writer who had already written about the Posner episode in German.

56 Cited in Feiner, *Moses Mendelssohn*, 162.

57 Moses Mendelssohn, *Jerusalem: A Treatise on Ecclesiastical Authority and Judaism*, vol. 2, trans. M. Samuels (London: Longman et al., 1838), 3–4.

58 Mendelssohn, *Jerusalem*, vol. 2, 21.

59 Ibid., 44.

60 Ibid., 61. Emphases in original.

61 Ibid., 80.

62 Ibid., 89.

63 Ibid., 89.

64 Mendelssohn launches into a detailed exposition of the workings of human memory and the status of symbols. He explains that in order to arouse these rational truths in the human mind, the symbols pointing to them must be continuously present. Thus God prescribed the Jews actual rules and actions to live by. Mendelssohn's idea was that our actions constitute us, inasmuch as restrictions on our behavior and recurring activities to which we are committed leave an imprint on our psyche, indeed our whole composition. He would agree with Ludwig Wittgenstein's dictum that "A pawn *is* the sum of rules for its moves"—Ludwig Wittgenstein, *Philosophical Remarks*, ed. Rush Rhees, trans. Raymond Hargreaves and Roger White (Oxford: Blackwell, 1998), 328.

65 Mendelssohn referred his readers to the words of the Sages, who declared that the day the Second Temple was destroyed, the laws of capital punishment were abolished and "all fines, so far as they were merely national, ceased to be legal." Mendelssohn, *Jerusalem*, vol. 2, 159.

66 Ibid., 161–62.

67 The German statesman Friedrich von Lynar asked the famous Jewish philosopher what he thought about such a proto-Zionist proposal. Mendelssohn replied that "the greatest difficulty that seems to me to stand in the way of this project is the character of my nation. It is not sufficiently prepared for such a great undertaking." He meant that the Jews were insufficiently strong and brave to take such an initiative on themselves, but it is not inconceivable that underpinning his resistance was also the position that he would develop later, namely that the Jews were not, fundamentally, a nation at all—but rather members of a common religious framework. See Shmuel Feiner, *Moses Mendelssohn* (Jerusalem: Zalman Shazar, 2002), 37 [Hebrew].

68 Batnitzky, *How Judaism Became a Religion*, 18.

69 Julius Guttmann, "Mendelssohn's Jerusalem and Spinoza's Theologico-Political Treatise," in *Studies in Jewish Thought*, ed. Alfred Jospe (Detroit: Wayne State University Press, 1981), 383.

70 Miriam Leonard, *Socrates and the Jews: Hellenism and Hebraism from Moses Mendelssohn to Sigmund Freud* (Chicago: University of Chicago Press, 2012), 20.

71 Cited in Mendes-Flohr and Reinharz, eds., *The Jew in the Modern World*, 114–15.

72 Ibid.

73 Cited in Mendes-Flohr and Reinharz, eds., *The Jew in the Modern World*, 257.

74 Immanuel Kant, *Religion within the Bounds of Bare Reason*, trans. Werner S. Pluhar (Indianapolis: Hackett, 2009), 139 (first published 1793).

75 Ibid., 136.

76 Immanuel Kant, "The Conflict of the Faculties," trans. Mary J. Gregor, in *Religion and Rational Theology*, ed. Allen W. Wood and George di Giovanni (Cambridge: Cambridge University Press, 2001), 276.

77 Ibid., 276.

78 This letter is discussed in Batnitzky, *How Judaism Became a Religion*, 25–28, and I am building on the author's commentary.

79 Friedrich Schleiermacher, "Letters on the Occasion of the Political-Theological Task and the Open Letter of Jewish Householders," in *A Debate on Jewish Emancipation and Christian Theology in Old Berlin*, ed. Richard Crouter and Julie Klassen (Indianapolis: Hackett, 2004), 85.

80 Ibid., 103–5.

81 Batnitzky, *How Judaism Became a Religion*, 26.

82 C. A. Bayly, *The Birth of the Modern World, 1780–1914*, 295.

83 Schleiermacher, "Letters on the Occasion of the Political-Theological Task and the Open Letter of Jewish Householders," 103.

84 Cited in Mendes-Flohr and Reinharz, eds., *The Jew in the Modern World*, 372. This declaration remained the official position of Reform Judaism until the Columbus Platform of 1937, which implicitly accepted that the Jews were also an ethnic and not only religious community, and which mentioned the Jewish resettlement of the Land of Israel in favorable terms. In time, Reform Judaism would gradually transition from an anti-Zionist to Zionist orientation.

85 Cited in Mendes-Flohr and Reinharz, eds., *The Jew in the Modern World*, 114.

86 Ibid., 119, 123–24.

87 Quoted in Immanuel Etkes, *Rabbi Shneur Zalman of Liady: The Origins of Chabad Hasidism*, trans. Jeffrey M. Green (Waltham, MA: Brandeis University Press, 2014), 259. The brackets in this quotation appear in the source material.

5. MEANING

1 Albert Camus, *The Myth of Sisyphus and Other Essays*, trans. Justin O'Brien (New York: Knopf, 1955), 39–44, emphasis in original.

2 Richard Dawkins, *The God Delusion* (London: Black Swan, 2007), 407.

3 Robert Darnton, *The Great Cat Massacre* (London: Allen Lane, 1984), 185.

4 Walzer, *The Revolution of the Saints*, 314.

5 Article VIII(2) of the 1796 Tennessee Constitution, available at http://www.dircost.unito.it/cs/pdf/17960206_UsaTennessee_eng.pdf.

6 Roy P. Basler, ed., *Collected Works of Abraham Lincoln*, vol. 7 (New Brunswick, NJ: Rutgers University Press, 1953), 542. It is open to debate whether Lincoln said so out of respect for his audience—Black Americans who had just presented him a copy of the Bible as a token of thanks in an official ceremony. For his own part, Lincoln was a devout Christian, but despite his famous grasp of the scriptures, in his youth he had expressed doubts about the tenets of the Christian faith; moreover, he was never formally a member of any Christian denomination.

7 Anselm, *Proslogium*, end of chap. 1.

8 See the discussion in Charles Taylor, *Sources of the Self: The Making of Modern Identity* (Cambridge, MA: Harvard University Press, 1989), 309–14.

9 Benedict de Spinoza, "Letter XXX," in *The Correspondence of Spinoza*, ed. and trans. A. Wolf (New York: Dial Press, 1985), 210.

10 "Letter XLIII," ibid., 2.

11 Locke, *A Letter Concerning Toleration*, 51.

12 Locke also argued against the toleration of Catholics, for similar reasons: atheists recognized no source of authority and therefore could not be trusted or relied upon to obey the law; Catholics did have a source of authority, but this was a rival source of authority to the laws of the state—namely, the pope—and therefore they could not be trusted either. The fact that Catholics were subordinate to the pope was connected to the principled case for the denial of their liberties: Locke believed that, since Catholics subordinated their consciences to the pope, they could not enjoy freedom of conscience anyway. Like Locke, Mendelssohn also excluded atheists from the circle of toleration. "Atheism and epicurism" were positions that "sap the foundation of civil society." Mendelssohn, *Jerusalem*, vol. 2, 49.

13 We find a similar position in a famous incident that happened more than one hundred years after Spinoza and Locke, when the Scottish philosopher Adam Smith praised his good friend David Hume, an illustrious Scottish philosopher in his own right. Hume died in 1776, and when Smith published an open letter in praise of the deceased, public uproar erupted. The reason was that Smith concluded his short text declaring that Hume approached "as nearly to the idea of a perfectly wise and virtuous man, as perhaps the nature of human frailty will permit." Such praise and testimony to moral uprightness was scandalous when consigned to Hume, who was a known sceptic and by many suspected of atheism. The idea that such a person can be virtuous was inconceivable, indeed offensive. See Dennis C. Rasmussen, *The Infidel and the Professor: David Hume, Adam Smith, and the Friendship That Shaped Modern Thought* (Princeton, NJ: Princeton University Press, 2017), 119–20.

14 Augustine, *Contra Epistolam Manichaei*, 5, 197.22.

15 Fisch, "Judaism and the Religious Crisis of Modern Science," 525–67.

16 Peter Harrison, *The Fall of Man and the Foundations of Science* (Cambridge: Cambridge University Press, 2007), 1.

17 Peter Harrison, *The Fall of Man and the Foundations of Science*, 7.

18 Ibid., 11. See also Charles Webster, *The Great Instauration: Science, Medicine, and Reform, 1626–1660* (London: Duckworth, 1975).

19 Peter Harrison, *The Fall of Man and the Foundations of Science*, 81–82.

20 Ibid., 97–102.

21 Ibid., 104.

22 St. Basil of Caesarea (329–379) wrote that "We were made in the image and likeness of our Creator, endowed with intellect and reason, so that our nature was complete and we could know God. In this way, continuously contemplating the beauty of creatures, through them as if they were letters and words, we could read

God's wisdom and providence over all things." Quoted in Giuseppe Tanzella-Nitti, "The Two Books Prior to the Scientific Revolution," *Perspectives on Science and Christian Faith* 57, no. 3 (2005): 235–48.

23 Peter Harrison, *The Bible, Protestantism, and the Rise of Natural Science* (Cambridge: Cambridge University Press, 1998).

24 Bernard McGinn, *The Foundations of Mysticism*, 71.

25 Peter Harrison, *The Bible, Protestantism, and the Rise of Natural Science*, 60–61.

26 Ibid., 198.

27 Quoted in ibid., 231.

28 Amos Funkenstein, *Theology and the Scientific Imagination: From the Middle Ages to the Seventeenth Century*, 2nd ed. (Princeton, NJ: Princeton University Press, 2018), 298, italics in original.

29 Ibid., 6.

30 Peter Harrison, *The Bible, Protestantism, and the Rise of Natural Science*, 200.

31 Amos Funkenstein, *Theology and the Scientific Imagination*, 346.

32 Ibid., 273.

33 John Toland, *Christianity Not Mysterious* (London: n.p., 1702), 6 (first published 1696).

34 I am deeply indebted to Charles Taylor's analysis on the subject. See Taylor, *Sources of the Self*.

35 Peter Gay, *The Enlightenment: An Interpretation: The Rise of Modern Paganism* (New York: W. W. Norton & Co., 1977), 122.

36 Voltaire, *A Philosophical Dictionary*, vol. 3 (London: John and Henry L. Hunt, 1824), 155–56 (first published 1764).

37 René Descartes, *Meditations on First Philosophy: with Selections from the Objections and Replies*, trans. Michael Moriarty (Oxford: Oxford University Press, 2008), 30.

38 It also reveals the will. Will, as Descartes explains later in his book, is infinite and therefore in itself hints that there exists something infinite in the cosmos, namely God.

39 The method of rational inquiry would enable us to know "the nature and behavior of fire, water, air, stars, the heavens, and all the other bodies which surround us, as well as we now understand the different skills of our workers, we can employ these entities for all the purposes for which they are suited, and so make ourselves masters and possessors of nature." René Descartes, *Discourse on Method*, trans. Laurence Lafleur (New York: Liberal Arts Press, 1956), 66 (first published 1637).

40 From Descartes's letter to Elisabeth, Princess of Bohemia. Cited in Taylor, *Sources of the Self*, 151, and see the discussion there on this.

41 Taylor, *Sources of the Self*, 151.

42 Cited in Jacob, *The Newtonians and the English Revolution*, 47.

43 Matthew Tindal, *Christianity as Old as the Creation: or, The Gospel, a Republication of the Religion of Nature* (London: n.p., 1732), 20 (first published 1730).

44 Ibid., 206.

45 Ibid., 169.

46 Ibid., 196.

47 Ibid., 11.

48 For more on D'Holbach's intellectual salon and the circles surrounding him, see Alan Charles Kors, *D'Holbach's Coterie: An Enlightenment in Paris* (Princeton, NJ: Princeton University Press, 1976).

49 See Jonathan Israel, *A Revolution of the Mind: Radical Enlightenment and the Intellectual Origins of Modern Democracy* (Princeton, NJ: Princeton University Press, 2010), 56.

50 Ibid., 215.

51 Carl Hammer, "Holbach According to Goethe," *Romance Notes* 1, no. 1 (1959): 18–21, quote from p. 19.

52 Paul-Henri Thiry (Baron D'Holbach), *The System of Nature*, vol. 2, trans. Samuel Wilkinson (1820), chap. 1, available online at Project Gutenberg, www.gutenberg.org.

53 Ernst Cassirer, *The Philosophy of the Enlightenment* (Princeton, NJ: Princeton University Press, 1951), 85.

54 D'Holbach, *The System of Nature*, vol. 2, chap. 12.

55 Ibid.

56 De Tocqueville, *Democracy in America*, 485.

57 Ibid., 485.

58 C. A. Bayly, *The Birth of the Modern World, 1780–1914*, 292.

59 As early as 1747, the French materialist philosopher Julien Offray de La Mettrie published his book *L'homme Machine* ("Man a Machine"), in which he argued, of course, that humans were machines. Unlike d'Holbach, La Mettrie assumed that the human machine was innately evil and incapable of developing or improving of its own accord. La Mettrie believed that virtue was a product of coercion, not of rational inquiry or the conscience, that there was no reason to be confident that the pursuit of personal happiness would advance happiness in general, and therefore that there was no alternative to a draconian system of law. Contrary to d'Holbach's humanistic optimism, La Mettrie was expressing a pessimism that was perhaps a much more natural consequence of their shared deterministic materialism. D'Holbach, as it happens, harshly criticized La Mettrie in his *System of Nature*, but La Mettrie invented nothing. This line of thinking originated with Hobbes, who outlined an entirely materialistic (and fairly pessimistic) picture of humanity, analyzing people as if they were moving mechanical systems. Spinoza also declared in his *Ethics* (part III, introduction) that he would treat "the powers of the mind" geometrically, "as if it were a question of lines, surfaces, or solids." In other words, that objects move in accordance with a fixed system of law. Benedictus de Spinoza, *Spinoza's Ethics*, trans. George Eliot, ed. Clare Carlisle (Princeton, NJ: Princeton University Press, 2020). Even earlier, Shakespeare's Hamlet had sworn to Ophelia that he pledged his love "while this machine is to him," meaning, as long as his body served him as vessel—or in short, as long as he was

alive. Hamlet does not think that humans are machines. In fact, he distinguishes himself from his body and thus maintains the body-soul duality that was considered obvious in the Christian world until modernity. The distinction between the (material, mechanical) body and the (immaterial, divine) soul makes it possible to position the human within the divine, locating selfhood within the soul. Both La Mettrie and d'Holbach imagined the human as a whole, bereft of a soul, as a machine, in order to reject the divine and locate selfhood within the body.

60 In the preface to his *Harmonices Mundi* (1619), Kepler writes that God waited 6,000 years for man to gain a correct knowledge—as Kepler himself finally had—of the world that he had created.

61 Newton used this phrase in a letter to Richard Bentley, the theologian and president of Trinity College, Cambridge. Cited in R. C. Jebb, *Bentley* (Cambridge: Cambridge University Press, 2009), 26 (first published 1882).

62 D'Holbach, *The System of Nature*, vol. 2, chap. 14.

63 Taylor dedicates a considerable portion of his *Sources of the Self* to an in-depth description of this process in the eighteenth century. In the latter part of chapter 5, I develop one perspective on the matter, connected to the idea of the image of God.

64 Taylor, *Sources of the Self*, 314.

65 The second source draws on the view of the cosmos as organized perfectly according to a divine plan. Everything exists in the place that God allocated for it. Nature is a sophisticated and harmonious system of entities existing in reciprocity, for the benefit of each and every species and form of life. This was how various Deist philosophers in the eighteenth century understood the world, but, contrary to a similar view from an earlier period, for them, the world and life in general did not exist for the sake of God's glory or in order to approximate him; they simply existed for themselves.

For the Deists, God created the world not for his sake, but for ours, so that we may be happy, here and now. This was a strikingly different perspective from the classical Christian view, according to which this world is a narrow, painful corridor on the road to the world to come. In fact, for the Deists, *this* world received the same importance that had once been attached to the next world: the hierarchy ascending toward the divine was broken, and good on earth became an end, not a means.

Nature came to be considered the bearer of God's imprint, of his infinite reason. And if nature was an expression of God's will, then examining our own nature was surely a way to understand his will. Moreover, if God's will was that we have good lives, then our feelings and desires were also fundamentally good. It was not a rational thought process, but feelings and intuitions, that formed the thrust of this inquiry and were the source of morality.

We are conscious of the cosmic order thanks to our inner nature, which points us to it not only through our thoughts but also through our senses. Like reason, this system, which was originally thought to be God-given, was detached from God and internalized. Nature came to be considered perfect without any external planning or instruction from above. The category of "nature" was expanded to encompass our internal nature, namely our desires, feelings, and imagination. It was out of this that natural harmony became an end in itself, not merely a means of worshiping God, reaching him, gaining knowledge of him, or pleasing him. In fact, divine worship could now be seen as a distraction and even as an obstacle to our internal connection to ourselves. There was no higher purpose for the cosmos than the cosmos itself. From this followed the possibility of a second, non-divine source of morality. See also Tomer Persico, *The Jewish Meditative Tradition* (Tel Aviv: Tel Aviv University, 2016), 135–36 [Hebrew].

66 Immanuel Kant, *Critique of Pure Reason*, trans. J. M. D. Meiklejohn (Buffalo, NY: Prometheus Books, 1990), 473.

67 Kant, who represents a continuation of Tindal, as far as concerns his conception of divine commands, straddles the border between this stage and the next. For Kant, autonomy was an indispensable condition for morality, but he also considered God a necessary condition for morality. Kant saw the existence of God (and of the eternal soul) as a necessity for morality because it was God who rendered the world a coherent moral and logical whole:

> It is only, then, in the ideal of the supreme original good, that pure reason can find the ground of the practically necessary connection of both elements of the highest derivative good, and accordingly of an intelligible, that is, moral world. . . . Thus God and a future life are two hypotheses which, according to the principles of pure reason, are inseparable from the obligation which this reason imposes upon us. (Ibid., 455).

Without faith in God's existence, Kant believes that his moral principles would be shaken in a way that would render him "hateful" in his own eyes (ibid., 465). On the other hand, he also insists that moral imperatives cannot be deduced from God's will:

> Moral theology is, therefore, only of immanent use. It teaches us to fulfil our destiny here in the world, by placing ourselves in harmony with the general system of ends, and warns us against the fanaticism, nay, the crime of depriving reason of its legislative authority in the moral conduct of life, for the purpose of directly connecting this authority with the idea of the Supreme Being. For this [deriving morality from God's will] would be, not an immanent, but a transcendent use of moral theology, and, like the transcendent use of mere speculation, would inevitably pervert and frustrate the ultimate ends of reason. (Ibid., 459–60).

In other words, Kant insists that morality must not be connected to God's will and that we must think only by ourselves. In fact, any attempt to derive morality from God's will is not only "fanaticism" but also a heresy, because God wants us to think by ourselves. The image of God is transformed here, once again, from the connection between us and God to the means that enables the *disconnection* between us and God, because although our capacity for reason and free choice came from God, Kant believes that they lead to moral action only if they are absolutely autonomous, that is, detached from God.

68 Voltaire, *A Philosophical Dictionary*, vol. 6, 358.

69 Giovanni Pico della Mirandola, *Oration on the Dignity of Man*, trans. A. Robert Caponigri (Chicago: Gateway Editions, 1956), 6–7.

70 Pico della Mirandola, "Heptaplus," in *Oration on the Dignity of Man*, trans. Douglas Carmichael (Indianapolis: Hackett Publishing Company, 1965), 135.

71 Pico della Mirandola, *Oration on the Dignity of Man*. See also Crofton Black, *Pico's Heptaplus and Biblical Hermeneutics* (Leiden: Brill, 2006), 44.

72 Taylor, *Sources of the Self*, 152.

73 Cassirer, *The Philosophy of the Enlightenment*, 190.

74 D'Holbach, *System of Nature*, vol. 1, chap. 12.

75 Ibid., chap. 15.

76 Mikhail Bakunin, "Man, Society, and Freedom," in his *Bakunin on Anarchy: Selected Works by the Activist-Founder of World Anarchism*, trans. Sam Dolgoff (New York: Vintage Books, 1972), 234–42, quote from p. 238.

77 Friedrich Nietzsche, *The Gay Science*, trans. Walter Kaufmann (New York: Vintage Books, 1974), 357 (first published 1887).

78 John P. Humphrey, "The Memoirs of John P. Humphrey, the First Director of the United Nations Division of Human Rights," *Human Rights Quarterly* 5, no. 4 (1983): 387–439.

79 Pew Research Center, "When Americans Say They Believe in God, What Do They Mean?," April 25, 2018, www.pewresearch.org.

80 Pew Research Center, "10 key findings about religion in Western Europe," May 29, 2018,www.pewresearch.org.

81 Philip S. Gorski and Ateş Altinordu, "After Secularization?" *Annual Review of Sociology* 34 (2008): 55–85.

82 Ibid., 62–64.

83 In the United States, the quintessential example of a Western country with different trends from the rest of the West, church membership (but not necessarily attendance, on which we have no data) began to rise in the 1820s.

84 These two phenomena were a sign of things to come, namely fundamentalist Islamism in general (Sunni and Shi'a) and the spread of Evangelical Christianity in the United States, Africa, and Asia.

85 Pew Research Center, "Russians Return to Religion, But Not to Church," February 10, 2014, www.pewresearch.org.

86 For Weber, secularization was the product of the rationalization and bureaucratization of society, which would leave it, unless "new prophets will arise," in "mechanized petrification"; Durkheim was more optimistic, apparently because he saw the civilian structures that replaced religion as operating similarly and fulfilling the same role.

87 Peter Berger, *The Sacred Canopy: Elements of a Sociological Theory of Religion* (New York: Doubleday, 1967), 107.

88 Ibid., 107–8.

89 José Casanova, *Public Religions in the Modern World* (Chicago: University of Chicago Press, 1994), 13.

90 That said, as David Sorotzkin eloquently explains, the whole world could equally become sacred. This is the reactionary project of fundamentalism, from religious-nationalist Judaism, through to fundamentalist Islam, Christian-national evangelicals and different apocalyptic sects. The sacred spills the bounds of the synagogue or the mosque and seizes control of the whole world. Every detail in one's daily life, or indeed in history, is suffused with religious meaning, and the sphere of politics has to conform. See David Sorotzkin, *Orthodoxy and Modern Disciplination: The Production of the Jewish Tradition in Europe in Modern Times* (Tel Aviv: Hakibbutz Hameuchad, 2011), 117–18 [Hebrew].

91 Casanova, *Public Religions in the Modern World*, 15.

92 Charles Taylor, "Western Secularity," in *Rethinking Secularism*, ed. Craig Calhoun, Mark Juergensmeyer, and Jonathan Van Antwerpen (Oxford: Oxford University Press, 2011), 31–53, quotation from p. 34.

93 Geertz, "Religion as a Cultural System," 87–125, quote from p. 98.

94 Ernest Gellner, *Nations and Nationalism* (Oxford: Blackwell, 1983).

95 De Tocqueville, *Democracy in America*, 485.

96 Jonathan Dewald, *Aristocratic Experience and the Origins of Modern Culture: France, 1570–1715* (Berkeley: University of California Press, 1993), xii.

97 Steve Bruce, "Cathedrals to Cults: The Evolving Forms of Religious Life," in *Religion, Modernity and Postmodernity*, ed. Paul Heelas, 19–35 (Oxford: Blackwell, 1999). See there a description of the entire process.

98 See Charles Taylor, *Varieties of Religion Today: William James Revisited* (Cambridge, MA: Harvard University Press, 2002).

99 Charles Taylor, *A Secular Age* (Cambridge, MA: Harvard University Press, 2007), 3.

100 In their brilliant book *Ritual and its Consequences: An Essay on the Limits of Sincerity* (Oxford: Oxford University Press, 2008), Adam Seligman, Robert P. Weller, Michael Puett, and Bennett Simon set out to show that the opposite of autonomy is not heteronomy (i.e., external law) but chaos. It is law, like ritual, that facilitates meaningful action in the world and thus facilitates *choice*, hence liberty. The absence of law means an absence of meaning and therefore an absence of the ability to choose. When there is no meaning, there can be no autonomy, because there can be no direction to our actions. If every action means the same as any other, there can be no autonomy, because there can be no such thing as purpose, reason, objective, value, or validity.

101 Emile Durkheim, *The Elementary Forms of Religious Life*, trans. Carol Cosman (Oxford: Oxford University Press, 2001), 92.

102 Durkheim defines the sacred as that which is separate and forbidden, a definition that coheres with the traditional Jewish definition.

103 The Spanish diplomat and author Salvador de Madariaga quipped that religion is "the relatively modest dogma that God is not mad," meaning it's the position that there exists a metaphysical order that operates according to a certain logic. In other words, religion holds the belief in meaning, in a cosmic order, in a responsible and consistent metaphysical authority, in the proposition that reality "works" and that we are not at the whims of meaningless chaos or in the clutches of a capricious demon.

104 William James, *The Varieties of Religious Experience* (New York: Modern Library, 1929), 32 (first published 1902).

105 Cicero (*De Legibus* 2.8.19) and Marcian (*Institutiones* 2). Cited in Guy Stroumsa, *The End of Sacrifice: Religious Transformations in Late Antiquity*, trans. Susan Emanuel (Chicago: University of Chicago Press, 2009), 138–39.

106 See ibid. See also Jan Bremmer, *The Greek Religion* (Cambridge: Cambridge University Press, 1999). It is true that starting in democratic Athens, citizens of the polis were able to join one of many philosophical schools and to adopt a "way of life" with its own systematic ethics and soteriological promise. We have already recalled the groundbreaking research by Pierre Hadot, which showed that philosophy in ancient Greece did not deal with theory in its contemporary sense (i.e., claims about the nature of reality), but rather with theory in its original sense, as θεωρία (*theoria*), meaning contemplative introspection, which itself was part of a philosophical "way of life," ethics, and spiritual quest. The array of philosophical schools and mystical cults increased in the Roman Empire, and although not all of them proposed a transformative spiritual path, they were focused on the individual and held within them a promise of private redemption, whether in this life or in the next. Similar ethical trends developed at the same time in India: Buddhism, Jainism, and various streams of Hinduism offered those in search of spirituality meditative practices and instructions to manage their private lives disconnected from society, in whole or in part. But these phenomena never won over a majority of the population, and even when they were relatively widespread, their intellectual impact was limited to specific spiritual movements. "In ancient culture the care of the self was in fact generalized as a principle," writes Foucault, "but always by being linked with this phenomenon of sectarian groups and practices." Michel Foucault, *The Hermeneutics of the Subject: Lectures at the Collège De France 1981–1982* (New York: Picador, 2005), 113. Moreover, with a few exceptions such as the Epicureans and the early Buddhists, these ideas and techniques did not take the place of the collective public religion, but rather complemented it. Thus the status of private religion was fundamentally different before the rise of Christianity, and certainly (in the Western world) before the middle of the twentieth century, when "spirituality" began to be taken as a substitute for religion and even regarded as its opposite.

107 Steve Bruce, "Cathedrals to Cults: The Evolving Forms of Religious Life," in *Religion, Modernity and Postmodernity*, ed. Paul Healas (Oxford: Blackwell, 1998), 40.

108 Martin, *The Dilemmas of Contemporary Religion*, 30. See also Marcel Gauchet, *The Disenchantment of the World: A Political History of Religion*, trans. Oscar

Burge (Princeton, NJ: Princeton University Press, 1997). Gauchet devotes his book to demonstrating how Christianity was the first religion to offer humanity a way out of a holistic religious perception of the world, and thus eventually a way to secularization. As he frames it, "Christianity proves to have been *a religion for departing from religion*" (ibid., 4, italics in original). Gauchet proposes that the roots of individuality and inwardness in the Axial Age, the Christian cultivation of those and its split between the religious and the political, and finally the rise of the modern state (in the West) served to break religion's hold on human civilization, by redefining the sacred as something transcendent and other than the world, and thus offering humanity a space for personal and political autonomy. The result, Gauchet suggests, is "this capitalist-rational-democratic world" (ibid., 144), which, while having Christian theology as its base, is completely secular.

109 Grace Davie, *Religion in Britain since 1945: Believing without Belonging* (Oxford: Blackwell, 1994).

110 Martin, *The Dilemmas of Contemporary Religion*, 65.

111 José Casanova, "The Secular, Secularisation, Secularisms" in *Rethinking Secularism*, ed. Craig Calhoun, Mark Juergensmeyer, and Jonathan Van Antwerpen (Oxford: Oxford University Press, 2011), 54–91. See also Henrich, *The Weirdest People in the World*, 484.

112 Ashis Nandy, "The Politics of Secularism and the Recovery of Religious Tolerance," in *Secularism and its Critics*, ed. Rajeev Bhargava (New Delhi: Oxford University Press, 2014), 321–44.

AFTERWORD

1 See Adam B. Seligman, *Modernity's Wager: Authority, the Self, and Transcendence* (Princeton, NJ: Princeton University Press, 2000).

INDEX

Abelard, Peter, 115
Absurd Man, 231–32, 262, 273
Académie Française, 255
acts, intentions contrasted with, 95
Acts of the Apostles, 316n10
Adam (biblical figure), 25, 28, 33, 89–90,
 111, 146, 242
adultery, 61, 64, 82–84, 314n68
Agobard (archbishop), 108–9, 324n87
Alcuin (theologian), 108
Alexandria, 78
Alexandria, Cyril of, 327n110
Altmann, Alexander, 34
American Reform Movement, 227
Ames, William, 153
Anabaptists, 130–31, 150–51
An Anatomy of the World (Donne), 166–67
ancestor worship, 315n74
"ancestral sin," 38
Ancien Régime, 234
ancient Near East, 32; image of God in,
 42; legal codes in, 36; Mesopotamian
 cultures contrasted with, 7
Anderson, Walter, 40–41
Anglican Church, 152–53, 156, 158, 169
animals, humans distinguished from,
 120–21
Anselm of Canterbury (theologian), 235
Anthony, Susan B., 165
antisemitism, 338n5
Antwerp, Tanchelm of, 137
Aquinas, Thomas, 120, 138, 235
Aristotle, 126, 293; on slavery, 29, 98–100,
 105, 124

An Arrow Against All Tyrants (Overton),
 159
Asad, Talal, 184
Assyria, 15, 17, 32, 36, 60, 202
ataraxia (ἀταραξία), 318n23
atheism, 248–49, 256, 258–59; as an ethos,
 231–33; dignity and, 271–74; ethos
 of, 274–76; historical fear of, 233–36;
 police officers thwarting, 234–35; tolerance excluding, 236–38
Athens (Greece), 353n106
Augustine, 197, 235, 243, 263, 314n60;
 on authority of the Church, 147, 241,
 248; on image of God, 90, 104, 119,
 138, 242; on inwardness, 78, 82, 244–
 45; on religion, 184, 186; on slavery,
 103–4
Augustodunensis, Honorius, 243–44
authenticity, 52, 132, 133, 232, 272, 287, 290,
 295–99, 304, 338n7
authority, 279; of conscience, 139; of divine
 revelation, 194; God and, 248; human,
 160; internalization of, 295–96. *See also*
 religious authority
autonomous individualism, secularization
 as, 288–91
autonomous thought, as virtue in its own
 right, 265
autonomy: ethos of, 291; freedom as, 56–
 57, 66, 166–67, 290–91, 294, 331n42; inner sphere guaranteeing, 108; of Jewish
 community, 179; laws juxtaposed with,
 291; as moral ideal, 264–66
Averroes (philosopher), 120

ABOUT THE AUTHOR

TOMER PERSICO is a Research Fellow at the Shalom Hartman Institute, a Rubinstein Fellow at Reichman University, and a Senior Research Scholar at the UC Berkeley Center for Middle Eastern Studies. His books include *The Jewish Meditative Tradition* and *Liberalism: Its Roots, Values and Crises*.